Through Early Yellowstone

Adventuring by Bicycle, Covered Wagon, Foot, Horseback, and Skis

Through Early Yellowstone

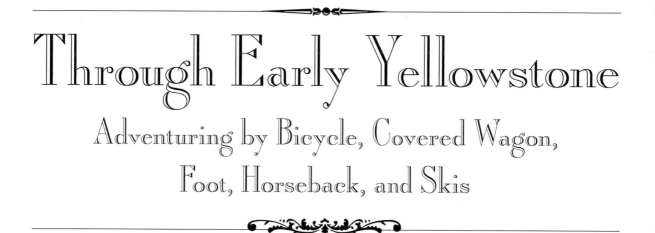

Adventuring by Bicycle, Covered Wagon, Foot, Horseback, and Skis

Selected and annotated by JANET CHAPPLE

Foreword by LEE H. WHITTLESEY

Watercolor sketches by THOMAS H. THOMAS

First Edition

GRANITE PEAK PUBLICATIONS

Lake Forest Park, Washington

Publisher's Cataloging-in-Publication Data
provided by Five Rainbows Services

Through early Yellowstone : adventuring by bicycle, covered wagon, foot, horseback, and skis / selected and annotated by Janet Chapple.

pages cm

Includes bibliographical references and index.

ISBN: 978-0-9858182-6-5 (pbk.)

1. Yellowstone National Park—Description and travel. 2. Voyages and travels—United States—History—19th century. 3. Bicycle touring—United States. 4. Travel with horses. 5. Travelers—Yellowstone National Park—History. 6. Thomas, T. H. (Thomas Henry), 1839-1915.   I. Chapple, Janet, editor. II. Title.

F722 .T57 2016

917.87`5204—dc23

2015955535

18 17 16   1 2 3 4

Designed by Ponderosa Pine Design, Vicky Vaughn Shea

Printed and bound in China

Published by Granite Peak Publications

Lake Forest Park, WA

www.ThroughEarlyYellowstone.com

Contents

Plates follow page 112.

Foreword

Anthologies help the forward progress of knowledge by collecting major information from numerous writers into single volumes and thus making that information more easily available to readers. It is a tribute to Yellowstone National Park as a subject that even though it has already been the subject and recipient of two anthologies—Paul Schullery's *Old Yellowstone Days* (1979, 2010) and Elizabeth Watry's and my *Ho! For Wonderland!* (2009)—it arguably needs one more. My friend Janet Chapple, long a Yellowstone student and writer, has produced this important addition, which concentrates on collecting the original, old-days works that were responsible for Yellowstone's being protected as the world's first national park and that inaugurated the very long bibliography (more than thirteen thousand published items!) of Yellowstone literature. I first met her some twenty years ago when she was working on her well-known book *Yellowstone Treasures* (2002), and she thereafter teamed with Suzanne Cane to produce *Yellowstone, Land of Wonders* (2013), which made Jules Leclercq's little-known European account available to Americans by translating it from its original French.

Chapple's collection begins with what is arguably the most important "origin" document for Yellowstone, namely N. P. Langford's "The Wonders of the Yellowstone," which essentially introduced the theretofore unknown region to American readers. Langford's article is known to some modern readers, but many of the accounts that Chapple has used are not so well known. Such pieces as Frank Lenz's "World Tour Awheel," Thomas Elwood Hofer's "Winter in Wonderland," Barton Evermann's "Two-Ocean Pass," C. Hanford Henderson's "Through the Yellowstone on Foot," and Ray Baker's "A Place of Marvels" are only some of the delightful early accounts presented here with their original illustrations. In addition, there are some rarer offerings: George L. Henderson's "Adventure at Norris Geyser Basin," Alice Parmelee Morris's "Yellowstone Trails Blazed by New York Woman," and Thomas H. Thomas's "Yellowstone Park Illustrated" are a few of these. In the case of the latter piece, Chapple has located and obtained the rights to reproduce Thomas's stunning full-color paintings of Yellowstone—long housed in Europe and never before seen by American readers. These illustrations alone are worth the price of the book.

So sit back, relax, and take your time as you savor these early accounts, whether you are a new reader or an old-time Yellowstone aficionado who has been wishing for years to read these gems.

Lee H. Whittlesey
Historian, National Park Service, Yellowstone National Park

Acknowledgments

Just after the first edition of my guidebook, *Yellowstone Treasures*, came out, a publishing industry acquaintance asked me if I had ever considered compiling early writings about the place so dear to my heart, Yellowstone Park. It took me almost no time to decide I would enjoy taking on the task of creating an anthology—which originally meant "a collection of flowers." Nearly three hundred explorer and visitor accounts later, I decided to focus on previously published articles visitors or staff wrote before the automobile was allowed to enter the park in 1915.

Few people had seen Yellowstone's marvels when the first of these articles were written. There were not even drawings or photographs of the canyon or the hot springs until 1870. Nothing in the previous experience of any of these early authors had prepared them for these marvels: colorful hot springs, spouting geysers, and jaw-dropping scenes like the Grand Canyon of the Yellowstone River. Almost all lived in a time when the "Indian question" had been settled, albeit unfairly, and the former wilderness had mostly been explored. While the first visitors had to travel by horseback, by 1883 travelers could cover most of the distance by train. With gradual improvements in the park's roads, horse-drawn coaches or wagons became commonplace.

Since Paul Schullery's 1979 collection *Old Yellowstone Days*, several Yellowstone historical anthologies have appeared. This volume, published in time to celebrate the centenial of the National Park Service, adds some perspectives not touched upon in previous collections, such as those of artists Thomas H. Thomas and Anne Bosworth Greene, and of "Billy" Hofer, who skied 225 miles through the park during a record-breaking cold winter. My criteria for choosing the "flowers" of literature presented here from the vast garden of sources available were readability, variety, and significance to Yellowstone's history.

My first thank-yous go to those who compiled the many helpful bibliographies I used: Paul Schullery, *Old Yellowstone Days*; Judith L. Meyer, *The Spirit of Yellowstone;* Aubrey L. Haines, *The Yellowstone Story;* Lee H. Whittlesey, *Wonderland Nomenclature;* Richard A. Bartlett, *Yellowstone: A Wilderness Besieged;* and Hiram M. Chittenden, *The Yellowstone National Park: Historical and Descriptive.*

Next, a warm thank you to the staff of the libraries I haunted for Yellowstone materials and especially to the helpful librarians on both coasts and in Wyoming. Among these were the Yellowstone Heritage and Research Center Library, especially Jessica Gerdes and Jackie Jerla and Yellowstone's archivist, Anne Foster; the American Heritage Center of the University of Wyoming Libraries and Tamsen Hert, then head of special collections; the John Hay Library, especially Andy Moul and Ann Dodge, and the Rockefeller Library, both at Brown University; the Providence Public Library; Yale University's Beinecke Library; the University of California Berkeley's Bancroft,

Doe, and Valley Life Sciences libraries; Stanford University's Green Library; San Jose State University's King Library; and the public libraries of San Francisco and Palo Alto.

Numerous people and institutions helped me find biographical information about my chosen authors: Graham Law of Waseda University, Tokyo, Japan; Thomas Crowther of the Charleston Renaissance Gallery; Michael McCue of Condar Press; the Vermont Historical Society Library; Ryerson Library of the Art Institute of Chicago; Judy Mulvaney Bunnell of Suffield, Connecticut, and Moose, Wyoming (who also provided hospitality during my research years); Tamsen Hert of the University of Wyoming libraries; Cheryl Oakes of the Forest History Society, Durham, North Carolina; the Harvard University Archives; Nancy R. Miller of the University of Pennsylvania Archives in Philadelphia; Christabel Hutchings of Virgin Media; and the South Whidbey Island Historical Society in Washington State. Kelly Corthell Bradford, Alan Corthell, and Sally Hill Mackey helped with biographical material about Nellie Corthell.

Curator of prints and drawings Beth McIntyre and image licensing officer Kay Kays at the National Museum of Wales went out of their way to assist in my viewing and reproducing the watercolors of Thomas H. Thomas that appear here courtesy of the National Museum of Wales for the first time in print. Stephen R. Howe and Dr. Alan Channing of Cardiff, Wales, helped me learn the whereabouts of these sketchbook watercolors.

For aiding my quest to learn about Yellowstone and especially its history, and for his thorough review of my original manuscript, I am indebted to Park Historian Lee H. Whittlesey, without whose assistance over the past many years my task would have been infinitely harder. Suggestions about publishing this collection came from Matthew Bokovoy of the University of Nebraska Press.

A warm thank you to others who have read my manuscript or otherwise assisted me: my husband Bruno Giletti, daughter Nancy Chapple; stepdaughter Ann Giletti; son-in-law Niklas Dellby; friends Helen Betts, Suzanne Cane, Elizabeth Jung, Erika Kunkel, Jo-Ann Sherwin, and Mary Van Buskirk; Yellowstone researchers Tamsen Hert and Judith Meyer; and Russ Taylor of Brigham Young University. Linton A. Brown not only read an early version of the manuscript but created the map (page 205) that shows the mountainous route Wilcox took. This volume would not have seen the light of day without my daughter Beth Chapple, my longtime editor and adviser in all things publishing who also became the publisher of Granite Peak Publications in 2014.

Notes on the Illustrations

Several factors make it difficult to trace the origin of a painting, drawing, or photograph, although sometimes we can find initials. In the late nineteenth century and into the early twentieth, published illustrations, even paintings, were almost always black and white. Also, late nineteenth-century publications rarely credited the creators of their illustrations, and copyright restrictions were not strong.

To reproduce an artwork for books and magazines, it had to be copied by hand. An engraver traced the lines and other markings onto thin paper and then carefully and laboriously cut V-shaped grooves from it into a wood, stone, or metal block or plate, so that the incisions would hold ink. He then rubbed ink into the plate and wiped the excess off the surface, covered the plate with a damp sheet of paper to pick up the image, and finally put the plate and paper through a press.

The halftone process for photoengraving became commercially viable as a method for printing multiple copies of a photograph only in the early 1890s. Images in Barton Warren Evermann's article and those of later authors represented in this volume were clearly reproduced by this method rather than by hand engraving.

To create a photoengraving, first the engraver coats a printing plate with a light-sensitive chemical (an emulsion). Then, by shining bright light through a grid (the screen) onto the plate, he prints a negative. The screen breaks the image into patterns of different-sized black dots small enough to look like varying shades of gray when seen from a slight distance. The dots are made acid resistant, then the plate is put into a bath of acid. This removes areas around the dots, raising the dots slightly, so they can be inked with a roller. The plate can then be put through a printing press.

Note that illustrations in this volume are in the public domain unless otherwise credited.

Nathaniel P. Langford, "The Wonders of the Yellowstone"

Only some of the sources of the illustrations in Nathaniel P. Langford's pair of articles are known. For example, the map that appears on pages 12–13 is not credited, but its representation of the outline and islands of Yellowstone Lake are exactly the same as Langford drew them in his later book.[1]

The images (probably woodcuts) with the initials *TM* were made by Thomas Moran, who was engaged by *Scribner's Monthly* to draw them, sometimes with only verbal descriptions to go by. Drawings were made in 1870 of Giant and Castle Geyser Cones (unsigned, but credited to explorer Walter Trumbull). Comparison of the Trumbull drawings with the engravings in Langford's *Scribner's* articles show that Moran copied them.[2] The following summer, in 1871, Moran took part in the Hayden exploration and "must have blushed at his faulty imagination when he saw the realities a few months later."[3] Moran is recognized now as the first and one of the best-known artists ever to paint Yellowstone scenes.

Among the other *Scribner's* illustrations, the least realistic is "The Grotto Geyser"; this one has no initials but had to be drawn by someone who had not seen Grotto's unique formation. One can only speculate about who might have drawn the delightful representation, "Bird's-eye View of the Geyser Basin" (page 40)—drawn from a perspective that is impossible at Upper Geyser Basin.

Elwood ("Billy") Hofer, "Winter in Wonderland"

Hofer's trip started on February 12, 1887. *Harper's Weekly* engaged C. T. ("Charles") Graham to draw a scene such as the Schwatka party would have encountered on their aborted January 1887 ski trip through Yellowstone, so *The Yellowstone in Winter—A Surprise* is from the same winter, though not originally with this article. Graham signed his name to the cover picture for April 9, 1887, and he may have been the engraver. This image was intended to illustrate the Haynes party's encounter with elk, but the only artist who went along with F. Jay Haynes on the tour a month before Hofer's was Henry Bosse.[4] Graham (1852–1911) had, however, painted western scenes for the Northern Pacific Railroad.

Hofer probably provided his own diagrams of the "lodge" he made for his winter trip and the pattern for it.

Thomas H. Thomas, "Yellowstone Park Illustrated"

Welshman Thomas H. Thomas painted over forty watercolors in his sketchbook while visiting Yellowstone; we include twenty-six in this volume's picture gallery, reproduced by permission from the National Museum of Wales. With his training as an artist, Thomas likely assisted the *Graphic* in turning some of his watercolor sketches into engravings for publication, perhaps even helping to select the engraver. However, there are no signatures or initials on most of them. Perhaps the desire to print so many engravings (forty-four) and the need to hire several engravers explains the fact that the *Graphic* took four years to publish Thomas's articles. (Note that Thomas's articles appeared in print in 1888, while Hofer's reached readers immediately after his 1887 winter trip.)

Unlike the majority of the early writers represented in *Through Early Yellowstone*, Thomas was careful to credit his sources at the ends of his articles. Four of the engravings were based on photographs by members of the same British Association for the Advancement of Science expedition with which Thomas traveled: two by Edgar W. Sollas (for whom he provides both a Trinity College, Dublin address in the first article and a London address in the second) and two by R. G. Brooks of St. Helen's, a town just northeast of Wales.

Seven engravings in the article were based on photos by F. Jay Haynes (whom Thomas misidentifies once as "Mr. W. E. Jay Haynes"). The Great Falls and Canyon photographs are replaced by two Thomas paintings in this volume. The young Haynes worked as photographer for the Northern Pacific railroad, but beginning in 1881 he was photographing in Yellowstone. Soon he became the park's "official" photographer, opening his own photo shop; later he settled permanently at Mammoth.

Three more photos are by T. W. Ingersoll of St. Paul, Minnesota, a civil engineer in his early years, who was photographing in Yellowstone throughout the 1880s. Ingersoll specialized in stereoscopic photography, invented in the 1830s. By the early 1900s Ingersoll's studio employed about twenty-five people "including young women who hand-tinted the color views."[5]

This is not the first time any engravings in Thomas's two articles have been reproduced in a book about Yellowstone.[6] However, curator Beth McIntyre of the National Museum Cardiff Wales informs us that Thomas's Yellowstone watercolors have never been publicly exhibited outside of Wales. Until now they have been totally unknown in the United States.

The art editors of the *Graphic* arranged the engravings based on Thomas's paintings and on photographs by his contemporaries in groups of three to eight images. These were chosen to fit on the magazine's sixteen-by-twelve-inch pages and did not always follow Thomas's route, so we have tried to rectify this.

In the gallery of watercolor plates, Thomas's original titles or any words Thomas wrote on the paintings are shown in quotation marks. For those watercolors he did not label or identify, we show the caption of the related engraving. If no engraving was made, we often give the current name of the feature.

With the text on page 148 we pair "Mrs. Finch's, Fire Hole Basin" with the engraving *Mrs. Finch's Camp Hotel, Fire-Hole Basin.* Here the publisher preferred creating an engraving from a photo by Edgar W. Sollas rather than from the

pencil sketch Thomas made from a different perspective. Note how Thomas's tree is ready to fall down in the next strong wind. He added "Tent Hotel Yellowstone" and "Sept 23" at the lower left.

Because the man and horse on page 156 ("A Parting Salutation, Yellowstone Park, Here's Luck Now and Always") were painted in black and gray tones, we include the picture with the text rather than in the full-color gallery.

Plates Following Page 112

Plate 1. "Approach to Rocky Mountains, from Yellowstone Valley W." Painted from the train, this is a view of the Crazy Mountains from a few miles east of Livingston. At this curve of the river is the gateway where the vast plains along the Yellowstone in Montana give way to mountain views to the north and south. The "W" must refer to the western stretch of the river; Thomas had traveled by rail paralleling the river since he entered Montana Territory. This area is also shown in "The Gate of the Mountains" by Albert Hencke accompanying "Lenz's World Tour Awheel" (page 168).

Plate 2. Boiling River on the Gardner River near Mammoth, "Sept 20th." This is the official name of a section of the Gardner River north of Mammoth where hot spring water mixes with cold river water. The water as it enters the river is actually scalding hot but not boiling. This spot is located three miles inside the park and almost exactly on the Montana-Wyoming state line. Thomas shows Electric Peak in the western distance.

Although he does not mention this place in his article, he dated the painting September 20, the day he arrived at Mammoth. However, he left a different clue in a letter to his friend Charles T. Whitmell: "On the last afternoon I spent in the Park, I went with Mr. Hobart, the proprietor of the Mammoth Hot Springs Hotel, to see the confluence of a boiling stream with the Gardiner river at the foot of the 'White Mountain.'"[7]

Plate 3. "Characters in Hall of Mammoth Hot Springs Hotel." Compare this original with the engraving on page 109. The engraver (WC) understandably created a clearer picture here than we can get from Thomas's obviously hurried sketch. Still, the man with the big fur coat, the (lone) stylishly dressed lady, the hurrying porter, the stances of the three men at the right (two in the engraving), the big stove, and, of course, the spittoons record the scene delightfully in both versions.

Plate 4. "Warm Pool at Mammoth Hot Springs Yellowstone Park." Compare with the engraving *The Bathing Pool at "Mammoth"—"Cleanliness is next to Godliness"* on page 138. The *Graphic's* engraver did not see fit to use the additional notes on Thomas's pencil sketch, "The 'Rustler' and the 'Sky-Pilot,'" added in blue ink, nor did he include the cattails on the far shore. Instead he provided the "rustler" with a hat and smoothed out the logs at the left to look more like a diving platform. This is the long-dry Bath Lake on the Upper Terrace at Mammoth.

Plate 5. Cleopatra Spring and Stalactite Terraces, Mammoth Hot Springs, "Sept 20." The National Hotel (at center right), as it was first called, was brightly painted in green with a red roof. This painting may be the only time it was ever represented in color.

Plate 6. "Interior of Extinct Fissure Geyser, Mammoth Hot Springs" [Devil's Kitchen].

Nowhere are the bulbous concretions near the top of this solution cave (never a geyser) at Mammoth Hot Springs, explained.

Plate 7. "The 'Orange' Geyser and the 'Chipmunk.'" Now known as Orange Spring Mound, it is made up of several cone-type formations grown together and a fissure ridge. A jet at the top sometimes spouts as much as one yard (1 meter) high.

Plate 8. Beaver Lake. Thomas wrote on the sketch, "Beaver Mound," "Beaver Dam," and "Sept 28/84." The beaver eventually deserted their dam, and the former lake has been a meadow for many years.

Plate 9. Lake of the Woods. This pretty lake is far off the present roads, with 10,336 foot Mt. Holmes in the background. The small floating circles are lily pads. Lee H. Whittlesey identified the subject of this painting.

Plate 10. In a Tent Hotel, Norris Basin—Strange Bedfellows. Compare with the engraving on page 142, which shows us only the light from a candle, while Thomas makes the candle, "elegantly sconced in a bottle," as he puts it, a central part of his fanciful drama in the tent.

Plate 11. Ford in Gibbon Cañon. Compare with the engraving on page 144. Bridges were rare in early Yellowstone.

Plate 12. Steam from "Hell's Half-Acre" and Lower Geyser Basin—Early Morning. Thomas could not have seen steam all the way from Midway Geyser Basin (his "Hell's Half-Acre") from this vantage point. Note that the puff of steam rising on the bank of and reflected in the Firehole indicates a hot spring still to be found there—but the footbridge is long gone.

Plate 13. Cone of "Grotto" Geyser. The *Graphic's* editor chose to represent Grotto with a photo by Ingersoll (not included in this volume) and passed up this small watercolor, which Thomas labeled "Grotto" and in which he included the cone of Grotto's neighbor, Rocket Geyser.

Plate 14. "Fire Hole Basin," "Sept 25, 1884." Compare with the engraving *Henderson and Klamer's Hotel, Fire-Hole Basin* on page 146. After comparing the painting and the engraving made from it and reviewing the history of the hotels in that area, I realize that the stream in Thomas's foreground is *not* the Firehole River but rather Nez Perce Creek. The hotel represented by Thomas is *not* the first one built in the area, on the west side of the Firehole, as I had thought, but the second one newly built between Nez Perce Creek and the Firehole. Thomas's painting and its caption represent the newer hotel, where he stayed.

In the engraving the distance from the hotel to the hill behind it is foreshortened, making it look impossible for a river to run behind the hotel. In the painting we don't see the river, but enough space for it can be imagined. Now we can mentally place the hotel between the streams and also realize that the steam from the left is coming from Hygeia Spring. This second hotel was located 75 meters north of the spring. Notice that the engraver has added some (nonexistent) steam behind the hotel and replaced Thomas's woman with a man, possibly carrying a rifle.

Plate 15. "Round the Stove Marshall's, Sept 22." Compare with the engraving *Round the Stove at Henderson's* on page 147. When Thomas stayed in the hotel in 1884 it was called Marshall and

Henderson's or Marshall House. But by 1888, when the *Graphic* published his articles, Marshall had sold out his share to Henry E. Klamer, and the hotel had become Henderson and Klamer's, or simply Henderson's.[8] The engraver kept the same number of men but changed their hats and turned one man into a cleric; he also eliminated the chandelier. But why did he move the spittoon?

Plate 16. Paint Pots, Lower Geyser Basin. This feature is now known as Fountain Paint Pot.

Plate 17. "Diana's Well" and "Castle" Geyser Plunging. This caption was used with the engraving (not reproduced in this volume). The use of the word "plunging" for erupting is very unusual. What Thomas called "Diana's Well" is now known as Crested Pool. Thomas includes Old Faithful erupting in the distance. The colors he uses between the hydrothermal features represent quite faithfully microbial growths in their runoff waters.

Plate 18. "Old Faithful Sept 22." Thomas painted the iconic geyser twice, but this is the more complete depiction.

Plate 19. "Giant Geyser, Yellowstone Park." Giant Geyser, the most powerful of Yellowstone's geysers next to Steamboat Geyser, erupts on its own unpredictable schedule, some years every few days, some years not at all. History records eruptions on September 4 and 10 in 1884.[9]

Plate 20. "Hell's Half Acre, 22 Sept / 84." Note the faintly written words "Excelsior" on the left at the top of the steam and "Prismatic" on the right.

Plate 21. Gulf of "Excelsior" Geyser. Thomas discusses this powerful geyser on pages 151–52.

Plate 22. Grand Prismatic Spring and Twin

Buttes. Thomas did not exaggerate the brilliant colors seen on a sunny day at this spring in Midway Geyser Basin. He has even indicated how the gentle waves break as the near-boiling water reaches the borders of the pool. The Twin Buttes are in the background.

Plate 23. Queen's Laundry, "25th Sept." This painting, which Thomas does not mention, was identified for this book by geyser expert T. Scott Bryan. The features shown are in the Sentinel Meadow Group in Lower Geyser Basin; the steaming hot spring is The Queen's Laundry, and the two geyserite cones are Flat Cone at the left and Steep Cone at the right. Queen's Laundry was named by Superintendent Norris in 1880, when the cooler pools below it were used by road workmen for laundering and bathing. Thomas probably rode a short distance out of his way to see these features when he stayed for the second time at Marshall and Henderson's Hotel.

Plate 24. "Hunter Yellowstone Sept. 26th." No doubt this was one of the men Thomas encountered at the hotel pictured in Plate 14.

Plate 25. "Great Falls of the Yellowstone." This Lower Falls image was probably painted from a North Rim canyon viewpoint not accessible today.

Plates 26 and 27. "Yellowstone," paired with the hand-colored engraving *The Grand Cañon of the Yellowstone, from the Great Falls.* That Thomas wrote only the word "Yellowstone" above his painting seems to reflect the wordless awe this canyon inspires in many viewers. This watercolor (or "drawing") was loaned by Thomas's friend Charles T. Whitmell to the *Graphic* to create their engraving. Rather than from the Great or Lower Falls,

it was much more likely painted when Thomas was farther down the canyon, perhaps at or near Inspiration Point. The colors are marvelous in the canyon, but Thomas has surely exaggerated the intensity of the red pinnacle. The engraving caption includes: "Facsimile of a drawing made from nature by T. H. Thomas, R.C.A., showing the exact colouring of the rock formations." R.C.A. stands for Royal College of Art.

Frank D. Lenz, "Lenz's World Tour Awheel"

Albert Hencke (1865–1936) contributed two paintings to the Lenz *Outing* articles about Yellowstone. He was born and studied art in St. Louis, Missouri, then studied in California and New York City. He was a book and magazine illustrator, known especially for children's paintings and pen-and-ink drawings.

Earley Vernon Wilcox, "A Visit to the Hoodoos of Wyoming"

Wilcox credited the photographs in his article to F. W. Traphagen, only mentioned in the text as "a professor." In the 1890s Traphagen was professor of chemistry and natural science at Montana Agricultural College in Bozeman, now Montana State University.

Ray Stannard Baker, "A Place of Marvels"

The artist who illustrated Baker's article, Ernest L. Blumenschein (1874–1960), was born in Albuquerque, New Mexico. He switched from violin to art as a student in Cincinnati, Ohio, and later studied art in New York and Paris. He became an illustrator for books and magazines, but a trip to Taos, New Mexico, resulted in his founding the Taos Society of Artists in 1898 with Bert G. Phillips. He then divided his time between Taos and New York but settled in Taos in 1919, where he painted Pueblo Indian portraits and southwestern landscapes.

We include a sampling of the original pictures. *The man who built the roads*, page 213, shows Hiram M. Chittenden, the Corps of Engineers officer who did the most to create the road system still in place in Yellowstone today. Chittenden also wrote a valuable history of the park, first published in 1895.

Anne Bosworth Greene, "Attempting Yellowstone"

In 1906 artist Anne Bosworth Greene received a commission to paint scenes both of Yosemite National Park (which had been fully turned over to the U.S. government the year before) and of Yellowstone National Park. Greene mentions having painted eight scenes in her "Attempting Yellowstone" chapter of the 1928 collection of her essays, *Lambs in March*. We reproduce only three of those she painted; these appeared in Robert Haven Schauffler's 1913 book *Romantic America* but were not printed in color.

About the Maps

Through Early Yellowstone contains five maps, the first two representing what was known about Yellowstone's topography and existing roads in 1871 and 1887. The third, 1897 Wilcox route map, was created by Linton A. Brown.

Our fourth map shows a portion of a modern (1996) USGS detailed topographic map of the remote Two Ocean Pass area just south of the Yellowstone border; we include it to compare with Evermann's relatively simplified map of an unusual phenomenon—where waters mingle and flow out to the oceans through different drainage systems.

The last map in this volume was sketched by Mrs. Robert C. Morris in 1917, who then personally financed the professional production of the map to show her suggestions for a Yellowstone bridle trail system.

For more historical Yellowstone maps, see Aubrey L. Haines's *Yellowstone National Park: Its Exploration and Establishment* (1974).

NOTES

1. Langford, *The Discovery of Yellowstone Park*, 64.
2. Chittenden credits Trumbull with the drawings in *Yellowstone National Park*, 168.
3. Bartlett, *Nature's Yellowstone,* 183.
4. Hassrick, *Drawn to Yellowstone*, 101–104. Charles Graham's elk in winter engraving appears on Hassrick's page 103.
5. Johnson, "Truman Ingersoll," 130.
6. Aubrey L. Haines included three engravings from Thomas's work in *The Yellowstone Story* 1: 199, 275. Art museum director Peter H. Hassrick reproduced "Characters in Hall of Mammoth Hot Springs Hotel" and "Gulf of 'Excelsior' Geyser" on pages 104 and 105 of *Drawn to Yellowstone.*
7. Whitmell, "American Wonderland," 96.
8. Whittlesey, "Marshall's Hotel," 44; Whittlesey, "Hotels on the Firehole," 14–17.
9. Whittlesey, *Wonderland Nomenclature,* 469.

Introduction

The national park idea, the best idea we ever had, was inevitable as soon as Americans learned to confront the wild continent not with fear and cupidity but with delight, wonder, and awe.
Wallace Stegner, *Marking the Sparrow's Fall:*
The Making of the American West, 1998

Step back in time for a moment to the American West of the early nineteenth century. Western Indian tribes, such as the Crows, Blackfeet, Shoshonis, and Bannocks, were still going about their lives with relatively little contact with the white man, since only the most intrepid explorers, fur trappers, and traders had yet entered the western plains and the Rocky Mountains. All travel was by foot, horseback, or small boat. Huge areas remained that descendants of European immigrants had not yet seen or reported on.

We have evidence that native tribes passed through or hunted in what is now Yellowstone Park as long as eleven thousand years ago. They made weapons from the hardened glassy lava of Obsidian Cliff.

In the early 1800s a few fur trappers and hopeful prospectors came to the area. The illiterate John Colter, who left the returning Lewis and Clark Expedition to trap and explore, gave his report to William Clark when he got back to St. Louis. Daniel T. Potts, Warren A. Ferris, and Osborne Russell produced written accounts of seeing spouting fountains and bubbling mud pots. Prospector A. Bart Henderson kept daily records between 1863 and 1871 but, like all the others, found gold only outside the present park boundaries, such as in the Cooke City area.

In the mid 1800s staggering changes were occurring in the West. Mormons had settled in Utah and southern Idaho beginning in 1847, and other immigrants from the East began after the Homestead Act of 1862 to settle on public land throughout the West.

Trappers had all but disappeared by 1840—out of work due to the whims of fashion, since beaver hats were no longer in style. The Plains Indian tribes, systematically deprived of their greatest source of livelihood, the buffalo, were decimated. Eventually, by the 1870s, most of these Indians were confined to reservations.

In the 1860s local newspapers in Montana Territory, such as the *Montana Post* of Virginia City and the *Helena Herald*, reported on exploratory trips into this fabulous unknown region, Yellowstone. Adventurous men who had read or heard stories about them were aching to see the area's marvels for themselves; a few exploring parties began to be organized but did not make the trip for various reasons.[1] Most important to the overall life of the West, the transcontinental railroad was completed in 1869.

Just after it became possible to travel across the continent by rail in about a week, three famous expeditions entered the area. The first was a loosely organized trip in September 1869 from Diamond City, a small mining town forty miles east of Helena, Montana Territory. Three men undertook a journey on their own that year: Charles W. Cook, who superintended the project; his former schoolmate, David E. Folsom; and William Peterson, an immigrant from Denmark.

Next, in 1870, came a semiofficial tour with a military escort led by Lt. Gustavus C. Doane. The writings and lectures of these explorers, especially Nathaniel P. Langford's *Scribner's Monthly* articles, and Walter A. Trumbull's pieces in the *Overland Monthly*, helped inspire the third famous exploration, led by Ferdinand V. Hayden. We present Langford's account along with excerpts from Trumbull's account. The journal of Lt. Doane was submitted to Congress but not widely read; it appears in volume 2 of Orrin H. Bonney and Lorraine Bonney's *Battle Drums and Geysers*. Expedition leader Henry D. Washburn and Harvard-educated lawyer and reporter Cornelius Hedges both kept diaries and published newspaper articles regarding the trip; other participants who kept diaries included Virginia City merchant Warren C. Gillette and former prospector Samuel T. Hauser, who later became governor of Montana Territory.

By 1871, convinced of the uniqueness of the region, the U.S. government decided to fund a geological expedition. Its leader, Ferdinand Vandiveer Hayden, was a medical doctor turned geologist. The extensive technical reports by Hayden and his colleagues from his 1871, 1872, and 1878 expeditions established Yellowstone as a site for scientific inquiry as well as a tourist destination. Also

in 1871, Gilman Sawtell led a privately funded trip up the Madison River into the park. One of the five adventurers, Calvin C. Clawson, wrote up the story, republished in 2003 as *A Ride to the Infernal Regions: Yellowstone's First Tourists.*

Even before the full Hayden report on the 1871 expedition could be published, a bill to set aside the Yellowstone area was introduced in the House and Senate and soon passed both houses. President Ulysses S. Grant signed it into law on March 1, 1872.

Three years earlier, the transcontinental railroad had joined West to East at Promontory Point, Utah. The park's unusual wonders began to attract visitors, but with the train tracks still hundreds of miles away, access was difficult. Understandably, many would-be visitors were also leery of entering "Indian country," still fearing attacks by Blackfeet, Nez Perces, and Bannocks, until the end of the 1870s. Most easterners who could afford travel would much rather spend an extended holiday in Europe than take the long train and stagecoach trip to an area where there were no hotels and all travel in the park was by horseback.

Given the difficulty of access and the slowness of communications in the 1870s, it is remarkable that guidebooks to the park began to appear in only one year. Some of them were in the form of travelogues, and some, such as Superintendent Philetus W. Norris's, even included poetry. Herman Haupt's 1883 guidebook instructed readers in how to prepare (or "outfit") for a horseback trip into the park.

A surprising number of Europeans heard about the "wonderland" in the western United

States and braved the discomforts and dangers to explore the new park, writing glowingly of their experiences. Probably the most popular—and the first descriptive book about Yellowstone that was *not* a guidebook—was *The Great Divide: Travels in the Upper Yellowstone in the Summer of 1874*, by W. T. Wyndham-Quin, usually referred to as the Earl of Dunraven.

Interest in visiting Yellowstone continued to be greater among European citizens of means than among similarly situated Americans even into the twentieth century. President Theodore Roosevelt observed, in his 1903 speech dedicating Yellowstone's North Entrance Arch, "At present it is rather singular that a greater number of people come from Europe to see it than come from our own eastern states." Back in 1887, a *Harper's Monthly* story's opening dialog reflected this attitude:

> "It is perfectly absurd for you to keep going to Europe in this way, summer after summer," remarked the Maiden . . . "Do you really mean, Mabel, that if you were I"—Mrs. Thayer here grasped faintly for the married dignity which was her only hope in the struggle—"you would give up the Tyrol for the Yellowstone?"[2]

In the story, of course, the family changed their itinerary and went west. Note how people used to speak of Yellowstone Park with "the" in front of the name, by analogy with other regions such as the Tyrol and the Rhine.

After the completion of the Northern Pacific Railroad line through Montana Territory in 1883, it was much easier to reach Yellowstone. Soon, other railroad companies began to build lines to terminal points near the park. In the 1880s wealthy travelers could choose either the NPRR to Livingston (or later Cinnabar, Montana) or the Union Pacific or Central Pacific to northern Utah and later to southern Idaho. They could then continue by horse-drawn coach on rough roads to Yellowstone's North or West Entrance and tour the park in another coach or on horseback. Transportation was becoming more affordable. In fact, most everyone's income increased during the decade from 1880 to 1890; for example, industrial workers' average wage gained 48 percent.[3] Families like that of Margaret Andrews Allen could now come in wagons, pitch their tents, and enjoy the park.

In the same decade, the new park in the West generated more jobs, including driving the horse-drawn coaches, working for the park administration or the concessionaires, or guiding parties through the park. But poaching and vandalism had become rampant. In response, in 1886 the government sent one company of U.S. Cavalry and later several more companies to Mammoth Hot Springs and a few men to remote posts throughout the park.

Yellowstone travelers came for one of two reasons: for adventure and recreation or because they had some mission, something they wanted to accomplish and often to write about. In many cases these two purposes were combined in one excursion. Paul LeHardy's short, unpublished autobiographical excerpt relates an unintended adventure that happened to him and a companion who were working in the park in its earliest days. A well-educated and literate man from Wales visited the park in 1884: Thomas H. Thomas took passage to the park with a group of British scientists. He wrote with humor and an interest in archeology and expressed his delight with everything he saw in watercolor sketches.

The U.S. Fish Commission sent ichthyologist Barton Warren Evermann to investigate how fish got into Yellowstone Lake while remaining absent in other Yellowstone bodies of water. Elwood ("Billy") Hofer had found his metier as a guide in Yellowstone back in 1878; nine years later the prominent eastern magazine *Forest and Stream* hired him to take a winter census of the elk and other wildlife. At the same time that Hofer was guiding sportsmen and scientists to remote parts (or backcountry) of Yellowstone, the incomparable guide and namer of park features George L. Henderson was sharing his vast knowledge of the "front country" with all the well-heeled hotel guests who would listen.

At the end of the nineteenth century a cycling enthusiast, an indefatigable walker, a botanist and agricultural expert, and a prominent journalist visited and wrote about the park in their own ways. Frank D. Lenz planned a world-circling bicycle tour in the days when bicycles with same-sized wheels and pneumatic tires were still new; his whirlwind trip through the park comprised a small part of the extensive reports he telegraphed to New York. Future educator C. Hanford Henderson walked an ambitious route that would be unpleasant if not impossible on today's crowded summer roads. Earley Vernon Wilcox and his party took a difficult high mountain route, with geological hoodoos as their goal. The 1902 Pulitzer Prize–winning Ray Stannard Baker related his experiences from horseback and observed the other tourists—who mostly toured in coaches.

Nowadays, when Americans decide to go camping in Yellowstone, they load up an SUV or other large vehicle with tent, sleeping bags, and all the gear needed to prepare meals; perhaps they reserve a space in one of the park's five reservation-only campgrounds—or else they take their chances in the nonreserved ones or stay outside the boundaries. *Through Early Yellowstone* includes stories of two early and very different family camping trips, both taken in horse-drawn wagons. The first is the brief tale Mrs. Allen told in 1885, and the second is a longer and more detailed trip from Laramie, Wyoming, to Yellowstone by Eleanor Quackenbush Corthell, a woman alone with her seven young children.

Enterprising men recognized the need for hotels even before the act creating the park had been introduced to Congress. The first hotel in Yellowstone was a log building at Mammoth Hot Springs that two local men named James McCartney and Harry Horr put up late in 1871. Other individuals and soon the railroads gradually built more facilities and also began providing coach tours from near the park's northern and western borders. At least eleven more hotels (some barely more than shacks) sprouted near scenic spots around the park:

- Marshall's Hotel at the confluence of the Firehole River and Nez Perce Creek (1880, Plate 14)
- the large National Hotel in 1883 and the modest Cottage Hotel in 1885 at Mammoth
- a tent camp (1883) and then the "Shack Hotel"

in 1885 at Upper Geyser Basin

- Yancey's, leased in 1884 in Pleasant Valley, a few miles from Tower Fall
- a temporary hotel at Canyon in 1887
- a small one at Norris in 1887 that burned but was replaced
- the first Lake Hotel and the Fountain Hotel bordering Lower Geyser Basin in 1891
- Old Faithful Inn in 1904
- and the biggest and most elegant, Canyon Hotel, in 1911.[4]

Inexpensive tent camps began appearing by the 1890s, in addition to the hotels. The brochure of one tent camp company, Shaw & Powell, assured the lady traveler that "carefully selected matrons" would look after her. "It is perfectly safe and proper for ladies to make the trip with us without escorts." A rival, the Wylie Permanent Camping Company, advertised nationwide to convince schoolteachers they could visit "Wonderland" inexpensively and safely traveling with their company.

Whether they were staying in hotels, in tent camps, or camping independently, Yellowstone visitors starting seeing bears frequently in the 1890s. By that time wild bears had had enough experience of the ways of man to learn where the hotels dumped their garbage. Soon, with the tacit approval of the acting superintendents (at that time, officers of the U.S. Cavalry), the ritual feeding of bears at the hotel dumps had evolved into a big show for the stagecoach travelers. Every visitor went home with stories and pictures of bears that they saw either begging along the roads or eating in the dumps.

During the park's early days, women rarely traveled to Yellowstone without family except as part of a supervised tour, but in 1906 intrepid horsewoman Anne Bosworth Greene toured the park alone—staying in Wylie tent camps, near one of which she had an adventure with a bear. She visited the park on a commission to paint scenery for a man she only identifies as "the Literary Person." Then, just before the United States entered World War I, another horsewoman, Alice Parmelee Morris, on her own initiative and at her own expense, rode at the head of a pack train through the entire park to plan a complete loop system of equestrian trails.

Late nineteenth-century prose is charming, even when wordy, flowery with adjectives, and sometimes fraught with hyperbole and poesy. In contrast to our hurried ways of writing and texting, the writers of a century or two ago allowed themselves to take time for everything. They presented us with delightful and skillfully written word-pictures. For example, Belgian visitor Jules Leclercq, describing the terraces of Mammoth Hot Springs in 1883, wrote,

> The eye loses itself in the multiple combinations of this magical architecture. How delicately are the sides of the basins chiseled! Their edges are outlined in scallops of an infinite richness of shape. Fountains in the most marvelous palaces born of the Oriental imagination would scarcely give an idea of these perfect bowls created by a caprice of nature; from them escape a thousand graceful cascades that lovingly bathe the sculptures of the stalactites and flow as pure and limpid as molten diamond.[5]

An Englishman, Sir Rose Lambart Price, who visited Yellowstone in 1897 as part of a Rocky Mountain hunting trip, wrote glowingly about what he had seen and his experiences:

> [Sights] too numerous to mention are embraced in the People's Park, and over a thousand miles of some of the best trout fishing in the world is thrown in to help them to enjoy it. Our American cousins have every right to feel proud of their magnificent playground, and they have conferred a benefit on the entire world by preserving it in its entirety for the national use. It makes me shudder to think what might have happened, but for the wise forethought that dedicated this grand property to the people of America and their heirs forever.[6]

President Roosevelt unwittingly echoed this when he called Yellowstone a "great natural playground" in his speech dedicating the North Entrance Arch in April 1903.

Noted western historian Patricia Limerick, in her keynote speech to Yellowstone's Fourth Biennial Scientific Conference (1997), said, "It is a treat to read these early accounts of early visitors to the park, because so many of them were so profoundly overcome by wonder at what they saw. Every one of them seems to have gone through a ritual of saying that words could not possibly capture what the eye could see in Yellowstone, and then every one of them wrote hundreds and hundreds of words anyway."[7]

Yellowstone remains a magnificent playground, counting four million American and foreign visitors in 2015. The park means something different to each of us. The selections in *Through Early Yellowstone* demonstrate that this has been true from its very inception.

By 1906, when Anne Bosworth Greene concluded her visit to Yellowstone, the United States had set aside several areas around the country as national parks, some of which are now designated national monuments or recreation areas. Ten years later the National Park Service (NPS) was formed through years of effort by forward-thinking men like Stephen T. Mather and Horace M. Albright and through national publicity in the *Saturday Evening Post* and *National Geographic Magazine*. Congress and President Woodrow Wilson created the NPS as a division of the Department of Interior on August 25, 1916. Now countries around the world have adopted America's national park idea.

NOTES

1. Cook, Folsom, and Peterson, *The Valley of the Upper Yellowstone*, xxi–xxxii.
2. Rollins, "The Three Tetons," 869–70.
3. Wikipedia article, "Gilded Age," note 2.
4. Detailed information about all Yellowstone hotels and other concessions is found in Culpin, *History of Concession Development in Yellowstone National Park, 1872–1966.*
5. Leclercq, *Yellowstone, Land of Wonders*, 51.
6. Price, *Summer on the Rockies*, 216–17.
7. Schullery and Stevenson, eds., *People and Place*, 239.

Accounts of the Washburn-Langford-Doane Expedition

At length we came to a boiling Lake about 300 ft in diameter forming a nearly complete circle. . . . The steam which arose for one third of the diameter of it was white, in the middle it was pale red, and the remaining third on the east light sky blue.
Osborne Russell, *Journal of a Trapper*, about 1840

Strong stimulus to national interest in the Yellowstone region and impetus for the creation of a national reserve came in spring 1871 with two accounts of the 1870 Washburn-Langford-Doane expedition in the popular press. In retrospect, these articles might be tagged the beginning of the historic literature of Yellowstone National Park. The new magazine *Scribner's Monthly* published a detailed and illustrated account by Nathaniel Pitt Langford of the biggest and best-organized exploratory foray into the area up to that time. In the same months (May and June), the *Overland Monthly* presented two articles by another member of the 1870 exploring party, Walter A. Trumbull.

Both these men had connections to the Northern Pacific Railroad. Langford was an informal scout for the railroad and later an enthusiastic popularizer of the beauties of Montana Territory, into which the railroad was planning to expand its tracks. Trumbull, fourteen years Langford's junior, was the eldest son of U.S. Senator Lyman Trumbull of Illinois, who also had interests in that railroad.

Both men, at the time of their Yellowstone adventure, were between jobs. Langford had served as collector of internal revenue from 1864 to 1868. For his part, Trumbull was assistant assessor of internal revenue for Montana Territory but was replaced at the beginning of Grant's presidency. Although Trumbull has always been considered an upright man and a trustworthy reporter, it must be noted that Yellowstone Park Historians from Aubrey L. Haines to Lee H. Whittlesey have considered Langford to be slippery and untrustworthy in some respects. One reason for this suspicion is that the pocket diary he carried on the Yellowstone trip and an important scrapbook of clippings have always been missing from the collection of papers he presented to the Minnesota Historical Society. "Were they disposed of for a reason?" the historians ask. If Langford's account needs to be considered not entirely factual, it is still entertaining reading and was unquestionably influential in leading to the establishment of the world's first national park.

As a young man Trumbull was a reporter for the *New York Sun*; after his Yellowstone trip he was a special correspondent to the *Helena Herald*. He contracted consumption as assistant consul to Zanzibar and died at the age of forty-five. Scattered throughout Langford's complete account here are several relevant quotations from the *Overland Monthly* articles by Trumbull.

Langford was one of thirteen children. His education—as a farmer's son—"was squeezed into the slack season between fall harvesting and spring plowing,"[1] according to historian Haines, but he nevertheless received a good education and entered banking in St. Paul in 1854. Eight years later, traveling west for his health, he joined an expedition to the Idaho gold fields, then moved in 1863 to Alder Gulch (later called Virginia City) in Montana Territory and became collector of internal revenue.

Langford became interested in exploring the upper Yellowstone River after hearing about "hot spouting springs" from famous mountain man Jim Bridger and about the findings of the Cook-Folsom-Peterson 1869 expedition from David Folsom in Helena. In 1870 he was able to interest a group in going there—a sufficiently large party to assuage fears of Indian attack.

Upon his return from the Yellowstone area, Langford lectured in Eastern cities about what he found there. He served as the park's first superintendent (with no compensation from Congress) from May 10, 1872, to April 18, 1877. At the same time, from 1872 to 1885, he was a bank examiner for the western states and territories. In his later years he worked in the insurance business in Saint Paul and as president of the county board of control.

Wrote Hiram M. Chittenden in his 1895 book, *The Yellowstone National Park: Historical and Descriptive*, "[Langford's] enthusiasm upon the subject in the early days of its history drew upon him the mild raillery of his friends, who were wont to call him 'National Park' Langford—a sobriquet to which the initials of his real name readily lent themselves."[2] In his *Scribner's* articles, the author vividly conveys the thrill of discovery, as well as suggesting the importance of access to this unique terrain to future generations, both for enjoyment and for scientific investigation. At the time he participated in the 1870 expedition, he was serving as a scout for the Northern Pacific Railroad, so it is no surprise that he ends his magazine articles with a brief verbal tour of that railroad's proposed route to the West.

The Wonders of the Yellowstone

1871

NATHANIEL P. LANGFORD
born Westmoreland, New York, 1832 • died Saint Paul, Minnesota, 1911

WITH EXCERPTS FROM "THE WASHBURN YELLOWSTONE EXPEDITION" BY WALTER A. TRUMBULL
born Springfield, Illinois, 1846 • died Zanzibar, 1891

I had indulged, for several years, a great curiosity to see the wonders of the upper valley of the Yellowstone. The stories told by trappers and mountaineers of the natural phenomena of that region were so strange and marvelous that, as long ago as 1866, I first contemplated the possibility of organizing an expedition for the express purpose of exploring it. During the past year, meeting with several gentlemen who expressed like curiosity, we determined to make the journey in the months of August and September.

The Yellowstone and Columbia, the first flowing into the Missouri and the last into the Pacific, divided from each other by the Rocky Mountains, have

their sources within a few miles of each other. Both rise in the mountains which separate Idaho from the new Territory of Wyoming, but the headwaters of the Yellowstone are only accessible from Montana. The mountains surrounding the basin from which they flow are very lofty, covered with pines, and on the southeastern side present to the traveler a precipitous wall of rock several thousand feet in height. This barrier prevented Captain Reynolds from visiting the headwaters of the Yellowstone while prosecuting an expedition planned by the Government and placed under his command, for the purpose of exploring that river, in 1859.[3]

The source of the Yellowstone is in a magnificent lake, nearly 9,000 feet [7,732 feet (2,357 meters)] above the level of the ocean. In its course of 1,300 miles to the Missouri, it falls about

9

7,200 feet. Its upper waters flow through deep cañons and gorges, and are broken by immense cataracts and fearful rapids, presenting at various points some of the grandest scenery on the continent. This country is entirely volcanic, and abounds in boiling springs, mud volcanoes, huge mountains of sulphur, and geysers more extensive and numerous than those of Iceland.

Old mountaineers and trappers are great romancers. I have met with many, but never one who was not fond of practicing upon the credulity of those who listened to his adventures. Bridger, than whom perhaps no man has experienced more of wild mountain life, has been so much in the habit of embellishing his Indian adventures, that they are received by all who know him with many grains of allowance. This want of faith will account for the skepticism with which the oft-repeated stories of the wonders of the Upper Yellowstone were received by people who had lived within one hundred and twenty miles of them, and who at any time could have established their verity by ten days' travel.

Our company, composed of some of the officials and leading citizens of Montana, felt that if the half were true, they would be amply compensated for all the troubles and hazards of the expedition. It was, nevertheless, a serious undertaking,

late: Everts had recently lost that political appointment.

cantinas: Mexican Spanish for "saddlebags."

needle-gun: Invented in the mid-nineteenth century, this gun used a needlelike firing pin to impact the percussion cap at the base of the bullet.

and as the time drew near for our departure, several who had been foremost to join us, upon the receipt of intelligence that a party of Indians had come into the Upper Yellowstone valley, found excuse for their withdrawal in various emergent occupations, so that when the day for our departure arrived, our company was reduced in numbers to nine, and consisted of the following-named gentlemen: General H. D. Washburn, who served with distinction during the war of the rebellion, and subsequently represented the Clinton District of Indiana in the Congress of the United States; Samuel T. Hauser, President of the First National Bank of Helena; Cornelius Hedges, a leading member of the bar of Montana; Hon. Truman C. Everts, **late** United States Assessor for Montana; Walter Trumbull, son of Senator Trumbull; Ben. Stickney, Jr.; Warren C. Gillette; Jacob Smith, and the writer.

The preparation was simple. Each man was supplied with a strong horse, well equipped with California saddle, bridle, and **cantinas**. A **needle-gun**, a belt filled with cartridges, a pair of revolvers, a hunting-knife, added to the usual costume of the mountains, completed the personal outfit of each member of the expedition. When mounted and ready to start, we resembled more a band of brigands than sober men in search of natural wonders. Our provisions, consisting of bacon, dried fruit, flour, &c. were securely lashed to the backs of twelve bronchos, which were placed in charge of a couple of packers. We also employed two colored boys as cooks.

Major-General Hancock, in favorable response to our application for a military escort, had given orders for a company of cavalry to accompany us, which we expected to join at Fort Ellis, in the Gallatin Valley—a distance of one hundred and twenty miles from Helena. We were none the less obliged to Gen. Hancock for his prompt compliance with our application for an escort, because of his own desire, previously expressed, to learn something of the country we explored which would be of service to him in the disposition of the troops under his command, for frontier defense; and if the result of our explorations in the least contributed to that end, we still remain the debtor of that officer for his courtesy and kindness, without which we might have failed altogether in our undertaking.

Our ride to Fort Ellis, through a well-settled portion of the Territory, was accomplished in four days. That portion of the valleys of the Missouri and Gallatin through which we passed, dotted with numerous ranches, presented large fields of wheat, oats, potatoes, and other evidences of thrift common in agricultural districts. Large droves of cattle were feeding upon the bunch grass which carpeted the valleys and foot-hills. Even the mountains, so wild, solemn, and unsocial a few years ago, seemed to be domesticated as they reared their familiar summits in long and continuous succession along the bordering uplands. At the three forks, where the Jefferson, Madison, and Gallatin unite and form the Missouri, a thriving agricultural community has sprung up, which must eventually grow into a town of considerable importance. Entering the magnificent valley of the Gallatin at this point, our course up the river lay through one of the finest agricultural regions on the continent. The soil is remarkably fertile, and the valley stretches away on either side, a distance of twenty miles, to immense mountain ranges, which traverse its entire length, enclosing a territory as large as one of the larger New England States, every foot of which is susceptible of the highest cultivation.

Bozeman, a picturesque village of seven hundred inhabitants, situated at the foot of the Belt Range of mountains, is considered one of the most important prospective business locations in Montana. It is near the mouth of one of the few mountain passes of the Territory deemed practicable for railroad improvement. Its inhabitants are patiently awaiting the time when the cars of the "Northern Pacific" shall descend into their streets. The village is neatly built of wood and brick. Its surroundings are magnificent. The eye can distinctly trace the mountains by which it is encircled, a distance of four hundred miles.

Fort Ellis, three miles distant, is built upon a table of land elevated above the valley, and which overlooks it for a great distance. Our party was welcomed by Colonel Baker, the commandant, and we pitched our tent near the post.

On the morning succeeding our arrival we were informed that, owing to the absence on duty of most of the soldiers, a fraction of a company—five cavalrymen and a lieutenant in command—were all that could be afforded for our escort; but, realizing that a small body of white men can more easily elude a band of Indians than can a large party, and without hesitating to consider the possible defense which we could make against a war party of hostile Sioux with this limited number, we declared ourselves satisfied, and took our

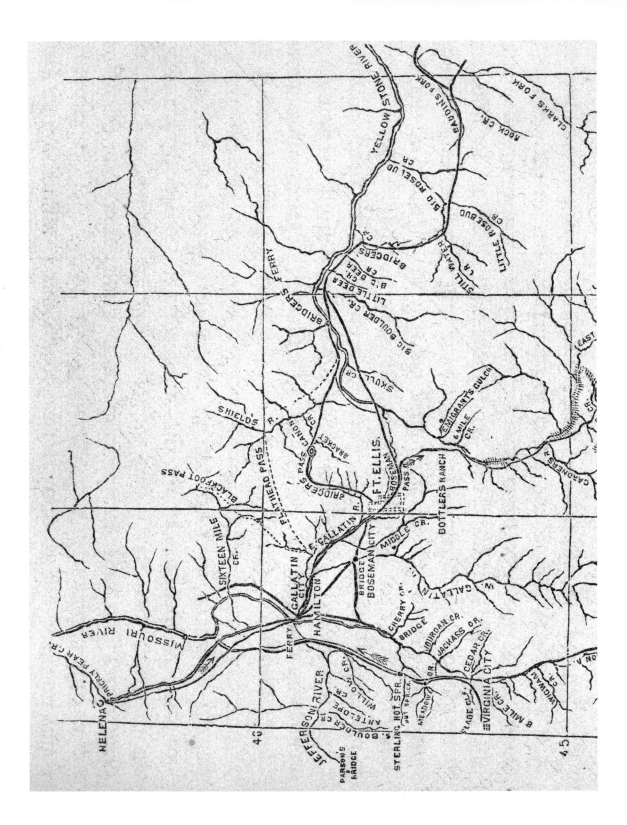

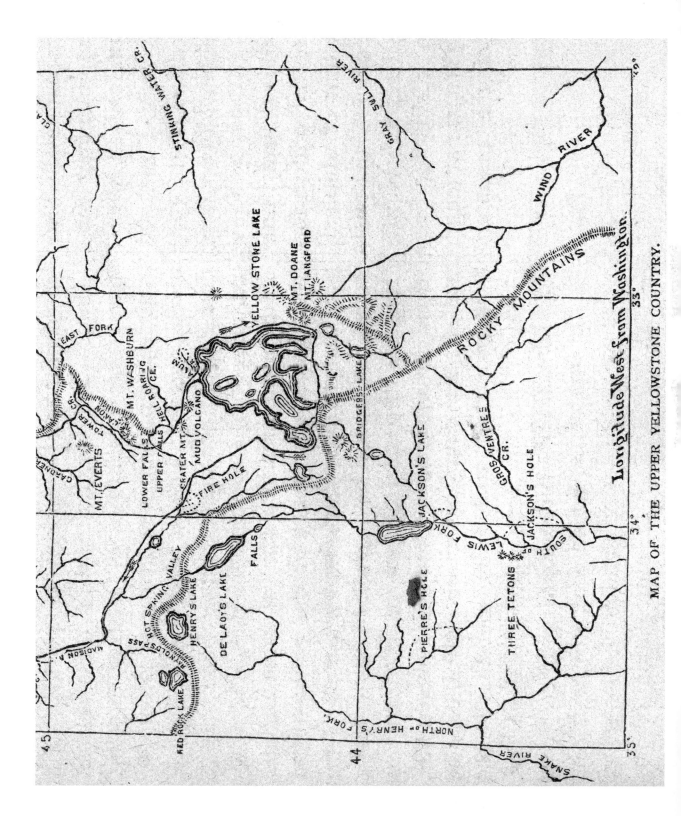

MAP OF THE UPPER YELLOWSTONE COUNTRY.

departure for the *terra incognita* as fully assured of a successful journey as if our number had been multiplied by hundreds.

Our pack-horses were brought up and their loads fastened to them with that incredible rapidity and skill which is the result only of life-long practice. The dexterity with which a skillful packer will load and unload his horses is remarkable. The rope is thrown around the body of the animal and securely fastened in less time than it takes to tell it. No matter what the character of the beast, wild or tame, it is under the perfect control of its master. The broncho is however, a refractory customer. He has many tricks, unknown to his well-trained brother of the East. Bucking is a frequent vice, for which there is small remedy; but as was proved in a single instance on the morning we left the fort, that horse must be more expert than was any in our train who can foil an experienced packer. Every leap of the enraged brute only increased the tension of the cord which bound him, and rendered him tractable.

Once under way, our little company, now increased to nineteen, presented quite a formidable appearance, as by dint of whip and spur our steeds gayly wheeled across the plain towards the mountains.[4] After a tedious ride of several hours up steep acclivities, over rocks, and through dark defiles, we at length passed over the summit of the mountain range, took a last look at the beautiful valley of the Gallatin, and descended into a ravine coursed by the waters of Trail Creek. Following this two days, we came to the Yellowstone, up which we rode to the solitary ranch of the brothers Boteler—the last abode of civilized man in the direction of our travels. These hardy mountaineers received and entertained us in hearty mountain style—giving us the best of everything their ranch afforded, together with a great deal of information and advice about the country, which we afterwards found to be invaluable. The Botelers belong to that class of pioneers, of which there are many in the new Territories, who are only satisfied when their location and field of operations are a little in advance of civilization—exposed to privation and danger—and yet unite with these discomforts some advantages of hunting, trapping, and fishing not enjoyed by men contented to dwell in safety. Free-hearted, jolly and brave, living upon such means as the country afforded, accustomed to roam for days and weeks in the mountains in pursuit of game and furs, their experience renewed our courage, and the descriptions which they gave us of the wonders they had seen increased our curiosity. It was not pleasant, however, to learn that twenty-five lodges of Crows had gone up the valley a few days before our arrival, or to be told by a trapper whom we met that he had been robbed by them, and, in common parlance, "been set on foot," by having his horse and provisions stolen.

In anticipation of possible trouble from this source, we organized our company, and elected Gen. H. D. Washburn, Surveyor-General of Montana, commander. It was understood that we should make but one march each day—starting at 8 AM, and camping at 3 PM. This obviated the necessity of unpacking and cooking a dinner. At night the horses were to be carefully picketed, a fire built beyond them, and two of the company to keep guard until one o'clock; then to be relieved by two others, who were to watch until daylight. This divided the labor among fourteen, who were to serve as picket-men twice each week.

These precautionary measures being fully understood, we left Boteler's, plunging at once into the vast unknown which lay before us. Following the slight Indian trail, we traveled near the bank of the river, amid the wildest imaginable scenery of river, rock, and mountain. The foothills were covered with verdure, which an autumnal sun had sprinkled with maroon-colored tints, very delicate and beautiful. The path was narrow, rocky, and uneven, frequently leading over high hills, in ascent and descent more or less abrupt and difficult. The increasing altitude of the route was more perceptible than any over which we had ever traveled, and the river, whenever visible, was a perfect mountain torrent.

While descending a hill into one of the broad openings of the valley, our attention was suddenly arrested by half a dozen or more mounted Indians, who were riding down the foot-hills on the opposite side of the river. Two of our company, who had lingered behind, came up with the information that they had seen several more making observations from behind a small butte, from which they fled in great haste on being discovered.[5] They soon rode down on the plateau to a point where their horses were hobbled, and for a long time watched our party as it continued its course of travel up the river. Our camp was guarded that night with

lower cañon: Historically called the Second Canyon of the Yellowstone, now known as Yankee Jim Canyon.

more than ordinary vigilance. A hard rain-storm, which set in early in the afternoon and continued through the night, may have saved us from an attack by these prowlers.

When we started the next morning, Gen. Washburn detailed four of our company to guard the pack train, while he, with four others, rode in advance to make the most practicable selection of routes. Six miles above our camp we ascended the spur of a mountain, which came down boldly to the river's edge. From its summit we had a beautiful view of the valley stretched out before us—the river fringed with cottonwood trees—the foot-hills covered with luxuriant, many-tinted herbage, and over all the snow-crowned summits of the mountains, many miles away, but seemingly rising from the midst of the plateau at our feet. Looking up the river, the valley opened widely, and from the rock on which we stood was visible the train of pack-horses, slowly winding their way along the sinuous trail, which followed the inequalities of the mountain-side. The whole formed a scene of great interest. Pursuing our course a few miles farther, we camped just below the **lower cañon** of the river. Our hunters provided us with a sumptuous meal of antelope, rabbit, duck, grouse, and trout.

⌐◦⌐

Trumbull described the scenery upstream from Bottler's ranch:

The view was exceedingly fine. The valley was in sight from the mouth of the cañon, *eight miles above, to a point at least forty miles below. The course of the river could be plainly discerned by an unbroken line of willows, stretching away to the north-east, while in the background the lofty, snow-capped peaks glistened midway between the earth and the cloudless firmament above. We camped at the mouth of the* cañon, *where the Yellowstone issues from the mountains. Above that point there is no open country, until you reach the basin of the great lake.*

During the day plenty of small game was killed, and the fishing was found to be excellent. Trout and white-fish were abundant—and such trout! They can only be found in the neighborhood of the Rocky Mountains, and on the Pacific Slope. Few of them weighed less than two pounds, and *many of them over three. They had not been educated up to the* fly; *but when their attention was respectfully solicited to a transfixed grasshopper, they seldom failed to respond.*

During the pleasant evening, and the long summer twilight peculiar to a northern latitude, some made rough sketches of the magnificent scenes by which we were surrounded; others wrote up their notes of the trip, while the rest serenely smoked their pipes, and listened to reminiscences from each other of by-gone times, or other scenes somewhat similar to those we *then enjoyed.* ("Washburn Yellowstone Expedition," 432)

The night was very cold, the mercury standing at 40° [F] when we broke camp, at eight o'clock the next morning. We remained some time at the lower cañon of the Yellowstone, which, as a single isolated piece of scenery, is very beautiful. It is less than a mile in length, and perhaps does not exceed 1,000 feet in depth. Its walls are vertical, and, seen from the summit of the precipice, the river seems forced through a narrow gorge, and is surging and boiling at a fearful rate—the water breaking into millions of prismatic drops against every projecting rock.

After traveling six miles over the mountains above the cañon we again descended into a broad and open valley, skirted by a level upland for several miles. Here an object met our attention which deserves more than a casual notice. It was two parallel vertical walls of rock, projecting from the side of a mountain to the height of 125 feet, traversing the mountain from base to summit, a distance of 1,500 feet. These walls were not to exceed thirty feet in width and their tops for the whole length were crowned with a growth of pines. The sides were as even as if they had been worked by line and plumb—the whole space between, and on either side of them, having been completely eroded and washed away. We had seen many of the capricious works wrought by erosion upon the friable rocks of Montana, but never before upon so majestic a scale. Here an entire mountain-side, by wind and water, had been removed, leaving as the evidences of their protracted toil these vertical projections, which, but for their immensity, might as readily be mistaken for works of art as of nature. Their smooth sides, uniform width and height, and great length, considered in connection with the causes which had wrought their insulation, excited our wonder and admiration. They were all the more

THE DEVIL'S SLIDE, MONTANA.

curious because of their dissimilarity to any other striking objects in natural scenery that we had ever seen or heard of. In future years, when the wonders of the Yellowstone are incorporated into the family of fashionable resorts, there will be few of its attractions surpassing in interest this marvelous freak of the elements. For some reason, best understood by himself, one of our companions gave to these rocks the name of the "Devil's Slide." The suggestion was unfortunate, as, with more reason perhaps, but with no better taste, we frequently had occasion to appropriate other portions of the person of his Satanic Majesty, or of his dominion,

in signification of the varied marvels we met with. Some little excuse may be found for this in the fact that the old mountaineers had been peculiarly lavish in the use of the infernal vocabulary. Every river and glen and mountain had suggested to their imaginations some fancied resemblance to portions of a region which their pious grandmothers had warned them to avoid. It is common for them, when speaking of this region, to designate portions of its physical features, as "Fire Hole Prairie,"—the "Devil's Glen"—or "Hell Roaring River," &c.—and these names, from a remarkable fitness of things, are not likely to be speedily superseded by others less impressive. We camped at the close of this day's travel near the southwestern corner of Montana, at the mouth of Gardiner's River [now the site of Gardiner, Montana].

Crossing this stream the next morning, we passed over several rocky ridges into a valley which, for a long distance, was crowded with the spires of protruding rocks, which gave it such a dismal aspect that we named it "The Valley of Desolation."[6] The trail was so rough and mountainous that we were able to travel but six miles before the usual hour for camping. Much of the distance was through fallen timber, almost impassable by the pack train. A mile before camping we discovered on the trail the fresh tracks of unshod ponies, indicating that a party of Indians had recently passed over it.[7] Lieutenant Doane, with one of our company, had left us in the morning, and did not come into camp this evening. One of our horses broke his lariat during the night and galloped through the camp, rousing the sleepers, who grasped their guns, supposing the Indians were really upon them.

We started early the next morning and soon struck the trail which had been traveled the preceding day by Lieutenant Doane. It led over a more practicable route than the one we left. The marks made in the soil by the travais[8] on the side of the trail showed that it had been recently traveled by a number of lodges of Indians,—and a little colt, which we overtook soon after making the discovery, convinced us that we were in their immediate vicinity. Our party was separated, and if we had been attacked, our pack-train, horses, and stores would have been an easy conquest. Fortunately we were unmolested, and, when again united, made

a fresh resolution to travel as much in company as possible. All precautionary measures, however, unless enforced by the sternest discipline, are soon forgotten—and danger, until actually impending, is seldom borne in mind. A day had scarcely passed when we were as reckless as ever.

From the summit of a commanding range, which separated the waters of Antelope and Tower Creeks, we descended through a picturesque gorge, leading our horses to a small stream flowing into the Yellowstone. Four miles of travel, a great part of it down the precipitous slopes of the mountain, brought us to the banks of Tower Creek, and within the volcanic region, where the wonders were supposed to commence. On the right of the trail our attention was first attracted by a small hot sulphur spring, a little below the boiling point in temperature. Leaving the spring we ascended a high ridge, from which the most noticeable feature, in a landscape of great extent and beauty, was Column Rock, stretching for two miles along the eastern bank of the Yellowstone. At the distance from which we saw it, we could compare it in appearance to nothing but a section of the **Giant's Causeway**. It was composed of successive pillars of basalt overlying and underlying a thick stratum of cement and gravel resembling pudding-stone. In both rows, the pillars, standing in close proximity, were each about thirty feet high and from three to five feet in diameter. This interesting object, more from the novelty of its formation and its beautiful surroundings of mountain and river scenery than anything grand or impressive in its appearance, excited our attention, until the gathering shades of evening reminded us of the necessity of selecting a suitable camp. We descended the declivity to the banks of Tower Creek, and camped on a rocky terrace one mile distant from, and four hundred feet above the Yellowstone.

Tower Creek is a mountain torrent flowing through a gorge about forty yards wide. Just below our camp it falls perpendicularly over an even ledge **112 feet**, forming one of the most beautiful cataracts in the world. For some distance above the fall the stream is broken into a great number of channels, each of which has worked a tortuous course through a compact body of shale to the verge of the precipice, where they re-unite and form the fall. The countless shapes into which the shale has been wrought by the action of the angry waters, add a feature of great interest to the scene. Spires of solid shale, capped with slate, beautifully rounded and polished, faultless in symmetry, raise their tapering forms to the height of from 80 to 150 feet, all over the plateau above the cataract. Some resemble towers, others the spires of churches, and others still shoot up as lithe and slender as the minarets of a mosque.⁹ Some of the loftiest of these formations, standing like sentinels upon the very brink of the fall, are accessible to an expert and adventurous climber. The position attained on one of their narrow summits, amid the uproar of waters and at a height of 250 feet above the boiling chasm, as the writer can affirm, requires a steady head and strong nerves; yet the

view which rewards the temerity of the exploit is full of compensations. Below the fall the stream descends in numerous rapids, with frightful velocity, through a gloomy gorge, to its union with the Yellowstone. Its bed is filled with enormous boulders, against which the rushing waters break with great fury.

Many of the capricious formations wrought from the shale excite merriment as well as wonder. Of this kind especially was a huge mass sixty feet in height, which, from its supposed resemblance to the proverbial foot of his Satanic Majesty, we

TOWER FALLS, ON TOWER CREEK, WYOMING.

Giant's Causeway: A basalt column formation located in County Antrim, Ireland.

112 feet: Tower Fall, which Langford called "Tower Falls," is 132 feet (40 m) high.

called the "Devil's Hoof." The scenery of mountain, rock, and forest surrounding the falls is very beautiful. Here, too, the hunter and fisherman can indulge their tastes with the certainty of ample reward. As a halfway resort to the greater wonders still farther up the marvelous river, the visitor of future years will find no more delightful resting-place. No account of this beautiful fall has ever been given by any of the former visitors to this region. The name of "Tower Falls," which we gave it, was suggested by some of the most conspicuous features of the scenery.

⌖

In their 1871 articles, neither Langford nor Trumbull explained how Tower Falls was named, but thirty-four years later Langford wrote:

> While in camp on Sunday, August 28th, on the bank of this creek, it was suggested that we select a name for the creek and fall. Walter Trumbull suggested 'Minaret Creek' and 'Minaret Fall.' Mr. Hauser suggested 'Tower Creek' and 'Tower Fall.' After some discussion a vote was taken, and by a small majority the name 'Minaret' was decided upon. During the following evening Mr. Hauser stated with great seriousness that we had violated the agreement made [at journey's outset] relative to naming objects for our friends. He said that the well known Southern family—the Rhetts—lived in St. Louis, and that they had a most charming and accomplished daughter named 'Minnie.' He said that this daughter was a sweetheart of Trumbull, who had proposed the name—her name—'Minnie Rhett'—and that we had unwittingly given to the fall and creek the name of this sweetheart of Mr. Trumbull. Mr. Trumbull indignantly denied the truth of Hauser's statement, and Hauser as determinedly insisted that it was the truth, and the vote was therefore reconsidered, and by a substantial majority it was decided to substitute the name 'Tower' for 'Minaret.' Later, and when it was too late to recall or reverse the action of our party, it was surmised that Hauser himself had a sweetheart in St. Louis, a Miss Tower. Some of our party, Walter Trumbull especially, always insisted that such was the case. The weight of testimony was so evenly balanced that I shall hesitate long before I believe either side of this part of the story."
> (Langford, *Discovery*, 21)

⌖

Early the next morning several of our company left in advance, to explore a passage for our pack-train over the mountains, which were very steep and lofty. We had been following a bend in the river,—but as no sign of a change in its course was apparent, our object was, by finding a shorter route across the country, to avoid several days of toilsome travel. The advance party ascended a lofty peak,—by barometrical measurement, **10,580 feet**

10,580 feet: Mt. Washburn's elevation is 10,243 feet (3,122 m).

above ocean level,—which, in honor of our commander, was called Mount Washburn. From its summit, 400 feet above the line of perpetual snow, we were able to trace the course of the river to its source in Yellowstone Lake. At the point where we crossed the line of vegetation the snow covered the side of the apex of the mountain to the depth of twenty feet, and seemed to be as solid as the rocks upon which it rested. Descending the mountain, we came upon the trail made by the pack-train at its base, which we followed into camp at the head of a small stream flowing into the Yellowstone.

Following the stream in the direction of its mouth, at the distance of a mile below our camp, we crossed an immense bed of volcanic ashes, thirty feet deep, extending one hundred yards along both sides of the creek. Less than a mile beyond, we suddenly came upon a hideous-looking glen filled with the sulphurous vapor emitted from six or eight boiling springs of great size and activity. One of our company aptly compared it to the entrance to the infernal regions. It looked like nothing earthly we had ever seen, and the pungent fumes which filled the atmosphere were not unaccompanied by a disagreeable sense of possible suffocation. Entering the basin cautiously, we found the entire surface of the earth covered with the incrusted sinter thrown from the springs. Jets of hot vapor were expelled through a hundred natural orifices with which it was pierced, and through every fracture made by passing over it. The springs themselves were as diabolical in appearance as the witches' caldron in Macbeth, and needed but the presence of Hecate and her weird band to realize that horrible creation of poetic fancy. They were all in a state of violent ebullition, throwing their liquid contents to the height of three or four feet. The largest had a basin twenty by forty feet in diameter. Its greenish-yellow water was covered with bubbles, which were constantly rising, bursting, and emitting sulphurous gas from various parts of its surface. The central spring seethed and bubbled like a boiling caldron. Fearful volumes of vapor were constantly escaping it. Near it was another, not so large, but more infernal in appearance. Its contents, of the consistency of paint, were in constant, noisy ebullition. A stick thrust into it, on being withdrawn, was coated with lead-colored slime a quarter of an inch in thickness. Nothing flows from this spring. Seemingly, it is boiling down. A fourth spring, which exhibited the same physical features, was partly covered by an overhanging ledge of rock. We tried to fathom it, but the bottom was beyond the reach of the longest pole we could find. Rocks cast into it increased the agitation of its waters. There were several other springs in the group, smaller in size, but presenting the same characteristics.

The approach to them was unsafe, the incrustation surrounding them bending in many places beneath our weight,—and from the fractures thus created would ooze a sulphury slime of the consistency of mucilage. It was with great difficulty that we obtained specimens from the natural apertures with which the crust is filled,—a feat which was accomplished by one only of our party, who extended himself at full length upon that portion of the incrustation which yielded the least, but which was not sufficiently strong to bear his weight while in an upright position, and at imminent risk

GETTING A SPECIMEN.

by white man. The name of **"Hell Broth Springs,"** which we gave them, fully expressed our appreciation of their character.

Our journey the next day still continued through a country until then untraveled. Owing to the high lateral mountain spurs, the numerous ravines, and the interminable patches of fallen timber, we made very slow progress; but when the hour for camping arrived we were greatly surprised to find ourselves descending the mountain along the banks of a beautiful stream in the immediate vicinity of the Great Falls of the Yellowstone. This stream, which we called Cascade Creek, is very rapid. Just before its union with the river it passes through a gloomy gorge, of abrupt descent, which on either side is filled with continuous masses of obsidian that have been worn by the water into many fantastic shapes and cavernous recesses. This we named "The Devil's Den." Near the foot of the gorge the creek breaks from fearful rapids into a cascade of great beauty. The first fall of five feet is immediately succeeded by another of fifteen, into a pool as clear as amber, nestled beneath over-arching rocks. Here it lingers as if half reluctant to continue its course, and then gracefully emerges from the grotto, and, veiling the rocks down an abrupt descent of eighty-four feet, passes rapidly on to the

of sinking into the infernal mixture, rolled over and over to the edge of the opening, and with the crust slowly bending and sinking beneath him, hurriedly secured the coveted prize.

There was something so revolting in the general appearance of the springs and their surroundings—the foulness of the vapors, the infernal contents, the treacherous incrustation, the noisy ebullition, the general appearance of desolation, and the seclusion and wildness of the location—that, though awe-struck, we were not unreluctant to continue our journey without making them a second visit. They were probably never before seen

"Hell Broth Springs": The party encountered these, called Washburn Hot Springs by 1904, along the western rim of the Grand Canyon of the Yellowstone.

Yellowstone. It received the name of "Crystal."[10]

The Great Falls are at the head of one of the most remarkable cañons in the world—a gorge through volcanic rocks fifty miles long, and varying from one thousand to nearly five thousand feet in depth [varies from about 800 to 1,200 feet (240–360 meters)]. In its descent through this wonderful chasm the river falls almost three thousand feet. At one point, where the passage has been worn through a mountain range, our hunters assured us it was more than a vertical mile in depth, and the river, broken into rapids and cascades, appeared no wider than a ribbon. The brain reels as we gaze into this profound and solemn solitude. We shrink from the dizzy verge appalled, glad to feel the solid earth under our feet, and venture no more, except with forms extended, and faces barely protruding over the edge of the precipice. The stillness is horrible. Down, down, down, we see the river attenuated to a thread, tossing its miniature waves, and dashing, with puny strength, the massive walls which imprison it. All access to its margin is denied, and the dark gray rocks hold it in dismal shadow. Even the voice of its waters in their convulsive agony cannot be heard. Uncheered by plant or shrub, obstructed with massive boulders and by jutting points, it rushes madly on its solitary course, deeper and deeper into the bowels of the rocky firmament. The solemn grandeur of the scene surpasses description. It must be seen to be felt. The sense of danger with which it impresses you is harrowing in the extreme. You feel the absence of sound, the oppression of absolute silence. If you could only hear that gurgling river, if you could see a living tree in the depth beneath you, if a bird

RUSTIC BRIDGE AND CRYSTAL FALLS.
by Philetus W. Norris, 1880

Will these feet that trip so lightly
O'er this structure rude but strong,
Or these eyes which beam so brightly,
E'er greet scenes more meet for song?

Skipping rill from snowy fountains
Dashing through embowered walls,
Fairy dell 'mid frowning mountains,
Grotto pool and Crystal Falls.

Charming dell, begirt with wonders,
Mighty falls on either hand,
Quiet glen amid their thunders,
Matchless, save in Wonder-Land.

O'er their mingled mists and shadows
Rainbows beauteous, tinted, rise,
And their ever-changing halos
Blend and vanish in the skies.

Shy beneath the crystal waters,
In the grotto of the glen,
Sylvan forms of nature's daughters
Sport and bathe unseen by men.

Here we part, perchance forever,
In our pilgrimage below;
Yet in scenes like this together,
Above may we each other know?

would fly past, if the wind would move any object in the awful chasm, to break for a moment the solemn silence that reigns there, it would relieve that tension of the nerves which the scene has excited, and you would rise from your prostrate condition and thank God that he had permitted you to gaze, unharmed, upon this majestic display of natural architecture. As it is, sympathizing in spirit with the deep gloom of the scene, you crawl from the dreadful verge, scared lest the firm rock give way beneath and precipitate you into the horrid gulf.

We had been told by trappers and mountaineers that there were cataracts in this vicinity a thousand feet high; but, if so, they must be lower down the cañon, in that portion of it which, by our journey across the bend in the river, we failed to see. We regretted, when too late, that we had not made a fuller exploration—for by no other theory than that there was a stupendous fall below us, or that the river was broken by a continued succession of cascades, could we account for a difference of nearly 3,000 feet in altitude between the head and the mouth of the cañon. In that part of the cañon which we saw, the inclination of the river was marked by frequent falls fifteen and twenty feet in height, sufficient, if continuous through it, to accomplish the entire descent.

The fearful descent into this terrific cañon was accomplished with great difficulty by Messrs. Hauser and Stickney, at a point about two miles below the falls. By trigonometrical measurement they found the chasm at that point to be 1,190 feet deep. Their ascent from it was perilous, and it was only by making good use of hands and feet, and keeping the nerves braced to the utmost tension,

that they were enabled to clamber up the precipitous rocks to a safe landing-place. The effort was successfully made, but none others of the company were disposed to venture.

From a first view of the cañon we followed the river to the falls. A grander scene than the lower cataract of the Yellowstone was never witnessed by mortal eyes. The volume seemed to be adapted to all the harmonies of the surrounding scenery. Had it been greater or smaller it would have been less impressive. The river, from a width of two hundred feet above the fall, is compressed by converging rocks to one hundred and fifty feet where it takes the plunge. The shelf over which it falls is as level and even as a work of art. The height, by actual line measurement, is a few inches more than **350 feet**. It is a sheer, compact, solid, perpendicular sheet, faultless in all the elements of grandeur and picturesque beauties. The cañon which commences at the upper fall, half a mile above this cataract, is here a thousand feet in depth. Its vertical sides rise gray and dark above the fall to shelving summits, from which one can look down into the boiling, spray-filled chasm, enlivened with rainbows, and glittering like a shower of diamonds. From a shelf protruding over the stream, 500 feet below the top of the cañon, and 180 above the verge of the cataract, a member of our company, lying prone upon the rock, let down a cord with a stone attached into the gulf, and measured its **profoundest depths**. We could talk, and sing, and whoop, waking the echoes with our mirth and laughter in presence of the falls, but we could not thus profane the silence of the cañon. Seen through the cañon below the falls, the river for a mile or more is broken by rapids and cascades of great variety and beauty.

Between the lower and upper falls the cañon is two hundred to nearly four hundred feet deep. The river runs over a level bed of rock, and is undisturbed by rapids until near the verge of the lower fall. The upper fall is entirely unlike the other, but in its peculiar character equally interesting. For some distance above it the river breaks into frightful rapids. The stream is narrowed between the rocks as it approaches the brink, and bounds with impatient struggles for release, leaping through the stony jaws, in a sheet of snow-white foam, over a precipice nearly perpendicular, **115 feet high**. Midway in its descent the entire volume of water is carried, by the sloping surface of an intervening ledge, twelve or fifteen feet beyond the vertical base of the precipice, gaining therefrom a novel and interesting feature. The churning of the water upon the rocks reduces it to a mass of foam and spray, through which all the colors of the solar spectrum are reproduced in astonishing profusion. What this cataract lacks in sublimity is more than compensated by picturesqueness. The rocks which overshadow it do not veil it from the open light. It is up amid the pine foliage which crowns the adjacent hills, the grand feature of a landscape unrivaled for beauties of vegetation as well as of

350 feet: The Lower Falls (named because of its position on the river) is 308 feet (94 m) high.

profoundest depths: In comparison, the Grand Canyon of the Colorado River, which was designated a national monument only in 1908, averages about one mile (1.6 km) deep.

115 feet high: Upper Falls is 109 feet (33 m) high.

rock and glen. The two confronting rocks, overhanging the verge at the height of a hundred feet or more, could be readily united by a bridge, from which some of the grandest views of natural scenery in the world could be obtained—while just in front of, and within reaching distance of the arrowy water, from a table one-third of the way below the brink of the fall, all its nearest beauties and terrors may be caught at a glance.

We rambled around the falls and cañon two days, and left them with the unpleasant conviction that the greatest wonder of our journey had been seen.

We indulged in a last and lingering glance at the falls on the morning of the first day of Autumn. The sun shone brightly, and the laughing waters of the upper fall were filled with the

UPPER FALLS OF THE YELLOWSTONE, WYOMING.

glitter of rainbows and diamonds. Nature, in the excess of her prodigality, had seemingly determined that this last look should be the brightest, for there was everything in the landscape illuminated by the rising sun, to invite a longer stay. Even the dismal cañon, so dark and gray and still, reflected here and there on its vertical surface patches of sunshine, as much as to say, "See what I can do when I try." Everything had "put a jocund humor on." Long vistas of light broke through the pines which crowned the contiguous mountains, and the snow-crowned peaks in the distance glistened like crystal. Catching the spirit of the scene, we laughed and sung, and whooped as we rambled hurriedly from point to point, lingering only when the final moment came to receive the very last impression.

At length we turned our backs upon the scene, and wended our way slowly up the river-bank along a beaten trail. The last vestige of the rapids disappeared at the distance of half a mile above the Upper Fall. The river, expanded to the width of 400 feet, rolled peacefully between low verdant banks. The water for some distance was of emerald hue which is so distinguishing a feature of Niagara. The bottom was pebbly, and but for the treacherous quicksands and crevices, of which it was full, we could easily have forded the stream at any point between the falls and our camping place. We crossed a little creek strongly impregnated with alum,—and three miles beyond found ourselves in the midst of volcanic wonders of great variety and profusion. The region was filled with boiling springs and craters.[11] Two hills, each 300 feet high, and from a quarter to half a mile across, had been formed wholly of the sinter thrown from adjacent springs—lava, sulphur, and reddish-brown clay. Hot streams of vapor were pouring from crevices scattered over them. Their surfaces answered in hollow intonations to every footstep, and in several places yielded to the weight of our horses. Steaming vapor rushed hissingly from the fractures, and all around the natural vents large quantities of sulphur in crystallized form, perfectly pure, had been deposited. This could be readily gathered with pick and shovel. A great many exhausted craters dotted the hillside. One near the summit, still alive, changed its hues like steel under the process of tempering, to every kiss of the passing breeze. The hottest vapors were active beneath the incrusted surface everywhere. A thick leathern glove was no protection to the hand exposed to them. Around these immense thermal deposits, the country, for a great distance in all directions, is filled with boiling springs, all exhibiting separate characteristics.

The most conspicuous of the cluster is a sulphur spring twelve by twenty feet in diameter, encircled by a beautifully scolloped sedimentary border, in which the water is thrown to a height of from three to seven feet. The regular formation of this border and the perfect shading of the scollops forming it, are among the most delicate and wonderful freaks of nature's handiwork. They look like an elaborate work of art. This spring [called both Sulphur Spring and Crater Hills Geyser] is located at the western base of Crater Hill, above described, and the gentle slope around it for a distance of 300 feet is covered to considerable depth with a mixture of sulphur and brown lava. The moistened bed of a small channel, leading from the spring down the slope, indicated that it had recently overflowed.

A few rods north of this spring, at the base of the hill, is a cavern whose mouth is about seven feet in diameter, from which a dense jet of sulphurous vapor explodes with a regular report like a high-pressure engine. A little farther along we came upon another boiling spring, seventy feet long by forty wide, the water of which is dark and muddy, and in unceasing agitation.

About a hundred yards distant we discovered a boiling alum spring, surrounded with beautiful crystals, from the border of which we gathered a quantity of alum, nearly pure, but slightly impregnated with iron. The violent ebullition of the water had undermined the surrounding surface in many places, and for the distance of several feet from the margin had so thoroughly saturated the incrustation with its liquid contents, that it was unsafe to approach the edge. As one of our company was unconcernedly passing near the brink, the incrustation suddenly sloughed off beneath his feet. A shout of alarm from his comrades aroused him to a sense of his peril, and he only avoided being plunged into the boiling mixture by falling suddenly backward at full length upon the firm portion of the crust, and rolling over to a place of safety. His escape from a horrible death was most marvellous, and in another instant he would have been beyond all human aid. Our efforts to sound the depths of this spring with a pole thirty-five feet in length were fruitless.

Beyond this we entered a basin covered with the ancient deposit of some extinct crater, which contained about thirty springs of boiling clay.

These unsightly caldrons varied in size from two to ten feet in diameter, their surfaces being from three to eight feet below the level of the plain. The contents of most of them were of the consistency of thick paint, which they greatly resembled, some being yellow, others pink, and others dark brown. This semi-fluid was boiling at a fearful rate, much after the fashion of a hasty-pudding in the last stages of completion. The bubbles, often two feet in height, would explode with a puff, emitting at each time a villainous smell of sulphuretted vapor. Springs six and eight feet in diameter, but four feet asunder, presented distinct phenomenal characteristics. There was no connection between them, above or below. The sediment varied in color, and not unfrequently there would be an inequality of five feet in their surfaces. Each, seemingly, was supplied with a separate force. They were embraced within a radius of 1,200 feet, which was covered with a strong incrustation, the various vents in which emitted streams of heated vapor. Our silver watches, and other metallic articles, assumed a dark leaden hue. The atmosphere was filled with sulphurous gases, and the river opposite our camp was impregnated with the mineral bases of adjacent springs. The valley through which we had made our day's journey was level and beautiful, spreading away to grassy foot-hills, which terminated in a horizon of mountains.

We spent the next day in examining **the wonders** surrounding us. At the base of adjacent

the wonders: The party had left Crater Hills and reached the Mud Volcano area.

foot-hills we found three springs of boiling mud [the Sulphur Caldron group], the largest of which, forty feet in diameter, encircled by an elevated rim of solid tufa, resembles an immense caldron. The seething, bubbling contents, covered with steam, are five feet below the rim. The disgusting appearance of this spring is scarcely atoned for by the wonder with which it fills the beholder. The other two springs, much smaller, but presenting the same general features, are located near a large sulphur spring of milder temperature, but too hot for bathing. On the brow of an adjacent hillock, amid the green pines, heated vapor issues in scorching jets from several craters and fissures. Passing over the hill, we struck a small stream of perfectly transparent water flowing from a cavern [Dragon's Mouth Spring], the roof of which tapers back to the water, which is boiling furiously, at a distance of twenty feet from the mouth, and is ejected through it in uniform jets of great force. The sides and entrance of the cavern are covered with soft green sediment, which renders the rock on which it is deposited as soft and pliable as putty.

About two hundred yards from this cave is a most singular phenomenon, which we called the Muddy Geyser [now Mud Geyser]. It presents a funnel-shaped orifice, in the midst of a basin one hundred and fifty feet in diameter, with sloping sides of clay and sand. The crater or orifice, at the surface, is thirty by fifty feet in diameter. It tapers quite uniformly to the depth of about thirty feet, where the water may be seen, when the geyser is in repose, presenting a surface of six or seven feet in breadth. The flow of this geyser is regular every six hours. The water rises gradually, commencing to boil when about half way to the surface, and occasionally breaking forth in great violence. When the crater is filled, it is expelled from it in a splashing, scattered mass, ten or fifteen feet in thickness, to the height of forty feet. The water is of a dark lead color, and deposits the substance it holds in solution in the form of miniature stalagmites upon the sides and top of the crater. As this was the first object which approached a geyser, we, naturally enough, regarded it with intense curiosity. The deposit contained in the water of this geyser comprises about one-fifteenth of its bulk, and an analysis of it, made by Prof. Augustus Steitz, of Montana, gives the following result:—Silica, 36.7; alumina, 52.4; oxide of iron, 1.8; oxide of calcium, 3.2; oxide of magnesia, 1.8; soda and potassa, 4.1 = 100.

◦◦◦

Mud (formerly Muddy) Geyser has not erupted significantly since the early twentieth century. But Trumbull was equally impressed with Mud Geyser:

> *Between the last-mentioned spring and the river is a boiling spring, a placid pond, a deep, dry funnel, or an active geyser, according to the time of one's visit [Mud Geyser]. In the course of a day we saw it in all its protean shapes. When in its funnel form, one would not dream that, from the small opening in the bottom, twenty or thirty feet below, would come a power capable of filling with water the funnel, which at the top is thirty feet by forty, and then so agitating it that the water would be splashed to a height of from thirty to fifty feet. If one saw*

it when the waters were troubled, he would be scarcely less astonished to hear it give one convulsive throb, and then see it quietly settle down in a single instant to the smooth surface of a placid pool. When the waters retired we went into the funnel, and found it rough, efflorescent, and composed of rock and hardened sulphur.

Though very different in character from the geysers afterward seen on the head-waters of the Madison River, and far less grand, this one was very peculiar, and we saw nothing resembling it during the rest of the trip. ("Washburn Yellowstone Expedition," 437)

⌒⌒⌒

While returning by a new route to our camp, dull, thundering sounds, which General Washburn likened to frequent discharges of a distant mortar, broke upon our ears. We followed their direction, and found them to proceed from a mud volcano, which occupied the slope of a small hill, embowered in a grove of pines. Dense volumes of steam shot into the air with each report, through a crater thirty feet in diameter. The reports, though irregular, occurred as often as every five seconds, and could be distinctly heard half a mile [away]. Each alternate report shook the ground a distance of two hundred yards or more, and the massive jets of vapor which accompanied them burst forth like the smoke of burning gunpowder. It was impossible to stand on the edge of that side of the crater opposite the wind, and one of our party, Mr.

Hedges, was rewarded for his temerity in venturing too near the rim by being thrown by the force of the volume of steam violently down the outer side of the crater. From hasty views, afforded by occasional gusts of wind, we could see at a depth of sixty feet the regurgitating contents.

This volcano, as is evident from the freshness of the vegetation and the particles of dried clay adhering to the topmost branches of the trees surrounding it, is of very recent formation. Probably it burst forth but a few months ago.[12] Its first explosion must have been terrible. We saw limbs of trees 125 feet high encased in clay, and found its scattered contents two hundred feet from it. We closed this day's labor by a visit to several other springs, so like those already described that they require no special notice.

The writer, in company with General Washburn, rode back three miles the next morning to resurvey Crater Hill and the springs in its vicinity. The large sulphur spring was overflowing and boiling with greater fury than on the previous visit, the water occasionally leaping ten feet high. On our return we followed the trail of the train [the expedition's pack train], fording the river a short distance above the camp. Here we found the first evidence, since leaving Boteler's, that the country had been long ago visited by trappers and hunters. It was a bank of earth two feet high, presenting an angle to the river ingeniously concealed by interwoven willows, thus forming a rifle-pit from which the occupant, without discovery, could bring down geese, ducks, swans, pelicans, and the numerous furred animals with which the river abounds. Near by we stopped a moment to examine another spring of boiling mud, and then pursued our route over hills covered with artemisia (sage brush), through ravines and small meadows, into a dense forest of pines filled with prostrate trunks which had piled upon each other for years to the height of many feet. Our passage of two miles through this forest to the bank of the lake, unmarked by any trail, was accomplished with great difficulty, but the view which greeted us at its close was amply compensatory. There lay the silvery bosom of the lake, reflecting the beams of the setting sun, and stretching away for miles, until lost in the dark foliage of the interminable wilderness of pines surrounding it. Secluded amid the loftiest peaks of the Rocky Mountains, **8,337 feet** above the level of the ocean, possessing strange peculiarities of form and beauty, this watery solitude is one of the most attractive natural objects in the world. Its southern shore, indented with long narrow inlets, not unlike the frequent fiords of Iceland, bears testimony to the awful upheaval and tremendous force of the elements which resulted in its creation. The long pine-crowned promontories stretching into it from the base of the hills lend new and charming features to an aquatic scene full of novelty and splendor. Islands of emerald hue dot its surface, and a margin of sparkling sand forms its jeweled setting. The winds, compressed in their

8,337 feet: Actually 7,732 feet (2,357 m) above sea level, Yellowstone Lake is the largest high-altitude lake in North America. Its overall width and length are about 14 by 20 miles (23 by 32 km).

beach: At Steamboat Point on the lake's northeast shore.

passage through the mountain gorges, lash it into a sea as terrible as the fretted ocean, covering it with foam. But now it lay before us calm and unruffled, save by the gentle wavelets which broke in murmurs along the shore. Water, one of the grandest elements of scenery, never seemed so beautiful before. It formed a fitting climax to all the wonders we had seen, and we gazed upon it for hours, entranced with its increasing attractions.

This lake is about twenty-five miles long and seventy-five or eighty in circumference. Doubtless it was once the mighty crater of an immense volcano. It is filled with trout, some of gigantic size and peculiar delicacy. Waterfowl, in great variety, dot in flocks its mirrored surface. The forests surrounding it are filled with deer, elk, mountain sheep, and lesser game; and in the mountain fastnesses the terrible grizzly and formidable amiss make their lairs.

In form, it was by one of our party not inaptly compared to a "human hand with the fingers extended and spread apart as much as possible. The main portion of the lake is the northern, which would represent the palm of the hand. There is a large southwest bay, nearly cut off, that would represent the thumb, while there are about the same number of narrow southern inlets as there are fingers on the hand."[13] Enclosing this watery palm, is a dense forest of pines, until now untraversed by man. It was filled with trunks of trees in various stages of decay, which had been prostrated by the mountain blasts, rendering it almost impassable; but as the beach of the lake was in many places impracticable, there was no alternative to recede altogether or work our way through it.

Our course for the first six miles lay along the **beach**, passing a number of hot sulphur springs and lukewarm ponds. Three steam jets, from incrusted apertures, discharged a hissing noise resembling the sound of steam escaping from an engine. The water of the lake was thoroughly impregnated with sulphur, and the edges, at a distance of twenty to fifty feet from the beach, bubbled with springs, which, like those on the bank, discharged through pipes of silicious sinter. These pipes, though completely submerged, were intensely hot, while the water of the lake was too cold for a pleasant bath.

At one point along the shore are scattered curiously wrought objects of slate, varying in size from a gold dollar to a locomotive. We gathered specimens of cups which had been hollowed out by the elements— discs, long pestles, resemblances to legs and feet, and many other objects which nature in her most capricious mood had scattered over this watery solitude. So strikingly similar were many of these configurations to works of art, that a fanciful old trapper who had seen them told us that we would find on the borders of the lake the drinking-cups, stone war-clubs, and remains of idols of an extinct race which had once dwelt there. These were doubtless the joint production of fire and water,—the former roughly fashioning, and the latter beautifully polishing and depositing them where they could be easily obtained. We gave to this locality the name of "Curiosity Point," and added to our collection a number of specimens from its ample store.[14]

Ascending the plateau from the beach, we became at once involved in all the intricacies of a primeval wilderness of pines. Difficulties increased

SLATE FORMATION. —DRINKING-CUP.

with our progress through it, severely trying the amiability of every member of the company. Our pack-horses would frequently get wedged between the trees or caught in the traps of a net-work of fallen trunks from which labor, patience, and ingenuity were severely taxed to extricate them. The ludicrous sometimes came to our relief, proving that there was nothing so effectual in allaying excitement as hearty laughter. We had a remarkable pony in our pack-train, which, from the moment we entered the forest, by his numerous acrobatic performances and mishaps, furnished amusement for the company. One part of the process of travel through this forest could only be accomplished by leaping over the fallen trunks, an exploit which, with all the spirit needful for the purpose, our little broncho lacked the power always to perform. As a consequence, he was frequently found with the feat half accomplished, resting upon the midriff, his fore and hind feet suspended over the opposite sides of some huge log. His ambition to excel was only equaled by the patience he exhibited in difficulty. On one occasion, while clambering a steep rocky ascent, his head overtopping his haunches, he literally performed three of the most wonderful backward head-springs ever recorded in equine history. A continued experience of this kind, after three weeks' toilsome travel, found him as sound as on the day of its commencement, and we dubbed him the "Little Invulnerable."

After fifteen miles of unvarying toil we emerged

from the forest to the pebbly beach of the lake. Here we found carnelians, agates, and chalcedony in abundance. The lake was rolling tumultuously, its crested waves rising at least four feet high. The scene was very beautiful and exhilarating.

Our route the next day was divided between the beach of the lake and the forest, and so much impeded by fallen timber that we traveled but ten miles. Part of this distance was along the base of a brimstone basin which stretched from the lake to a semicircular range of mountains.[15] In company with Lieutenant Doane the writer ascended this range, traversing its slopes a distance of three or four miles, and found it covered half way to the summit with a mixture of carbonate of lime and flowers of sulphur. Exhalations, issuing from all parts of the surface, impregnated the atmosphere with strong sulphurous odors. Small rivulets of warm water, holding sulphur in solution, coursed

"LITTLE INVULNERABLE" IN A FIX.

their way down the mountain, uniting at its foot in a considerable stream. The surface over which we rode was strongly incrusted, and sounded hollow beneath the tread of our horses. It was filled with vents and fissures, surrounded with sulphur deposits nearly washed away. This mountain exhibited the same general phenomena as Crater Hill, though not in an equal state of activity.

Our course during the two following days was nearly southeast, on a line parallel with the Wind River Mountains[16]—that remarkable range which forms so conspicuous a feature in Mr. Irving's *Astoria* and *Bonneville's Adventures*. The faint outline of their distant peaks had been visible on the northeastern horizon [southeastern horizon] for several days. On our right, seventy-five miles distant, were the towering summits of the three Tetons, the great landmarks of the Snake River valley. The close of the day, on Sept. 6th, found us near the southeastern arm of the lake, into which a large river flows. The ground was low and marshy, and being unable to find a fording-place, we were compelled to make our camp at the base of a range of bluffs half a mile away. During the night we were startled by the shrill and almost human scream of an amiss or mountain lion, which sounded uncomfortably near. This terrible animal is much larger than the panther of the eastern forests, but greatly resembles it in shape, color, and ferocity. It is the terror of mountaineers, and furnishes them with the staple for many tales full of daring exploits.

Early the next morning our commander and several others left camp in search of a ford, while the writer and Lieutenant Doane started in the direction of a lofty mountain, from the summit of which we expected to obtain a satisfactory observation of the southern shore of the lake. At the expiration of two hours we reached a point in the ascent too precipitous for further equestrian travel. Dismounting, we led our horses for an hour longer up the steep side of the mountain, pausing every few moments to take breath, until we arrived at the line of perpetual snow. Here we unsaddled and hitched our horses, and climbed the apex to its summit, passing over a mass of congealed snow more than thirty feet in thickness. The ascent occupied four hours. We were more than 600 feet above the snow line, and by barometric calculation 11,350 feet above the ocean level.[17]

The grandeur and vast extent of the view from this elevation beggar description. The lake and valley surrounding it lay seemingly at our feet within jumping distance. Beyond them we saw with great distinctness the jets of the mud volcano and geyser. But beyond all these, stretching away into a horizon of cloud-defined mountains, was the entire Wind River range, revealing in the sunlight the dark recesses, gloomy cañons, precipices, and glancing pinnacles, which everywhere dotted its jagged slopes. Lofty peaks shot up in gigantic spires from the main body of the range, glittering in the sunbeams like solid crystal. The mountain on which we stood was the most westerly peak of a range which, in long-extended volume, swept to the southeastern horizon, exhibiting a continuous elevation more than thirty miles in width; its central line broken into countless points, knobs, glens, and defiles, all on the most colossal scale of grandeur and magnificence. Outside of these, on either border, along the entire range, lofty peaks rose at intervals, seemingly vying with each other in the varied splendors they presented to the beholder. The scene was full of majesty. The valley at the base of this range was dotted with small lakes and cloven centrally by the river, which, in the far distance, we could see emerging from a cañon of immense dimensions, within the shade of which two enormous jets of steam shot to an incredible height into the atmosphere.[18]

This range of mountains has a marvelous history. As it is the loftiest, so it is the most remarkable lateral ridge of the Rocky Range. The Indians regard it as the "crest of the world," and among the Blackfeet there is a fable that he who attains its summit catches a view of the land of souls, and beholds the happy hunting-grounds spread out below him, brightening with the abodes of the free and generous spirits.

In the expedition sent across the continent by Mr. Astor, in 1811, under command of Captain Wilson P. Hunt, that gentleman met with the first serious obstacle to his progress at the base of this range. After numerous efforts to scale it, he turned away and followed the valley of the Snake, encountering the most discouraging disasters until he arrived at Astoria.

Later, in 1833, the indomitable Captain Bonneville was lost in this mountain labyrinth, and after devising various modes of escape, finally determined to ascend the range. Selecting one of the highest peaks, in company with one of his men, Mr. Irving says: "After much toil he reached the summit of a lofty cliff, but it was only to behold gigantic peaks rising all around, and towering far into the atmosphere. He soon found that he had undertaken a tremendous task; but the pride of man is never more obstinate than when climbing mountains. The ascent was so steep and rugged that he and his companions were frequently obliged to clamber on hands and knees, with their guns slung upon their backs. Frequently, exhausted with fatigue and dripping with perspiration, they threw themselves upon the snow, and took handfuls of it to allay their parching thirst. At one place they even stripped off their coats and hung them upon the bushes, and thus lightly clad proceeded to scramble over these eternal snows. As they ascended still higher, there were cool breezes that refreshed and braced them, and springing with new ardor to their task, they at length attained the summit."

As late as 1860, Captain Raynolds, the commander of the expedition sent by Government to explore the Yellowstone, from his camp at the base of this formidable range writes: "To our front and upon the right, the mountains towered above us to the height of from 3,000 to 5,000 feet in the shape of bold, craggy peaks of basaltic formation, their summits crowned with glistening snow. It was my original desire to go from the head of Wind River to the head of the Yellowstone, keeping on the Atlantic slope, thence down the Yellowstone, passing the lake, and across by the Gallatin to the Three Forks of the Missouri. Bridger said at the outset that this would be impossible, and that it would be necessary to pass over to the head-waters of the Columbia, and back again to the Yellowstone.[19] I had not previously believed that crossing the main crest twice would be more easily accomplished than the transit over what was in effect only

a spur, but the view from our present camp (head of Wind River) settled the question adversely to my opinion at once. Directly across our route lies a basaltic ridge, rising not less than 5,000 feet above us, its walls apparently vertical, with no visible pass or even cañon. On the opposite side of this are the head-waters of the Yellowstone."[20]

We were an hour and a half making the descent of the mountain. At its base we struck the trail of our pack-train, which we followed to a point where the direction it had taken would have been lost, but for the foresight of one of our companions, who had formed a tripod of poles, one of which, longer than the others, pointed to the right. Obeying this Indian indication, we descended the bank and crossed the bottom to the river, fording which we followed the trail through a beautiful pine forest, free from undergrowth and other obstructions, the distance of a mile. Here night overtook us, and mistaking for the trail a dark serpentine line, we soon found ourselves clambering up the side of a steep mountain. The conviction that we were following a band of Indians, and possibly were near their lodges, suggested no pleasant reflections. Alighting from our horses, we built a fire upon the track, and, carefully examining it, could not find the impression of a single horseshoe. Further investigation revealed the fact that we had been for some time pursuing the path worn by a gang of elk that had crossed the trail of the pack-train since the twilight set in.

A night on the mountain, without supper or blankets, was not to be endured. We retraced our route to the base of the mountain, and struck out boldly in the darkness for the beach of the lake, where we supposed our party had camped. Our ride through fallen timber and morass until we reached the shore was performed more skillfully than if we had seen the obstacles which lay in our path. We reached the lake in safety, and after a ride of two miles on the smooth beach rounded a point from which we saw the welcome watch-fire of our company. A loud halloo was responded to by a dozen sympathetic voices, showing that our anxiety had been shared by our companions. Our camp was on the eastern inlet of the south shore of the lake, distant but four miles from the camp of the preceding night.

Thirteen miles of toilsome travel, zigzagged into only seven of progress, found us encamped, at the close of the next day, two miles from the mouth of a small stream flowing into the lake. Our party was separated nearly all day, searching for routes. Two members, after suffering all the early sensations incident to a conviction of being lost in the wilderness, came into camp at a late hour full of glee at their good fortune. At one of their halts, after they had dismounted to reconnoiter, a huge grizzly jumped at one of them from the bushes, frightening his horse so that he broke his bridle and ran away. They caught him with difficulty. Our commander and Mr. Hauser, in company, while seeking a route for future travel, came suddenly upon a female grizzly and two cubs, about half a mile from camp. On their return, six of the party started in pursuit, but Madame Bruin, meanwhile, had made good her retreat.

Our journey of five miles, the next day, was accomplished with great difficulty and annoyance. Almost the entire distance was through a forest piled full of fallen trunks. Traveling was but another name for scrambling; and as man is at times the least amiable of animals, our tempers frequently displayed alarming activity, not only towards the patient creatures laden with our stores, but towards each other. Once, while involved in the reticulated meshes of a vast net of branches and tree-tops, each man, with varied expletive emphasis, clamorously insisting upon a particular mode of extrication, a member of the party, who was always jolly, restored us to instant good-humor by repeating, in theatrical tone and manner, these beautiful lines from **Childe Harold**:—

"There is a pleasure in the pathless woods,
There is a rapture on the lonely shore."

Our "Little Invulnerable," too, was the unconscious cause of many bursts of laughter, which, like the appreciative plaudits of an audience, came in at the right time. We were glad, however, at an early hour in the afternoon, to pitch our tent on one of the small tributaries of Snake River—three miles distant from the lake. In the search made by every member of the party for routes, our company was unavoidably much scattered. Our first care being for the pack-train, when it came up we missed therefrom the little animal whose frequent mishaps had been to all a source of so much amusement. An instant search was instituted, and at a

"Childe Harold's Pilgrimage": Lord Byron's long narrative poem from the early nineteenth century, describing his travels in foreign lands. Langford's quote is from verse 178 of the Fourth Canto.

late hour we found him three miles from camp. He saluted us with a low neigh, and with hurried pace soon rejoined his companions. One of our comrades (the Hon. Truman C. Everts, late U.S. Assessor of Montana) had failed to come up with the rest of the company; but as this was a common circumstance, we gave it little heed until the lateness of the hour convinced us he had lost his way. We increased our fire and fired our guns, as signals; but all to no purpose. It had been a sort of tacit agreement among us only the night before, that should any one get parted from the company, he would at once go to the south-west arm of the lake (that being our objective point) and await there the arrival of the train. The belief that we should find our companion there, hastened us into the commission of an error, which was designed by all as a measure of speedy relief. If we had not continued our journey with all possible expedition towards the point indicated, Mr. Everts would probably have rejoined us within three or four days, as he has informed us since that he visited our camp, but the falling foliage of the pines had entirely obliterated our departing trail.

The narrative of this gentleman, of thirty-seven days spent in this terrible wilderness, will furnish a chapter in the history of human endurance, exposure, and escape as incredible as it must be painfully instructive and entertaining.[21]

Seven miles of struggling took us through the timber to another inlet, five miles further on our way. No sign of our missing comrade. We built a large fire on a commanding ridge, and ascended a mountain overlooking the north and west shores of the lake, where we kindled another fire, which could be seen at a great distance. Eight hundred feet above Yellowstone Lake, nestled in a dark mountain glen, we found two small lakes, completely environed with frightful masses of basalt and brown lava, seemingly thrown up and scattered by some terrible convulsion. Two of our company took the backward trail at night, searching for Mr. Everts; and our anxieties were greatly increased lest they too meet with some disaster.

We rose early the next morning, after passing a sleepless night. While at breakfast, our two companions came in. They had followed the beach to a point east of our camp of two days before, and found no trace of Mr. Everts. More than ever assured that we should find him at the west arm of the lake, we struck out for that point,—three of our party, Mr. Hauser, Lieut. Doane, and myself, in advance, to explore a route for the train and make all possible search by the way. We posted notices on the trees to indicate the route we had taken, and made caches of provisions at several points. Late in the afternoon, at the close of a fatiguing day's travel, mostly through forest, we arrived at our objective point, and were greatly distressed to find there no trace of our lost friend. While gathered around our camp-fire in the evening, devising a plan for more systematic search, our ears were saluted with a screech so terribly human, that, for a moment supposing it to be our missing comrade, we hallooed in response, and would have started to his relief but that a minatory growl warned us of the near approach of a mountain lion.

Three parties, of two each, struck out the next morning in different directions, in pursuit of our companion. One followed the lake shore; one the back trail through the forest; and the third, southerly from the lake to a large brown mountain. The party following the lake shore returned to camp early in the afternoon, with the report that they had seen Indians. The story of their adventures, written by one of them, runs thus: "He and his companion having penetrated several miles through the inhospitable wilds of that region, dismounted and unsaddled their horses. Mr. T. commenced to fish, and prepare them a little dinner, while Mr. S. went ahead with his gun, to continue the search on foot. The former had just caught four fishes, and kindled a fire, when the latter returned in some haste, but perfectly cool and self-possessed, and stated that there were six Indians on a point jutting out into the lake, about a mile distant. They concluded that neither had a mouth for fish, which they left sweltering in the noon-day sun, and, saddling their horses, they advanced towards the foe. Mr. S. saw them distinctly; but Mr. T. could not, probably because he was somewhat near-sighted. Finally, the former gentleman saw them flitting, phantom-like, among the rocks and trees, at which juncture the party retired to camp in platoons, and in good order, at the rate of a mile in every three minutes." This tribe of Indians, being one of the curiosities of the expedition, and hitherto unknown, was named after the person who discovered it.

Both of the other parties returned, after a fruitless search. In their trip to the brown mountain [Mt. Sheridan], the two who went south crossed the main range of the Rocky Mountains through a very low pass, which on the western side terminated in a brimstone basin containing forty or fifty sulphur and mud springs, and a large number of craters, from which issued jets of vapor.[22] This slope of the mountain was covered with a hollow incrustation through which the water from the springs, percolating in different channels, had spread out over the little patches of soil with which they came in contact, covering them with bright green verdure. In crossing one of these the horse of one of the party broke through to his haunches, and being extricated, he plunged more deeply into another trap, throwing head-long his rider, whose arm as he fell was thrust violently through the treacherous surface into the scalding morass, from complete submersion in which both man and beast were with great difficulty saved.

At the base of the brown mountain the party saw a lake of considerable size, which they believed to be the head-waters of Snake River—the Lewis Fork of the Columbia.[23] They could not approach it nearer than a mile, on account of the treacherous character of the soil. The other party were absent two days. They had visited all the camps of the six preceding days, following the trail between them, mostly obliterated by the falling foliage of the pines, with great difficulty, but without discovering the slightest indication that Mr. Everts had come upon it. On full consultation we came to the conclusion that he had either been shot from his horse by an Indian, or had returned down the Yellowstone, or struck out upon some of the head-waters of Snake River, with the intention of following it to the settlements. It was agreed that we should pursue the search three days longer from this point before renewing our journey. Snow began to fall early in the evening. Through the hazy atmosphere we beheld, on the shore of the inlet opposite our camp, the steam ascending in jets from more than fifty craters, giving it the appearance of a New England village.

Snow continued to fall all night and the next day, and we made our camp as comfortable as possible. At night the snow was more than two feet deep. It turned to rain the following morning. Showers, alternated with sunshine through the day, removed the snow rapidly. We were now so completely environed by forest, and so far away from any recognized trail, that all our fear of molestation by Indians, or of danger from any other cause was thoroughly dissipated. With true Falstaffian philosophy we felt that we could take our ease in our inn, and the figure one of us presented has been graphically delineated by our artist upon the spot.

We made a circuit round the head of the inlet to the springs we had seen, the next day [West Thumb Geyser Basin]. They were widely different from any we had visited before. In all they numbered 150, and were scattered along the lake shore

ON GUARD ON YELLOWSTONE LAKE.

about a mile, at a distance of 100 yards from the beach. Those farthest inland resembled boiling mud of various degrees of consistency, some not thicker than paint, others so dense that as they boiled over, the contents piled into heaps, which gradually spread over the ground, forming an extensive vitrified surface. This sediment varies in color—that flowing from some of the apertures being white as chalk, that from others of a delicate lavender hue, and from others, of a brilliant pink color. The following are the results of analyses of the various specimens which we gathered, by Professor Augustus Steitz, of Montana:—

White sediment.

Silica. 42.2
Magnesia 33.4
Lime. 17.8
Alkalies. 6.6
Oxide of calcium 4.2
                                                                    ————
                                                                    100

Lavender sediment.

Silica. 28.2
Alumina 58.6
Boracic acid .3.2
Oxide of iron 0.6
Water and loss. 2.5
                                                                    ————
                                                                    100

Pink sediment.

Silica. 32.6
Alumina 52.4
Oxide of calcium 8.3
Soda and potassa. 4.2
Water and loss. 5.2
                                                                    ————
                                                                    100

In close proximity to these springs are others of pure, odorless water. Near the shore were several boiling springs, around which the sedimentary increment had formed into mounds of various sizes and heights. The deposit around one of these springs resembles a miniature forest of pines.

The most remarkable springs in this group, six or seven in number, are of pure ultra-marine hue—very large, and wonderfully transparent. The largest is forty feet wide by seventy feet long. The sides are funnel-shaped, converging regularly to the depth of forty feet, where they present a dark and apparently unfathomable chasm. From the surface to this opening the sides of the funnel are furrowed and sinuous, coated with a white sediment, which contrasts vividly with the dark orifice at its base.

❧

Langford omits any mention of what may well be the first record of catching a fish at Yellowstone Lake's subsequently famous Fishing Cone, but Trumbull wrote:

Several springs were in the solid rock, within a few feet of the lake-shore. Some of them extended far out underneath the lake; with which, however, they had no connection. The lake water was quite cold, and that of these springs exceedingly hot. They were remarkably clear, and the eye could penetrate a hundred feet into their depths, which to the human vision appeared bottomless. A gentleman was fishing from one of the narrow isthmuses, or shelves of rock, which divided one of these hot springs from the lake, when, in swinging a trout ashore, it

accidentally got off the hook and fell into the spring. For a moment it darted about with wonderful rapidity, as if seeking an outlet. Then it came to the top, dead, and literally boiled. It died within a minute of the time it fell into the spring. ("Washburn Yellowstone Expedition," 492)

❧

This group of springs exhibit in their deposits a great variety of shades and colors—no two of them being alike. Their constant overflow has fashioned a concrete bank of commingled tufa, eight feet in height and a quarter of a mile in length, on the margin of the lake. The waves have worn this bank into large caverns, which respond in hollow murmurs to their fierce assaults. Between the springs are numerous vents and craters, from which heated vapor is constantly rising. Along the edge of the water, and ten or twenty feet from shore, many springs are bubbling, none of which seem to be strongly impregnated with sulphur. The beach for a mile or more, is strewn with fragments of sinter of various colors, which have been worn by the waves into many fantastic forms.

The five days during which we camped at this locality were occupied by every possible effort to find our missing friend, but the labors of each day only served to increase our fears for his safety. One hope, that of meeting him at Virginia City, was still indulged;[24] but opposed to this were many painful conjectures as to his possible fate—not the least prevalent of which was the one that he might have been shot from an ambush by an Indian arrow. Our provisions were rapidly diminishing, and our longer stay gave promise of unfavorable results. The force of circumstances obliged us to adopt the gloomy alternative of moving forward the next day, leaving one of our own party and two of the cavalrymen to prosecute a further search.

The loss of our comrade and friend was to us all a source of much unhappy reflection, and the hope of finding him so entirely absorbed our attention that we had little curiosity to examine, and so escaped very many of the wonders of this region, which we should otherwise have seen. In our constant passing to and fro in different directions through the forest, along the lake, and over the surrounding mountains, we had glances of objects which, had we been free from a heavy charge, it would have been pleasant to visit and describe. These, however, are reserved for future investigation.

The plan of our route led us in a northwesterly direction from the lake towards the head-waters of the Madison. We traveled through a dense pine forest, unmarked by trails and encumbered by fallen timber for most of the distance. The close of the first day's travel found us only twelve miles from the lake, still in the midst of the deep snow, with no place to pitch our tent, and each man seeking, unsuccessfully, a dry spot whereon to spread his blankets, under the shelter of the trees. The next day we reached the east bank of the Fire Hole River, the largest tributary of the Madison, down which we traveled, passing several cascades, many craters and boiling springs, to a large basin,

BIRD'S-EYE VIEW OF THE GEYSER BASIN.

two miles above the point of the union of the Fire Hole and Burnt Hole Rivers.[25]

We bade adieu to Yellowstone Lake, surfeited with the wonders we had seen, and in the belief that the interesting portion of our journey was over. The desire for home had superseded all thought of further exploration. We had seen the greatest wonders on the continent, and were convinced that there was not on the globe another region where, within the same limits, nature had crowded so much of grandeur and majesty, with so much of novelty and wonder. Our only care was to return home as rapidly as possible. Three days of active travel from the head-waters of the Madison, would find us among the settlers in the beautiful lower valley of that picturesque river, and within twelve miles of Virginia City, where we hoped to meet with Mr. Everts, and realize afresh that "all is well that ends well."

Judge, then, what must have been our astonishment, as we entered the basin at mid-afternoon of our second day's travel, to see in the clear sunlight, at no great distance, an immense volume of clear, sparkling water projected into the air to the height of one hundred and twenty-five feet. "Geysers! geysers!" exclaimed one of our company, and spurring our jaded horses, we soon gathered around this wonderful phenomenon. It was indeed a perfect geyser. The aperture through which the jet projected was an irregular oval, three feet by seven in diameter. The margin of sinter was curiously piled up, and the exterior crust was filled with little hollows full of water, in which were small globules of sediment, some having gathered around bits of wood and other nuclei. This geyser is elevated thirty feet above the level of the

SECTION OF LARGE SPRING.

surrounding plain, and the crater rises five or six feet above the mound. It spouted at regular intervals nine times during our stay, the columns of boiling water being thrown from ninety to one hundred and twenty-five feet at each discharge, which lasted from fifteen to twenty minutes. We gave it the name of "**Old Faithful**."

In our journey down the valley, looking down through a crevice in the crust upon which we were traveling, we discovered a stream of hot water of considerable size, running nearly at right angles with and away from the Fire Hole River.

On the summit of a cone, twenty feet high, was a boiling spring, seven feet in diameter, surrounded with beautiful incrustations, on the slope of which we gathered twigs and pine-tree cones, encased in a silicious crust a quarter of an inch in thickness. But all the curiosities of this basin sink into

Old Faithful: This geyser erupts to an average height of 145 feet (44 m) and has always been regular enough to predict within a few minutes.

insignificance in comparison with the geysers. We saw, during our brief stay of but twenty-two hours, twelve in action. Six of these, from vents varying from three to five feet in diameter, threw water to the height of from fifteen to twenty-five feet, but in the presence of others of immense dimensions these soon ceased to attract attention. One, which we named **"The Fan"** [called Fantail by some members of the 1870 party], has an orifice which discharges two radiating jets of water to the height of sixty feet, the falling drops and spray resembling a feather fan. It is very beautiful. Its eruptions are very frequent, lasting usually from ten to thirty minutes. A vent connected with it [Mortar Geyser], about forty feet distant, expels dense masses of vapor fifty or sixty feet high, accompanied by loud, sharp reports, during the time the geyser is in action.

"The Grotto" was so named from its singular crater of vitrified sinter, full of large, sinuous apertures. Through one of these, on our first visit, one of our company crawled to the discharging orifice; and when, a few hours afterwards, he saw a volume of boiling water, four feet in diameter, shooting through it to the height of sixty feet, and a scalding stream of two hundred inches flowing from the aperture he had entered a short time before, he concluded he had narrowly escaped being summarily cooked. The discharge of this geyser continued for nearly half an hour.

"The Castle," situated on the summit of an incrusted mound, has a turreted crater through which a large volume of water is expelled at intervals of two or three hours to the height of fifty feet, from a discharging orifice about three feet in diameter. The architectural features of the silicious sinter surrounding it, which is very massive and compact, indicating that at some former period the flow of water must have been much greater than at present, suggested its name. A vent near it is constantly discharging a large stream of boiling water, and when the geyser is in action the water in this vent boils and bubbles with great fierceness.

"The Giant" has a rugged crater, ten feet in diameter on the outside, with an orifice five or six feet in diameter. It discharges a vast body of water, and the only time we saw it in eruption the flow of water in a column five feet in diameter, and one hundred and forty feet in vertical height, continued uninterruptedly for nearly three hours. The crater resembles a miniature model of the Coliseum.

Our search for new wonders leading us across the Fire Hole River, we ascended a gentle incrusted slope, and came suddenly upon a large oval aperture with scalloped edges, the diameters of which were eighteen and twenty-five feet, the sides corrugated and covered with a grayish-white silicious deposit, which was distinctly visible at the depth of one hundred feet below the surface. No water could be discovered, but we could distinctly hear it gurgling and boiling at a great distance below. Suddenly it began to rise, boiling and spluttering, and sending out huge masses of steam, causing a general stampede of our company, driving us some distance from our point of observation. When within about forty feet of the surface it became

Fan and its neighbor Mortar now nearly always erupt simultaneously.

stationary, and we returned to look down upon it. It was foaming and surging at a terrible rate, occasionally emitting small jets of hot water nearly to the mouth of the orifice. All at once it seemed seized with a fearful spasm, and rose with incredible rapidity, hardly affording us time to flee to a safe distance, when it burst from the orifice with terrific momentum, rising in a column the full size of this immense aperture to the height of sixty feet; and through and out of the apex of this vast aqueous mass, five or six lesser jets or round columns of water varying in size from six to fifteen inches in diameter, were projected to the marvellous height of two hundred and fifty feet. These lesser jets, so much higher than the main column, and shooting through it, doubtless proceed from auxiliary pipes leading into the principal orifice near the bottom, where the explosive force is greater. If the theory that water by constant boiling becomes explosive when freed from air be true,

THE GROTTO GEYSER.

CRATER OF THE GIANT GEYSER.

this theory rationally accounts for all irregularities in the eruptions of the geysers.

This grand eruption continued for twenty minutes, and was the most magnificent sight we ever witnessed. We were standing on the side of the geyser nearest the sun, the gleams of which filled the sparkling column of water and spray with myriads of rainbows, whose arches were constantly changing—dipping and fluttering hither and thither, and disappearing only to be succeeded by others, again and again, amid the aqueous column, while the minute globules into which the spent jets were diffused when falling sparkled like a shower of diamonds, and around every shadow which the denser clouds of vapor, interrupting the sun's rays, cast upon the column, could be seen a luminous

THE BEEHIVE.

found to be two hundred and nineteen feet in height. The stream did not deflect more than four or five degrees from a vertical line, and the eruption lasted eighteen minutes. We named it "The Beehive."

How many more geysers there are in this locality it would be impossible to conjecture. Our waning stores admonished us of the necessity for a hurried departure, and we reluctantly left this remarkable region less than half explored. In this basin, which is about two miles in length and one mile in width, more than a thousand pipes or wells rise to the surface, varying in diameter from two to one hundred and twenty feet, the water in which varies in temperature from 140° [F] to the boiling-point, upwards of a hundred of which give evidence, by the calcareous and silicious deposits surrounding them, that they are geysers; and to all appearances they are as likely to be as any we saw in action.

The sides of these wells were covered with silicious incrustations, and were funnel-shaped; and in many of the larger ones gradually converged for a distance of from twenty to fifty feet from the edge, below which point the apertures enlarged laterally in all directions like a jug below the neck, and were apparently unfathomable. None of the springs in this locality appear to be impregnated with sulphur. In this basin there are to be found no mud springs, of which we discovered so many in the valley of the Yellowstone; and we found but one spring of cold water.

circle radiant with all the colors of the prism, and resembling the halo of glory represented in paintings as encircling the head of Divinity. All that we had previously witnessed seemed tame in comparison with the perfect grandeur and beauty of this display. Two of these wonderful eruptions occurred during the twenty-two hours we remained in the valley. This geyser we named "The Giantess."[26]

A hundred yards distant from The Giantess was a silicious cone, very symmetrical but slightly corrugated upon its exterior surface, three feet in height and five feet in diameter at its base, and having an oval orifice twenty-four by thirty-six and one-half inches in diameter, with scalloped edges. Not one of our company supposed that it was a geyser; and among so many wonders it had almost escaped notice. While we were at breakfast upon the morning of our departure a column of water, entirely filling the crater, shot from it, which, by accurate triangular measurement, we

At this point in his account, Trumbull described the hot lakes of Midway Geyser Basin and the two canyons the party passed through:

Steam-jets and clear, deep pools occurred in great numbers, all over the geyser basin. The latter were very beautiful. Four or five miles below the geyser basin, on the west side of the Fire Hole, were four hot lakes [in Midway Geyser Basin]. They were similar to the clear, pale-violet pools which we saw above, and at the point where we left the lake, but were very much larger. Three of the party paced around the largest one, making the circumference four hundred and fifty paces. It looked very deep. The sides, of the whitest subsilica, converged at an angle of about forty-five degrees. It was full to the brim, and a track, about twenty feet wide all around it, was covered with two inches of water, which was so hot that it almost scalded our feet, through heavy boots. Before our pacers got all the way round, they stepped not only very high, but in quite a lively, animated style. Beyond the track of water which circled the lake, the ground, covered with subsilica, sloped away gradually on all sides. Immense volumes of steam rose from all these lakes, and first attracted our attention to them. So much hot water flowed from them that the Fire Hole was tempered for several miles below. We found no fish anywhere in the Fire Hole, though after its junction with the Madison they were quite plentiful.

Leaving the hot lakes, we continued homeward. On the way we passed through two beautiful cañons; *one on the Fire Hole, and one on the Madison. The* cañon *on the Fire Hole is grand and beautiful. Its sides are granite, nearly perpendicular, and from eight hundred to a thousand feet high. It is cut on both sides by small, lateral ravines, which are filled with evergreens; and on both sides of the river is a narrow bottom, also covered with trees and verdure. The cañon on the Yellowstone is grand and gloomy. This one is beautiful and cheerful. The first was seen from above, the last from below. The former inspires one with awe, the latter with delight.*

The Madison Cañon may be less grand, but scarcely less beautiful. Its walls are not so high, and generally not quite so precipitous. It is filled with fine timber, affords splendid and picturesque camping-places, and is watered not only by the Madison River but by pleasant, clear, rippling brooks, which flow through ravines entering the sides of the cañon. ("Washburn Yellowstone Expedition," 495)

This entire country is seemingly under constant and active internal pressure from volcanic forces, which seek relief through the numberless springs, jets, volcanoes, and geysers exhibited on its surface, and which, but for these vents, might burst forth in one terrific eruption and form a volcano of vast dimensions. It is undoubtedly true that many of the objects we saw were of recent formation, and that many of the extinguished craters recently ceased their condition of activity. They are constantly breaking forth, often assuming new forms, and attesting to the active presence of volcanic force.

A mountaineer,[27] who visited a portion of this region a year ago, found at one place a small volcano which was constantly overflowing with liquid sulphur and lava, and emitting smoke; showing that the genuine volcanic elements were there, and needed but the concentration of the forces now dissipated through thousands of vents to present a spectacle of grandeur surpassing that of Vesuvius or Aetna.

The geyser is a new and, perhaps, the most remarkable feature in our scenery and physical history. It is found in no other countries but Iceland and Thibet.[28] The geysers of the country last named are inconsiderable when compared with either those of Iceland, or the Fire Hole or Madison Basin; and those of Iceland, even, dwindle into insignificance by the side of those of the Madison. Until the discovery of the Madison geysers there were but two of any note known to the world—the Great Geyser and the Strokr of Iceland. The phenomena presented by these have been sufficient at various periods during the past century to invite the personal investigation of some of the most distinguished of European savans. Von Troil, Stanley, Ohlsen, Hooker, MacKenzie, and at a later day, Bunsen, have visited Iceland for the purpose of witnessing these aqueous eruptions, and forming some satisfactory conclusion relative to the causes in which they originate.

The theory published by Sir George MacKenzie, that the outbursts were produced by pressure on the air contained in cavernous recesses underground, for many years received the sanction of the scientific world. The periods intervening between the eruptions of the Great Geyser of Iceland have been very irregular until within the past forty or fifty years, since when it has generally projected a small jet to the height of twenty feet every two hours, and a large one to the height of eighty feet every six hours. Mackenzie's theory was that there were two subterranean cavities connected with the main pipe, one much deeper and larger than the other, which rapidly filled with water after each eruption, and that the pressure of the vapors upon them produced these periodic explosions.

Ingenious as this theory appeared to be, it was dissipated by the experiments made upon water by M. Donny, of Ghent. He discovered that water long boiled became more and more free from air, by which its molecular cohesion is so greatly increased, and that, when it is exposed to a heat sufficient to overcome the force of cohesion, the production of steam is so instantaneous and so considerable as to cause explosion. Bunsen ascribes the eruption of the geysers to a constantly increasing temperature up to the moment of an eruption. On one occasion it was as high as 261° Fahrenheit. His idea is that on reaching some unknown point above that temperature ebullition takes place, vapor is suddenly generated in enormous quantities, and an eruption of the superior column of water is the consequence. The geysers of the Madison exhibit precisely the same physical features, and, doubtless, originate in the same causes. They are surrounded too, as are those of Iceland, by innumerable springs of hot water. The bursting of a column into millions of particles resembles an explosion more than a mere eruption; and the vast clouds of vapor which enshroud them and mingle with them in their ascent sometimes give an appearance of bulk to the upper part of the columns much greater than their real magnitude.

The water of the Madison geysers, like that of the geysers of Iceland, appears perfectly pure, and, doubtless, could be used for cooking or drinking. We had not the means of analyzing it on the spot. The sinter was both carboniferous and silicious, the latter characteristic predominating, but both prevailing sufficiently to have produced large incrusted mounds, and numerous illustrations of petrifaction in various stages of progress. All this, where such immense volumes of water are being constantly ejected, could be effected with a moderate infusion of silica or soda. Dr. Black gives the following result of an analysis of a quantity of 10,000 grains (about one-sixth of a gallon) of water from the Great Geyser of Iceland:—

Soda	0.95
Alumina	0.48
Silica	5.40
Muriate of soda	2.46
Dry sulphate of soda	1.46
Total	10.75

That the same elements are held in solution in the waters of the Madison geysers, we have abundant proof in the vast incrusted field by which they are surrounded. They are but a reproduction, upon a much grander scale, of the phenomena of Iceland.

A wider field for the investigation of the chemist than that presented by the geysers may be found in the many-tinted springs of boiling mud and the mud volcano. These were objects of the greatest interest to Humboldt, who devotes to a description of them one of the most fascinating chapters of *Cosmos*.[29] It would be rash in us to speculate where that great man hesitated. We can only say that the field is open for exploration—illimitable in resource, grand in extent, wonderful in variety, in a climate favored of Heaven, and amid scenery the most stupendous on the continent.

By means of the Northern Pacific Railroad, which will doubtless be completed within the next **three years**, the traveler will be able to make the trip to Montana from the Atlantic seaboard in three days, and thousands of tourists will be attracted to both Montana and Wyoming in order to behold with their own eyes the wonders here described. Besides these marvels of the Upper Yellowstone, one may look upon the strange scenery of the lower valley of that great river, the Great Falls of the Missouri, the grotesque groups of eroded rocks below Fort Benton, the beautiful cañon of the Prickly Pear, and the stupendous architecture of the vast chains and spurs of mountains which everywhere traverse that picturesque and beautiful country.

three years: Due to major financial setbacks, the Northern Pacific was not completed until 1883.

NOTES

1. Haines, *Yellowstone Story* 2: 448.
2. Chittenden, *Yellowstone National Park*, 302–3.
3. Capt. William F. Raynolds's unsuccessful attempt to reach the Yellowstone River drainage from what is now Wyoming occurred in 1860.
4. The completely assembled party left Fort Ellis for the Yellowstone area on August 22, 1870.
5. It is interesting to compare the written reports about an Indian encounter by the various exploring party members. In Langford's book *The Discovery of Yellowstone Park*, published thirty-five years after the Yellowstone adventure, he wrote, "Today we saw our first Indians as we descended into the valley of the Yellowstone," and "there were one hundred or more of them watching us from behind a high butte" (9). But in his 1871 *Scribner's* story he first mentions seeing Indians two days later, when he learned "that twenty-five lodges of Crows had gone up the valley a few days before our arrival." The study by Yellowstone Park Historian Aubrey L. Haines, *Yellowstone National Park, Its Exploration and Establishment*, quotes Doane as reporting, "In the afternoon we met several Indians belonging to the Crow Agency 30 miles below" (67); in Hedges's diary there were "many Indians on the river observing us with the eye of a horse thief" (14); Gillette wrote, "About 4 o'clock PM saw 3 Crow Indians on the other side of the Y. S. [Yellowstone River]" (Haines, 168n98). And Trumbull's 1871 article relates, "As the skirmishers neared the river they discovered three Crows; not sitting on a tree, but riding in their direction. With keen military sagacity, they appreciated the position, and rallied on the main body with astonishing rapidity" (Trumbull, "Washburn Yellowstone Expedition," 432).
6. Langford is describing what was soon to be dubbed the Third Canyon, now called the Black Canyon of the Yellowstone. This exploration party did not ascend the Gardner River to Mammoth Hot Springs but rather followed the Yellowstone River and did not see the hot spring terraces.
7. Walter Trumbull makes no mention of Indian sign in his account but does mention that "some blazed trees" were seen at this camp, "showing that enterprising miners had preceded us."
8. A travois (misspelled here as "travais") was a device used by Plains Indians for transporting goods, consisting of two long poles, attached on either side of a horse, and a platform made from animal hide or woven branches, dragged behind the horse.
9. The spires or towers on Tower Creek are formed of volcanic debris that was eroded locally to form sedimentary beds that in turn were eroded, leaving strange forms. They are not simply made of shale and slate but are probably a mixture of all those as well as other rocks.
10. Five years after the Washburn expedition, second Yellowstone Superintendent Philetus W. Norris renamed the area above Crystal Falls "Grotto Pool," declaring it his favorite spot in the park, and even wrote two poems about it: "Rustic Bridge and Crystal Falls" and "Afar from the Cities and Hamlets of Men" (Norris, *Calumet of the Coteau*, 132).
11. This area of boiling springs and craters is the Crater Hills hydrothermal area, which is situated well away from the present roads and maintained trails of the park. An even older name for the area is Sulphur Mountain. Whittlesey, *Yellowstone Place Names*, 75 and 242.
12. When Langford returned to Mud Volcano (as his party named it) two years later, he found that a major explosion had changed it and the surrounding landscape entirely.
13. Langford drew the quote about the shape of Yellowstone Lake from an article by Cornelius Hedges in the *Helena Daily Herald*, November 9, 1870, 2.
14. Strange specimens like those described by Langford had also been found and collected at this shore point by prospector A. Bart Henderson in 1867. No such specimens can be found today, due to avid collecting by early visitors.
15. In his report, Lt. Doane capitalized Brimstone Basin here, perhaps inadvertently, and this name is still used today for this feature. Whittlesey, *Yellowstone Place Names*, 57.
16. Here and in his discussion of exploration parties through page 34, Langford is confusing the Wind River Range with the Absaroka Range. The mountains east of Yellowstone Lake and the peak he and Lt. Doane climbed are in the Absarokas. The Wind River Range, over eighty miles away, could not have been visible above the 11,000-foot peaks of the Absaroka Range to a party traversing the east shore of Yellowstone Lake. Langford is correct, however, that it was in the Wind River Mountains that Capt. Bonneville climbed in 1833, according

to Washington Irving's book, *The Adventures of Captain Bonneville.*

17. Aubrey L. Haines identified this mountain as Colter Peak, elevation 10,683 feet (3,256 meters) (Bonney and Bonney, *Battle Drums and Geysers*, 312–13).

18. Bonney and Bonney, *Battle Drums and Geysers*, 310n22, suggest that these "jets of steam" could have come from hot springs at the northern end of Jackson Lake thirty miles to the southwest, or they might have been smoke from forest fires or even peculiar clouds. Huckleberry Hot Springs is located near Flagg Ranch in the Rockefeller Memorial Parkway.

19. Jim Bridger also said, "A bird can't fly over that without taking a supply of grub along," according to Haines, *Yellowstone Story* 1, 87.

20. The Raynolds party simply arrived too early in the season (early June) to cross the snow-covered Absarokas into the Yellowstone area.

21. Evert's story originally appeared in *Scribner's Monthly* in November 1871 and has most recently been published as Truman Everts, *Lost in the Yellowstone* (2015). Langford does not say that Everts was found (as he was) but only implies it by mentioning his "escape."

22. The search party encountered Heart Lake and the hot springs of Heart Lake Geyser Basin, mostly north of Mt Sheridan.

23. Heart Lake is not the source of the Snake River (which empties into the Columbia River in southeastern Washington State). The source of the Snake is actually in some tiny lakes near the southern boundary of the park and Mariposa Lake on Two Ocean Plateau.

24. Virginia City, which was on the explorers' route back to Helena, was established in 1863 as a mining center and became the capital of Montana Territory in 1865.

25. Burnt Hole River is a puzzling designation here: some confusion has existed over the similarity of the name Burnt Hole to Fire Hole. The Burnt Hole was the trappers' name for part of the Madison River valley some thirty miles northwest of Upper Geyser Basin. Langford could have been referring to the confluence of the Little Firehole River and the Firehole about two miles north of the basin.

26. For the party to have witnessed two eruptions of Giantess and one of Giant Geyser in less than one day at Upper Geyser Basin was an incredible stroke of luck. Today Giantess erupts only a few times each year; its eruptions alternate between forceful high jets of water and raucous steam emissions. Over many years Giant Geyser has alternated between absolute dormancy and eruption intervals of a few days. The halo effect Langford's party saw is called the Specter of Brocken.

27. The "mountaineer" Langford refers to is probably Charles W. Cook, who in 1869 with two companions found "a vast number of hot sulphur springs," "a considerable amount of lava," and "several gallons of black-looking liquid" about one mile below Tower Fall (Cook et al., *Valley of the Upper Yellowstone*, 24–25). This is Calcite Springs, so named by the Hague party of geologists in 1885. "These springs are unusual in that they sometimes discharge organic liquids (essentially crude oil) along with water" (Bryan, *Geysers of Yellowstone*, 397).

28. Geysers are found in many other places, including the Kamchatka Peninsula of Russia, New Zealand, Indonesia, Papua New Guinea, Peru, Chile, Mexico, and Alaska.

29. *Cosmos* (spelled *Kosmos* in the original German) is five volumes of lectures on science and nature that the highly esteemed scientist Alexander von Humboldt (1769–1859) delivered at the University of Berlin between 1845 and 1862. This work was widely read for decades thereafter.

The Organic Act Creating Yellowstone National Park

U. S. Statutes at Large, vol. 17, chap. 24, pp. 32–33, 1872

An Act to set apart a certain Tract of Land lying near the Head-waters of the Yellowstone River as a public Park.

Be it enacted by the Senate and House of Representatives of the United States of America in Congress assembled, that the tract of land in the Territories of Montana and Wyoming, lying near the head-waters of the Yellowstone river and described as follows, to wit, commencing at the junction of Gardiner's river with the Yellowstone river, and running east to the meridian passing ten miles to the eastward of the most eastern point of Yellowstone lake; thence south along said meridian to the parallel of latitude passing ten miles south of the most southern point of Yellowstone lake; thence west along said parallel to the meridian passing fifteen miles west of the most western point of Madison lake; thence north along said meridian to the latitude of the junction of the Yellowstone and Gardiner's rivers; thence east to the place of beginning, is hereby reserved and withdrawn from settlement, occupancy, or sale under the laws of the United States, and dedicated and set apart as a public park or pleasuring-ground for the benefit and enjoyment of the people; and all persons who shall locate or settle upon or occupy the same, or any part thereof, except as hereinafter provided, shall be considered trespassers and removed therefrom.

SEC. 2. That said public park shall be under the exclusive control of the Secretary of the Interior, whose duty it shall be, as soon as practicable, to make and publish such rules and regulations as he may deem necessary or proper for the care and management of the same. Such regulations shall provide for the preservation, from injury or spoliation, of all timber, mineral deposits, natural curiosities, or wonders within said park, and their retention in their natural condition. The Secretary may in his discretion, grant leases for building purposes for terms not exceeding ten years, of small parcels of ground, at such places in said park as shall require the erection of buildings for the accommodation of visitors; all of the proceeds of said leases, and all other revenues that may be derived from any source connected with said park, to be expended under his direction in the management of the same, and the construction of roads and bridle-paths therein. He shall provide against the wanton destruction of the fish and game found within said Park, and against their capture or destruction for the purposes of merchandise or profit. He shall also cause all persons trespassing upon the same after the passage of this act to be removed therefrom, and generally shall be authorized to take all such measures as shall be necessary or proper to fully carry out the objects and purposes of this act.

Approved, March 1, 1872.

How LeHardy's Rapids Got Its Name

Autobiography of Paul LeHardy, pp. 98–100, 1873

When Paul LeHardy de Beaulieu was a small child, his family immigrated to the state of Georgia from their native Belgium, where his father had been imprisoned for his political views. In 1873 he was employed as a topographer on Captain William A. Jones's expedition, which entered Yellowstone across a difficult pass on the eastern border, now called the Jones Pass.

*M*any were the minor accidents that occurred during that long, tedious crossing of the divide. Pack mules would sometimes lose their footing while zigzagging down the steep side of a sharp spur, sometimes damaging some of the goods; again while crossing a rapid stream full of slippery boulders a mule would lose her footing, go floundering a few yards, soaking bags of flour or of sugar. Finally we went over the ridge and camped by a little, very little brook of sparkling water bordered with nicely perfumed mimulus [monkey-flowers]. In the morning we found the little brook nearly completely frozen over, cool water for scrubbing one's teeth, but the delicate little flowers, having for ages been born there, did not mind the cold. By evening we found ourselves by the lakeshore at the beginning of the Yellowstone River.

We camped there about a week; as it was the intention to return on the west side of the lake, a raft was built to transfer to the other side of the river a mass of stuff, geological specimens, etc. In the meanwhile Gabbett and I discovered that the lake abounded with big salmon trout and were very easy to catch. We also discovered that the coarse sand of the lakeshore was quite largely composed of small particles of semiprecious stone. We wished to collect these minute gems. Quite a number of pelican quills were found to be just what we needed: with a smallish quill trimmed as a long toothpick and moistened between the lips we would pick up the little particles and drop them into the larger quills, which were plugged when full with a piece of the feather stem.

Gabbett and I wished to explore an island in the lake, but the wind was against us, and we could not have polled the raft to it, so we gave that up; but as the outfit was going to cross the river somewhere between the foot of the cañon and the Mammoth Hot Springs, we decided to use the raft to carry us downstream toward the Falls.

On the raft we loaded our bedding, some food and a gridiron, guns and ammunition. We floated down on clear water [two] feet deep over clean gravel and cobblestone bottom, but under us for several miles circled about a dozen of those salmon trout. After a while we saw that a steep bluff would cause a sharp bend in the stream, indeed the water on the inside of the curve, which we hugged because it was the shortest way, became shallow and quite rapid as we approached the bend. Realizing that there would be more water for our clumsy unwieldy raft on the other side we tried but in vain to cross over, now we perceived that we were fast approaching a fall or rapids. It was now too late for anything except trust to luck. On the crest of the rapids there appeared an opening we could shoot through, but upon reaching this gap we perceived, half way down the chute, a conical rock, and instantly our heavy raft straddled it, the rear end being at once sucked to the bottom. The water fortunately was only about two feet deep. We quickly pushed our paraphernalia up out of reach of the water and then considered what to do next. As we looked at the galloping waters at the foot of the bluff and wishing we had gone down that side, we saw our outfit filing past up above and looking down at us. They could not have done anything to help us. Gabbett stripped, I tied a rope about his waist and he let himself down in the eddy below the rock, then worked his way to the stony shore. I had tied the rope to the submerged side of the raft, and the idea was that when we had transferred our stuff to the shore, I would go over and we two would pull to dislodge the raft if possible. The rope broke and there we were, marooned on the wrong side of the river. We "cached" much of our surplus, including my precious Lefaucheux [or Le Falcheux] shotgun, which had got broken when thrown ashore. Then we followed a game trail down the river.

Before dark we reached some spouting mud springs, considered that a good camping place, and proceeded to gather wood, for the nights were cool and we wanted a fire anyway. We made us a good mattress of pine boughs, gathered our tired bodies between two buffalo robes, and went to sleep to the tune of sputtering hot mud.

Next morning early while bathing in the edge of the river, I saw Gabbett stirring the fire to prepare a little breakfast. I reached for my little fish line and in an instant hauled out a fine salmon trout and handed it over to the astonished partner.

Farther down the river I was fortunate enough to bring down from above a big wild goose. I reduced its weight and packed it for several miles, tramping over low flat land frequently intersected by shallow bayous, the water never deeper than about two and one-half feet. Finally we ascended a grassy rounded elevation, perhaps about 40 feet above the river, and from this point we could see part of our camp and the stock picketed out to graze. On this little hill was one solitary small bush pine. I gathered up a lot of dry branches from the neighborhood to stick among the branches of the tree, intending to set fire to it, as a signal to camp; embers falling from the tree set fire to the grass and in a few minutes dense smoke was rising from an acre of hillside. Within half an hour or less our camp seemed to be about five miles away. Two of our men came on horseback to reconnoitre. They had brought their lariats. Gabbett spied a couple of pine poles about the size of telegraph poles a little way upstream; he swam to them with the aid of those lariats, [and] made a long raft upon which we loaded our belongings.

But while waiting for this help from camp we cleaned the goose and cooked it [on] our gridiron, and it was certainly very fine eating; what was left of it was not worth looking at.

It took us about an hour and a half to reach camp, and after briefly recounting our adventure, we turned in for a needed siesta.

We had burned our signal fire at precisely the right spot; had we gone a very few yards beyond this, we would no longer have seen the camp nor been seen from it, and what is more important is that beyond this point the river begins to be narrowed between bluffs and finally confined between vertical walls— and then occur the Upper Falls. Had we not crossed where we did, we would have been entirely cut off from the outfit for perhaps two weeks and had to travel over what we later found to be very bad land, and besides, we had no provisions and no means whatever of procuring any. The Grand Cañon would have separated us from the party.

A Sunset Descent from Mount Washburn

Windham Thomas Wyndham-Quin, *The Great Divide*, pp. 332–34, 1876

The Earl of Dunraven (1841–1926) was a nobleman from Limerick County, Ireland. On his third trip to North America in the summer of 1874, he had traveled to the West to hunt but put his guns away to enjoy Yellowstone's wonders. Near his trip's end, he and guide Fred Bottler ascended Mount Washburn, elevation 10,243 feet (3,122 m), and stayed as long as possible to appreciate the stupendous view.

I jumped to my feet. It was indeed high time to be moving. The sun was getting very low, and the valleys were already steeped in shade. To the east all was dark, but in the western heavens long flaming streaks of yellow were flashing across a lowering sky. The masses of black white light of a watery sun had changed into broad streaks of flaunting saffron. Across all the hemisphere opposed to it, the setting orb was shaking out the red and yellow folds of its banners, challenging the forces of cloudy warriors resplendent in burnished gold. As I looked the sun sank into a mass of cumulus, and all was grey.

So we turned to descend the mountain; but, as we went, the sun, invisible to us, broke through some hidden rift in the cloud strata, and shone out bright and strong, splashing its horizontal rays full against the opposite slope, and deluging the lower portions of the valley with a flood of intense cherry-coloured lurid light. The hills reddened as if beat upon by the full glare of a great furnace. It was a sight most glorious to see. The beauty of it held us and forced us to stop. The glow did not gradually ripen into fullness, but suddenly and in all its intensity struck upon a prominent ridge, lighting up the crags and cliffs, and even the rocks and stones, in all their details; and then by degrees it extended and spread on either side over the foot-hills, bringing out the projecting slopes and shoulders from deep gloom into clear light, and throwing back the valleys into blackest shade. Every rock and precipice seemed close at hand, and shone and glowed with such radiance that you could trace the very rents and crevices in the cliff-faces, and mark the pine-trees clinging to the sides; while in comparison the deep recesses of the chasms and cañons seemed to extend for miles back into dark shadow.

As the sun sank so rose the light, rushing upwards, surging over the hills in a wave of crimson most rarely beautiful to behold, and illuminating the great bulk of the range, while the peaks were still darkly rearing their sullen heads above the tide, and the valleys were all filled with grey vapour. At last the glare caught the mist, and in an instant transformed it from grey cloud into a gauzy half-transparent veil, light, airy, delicate exceedingly, in colour like the inner petals of the rose. Then, as the sun dropped, suddenly the light flashed upon the summits; the peaks leaped into life for a moment, and sank back into their clay-blue shrouds. . . .

THE WONDER-LAND
by Philetus W. Norris, 1878

Ho, ye pilgrims, seeking pleasure,
Or for health in vain,
Listen to me, while I truly
Tell where both to gain.

Chorus.

'Mid encircling snowy mountains,
Falls and canyons grand,
Bathing-pools and spouting fountains,
Of the "Wonder-land."

There, enraptured, have I wandered
Through the glades and dells,
Where the big-horn, elk, and beaver
Each in freedom dwells.

Where the azure pools of healing
Terrace from the snow,
Like a glist'ning cascade frozen,
To the glens below.

Where the spray from spouting fountains
Forms a halo crest,
Looming up the snowy mountains
Rainbows where they rest.

Where the halo's quivering shadows,
O'er the Triple Falls,
Tint the canyon, where wild waters
Echo 'long its walls.

Where the swan with snowy plumage,
Brant, and crested drake,
O'er the yellow trout and speckled,
Skim the crystal lake.

Where the screams of mountain-lion
Pierce the midnight air,
Like the fabled Indian warrior
Wailing in despair.

Where the moose and curly bison,
Monarchs of the glades,
Like the mammoth loom in roaming
'Mid the twilight shade.

Where the ancient forests vernal,
Now in lava cased,
Matchless opal, crystal caskets,
Ruthless are defaced.

Where thin-crusted earth seems bending
From the fires below,
Threat'ning, as of old, the rending
And lava overflow.

Where the bowers of Eden, blooming
'Mid the glens of earth,
Nestle, 'neath fierce tempests howling,
Like creation's birth.

Where on earth are matchless blended
Vernal flowers and snow,
Eden glens and glens of sulphur,
Elysium and woe.

Oh, for wisdom in the councils
Of our nation great,
To protect these matchless wonders
From a ruthless fate! [Note 43]

[Norris's Note 43] This poem was written in Washington, and used in manuscript in the spring of 1878 to aid in securing the first appropriation of funds ever made by Congress to protect, preserve, and improve the people's heritage of wonders in the Yellowstone National Park, and hence the language of the last verse.

Source: Norris, *Calumet of the Coteau*, 70. Philetus W. Norris (1821–1885) received little formal schooling. He served as the park's second (at first unpaid) superintendent from April 18, 1877 to March 31, 1882. He convinced Congress to appropriate $10,000 to fund the park, built roads, explored previously unknown areas and features, and submitted thorough annual reports. His enthusiastic writings about Yellowstone's wonders continue to help and inspire historians.

Preparing for a Trip to the Park

Herman Haupt, *The Yellowstone National Park*, pp. 17–20, 1883

Herman Haupt (1817–1905) was an expert on bridge construction before the Civil War. He was a Union Army general and from 1881 to 1885 served as general manager of the Northern Pacific Railroad. He visited Yellowstone in 1882 with Dr. Eccleston, a Baptist minister from Baltimore, and published his guidebook the next year. His detailed book "was cleverly published in a fold-around binding that protected it from inclement weather."[1]

Haupt's was not the only guidebook available in the park's earliest years. Whittlesey listed seven others in his 1988 names book. The first two guidebooks of the park were by James Richardson and Harry Norton (in 1872) The 1880s saw four more, by William Wylie, Henry Winser, Superintendent P. W. Norris, and the Northern Pacific Railway (published from 1884 to 1906). From 1890 on and until 1966, visitors such as those represented in this volume could have used the guides published by F. Jay Haynes and his son Jack Haynes.

OUTFITTING

To Bozeman the tourist will repair in order to outfit, which means to procure his outfit for the trip through the Park. This includes the purchase of everything he needs on the way, from a needle and thread to his cayuse (Indian pony).

The manner in which he expects to make the tour of the Park will determine the extent of the outfit he will be obliged to purchase. For instance, if he be a prospecting miner, he will buy him two cayuses and shovel, pick, blankets and "grub-stake," consisting of flour, bacon, dried fruit, sugar, coffee, salt, tea, etc. and, with a gold-pan and a frying-pan, he is "made up," with the exception of rifle and ammunition.

If he be not a miner, but a "tenderfooted gentle-man from the States," or a "pilgrim" and not accustomed to "rustle," he will much prefer to have a guide provide all the necessaries and he will foot the bills.

He buys neither his horse nor any other part of his outfit, but leaves the whole matter to the dragoman whom he may be fortunate enough to have secured. This is a convenient way to do, as it relieves from all care. But there are certain little comforts that every-one wants to provide for himself—as a good heavy pair of blankets, an overcoat long enough to wrap well up in or an ulster, a rubber blanket or rubber coat. A rubber pillow from the States will be a very pleasant adjunct to the outfit. A strong suit of clothes, with a change or so of underwear, as the tourist may please, and a helmet or cork hat brought from St. Paul or the States with a pocket-flask and a pair of convex smoked glasses or spectacles will materially enhance the comforts of the trip. Of course you will need soap and other toilet articles, and a good field-glass will not be amiss. But let me advise the tourist of one thing—namely, to avoid a "gripsack" or valise. Put all your traps in a pair of saddle-pockets, or, if you cannot get that, secure a good strong duck sack, such as is used for grain, with a cord tied around the neck, and you will have more comfort on your trip, and less swearing on the part of the guide, than you can imagine. "We have been there," and speak by the card.

The tourist who wants to reduce his expenses will spend a day at Bozeman and buy his horses, which on his return he can sell for almost, if not quite, the price which he paid for them, either to a speculator or to some pilgrim just from the States. In fact, an entire outfit, except the grub-stake, may frequently be procured in this way from a returned party, and sold on the return, which is certainly the cheapest way of doing the Park.

GUIDES

As to guides, there are in and around Bozeman a few men whom I have met that will conduct parties through the Park in safety and with satisfaction to the tourist. Among this number may be mentioned Jack Barronett, Samuel Jackson, Nelson Catlin and James S. Bennett. And the tourist should look well to this matter if he does not wish to spoil his trip by a surly and obstinate guide. Every year adds new names to the list of efficient guides, and it will be a great while till they will be too plenty.

STARTING OUT

The guide being selected and the outfit got ready, the hour for starting out arrives, and the sacks of flour, bacon and sugar and the buffalo-robes are carried out to the appointed place and the pack-animals brought up, and saddled. The pack-saddle consists of four pieces of wood secured together like a saw-buck, with two additional pieces fastened longitudinally, beneath the lower arms, on which the whole structure rests, on the animal's back, being protected by a few folds of blanket. The four upper arms fasten the cords holding the load, which is secured by a diamond-hitch and a cinch. The small Indian pony, or cayuse, will readily convey a load of two hundred and fifty pounds for a whole day and seem as frisky and playful after his load is removed at evening as ever before. In fact, these little "beggars" have a most effectual way of ridding themselves of a troublesome burden by a trick, peculiar to themselves, known in the vernacular as "bucking" (a name taken from the habit of the elk and the deer of putting all four feet together and stamping with all four simultaneously on the ground, with head down and tail depressed), with a succession of shocks so quickly succeeding each other that rider, pack, or whatever it may be, comes off his back. Then all is quiet, and the animal seems as gentle as a kitten. It does not make any difference where the cayuse may happen to be when he is taken with the notion to buck; for buck he will—even on the side of a steep mountain, as we know from dire experience. We were going up the side of Mount Henderson on one occasion, and we had on "Old Pinto" a miscellaneous pack of frying-pans, flour, etc., together with a pair of elk-antlers, and just at the steepest part of the ascent the antlers turned a bit and took Old Pinto in the soft parts of his anatomy, whereupon he stopped and went through such a series of evolutions as would have puzzled an acrobat; and the result was that we were full half an hour carrying the scattered items of his pack up the hill again and readjusting them on his back. But almost any horse would have bucked under such circumstances.

With all their bucking propensities, the cayuses are very sensible little beasts, and soon become so well trained that they will carry a heavy load in perfect safety over a narrow foot-bridge or log with the top side flattened, and along the edge of a yawning chasm with more steadiness than a man can walk; and to those with unsteady heads I would say, "Trust your cayuse to carry you through, and, shut your eyes if you are nervous"; it will be all right.

It is a motley crew, and a grotesque sight to see the train start out of the town with its freight, bound for the Wonderland. Indeed, it is a wonder in itself, when we consider the fact that on the backs of that band of small ponies is stowed away the endless confusion of pots, pans, bags, cans, bundles, tents, buffalo-robes, blankets, guns, ammunition, etc., that a short time before lay, a helpless mass, in Catlin's back yard.

Well, off they go, Catlin in the lead on his big bay, with old frosted-ear "Pinto" following hard on his heels, succeeded by "Black Jack" and the others— all in a line, with no straps to hitch them together; and finally, on the gray rides Deam, with pipe in his mouth and his long persuader cracking about the flanks of his unwilling brute.

1.   Whittlesey, *Yellowstone Place Names*, 1st ed., 136. (The section on guidebooks was cut from the second edition.)

A Family Camp in Yellowstone Park

Margaret Andrews Allen, *Outing*, vol. 7, pp. 157–59, November 1885

About six o'clock on a July evening our heavy emigrant wagon rumbles along the road leading into the Upper Geyser Basin of the Yellowstone. All around us the soil is white as the winter snow relieved on our right by a grove of scattered pines. In this grove we make our camp, while our opposite neighbor, the Castle Geyser, just across the road, rumbles and grumbles a welcome.

We are tired with our long drive, so we busy ourselves with supper,—roasted potatoes, bacon, and batter-cake, with a can of apples for refreshment. We pitch our tent, unroll our bedding, spread it on the dry pine-needles, and prepare for sleep.

Suddenly a shout rings through all the valley, and, dropping dishes, blankets, and bedding, we rush out to see an eruption of the Grand Geyser across the river, but in full view from the road where we stand.

Early in the evening I had heard some men passing on the road say, "There's a bonfire by the Grand," but I thought nothing of it. Now, when we see the

Grand itself, sending its great column of water two hundred feet toward the sky, rosy in the firelight, we are thankful to the fire-builders. Again and again it rises for ten "pulsations" and then falls back into its basin, leaving only rosy clouds of steam, and we go back to our tent, gather our scattered belongings, prepare our beds, and sleep, lulled by the bubble and splash of our Castle.

Morning comes gray and cloudy, and we start to explore the Basin. It is an ideal day for exploration, for the bright sunshine makes the glare of the white "formation" almost insupportable.

First, of course, we visit Old Faithful, the Clock of the Valley, hardly varying five minutes in its hourly eruptions. Its low, broad cone of scale-like layers is firm as the solid rock. No thought of danger here. Everything gives us the idea of regularity and order. We are in position, the curtain rises, and the play begins. The eruption is fine, the geyser sending up a solid column of water, with clouds of hot steam, for over a hundred feet. But it is soon over, and we add to our experience by drinking of the hot sulphur water it has left in all the little hollows of the crust. This is merely to add to our experience, for the taste is far from agreeable. This geyser is the great resource of hurried tourists, from its regularity. We met many parties who had seen only this one—and that one alone is well worth seeing. But what one is sure of seldom fascinates. The freaky ones are most sought after and admired.

We cross the rushing Firehole, and I shall leave it for the guide-book to tell the variety of craters and pools, extinct and active geysers and formations, all the way from Cauliflower to Coral. We come back to our tent already feeling like old residents, ready to initiate ignorant new-comers.

We have seen various men pass with mysterious bags on long poles, and, on questioning one of our neighbors (a very old resident, for she has been here a month) we find it is merely the family washing. The bag contains soap and clothes, and is to be hung in a boiling spring, when, in a few hours, the dirt will be boiled out. We follow suit, and immediately our bag of clothes is hanging in a lovely little blue pool not far from our tent.

A wilderness guide on skis

Elwood "Billy" Hofer was not the first man to traverse Yellowstone on skis,[1] but his report is surely the most complete. When he submitted his five-part story,[2] titled "Winter in Wonderland," to *Forest and Stream* magazine's "The Sportsman Tourist" section in 1887, the magazine was owned by George Bird Grinnell—a man the *New York Times* called "the father of American conservation." Grinnell ran many articles as well as editorials and letters supporting good management and wildlife conservation in Yellowstone.

Hofer set out only a few weeks after the start of the much-publicized winter expedition of Lieutenant Frederick Schwatka, a well-known Arctic explorer, whose trip was sponsored by the *New York World* newspaper. A few days after leaving Mammoth Hot Springs on January 5, 1887, Schwatka had become ill and was obliged to turn back. However, the photographer F. Jay Haynes and three other men continued, overcoming great difficulties. Haynes took the first winter pictures of Yellowstone. His party's story was told in several publications, and some of Haynes's pictures and a striking lithograph of elk and skiers (see page 63) were published in an issue of *Harper's Weekly*. But Hofer's remarkable trip that same winter and his superbly readable account, with its outstanding word pictures, received less attention.

Emerson Hough's version of the Schwatka expedition, in the article he wrote about his own 1894 winter trip, puts it this way:

The Schwatka expedition, as is well known, was sent out by the New York World, and it made a magnificent and elaborate failure. Schwatka had along enough baggage to supply an army. He had long-tailed reindeer coats, plenty of furs, sledges, etc., and in short was equipped for an Arctic trip. Unfortunately one cannot sit in a sledge and be hauled by dog team through the Park, because the snow is too soft and it snows too much and too often there, and the hills are too high and steep. The only way to go is by one's own muscle. Schwatka got his big party and all his lumber into the Park just 20 miles, and then he found he had enough of it, and so marched down the hill again. ("Yellowstone Park Game Exploration," Part 5, *Forest and Stream* 42, 508)

Although they had no way of knowing it at the time, the men of these winter parties had chosen to brave the Yellowstone wilderness during the most severe winter the West had seen in decades (1886–87). In his excellent study of nineteenth-century winter ski visits to Yellowstone, *Yellowstone's Ski Pioneers*, Paul Schullery says that Hofer "was on park business, even though not funded by park management. His detailed accounting of wildlife numbers and distribution, and his many observations on what winter was really like, were the first such report produced." Hofer also "left us a singular vignette of an earlier Yellowstone—a colder, more isolated, and considerably less disturbed park, in the throes of one of American history's great winters, and he did it in a calm, matter-of-fact, and often quite charming manner surpassed by few other park visitors before or since."[3]

Hofer's instructions for making his own "snowshoes" (Norwegian skis) and his inventory of appropriate clothing were so precise they could have been copied by subsequent adventurers. His struggles through the park were rewarded by the sight of marvelous snow and ice formations not seen in milder winters. The details he presents of his visit to Norris Geyser Basin (in his second article) may be the most lyrical and complete description of the basin in winter ever written. He was a sensitive observer as well as a consummate outdoorsman, and he introduces us to some of the people—including children—who lived in the park in the winter.

Hofer's main goal on his trip was to observe the big game of Yellowstone, to assess their condition and estimate their numbers, since these were primary interests of the sportsmen who read *Forest and Stream* magazine. These readers, as responsible hunters, knew that their success in hunting outside the park depended on the well-being of game animals preserved inside Yellowstone's borders. Concern that the buffalo would become extinct was widespread, not just among hunters. Sportsmen also wanted reassurance that elk were still plentiful. In the fifth part of his report, Hofer's writing reflected the then-prevalent thinking about "good" and "bad" fauna: "Expecting to get a shot at a mountain lion at the mill, or have a crack at a lynx, we took a .40-90 Sharps [popular nineteenth-century rifle] along and a small revolver." At that time, even inside the park, it was permissible to kill predators, such as mountain lion, lynx, and wolf, while doing everything possible to help their prey, that is, the elk, deer, and pronghorn antelope.

Hofer concluded his report predicting that visitors, flocking to see the game and the interesting ice features, would soon be common in winter. But he was off by more than eighty years; winter visitation to Yellowstone did not really begin until the advent of over-snow vehicles in the mid-nineteenth century.

"Winter in Wonderland" was one of the myriad Yellowstone reports and letters that Billy Hofer supplied to *Forest and Stream* magazine. He wrote such reports for over forty years, from 1885 to 1925, beginning with his first and longest article for the magazine, "Through Two-Ocean Pass." (See a slightly later report on this unusual mountain pass by Barton Warren Evermann starting on page 180.) He surely did not consider himself a hero, but what he accomplished despite nearly insurmountable odds was truly remarkable. His report is long, but it is good reading and provides a unique historical account.

Born in 1849 in New Haven, T. E. "Billy" Hofer moved west and worked as a miner and a mail carrier—on skis—in Colorado before he first entered Yellowstone in 1878. A few years after coming to the park, he built his own sailboat with his brother to transport tourists on Yellowstone Lake, but it was soon wrecked.

Hofer became renowned in the park as a guide for parties of tourists, scientists, and hunters. When a special agent of the Department of the Interior was sent in 1885 to investigate irregularities among the concessionaires in the park, he reported that Hofer was a man of "high character and in every way worthy of the confidence in the Department."[4] Popular western writer Hough credits him thus in his 1894 *Forest and Stream* article: "The only man ever successful enough to go through the Park in winter, and intelligent enough to make a newspaper account of it, was Mr. Elwood Hofer" and "[We were] highly fortunate in having Mr. Hofer as a member of the party. His guidance, counsel and assistance constituted the difference between success and failure. Without him the trip could not have been what it was."[5] And in 1904 the same magazine mentioned, "A few years ago Mr. Elwood Hofer taught a few people in New England the use of the ski, and the time will come when in the northern portions of the United States these shoes will be extensively used."[6]

Hofer led such eminent American park guests as Theodore Roosevelt, Henry Adams, geologists Arnold Hague and J. P. Iddings, and ichthyologist David Starr Jordan. Hofer was also a scout for the U.S. Cavalry when it first arrived to patrol the park. In the 1890s he built an enclosure at Alum Creek in Hayden Valley in an attempt to entrap and feed the scarce buffalo (not a success), and he trapped wildlife for shipment to the National Zoo.

In 1910, having formed his own company, Hofer was again boating on Yellowstone Lake, where he transported tourists for two summer seasons. The last years of his life were spent with his sister and niece in Clinton, Whidbey Island, Washington, where he was known as "Uncle Billy."

Winter in Wonderland

Through the Yellowstone Park on Snowshoes

1887

ELWOOD ("BILLY") HOFER

born New Haven, Connecticut, 1849 • died Clinton, Washington, 1933

1.

Mammoth Hot Springs, Yellowstone National Park, March 7, 1887

—To Editor *Forest and Stream.*

Having completed the midwinter snowshoe expedition through the National Park, undertaken at the instance of the *Forest and Stream*, and as a special commissioner of that journal, I submit herewith my report of the trip.

To see the Park in its Arctic attire, one must visit it after the 15th of January; before that date the frost has not had time to do its best work. I desired to make the trip with only one companion, and this only after my friend had requested me to take him. I prefer to make most of my trips alone. A young man, Jack Tansey, said he would go with me. He had had no experience in snowshoeing, but as I intended to travel slowly, I thought he could make the stations and camps without any trouble. He was acquainted with some parts of the Park, and had been over most of the route with me last summer. He proved to be a very agreeable camp companion.

The outfit I thought necessary to take with us included an Indian lodge for shelter while camping out. This was 10 ft. in diameter on the ground, made of heavy sheeting, and weighed complete,

"The Yellowstone in Winter—A Surprise," drawn by Charles Graham.

63

7½ lbs. A small chopping hatchet, handle and all, 2½ lbs. A pocket knife for each of us, two sheath knives and one revolver between us, a small .38-cal. Smith & Wesson—carried for fear of an accident. I could use it to build a fire or kill small game if we ran out of provisions. Then there were a small compass, a package of small screws of various sizes under 1½ in. to mend broken snowshoes, and two miner's candles each. We took a change of underclothing and socks, which were also to be used for extra clothing in extreme cold weather. Each had a pint cup. I took from here 5 lbs. of sugar, l lb. of best black tea, salt. 1,000 matches, ½ lb. extract of beef, 2 lbs. condensed soup. Bedding and provisions for the camping out part of our trip I intended to get at the Upper Geyser Basin.

To make my Indian Lodge, I drew a half circle on a floor 21 ft. in diameter, laid down the sheeting on the straight line, cut off at the circle, allowing for hem; lapped on ½ in. and cut off, until I had the marked space covered. Then I lapped the long piece on to the shorter pieces and trimmed the edges, allowing for a hem 1 in. wide. I cut two triangular pieces, 3 ft. wide, 4 ft. long, to a point. I had these sewed to the straight side, the wide ends

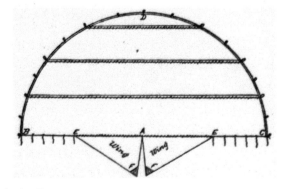

Lodge Pattern

butting at the middle (*A*). I had pockets sewed on to the outer corners of the wings at *F*. Strings on the straight edge from *E* to *C* and *E* to *B* with loops for lodge stakes on the half circle. The seams were sewed on a machine, double stitched. The pockets on the wings are for the wing poles to keep the wings in place and regulate the draft.

Clothing for a winter's trip through the mountains is one of the most difficult things to decide on, as it is very important that one should have sufficient, and still not be burdened with superfluous or useless garments. I used next to my body a fine undershirt, then an antelope skin—short sleeveless—shirt Indian dressed, a California flannel shirt, a woolen overshirt, vest and buckskin jumper; for my legs a pair of mission drawers, pantaloons and canvas overalls; for my feet fine cotton socks, calf boots and arctic overshoes, with canvas leggings tied on with buckskin strings. I used a common white felt hat, and for cold weather I had a jersey cloth hood and mask to draw down over my face, with two silk handkerchiefs to tie around my neck in windy weather, and smoked spectacles to protect my eyes from snow blindness. I had gloves and leather mittens for my hands, and I used long snowshoes—"skeys" or Norwegian— made of red fir.

The snowshoes were 9 ft. long, 1 in. thick, 4 in. wide in the middle, tapering to 3¾ in. at the front, and 2¾ in. at the back end. Fourteen inches of the front was thinned down to ½ in., steamed and bent up so that the end was 8 in. off the ground. The tops of the shoes are beveled off, to allow the snow to slide off readily. The shoes were saturated with melted beeswax, candles, linseed oil of equal parts, with a little rosin to harden the mixture; this preparation was put on the shoes after first heating them before an open fire. The bottoms were heated enough to scorch them a little. After allowing them to cool, I put a coat of shellac on the tops to keep melted snow from wetting the wood. Measuring from the front end of the shoe back 4 ft., I put on a hard wood cross piece or cleat, 4 in. long, ⅝ in. wide, 1½ in. thick, thinned down to ½ in. in the middle to allow the foot to fit in well. The projections assist the foot in guiding the shoe. Two inches in front of the cross piece, two pieces of leather 4 in. wide and 3 in. long were well fastened with screws to the side of the shoe in a groove as deep as the leather was thick, so that nothing should project beyond the side of the shoe. These pieces were laced together to fit the foot. They came over the toe and well back on the instep. The latter must not interfere with the easy movement of the foot while walking. Some prefer an inch strap, tying the foot to the shoe with straps passing back of the foot and over the instep, covering the top of the shoe with tin to prevent the snow's packing under the foot, and using no cross piece. One cannot steer shoes rigged in this way as well as he can those with the cross piece. I covered the top of my shoes (that part under the foot) with part of a rubber bootleg, and found it to work well. To assist one while walking up hill, and steer with while sliding down, a long pole is used. I used a 7 ft. pine pole, which I used also to measure the depth of snow, until the snow was too deep for the pole to touch bottom.

On Saturday, Feb. 12, we left Gardiner, Montana, for the Mammoth Hot Springs, four miles within the Park. Our route was up the Gardiner River, which we found open, owing to the great volumes of hot water running into it from the Boiling River at the foot of the old hot spring terraces, four miles above. [Boiling River, painted by Thomas H. Thomas, is reproduced in Plate 2]

The road follows along the river most of the way to the Hot Springs, crossing it twice. Often we could see trout in the clear water. I counted seventeen small ones near one rock, at a point less than 1½ m. [miles] from Gardiner. I saw no large fish. A little further on we crossed the river to where the road runs under some cliffs. Here I saw a band of six mountain sheep, feeding within ten feet of the road on a hillside and above the roadway. Seeing us, two of them walked up on the hill, a little further to a point where they had a better view of us. After satisfying their curiosity, they went on feeding, for there was little snow. They showed no fear whatever; some of them only looked up once, but paid no attention to us. Though we passed within 20 yds. of them they were as unconcerned as possible, pawing snow and feeding as though there were no such thing as a rifle or hunter in the world. The band consisted of four ewes and two lambs. One of the lambs had patches of hair off from its sides; this I attribute to a parasitical disease similar to the scab of domestic sheep; I have often noticed that mountain sheep are afflicted with it in the spring. I have found old rams dead that had very little hair on them, the skin being hard, dry and cracked. I have often noticed the same trouble with elk, especially bull elk; the first one I ever killed was in a sorry plight, with scarcely a hair on his sides, shoulders, or neck; the skin looked like scales—all cracked and bleeding—he was very poor, and

unfit for any use except wolf bait. The other sheep in this band appeared in fair condition. The band have been in the Gardiner cañon all winter; they are so tame that they will lie down within less than 20 yds. of passing teams. An old ram belonging to the band, but not with it when I passed, once thought of disputing the road with the Post Surgeon on his way to Gardiner; the ram finally concluded to let his team go by, so he hopped up on a rock beside the road, went up on the hill a little way and lay down.

I did not see any of the antelope on Mt. Evarts as we were down in the cañon. In the river I observed, besides the fish, several kinds of ducks, the names of which I do not know. Water wrens [*Cinclus mexicanus* or American dipper], queer little birds, were dashing in and out of the water seeking their food; they would sit on a rock, bob up and down a few times, then with a squeak dash into the water and out of sight, popping up in an unexpected place. Snowbirds, camp or moose birds, Clark's crows [*Nucifraga columbiana* or Clark's nutcracker], and several small birds were

also noted on our way up. The snow on the river was about 2 ft. deep. As we began to climb the old terraces to the main Hot Springs proper, the snow deepened very fast until in the vicinity of the hotels there was on an average about 4 ft. of settled snow, packed quite hard by the wind and very much drifted.

Striking across the flats, we stopped at the Cottage Hotel [at Mammoth Hot Springs]. Here I learned that the mail carrier had not been heard from for over two weeks, and fears of his having lost his life were expressed. One of the teamsters whose teams are snowed in at the Norris Hotel, Con Sheehan, had come down for the mail and intended to start back in the morning; so I was to have company part way up.

I did not visit the active Hot Springs, as they are for the most part snowed under. Only the hot water is exposed. Soon after the water leaves the springs it cools down and freezes, and the snow falls on the ice, hiding anything worth seeing in the way of frost work. Then, too, the coloring that adds so much to the beauty of the formation and attracts so much attention, is very much dimmed; it is not nearly so brilliant as in summer.

Sunday morning I was up for an early start, but found it snowing hard with a heavy wind from the south and southwest, which I would have to face, and that, too, in an open country. Con had started, but turned back, so we put in Sunday visiting the people around the Springs. One of the men who had packed for the Schwatka party and, later, for Mr. Haynes, told me his experience on the trip. The party were taken to Indian Creek with teams, to a barn, where everything was left.

The whole of the next day was spent making less than a mile, where a camp was made. The party rested up here, then started for Norris, distance some 12 or 14 miles; some of the party did not get in until very late. Almost all of their baggage was left at the barn. At Norris Lieut. Schwatka, Mr. Brackett and the guide, Jack Barronett, stopped. The rest of the party went on to the Lower Basin, and most of them to the Upper Basin, returning to Norris the same way they had come. Then all the party went from there over to the Falls, 12 miles. At the Lower Basin, Mr. Haynes, the photographer, left the party, and with three men as packers, visited the Lower and Upper Basins, Grand Cañon and Falls, returning to the Mammoth Hot Spring via Mt. Washburne and Yancey's. In going over Washburne, the party were lost three days and were without blankets or provisions.

I had been told of snow slides and dangerous places in the Gibbon Cañon, until I began to dread that part of my trip, as I have had one snow slide catch me and carry me part way down a mountain, besides having very narrowly escaped three others; still I decided to make the "grand round," if possible. I intended to go from here to the Norris Basin and Lower and Upper Basin; from there go over on to the Pacific Slope, crossing the Continental Divide to Shoshone Lake; visit that, recross to the Yellowstone Lake, follow down that to the river, then on down stream to the Falls of the Yellowstone, then over Mt. Washburne to the Tower Falls; look up the game, and return to the Hot Springs.

We had enough lunch put up for two days, then on the morning of Feb. 14, with 18 lbs. packs each, we started for Norris, 22½ miles distant. We were joined by Con and passed the **quarters of the soldiers** stationed here for the protection of the Park. Their buildings, barracks, storehouse, guard house, stables, hospital and others are built under the principal Hot Springs terraces. We soon came to the dead timber, which extends for miles around the springs, and which was killed by a fire in October, 1882, started in the Swan Lake Basin.

Within two miles of the Springs we came to the fresh trail of a band of elk. I saw their beds to the left of the road where they had passed the night. I think there must have been twenty in the band. Arriving at Golden Gate, we found that the wind had swept the snow off the road, and even out of the gulch, except where it was piled in immense drifts. The wind sweeps through this pass with frightful force from the open country beyond. The trees exposed to the wind are all leaning from it, and every limb is pointed in the same direction. As we came in sight of the Pass we saw it would be very difficult to get out that way unless we descended into the gulch and then climbed out over the Rustic Falls. This we thought worse than climbing the cliffs to our right, which we did, passing our snowshoes to one another.[7] We had to go up about 75 ft. to get out on to a country where we could use our shoes again. In a few minutes we were out in the open country known as the Swan Lake Basin.

quarters of the soldiers: The first army headquarters in Yellowstone was Camp Sheridan, located just east of the Mammoth terraces. The camp was used from 1886 to 1891.

It was snowing a little, still we could see a few miles. There was very little wind; the day was cold and good for traveling. Going about half a mile I turned to look south toward Electric Peak.[8] All the high ridges exposed to the west wind were blown free from snow, and on them were several bands of elk feeding, I counted up to 120 in all; only four of them were old bulls; they were off to one side. The elk were in small bands of ten and fifteen; it was a beautiful sight. I could not resist the temptation to shout, and I gave one *whoo-pee*! I think every elk heard it and started for higher ground; not knowing what was wrong, they collected on some high points, where they remained so long as in sight. All these elk were within less than four miles of the Mammoth Hot Springs and do not include those on Sepulchre Mountain, Electric Peak or the ridges between them. Cows, calves and spike bulls made up the band. I was within half a mile of the most distant of those I saw until I shouted.

Following the open country south, we soon came to the Gardiner River, which we crossed on a bridge just below where the stream is joined by Panther and Indian Creeks. The streams were open most of the way, and every rock or snag in the stream was capped with a huge ball of snow out of all proportion to the size of the rock or support. Through this section of the country the snow was from 4½ ft. to 5 ft. deep, and increasing in depth as we went south.

Two miles from the bridge we came to Lieut. Schwatka's second camp, a Sibley tent, crushed down by snow, with only the pole and stovepipe standing. Con proposed to dig it out and camp here for the night. It was rather early to camp, only

1 PM. We had the tent partly uncovered when the mail carrier came along on his way to the Springs. He had been very sick from a wetting he received in the Gibbon River on his way out. He had to cross on a log, at the further end of which there was a large snowdrift, in which he tried to beat a foothold with his snowshoe pole, when suddenly the whole drift gave away, knocking him off the log into the river, where the water was four feet deep. The snow rolled over him, and kept him under water for quite a while. When he finally got out, his matches were wet, so he could not build a fire to dry himself. He was six miles from Norris and twelve miles from the Lower Basin Hotel. He concluded to go on to the Geyser Basin. His clothing soon froze like armor. He was hardly able to move. About half a mile further on, at the Beryl Hot Springs, he warmed up and thawed out his stiffened garments. Then by moving fast he kept warm; went on the next day to the Upper Basin, and there was taken sick from the effects of his wetting and exposure. This accounted for his being out in the Park so much longer than usual. We were glad to learn of his escape, for Pete Nelson is a good, reliable man and a first-class snowshoer.

We soon had the tent cleaned off and propped up with poles, and a fire started. Making some tea, we lunched. While engaged in cutting some wood for the night, we heard a dog bark, and looking up saw Mr. Kelley (the man in charge of the Norris Hotel) coming down on Pete's trail with two small dogs following. Mr. Kelley was out looking for Con who was overdue at Norris. I began to think the woods were full of people. I had not expected to meet any one when I started out. Kelley was glad to find us and a comfortable fire to camp by; if he had not found us here he had intended to go on to the Mammoth Hot Springs. We found in the tent some blankets, sleeping bags and robes left here by the Schwatka party. We made ourselves comfortable and passed a very pleasant night.

In the morning Con noticed a bottle hanging up on a tree, some 12 ft. from the level of the snow. Thinking it would be good to carry tea in to drink on the road, he climbed the tree and took it down. Noticing some writing on it he brought it to me, and it was a surprise. Written on the label was a note that the bottle was "placed on the level of the snow. Thermom. -51°," signed, "Schwatka, Jan. 7." On Jan. 7 the snow was not deep enough to prevent teams passing back and forward between the Mammoth Hot Springs and Norris—about 3 ft. of snow. The thermometer did register rather low, -31° at the Lower Geyser Basin, and -26° at the Mammoth Hot Springs. I took off the label as a curiosity. I suppose the snow must have been very deep when the bottle was "placed on the level of the snow," and the weather very much colder here than anywhere else in the Park. As there was nothing in the bottle but air I concluded that the whole thing was a misstatement and that the high winds had blown and lodged the bottle in the tree, even with a telephone insulator spiked to the other side of the tree. Strange things happen in the Park.

I mentioned the matter of bedding, which I wished to obtain at the Upper Basin Hotel to use while going from there to the Falls, via Shoshone and Yellowstone Lake. Mr. Kelley, who had charge of some of the stuff left by Lieut. Schwatka, suggested that we take one of the Arctic sleeping bags, which we did, to be left at the Mammoth Hot Springs on our return. This saved the trouble of packing blankets, but I think a pair of blankets each would have answered our purpose better than the bag.

Leaving this camp we started out through Willow Park, taking turns of fifteen minutes each breaking trail, as it is quite hard on the man ahead, when one sinks in the snow from six to ten inches. In this order we came to Crystal Springs; here there was a very dangerous bit of snow on an exposed side of the cañon with no timber to hold it. There was danger of its sliding down at any moment. We passed here safely, however, and soon came out to the Obsidian Cliffs and Beaver Lake. The cliffs were draped with snow, which hung to every projection and point, hiding most of the obsidian. The little of the cliffs that could be seen looked blacker than usual from being brought into contrast with the pure white of the snow.

Beaver Lake was frozen over and covered with about two feet of snow. We crossed it lengthwise, passing near the beaver house, which tourists can see from the road in summer. From indications there is a family of beavers in it now.

We soon came to Roaring Mountain, where the steam rushes from the mountain with a loud noise. There is considerable bare ground on the mountain owing to the heat melting the snow off as fast as it falls; but every detached rock is cold enough to hold snow; on these it accumulates in globe-like masses, looking like white islands scattered over the bare ground.

Twin Lakes were soon passed; these were interesting. We crossed on the snow and ice; and took the short cuts every time. While passing the Roadside Springs,[9] we found more bare ground; at one place the road was bare for a hundred yards, except where there was a small bridge; the snow on this was 4 ft. deep; it looked like a white marble tomb. Some of the shapes taken by the snow on the loose rocks were queer. Tam O'Shanter hats, rabbits, bears, and hundreds of forms resembling animals and buildings, forms that only a photographer could illustrate.

At about 11 o'clock we were all startled by a loud rumbling report in the direction of the Falls [that is, to the east, where the Yellowstone falls are located]. We thought at first it was an earthquake, but we felt no tremor or movements of the ground. This was a beautiful clear day, the third clear day since Jan. 11; up to this time it had snowed every day with the two exceptions.

The bright sunshine made it hard snowshoeing for Con and Kelley, their shoes clogging considerably. Jack's and mine ran very smoothly with an application of the candles a few times, rubbed on the bottoms of the shoes. At 3:15 we arrived at the Norris Hotel, where we were taken good care of.[10] Maj. Lyman telephoned over that he had heard a loud report in the direction of the Norris Geyser Basin. No one knew about the cause—an additional Park mystery.

2.

On February 16 I visited Norris Geyser Basin. A heavy fog hung over the country, with a light snow. As I approached the Basin, I was startled by the resemblances to men and animals the ice-laden trees showed, as, standing sentinel duty on each side of the road, they appeared to be watching our approach. Everything was loaded down with the steam frozen as it had drifted from the geysers. There were fantastic forms of men and women looking into the pools. Up the road were seen hogs, rabbits, mules, elephants, leopards, tigers, cats and dogs; animals of all kinds and shapes, creatures that outside of the Park nothing but a disordered mind could conjure up. All were in white, but often with dark eyes, ears and mouth, or limbs or faces, where the deep green of the pines showed through the white ice. Now and then a bough free from frost projected through the ice to form the plume of a soldier or the ears of a mule or rabbit. Again there appeared the form of a woman holding a child, bending over it as if to protect it from the wintry blasts. Others there were with groups of children gathered about them, all in white, as though just escaping from their burning homes; and it wanted but the red glow of a sunset to make the illusion complete; the steam looked like smoke, while the confused sounds of the geysers resembled the burning and crackling of flames and the crash of falling buildings. I was alone with all this mysterious, ghostly band, and I confess to a strange sensation amid these weird surroundings as I descended into the basin through the fog. On every side could be heard the rush and roar of hot water and steam. Even under foot was heard the hissing of escaping steam and gases, and the bubbling and sputtering of waters through the sand and decomposed formations. Mud pots were puffing and splashing their inky contents, or whirling and dashing their turbid waters against the banks of the caldrons, all invisible until one was within five or ten feet of the brink of the pool and geysers.

I soon noticed an increase in the activity of most of the geysers through the Basin. I timed the Five Minute, or Constant Geyser, the eruptions occurring every twelve to fifteen seconds. It threw its clear waters from 15 to 20 ft. high. There would be several thuds, agitating the waters considerably, then a burst of steam and gases which threw the waters to their fullest height.

Wandering around among the pools in the mystery of the fog, alone in the world—like one at sea on a raft without a sail in sight—I could not see the ghostly goblin band over the hill I had left behind, but I could feel their presence; and now and again I would suddenly come in sight of more of them as I approached the timber either on my right or left. I found ice and snow everywhere in the valley. I could travel on my snowshoes on snow and ice 8 ft. deep, by the side of streams of hot water, while snow was falling on me, and white rabbits were mysteriously disappearing from sight among the snow-laden trees on my left. Flies were seen on the surface of the stream, and where the water was collected in shallow pools a **water insect like a worm** could be seen on the bottom moving sluggishly about. Most of the colors of the rainbow lined the bottom of the stream, though the shades were pale. I followed down the stream of the waters running from Constant, Black Growler, Ink Geyser, and the pools in the northern part of the Basin, until it was joined by the waters from the Monarch, New Crater, Vixen, Spiteful, Coral and the other beautiful pools, springs and geysers in the main basin. This stream I then followed up until I had visited every point of interest. I was often cautioned by signs "not to drive over the formation." Once seeing a queer ice mound I could just make out a sign, and breaking away some of the ice I was notified "to extinguish my fires." Well, hardly, on this cold day, if you please. The snow, which was from 4 to 5 ft. deep, was seamed everywhere by little streams of hot water, all leading to some hot spring or geyser; the snow and ice extended up close to the hot water, sometimes within 1 or 2 in. I could step across most of the streams without getting off my snowshoes.

As I approached Coral Spring [north of Yellow Funnel Spring in Back Basin] I was almost tempted to shoot at a large polar bear; he was ten feet up a dead tree near the spring; he had climbed up the tree and was looking back at the hot water as if afraid of it; I could have believed him to be alive as I first saw him through the fog and falling snow. He was only ice, however, and had grown right there where he was, as the frozen steam had added to his bulk. He was at least ten feet long; and as he grasped the tree with all his legs, one foreleg thrown over a dead limb, he was a perfect picture of a great white bear. If carved from a block of ice by an artist he could not have looked more natural. All the trees in and near the basin are small second growth pines, the fires having killed off all the large timber. These trees are just large enough to form ice figures of proportions to make their resemblance to human beings and animals perfect.

---

water insect like a worm: In Yellowstone's hot spring runoff streams, ephydrid flies live and lay their eggs; Hofer likely saw the larval stage of this fly.

Following up the waters from the new Crater Geyser [Steamboat Geyser], I soon came to the geyser and saw it in eruption. There has been some increase in the size of the Crater since I saw it last summer. Leaving this I followed the high ground to the Emerald, a beautiful pool, whose bright green shone more brilliant by being brought into strong contrast with the white of the surrounding snow. Further on I came to the **Schaum Kessel**, the only object **Mr. Arnold Hague**, of the Geological Survey, personally named. It is a very interesting mud geyser. The bottom and sides of the basin are lined with a pearly formation, and when dry the points show a bluish-white tinge, looking very pretty against the dark background of the basin. When in action this geyser is as attractive as any I have seen; it throws jets of lead blue colored waters up through a whirling, dashing, waving mass seven feet in diameter. Its action is different from those of the other geysers; they all differ very much when closely noticed. Some Park visitors say: "Well, I have seen one; I've seen all." This is a great mistake. I know of no two alike, either in action or formation. In mound, terrace, or cone all are different, and one who is so well acquainted with their formation as is Mr. Hague can tell from a specimen which one of the principal geysers it came from.

From this point I went up on a very perfect

Schaum Kessel, German for "foam kettle," should be Schlammkessel (mud kettle), an old name for today's Bathtub Spring.

Dr. Hague worked in and wrote about Yellowstone from 1883 until at least 1913, contributing greatly to geological knowledge and naming many features.

cone of ice, 6 ft. high by 10 ft. in diameter, formed by the frozen spray and steam from the "safety valve," which was blowing off as though on its efforts depend the integrity of the whole crust of the basin.[11] Sliding off the cone I visited the Black Growler. Here, too, I think there is some increase in the action. Following the hillside a little way from the Growler, one leg, snowshoe and all, suddenly dropped down with the snow, throwing me on my side. For an instant I thought I was over a hot hole, but could not remember any in the immediate vicinity; and soon righting myself I looked into the hole and saw logs there. I think the warm ground had melted the snow away, the logs supporting the crust until I had stepped on it. My foot and snowshoe passed between two logs. There was not the least danger, but it taught me to be a little more cautious unless I was sure the ground under me was safe.

Further east I came to another steam escape, somewhat sheltered from the wind. Near this was an ice-covered tree, which had taken the form of a woman, her garments covered with the most delicate frost work lace, fringes and tassels, more delicate than the finest silk, and that a breath of wind would disturb and break; a gossamer-like bridal veil of frost hung over all, looped and gathered into folds. It was the most delicate frost work I have yet seen. With one beam of sunlight all would have disappeared. The whole fabric was so fine that parts were continually breaking off and falling on the snow below, making a train for the dress.

I had now been in the Basin several hours, had seen boiling water and solid ice within less than a foot of each other, and little mounds of green and blue tinted ice, where the spray from the small geyser jets fell; and I had stepped across running streams of hot water, with my snowshoes elevated above the stream by two or three feet of snow and ice. In summer no such extremes meet; nothing so beautiful and delicate as the frost work is then to be seen. Before I left the Basin the fog lifted; the wind began to blow, swaying the trees about, rattling their icy garments; the ghosts and goblins were going through a weird dance, bowing and swaying to each other, accompanied by the mournful music of the wind as it sighed and moaned through the pines.

The clouds lifting showed Mt. Holmes in the northwest. This beautiful peak with its snow-capped summit rose from the dark masses of green timber. In places the trees were so laden with snow as to give the whole forest a white appearance; the last snow had covered every limb and bough, and one could call it a forest of silver trees. In a few places the wind had blown the snow off, revealing a dark green and giving to the landscape the appearance of shadows of passing clouds.

Returning to the hotel, I learned the history of the Schwatka Exploring Expedition, the true cause of its failure and the extent of its explorations. There is much humbug about the whole thing. As well talk of "exploring" Central Park, New York, as the National Park. The National Park is a well-known country; everything worth seeing is mapped out and described in reports and geological surveys, guide books and newspaper letters. The extent of the Schwatka "explorations" consisted in following a first-class wagon road, 80 ft. wide, cut through the forest, and planted with telephone poles every 200 feet. The party, after being helped almost half way with teams, consumed three days in going to the Norris Hotel from the Mammoth Hot Springs. The "explorers" had no packs to carry, having several men as assistants. The trip was very poorly managed; enough baggage was taken for twenty men. Not only were the men burdened with packs, but there were a "master of transportation" and guides, who would carry no baggage. On a trip of this kind every man ought to carry his proportion. As, when starting out, they had more baggage than they could get through with, the surplus was left in a log barn on Willow Creek,[12] and in a tent, three-quarters of a mile this side, where they made their last camp. Mr. Ross, the snowshoer, was the first into Norris, Coho and Schwatka coming in last. Mr. F. Jay Haynes, the photographer, packed his portion of the baggage.

After resting, most of the explorers started for the Lower Basin, leaving Mr. Brackett, an old gentleman of 76, at the hotel. The Lieutenant got as far as the Dude's Head, a peculiar stump beside the road, not quite four miles from the hotel. There is here an abnormal growth on a tree about 4 ft. high, the road builders having cut the tree off at this swelling and leaving the stump as a landmark. Here it is said he had a hemorrhage of the lungs, and with the assistance of Baronnett, the Government scout, he returned to the hotel and his base of supplies until the party returned from the Basins, when he mustered sufficient vitality to go to the Falls. Mr. Brackett, with his burden of 76 years, also made this trip, some twelve and a half miles.

That part of the expedition that made the trip to the Basins returned to Norris on about Jan. 12.

At the Lower Geyser Basin Mr. Haynes dropped the explorers. Selecting two men and sending for Ed Wilson, with these three he visited the Geyser Basins, returning by the way he had come, and reaching Norris on Jan. 19, during a very severe wind storm, which blew and broke down hundreds of trees along the roads in the park. The storm disabled the telephone wire from the Mammoth Hot Springs to the Lower Basin, where it is down in over fifty places, and rendered it useless for the winter.

From the Norris Basin Mr. Haynes visited the Falls and Grand Cañon, going out over Mt. Washburn, on which he and his party were lost for three days. They were lost before reaching the top of the Pass on the east trail. They had no bedding, no ax, and little provisions, but fortunately enough were provided with matches, and as they were on a well timbered country they did not suffer for the want of a fire. Their exploits have been described in several papers, in some greatly exaggerated. One writer for a Montana paper, not knowing the geography of the country, has them at noon on the summit, later lost, then looking into Tower Creek Cañon, then back on the south side of the mountain, then well down in the Yellowstone Cañon— jumping them about by prodigious leaps of from ten to twelve miles at a bound, before finally rescuing them. The fact is, that they were lost before they began the ascent of the mountain; wandering around on the south side they finally made their way around the mountain on the east, between it and the Yellowstone Cañon. They crossed a spur that is the highest point in the cañon, and here they passed over one very dangerous place, where they were likely to start a snow-slide which would

have swept them to certain death. While crossing this place not a word was spoken, for each one realized the danger. I am quite familiar with all the trails over and around the mountains, and I know that even in summer there is much danger in riding around this point. Tourists never travel this trail, but take one further to the west known as the East, or Cañon Trail.

After rounding this point they were soon on the waters of Antelope Creek, and in an open country. Striking across the country they soon descended to Tower Creek. The party were too much exhausted to photograph this beautiful fall, or a band of elk which they saw. Pushing on, they arrived at Yancey's Station about 2 PM on the third day from the Falls. Resting here a day, they then went in to the Mammoth Hot Springs, glad to get safely out of the Park. Lieut. Schwatka and friends had returned to the Mammoth Hot Springs by the way they came, before Mr. Haynes had got down from the geysers.

I saw a clipping from the *New York World* telling of the wonderful things the expedition was going to do in the Park. The most wonderful of all was that they were going to take with them some fifty Crow scouts. It would take more than the whole United States Army to drive a Crow Indian through the Park in winter. They know nothing about the geyser country. They are afraid of it. It is "bad medicine" for the superstitious Indians. To ask one to go in there would be to get an answer to the effect that a white man was "heap a damn fool, heap crazy."[13]

Going over the hotel on my return from the Basin, I saw the cracked walls and chimneys broken by the shaking up the building had received by an earthquake shock in November. It had shaken dishes off the shelves and broken many of them. Throughout this region the snow was about seven feet deep; one bank in front of the hotel reached up to the second story. White rabbits were very thick about here. Wolverine and lynx tracks were seen every few rods [one rod equals 16.5 feet]; one can follow with his eyes the attempts of the lynx to catch a rabbit for his dinner. They never make many jumps, only about three; if they miss a rabbit then they give it up and try another. These rabbits can make as long a jump as a lynx, and can out-run a lynx on the snow. When a rabbit hides in the snow he is unsafe. I noticed places where a lynx had been diving for a rabbit; into his hole he would go, the rabbit getting away from it and making for another place to hide, only to have the lynx down on him again; and so it went on until the rabbit was overtaken by the lynx. A little blood stain showed where the hunt had ended. A lynx sinks but little in the snow, its very large feet prevent its light body from sinking much more than a rabbit.

Soon after 3 AM on the 17th, we started for the Lower Basin. It was quite dark and snowing a little when we set out. We passed through the basin I had visited the day before, coming out through the fog and steam on the other side. We could see a little better, as it was getting daylight. In due time we came to the Dude's Head, the top of which was below the level of the snow, only a little mound of white showing where it was. With some difficulty I could run my snowshoe pole to the ground, and I found that through this stretch of timber the snow was from six to seven feet deep. We sank from four to six inches deep in the snow while on the shoes, without them we would go down to our knees.

When we came out in sight of the Gibbon Meadow, we were favored with a lifting of the clouds, giving us a view of the meadow and surrounding country. We could look down the Gibbon Cañon a short distance and see great clouds of steam rising from the Monument Geysers, the Artist Paint Pots and geysers on the head of Geyser Creek, and on our right Sylvan Spring. A dark snow cloud hid Mt. Holmes and all the peaks in the Madison Range. We ran down to the meadow in a few seconds, a delightful slide after the steady tramping in the snow through the timber. Shortly after descending the hill, a severe snow storm struck us, followed by a strong wind, which drove the snow against us in horizontal lines; but as it came from our right it was not so difficult to travel in, though had it been driving in our faces it would have been hard work making headway.

The Gibbon River was open and free from ice; all the open creeks that flow into it were steaming. Drifted snow curled over its banks and hid them, the river coming through a white field. Long bright green grasses and water plants grow on the bottom, waving with the current.

Through this part of the Park I expected to see moose, for there are a few in here and to the north nearer Mt. Holmes. I expected to find them feeding on the grasses in the water, or at least to discover some signs of them; but we saw nothing that I was sure of, for the fast falling snow hid whatever tracks there might have been. I noticed several flocks of ducks on the river, most of them wooducks, with a few mallards and a black duck with white cheeks and white tipped wings.

We soon entered the cañon which I had been dreading [Gibbon Canyon], for I was fearful of snowslides and the dangerous places I had been told of. I was tempted to go around to avoid the bad part; but we concluded that we could slip through and by taking due note of the dangerous places shoot across them. We soon came to the Hot Springs on the left of the old road. Here a log had been thrown across the stream, as there was no bridge on the new road. We were obliged to cross on this log, the one that had caused Pete Nelson, the mail carrier, so much trouble. Taking both snowshoe poles, I balanced myself with one, breaking the snow and ice off with the other. The log sagged so that the water ran almost over it, making it slippery; and it required caution to cross without a wetting. Although encumbered with packs and long snowshoes, we managed to pass over in safety. In this cañon I noticed the effects of the storm of Jan. 19; many trees had been blown down, some were broken off 20 ft. up and had brought down in their fall telephone wires and poles. The wide wagon road was piled up with snow fully 12 ft. deep, drifted in long ridges, the tops of which we were obliged to follow as if traveling on the comb of a house. At the Beryl Spring we paused a few minutes to see the effect of the cold. All the trees were covered with ice, in interesting and strange shapes. We then crossed two bridges over gulches, the snow being piled above the railing. Through here there was some 7 ft. of snow, on the meadow above from 4 to 7 ft.

Constantly looking for danger we recrossed the river on a bridge, and soon after I noticed the trail of two small snowslides, and walking back saw the trail of another above the bridge. That was the only dangerous ground I saw. To be sure, the sides of the cañons are very steep and the snow deep, but fortunately the cañon is well-timbered and holds the snow in place. I really think there is no danger here at all. Climbing a long hill we soon came to the Gibbon Falls, to see which we must descend into the cañon again; this was so difficult in the deep snow, to say nothing of the trouble we would have in getting back, that we concluded to go on.

The storm was over and the sun out, with now and then passing clouds. When we came to the Cañon Creek hill, we had a view of half a mile, descending some 400 ft. While resting here and lunching, I looked for fish, as this is the first stream in which one can find trout after leaving the Mammoth Hot Springs. I saw but a single fish and that but a small one. Having rested an hour we pushed on our way, and before sunset came to the Teton Hill, from which, on a clear day, one can see the top of the Grand Teton.[14] We could discern steam rising from the Great Fountain, Fountain, and Excelsior Geysers. The whole of the Lower Basin was before us; flowing to our right was the Fire Hole River; further north the Cañon of the Madison, 1,700 ft. deep. The whole river was open, with ducks and brant on the surface, and now and then a gull.

Running down the hill we crossed an exposed space where the snow was only 4 ft. deep. Just before entering the Lower Basin we crossed immense drifts, and making our way over Nez Percé Creek, came to the hotel, reaching there a little after 6 PM.

3.

At the Lower Basin we found Mr. James Dean and wife in charge. They were living in one of the comfortable log cottages belonging to the hotel.[14] Mr. Dean is one of the old assistant superintendents, who for years did more to save the Park from destruction by fire than any other assistant. Stationed in the cottage at Norris he daily rode each way on the road, putting out fires and removing obstructions from the geysers and springs; keeping a sharp lookout for specimen fiends. It is to be regretted that Congress did not appropriate money for the protection of the Park and place such men as Mr. Dean in charge. The Yellowstone Park Association have had him in charge of their hotel at this place ever since they started. During the winter he has been keeping a record of the maximum and minimum thermometer readings, the depth of snow fall and earthquake shocks. The latter occurred first on the 5th of November [that is, three months previously]. There was first a slight shock, with a long rumbling sound accompanied with a jar, the sound coming from the east and passing on west, where it appeared to strike the hill on the west and stop.

On the 7th, or more properly the 8th, at 12:50 AM, occurred a second shock. There was a rumbling, and then a shaking and swaying of the cabin so that the dishes rattled. Mr. Dean was awakened by the movement of the house; a large dog asleep in the next room was frightened, and going to the door begged to be let out. This was the heaviest shock felt, and, I believe, the one that was so heavy at Norris. The next night, Nov. 9, there was a rumbling sound which came from the east,

a very sudden shock or jar, the sound passing on and ending apparently at the hill on the west; the whole thing was over in less than ten seconds. On Nov. 27 the same rumbling sound was heard coming from the east; as it passed under the cabin there was a slight shock felt. On Dec. 20, at 7:30 PM, a slight jar and shock was felt, accompanied with the usual rumbling noise. This account is as Mr. Dean gave it to me, and can be depended on as reliable, without any sensational additions.[16]

The thermometer readings for that part of January while the Schwatka explorers were finding the snow so deep on Willow Creek, and the cold so intense (−51°) I give below. The readings are taken at noon from self-registering thermometers:

	Max.	Min.		Max.	Min.
Jan. 6	+20°	−1°	Jan. 8	−13°	−31°
Jan. 7	+5°	−5°	Jan. 9	0°	−22°

The highest in January was on the 3d, +33°, and the lowest the 8th, or night of the 7th, −31°.

The snowfall up to date was for October, November and December, 58 in.; January, 51 in.; February 1 to 18, 44 in., a total of 153 in. or 12 ft. 9 in., a very respectable amount of snow, considering that March and April are very snowy months, some years as much falling in these two months as in all the others put together. The snow was drifted around the buildings in immense piles. This hotel is the only one at all exposed to the wind, the others are sheltered either by timber or hills. Around each building on three sides would be a narrow space, the snow drifted in perpendicular walls. On the other or north side it will be piled up against the building 7 and 8 ft. deep.

On Feb. 18 I made a new pair of snowshoes for Jack [Tansey, Hofer's traveling companion], his being, for him, unmanageable. This took most of the day. Flocks of ducks were often seen flying up or down stream. Their "quack, quack" could be heard in the streams on each side of the group of houses.

On the 19th, a clear day, I visited the Lower Basin, crossing the open meadow between the hotel and the Fountain Geyser. On this flat I found the snow from 1 to 3 ft. deep. I turned aside to the **Third Geyser Group**, but saw nothing unusual here. The Surprise Geyser showed no signs of having had an eruption this winter, and the other pools and springs on the flat were about as usual. At the Fountain [Geyser] I was rewarded by a beautiful sight. A small grove of trees about a hundred yards to the northeast were a mass of ice formed from the steam that had drifted to them from the Fountain Geyser. The central tree was a white monument, a tower resting on a base seemingly formed by arches of ice uniting around the tree some 10 ft. from the ground, making a grotto through whose passages one could walk, the tree's trunk supporting the whole. This monument was surrounded by others, each one glittering in the bright sunshine and well worth a fifty-mile snowshoe trip to see.

Third Geyser Group: Hofer no doubt means to refer here to the Thud Geyser Group in Lower Geyser Basin, east of the Grand Loop Road near the Fountain Paint Pots area.

Approaching nearer and going around the group, I noticed a great change. Most of the limbs and twigs had no ice or snow on them on the side away from the geyser. Toward the geyser there was a thin ribbon of ice fastened by one edge to the twigs and small limbs, while on the body and large limbs the ice was in masses. These ribbons were two inches wide and less than a quarter inch thick. They were made up of bands of different shades of ice. Next [to] the limb was a clear, transparent strip a quarter inch wide, then came a band of white ice, then a thread which was perfectly clear, next a line beautifully shaded, like porcelain. The whole was like a ribbon of banded agate, the outer edge being a pure dead white. The last addition of frost to the ribbon was a little thicker than the rest and somewhat more wavy—sometimes almost like a fringe. These ribbons followed the line of everything that supported them. In a few places they were broken off; but on the whole, everything that could support their weight was thus ornamented.

Leaving here after spending an hour and only once attempting to make a sketch of this beautiful grove, I moved on to the great Paint Pots and other geysers. Here I saw nothing as interesting as the frost work. The coloring was not as brilliant as in summer.[17] The ice and snow came up to within a few inches of the pools and to where the water fell from the geysers. Wherever the hot water had cut channels through the fields of ice, the bottoms of the streams were colored, as is usual where the water is hot.

Returning to the Fountain I enjoyed, before I left, another look at the Monument Grove. While looking at it the Fountain went off, and I was soon surrounded by clouds of steam from the overflowing water. As a strong cold wind was blowing from the southwest, I left here to get away from the steam, following down one of the channels on a run with the hot water only a little way behind me. Getting to the flat I used my snowshoes again. In recrossing the meadow I saw many very thin places in the snow, and some spots where the ground was bare. Either the ground is warmer here from internal heat or the snow has blown off, as there were many wet places. It seems probable that the slight depth of snow here may be accounted for by the heat having melted most of it.

Rabbit, fox, coyote, wolverine and lynx tracks crossed and recrossed one another on the flat. They tell me here geese and swans have been seen in the Fire Hole River this winter, but I saw none.

Soon after my return to the hotel, Mr. Kelly came in from Norris with a man Sullivan, whom Mr. Dean had sent for to work around the place. Sullivan had started from the Mammoth Hot Springs with a very poor pair of snowshoes. Foolishly passing the tent we had propped up, he went on a little further, and when night overtook him, camped in the snow. Breaking off dead limbs he lit a fire by some dead trees and this he kept up all night. In the morning he was down in a hole in the snow, out of which he could not see. He had frosted his feet during the night while gathering firewood. The next day he made in to the Norris Hotel in an exhausted condition. He went to bed soon after arriving and Mr. Kelly let him sleep some sixteen hours. The third day, after having rested up, Sullivan started for the Lower Basin. Mr. Kelly accompanied him, intending to go only part way, but finding that S. was inclined to stop too often, Kelly concluded to come on to the Basin with him, fearing that if he was left alone he would not make it in or [would] freeze to death in the night. By alternately encouraging and threatening, Kelly induced him to keep on until he got him safe to the hotel. If left alone there is little doubt that Sullivan would have frozen to death that night, as it was very cold, −21°. Mr. Kelly, although a new hand snowshoeing, has been out frequently on the road, helping men in, and looking for the overdue. He was out after some of the Schwatka party when their own men would not go, was out looking for Con when he came to our camp, helped Sullivan through, and rescued for Mr. Jones a horse that had been left on the road exhausted.

On the 20th, a bright cold morning, the thermometer reading −21°, we started from [for] the Upper Basin [leaving the Lower Geyser Basin]. As the telephone wire was down we took a piece to repair it, expecting to find it broken where it passes over a hot spring where, when it is very cold, the wire gets heavily loaded with frost from the steam. The road was often crossed by small game tracks. We flushed two dusky grouse, saw several pine squirrels and a flying squirrel. These last I did not suppose, a year ago, were to be found in the Rocky Mountains, but they are very abundant about some parts of the Park. I have seen them only at nightfall. I think they are about but little in the daytime. Soon after crossing the Fire Hole River, I saw a very large lynx. I called Jack's attention to him and he thought it was a lion until he saw there was no long tail. A little further on we came to a place where the lynx had watched our approach.

Wishing to know more about us he had crossed the road and was passing to the windward of us when I saw him. He was grayish on his back, had reddish gray sides and light gray belly—a Canadian lynx and a very large animal of its kind. Its track measured 4 in. wide and 6 in. long. It did not stop long in sight, but soon disappeared in the timber. I gave a cat-like call, hoping to stop it, which I did, but it was behind some brush and out of sight. Here it stayed a moment and then trotted on.

While traveling through this section I was constantly on the watch for bison or their sign, as I have reason to believe there is a small band wintering within a circuit of two miles or so of this locality from signs seen in the early spring last year. I was disappointed in not seeing them. Had I had the time, I would have devoted a week to looking them up.

We soon came to the Midway Geyser Basin, a part of the Lower Basin, and sometimes called "Hell's Half Acre." Here are the Excelsior Geyser, Prismatic and Turquois Springs [Turquoise Pool], with several others of lesser note. The whole surface of the formation was covered with snow and ice, except in a few narrow channels made by the overflowing waters. Even some of them ended in fields of ice and snow, especially those from the Prismatic Spring, only one or two streams finding their way to other pools of hot water, the rest disappearing in the snow. Leaving our snowshoes we traveled from place to place in these channels, which we could easily do, as the water in them is very shallow. At the Turquois spring the snow and ice came so close to the hot water that I could not walk along the edge of the spring without stepping

in the hot water. The spring was as beautifully blue as in summer—even more so by contrast with surrounding banks of snow. We could walk around the Prismatic Springs without trouble, as the overflow is about the same everywhere, melting the snow off for from 10 to 50 ft. Here the coloring, as usual in winter through the Park, was dull.

Wading through banks of snow we came to the great Crater of the Excelsior, the largest and most powerful geyser in the Park and in the world when it was in action. It was boiling and bubbling all over, and most of the surface was hidden by dense clouds of hot vapor. The center was boiling more violently at times. Now and then one could catch a glimpse of a mass of water 25 ft. in diameter, thrown up from 5 to 6 ft., sending to the shore waves which constantly wear the banks away, undermining the sides until they cave in, only to be worn out again by the constant wave motion of the hot water. There is often a roar as the steam rushes up through the water, giving one the impression that there is going to be an eruption at once.

There has been a great amount of sensational stuff written about this geyser. One writer has it in eruption at the time of the Charleston earthquake, throwing out red hot rocks, flames, water, steam, sulphurous gases, smoke; in fact, a volcano. Others have seen every indication of "its having just gone off, it was so wet around there," forgetting that the waters of the Prismatic Spring flow all around it. No reputable witness claims to have seen it in action since the fall of '82, which was the only time I was fortunate enough to see it in all its glory. It did throw out pieces of geyser formation some 4 in. in diameter and 2 in. thick; they were the largest pieces I saw thrown out. I have heard people say that they have seen it "throw out rocks as big as that stove."[18]

As a proof that no eruption has taken place this winter, on all sides banks of ice and snow, from 1 ft. to 5 ft. deep, came down close to the edge of the crater. On the west and south sides there was no room to walk, and we had to keep back on the snowbanks. On the side toward the Prismatic Spring great icicles hung, from the formation almost to the surface of the water. On a piece of fallen formation, forming a little island near the shore, was a little snow. The porous nature of the formation makes this rock a very poor heat conductor, and I believe this to be the cause of so much ice and snow so near the great bodies of hot water. We visited the other pools, but saw nothing of special interest. Just before reaching the bridge where we recross the Fire Hole, we met the man in charge of the Upper Basin Hotel, Mr. Roake, and his son Willie, a 12-year-old boy, both out on snowshoes, the boy being able to do his ten miles in a day with anyone. They had just repaired the broken wire where the break was supposed to have been, and were looking for us, expecting to see us on the road. With this addition to our company we went on, noticing many ice-covered trees like those at the Fountain Geyser, wonderful and beautiful beyond words. Soon after Mr. Roake turned back with us, we came to a large lynx track which had struck his trail, followed it a little way, and then crossed the road back and forth, ten or fifteen times, traveling like the letter S. Just before getting to the Basin, another son of Mr. Roake came to us, Bert, a boy 14 years old, and a good snowshoer.

Mr. Roake and his family were living in the log-house in front of the hotel, which they had fixed up for the winter. We soon came in sight of a stove-pipe above a bank of snow which showed where the cabin was. We could just see the top of the house when we got on the same level with it. The snow through this section had settled considerably, as was shown by little mounds 2 ft. high around every tree, bush and stump; still, on a level, there was 7 ft. of snow. Soon an object came up out of the snow which proved to be another son of Mr. Roake, Harry, a little fellow seven years old, and soon a little girl four years old popped up out of the entrance to the cabin to tell us that the telephone was all right. We soon descended into the cabin, and were surrounded by these children, whose nearest neighbors were ten miles away—too far for a call except over the telephone, which they all use. Sending to Mr. and Mrs. Dean word of our arrival, we were soon sitting down to a good meal, and, as this was to be our last stopping place before striking out for the forests and streams, and lakes and rivers of the Shoshone and Yellowstone country, we made the most of it.

We built a fire in a tent which had been standing here ever since the old Y. P. I. Co. started.[19] This we made comfortable for our sleeping room.

Before dark we saw a fine display by the Beehive and Old Faithful geysers. The evening we spent with Mr. and Mrs. Roake's happy family. All the children know how to play chess, an unusual thing in the mountains. Even the four-year-old Topsy played two games. I left my king exposed to see if she would notice it, which she did, mating me at once.

The morning of the 21st, in company with Mr. R. and son, I visited the whole of the Upper Geyser Basin, going out past the Castle to Iron Creek [Iron Spring Creek], which was open, crossing it twice on a snow bridge without getting off our shoes. Along this stream down to the Specimen Lake and Black Sand Geyser [now called Black Sand Pool] there were many bare spots with bright green grasses, and several water plants growing in the warm water and earth, some even showing flower buds. The bright green mosses and plants looked doubly green beside the white snow. All along this creek was to be seen the usual number of ice forms. One in particular was very life-like. It looked like an Esquimau [Eskimo], dressed in white bear robes, with a bundle of sticks in his arms. He had a woe-begone expression on his face, as though in trouble because he had so little wood.

We passed across Specimen Lake on snowshoes and by the Black Sand Geyser, the Devil's Punch Bowl [Punch Bowl Spring] to the Splendid Geyser. This went off very soon after we had reached it, giving us one of the finest displays I have ever seen it make. I was under the impression that the geyser action would not be as attractive in winter as in summer, owing to the great amount of steam thrown off in cold weather, but I find that I was mistaken. The steam only adds to the general effect, the jets of hot water shooting up through the clouds leaving a trail of steam behind, turning in the air and descending like a comet with the tail of steam following them until lost in the rolling masses of vapor lower down. This geyser I believe

to have increased in action since last summer. Crossing the Fire Hole River on a snow bridge we saw all the great geysers. Near the Giantess was the usual display of ice-covered trees. This geyser has been in eruption all winter with intervals of nine to fourteen days. We returned by Old Faithful, which has been regular all winter in its hourly eruptions.

On the 22d, with Mr. Roake and his son Bert, I went out to the Lone Star Geyser. We traveled among the snow-laden pine timber, zigzagging up a long hill until we had reached the summit of the ridge. Keeping along this for a mile we then went down the open meadow on the Fire Hole, and turning to our left around a point of timber we came out to the geyser, which was not in action. We thus had an opportunity to examine the most beautiful cone in the whole Park. For 10 ft. around the cone there was no ice or snow, but to the east there was a great mound of ice, a dome-shaped pile 15 ft. high. While we were on top of this looking at the "pepper box" like top of the cone, the geyser suddenly began to play, sending showers of water on us. We soon got away from there. A strong wind was blowing from the west, quite cold, although a bright sun was shining from a clear sky. Going around to the north side we had a fine view of the geyser in eruption as it shot its hot waters 60 ft. above the cone. The clear waters and the white steam clouds showed finely against the bright blue of the sky for a background. Several little holes in the top of the cone were shooting little jets of hot water that, descending, left a trail of steam behind them as they fell over the sides of the cone and added very much to the beauty of the display. This lasted twenty minutes.

Off to our left on the side of the hill across the river, in a sheltered gulch, were some ice-laden trees over 60 ft. high, looking like huge giants standing guard over some steam vents in the hillside. The sun just touched the tops of the trees, giving the figures the appearance of wearing burnished silver helmets. As we were leaving this place, I noticed a sort of opening through a screen of icicles in the northeast side of the ice mound mentioned. Going to it we broke away some of the screen and saw a cave-like tunnel into which we walked some distance. It soon became dark and I lit a candle, with which we went on for 50 ft., though often obliged to stoop. The passage continued 25 ft. further to where we could see a pale, blue light, made by the sunshine on the ice where it was getting thin on top. After getting out of here we noticed that our hats and coats were covered with a white, pasty substance, rubbed off the roof of the cave. This I presume was silica, thrown out with the geyser water and deposited with the ice. As the ice gradually melted from beneath, the silica was left on the surface in a pasty form. I had noticed the same thing as sediment around all the active geysers on this trip, something I have not seen in summer.

We decided to return by following the Fire Hole down to the Basin. This we did, keeping to the river, first on one side then the other, crossing the open waters on snow-covered trees which had fallen across the stream. Over these bridges we walked on our snowshoes. We passed Kepler's Falls and Cascades, but the effect of these was spoiled by the depth of the snow which hid them from view. The cañon below was very pretty with its tall, dark firs laden with snow, the points of rock in the cañon covered with masses out of all proportion to their support hanging over the edges ready to drop with the slightest touch.

Before reaching the Basin we came to a small open stream on the east side of the Fire Hole. Here is the home of several beaver, and as we were crossing on a snow bridge one of them swam out to see what was going on overhead. We had but a glimpse of him. Along here in this stream and the Fire Hole some twenty beaver live in the banks, and as they increase very fast, the stream will soon be restocked. Now and then a tourist sees one.

As we passed the hotel on our return we went up to the second story verandah for a slide down the hill. Off the roof we went, getting headway enough to take us to the cabin door. Before the snow had settled around here the cabin was completely buried. One morning Mr. R. had to crawl up through a small hole dug from the inside of the house with a fire shovel, to get out, and then to work for a long time to clear the snow away from the only door the family could use. From the record Mr. Roake has, he makes the snowfall at the Upper Basin from Oct. 1 to date, Feb. 22, 15 ft. 10 in. From all the indications I think that is not far from correct, as there appears to be more snow here than at the other basins.

The last part of the day was devoted to preparing for our trip around the lakes. Mrs. Roake had baked for us a lot of oatmeal biscuits. With 8 lbs. of them for bread, 5 lbs. of fresh beef, 2 lbs. of bacon and 2 lbs. of boiled corned beef; a few cookies and the provisions we had with us, we made up our packs, which weighed about 25 lbs. each.

4.

On the morning of the 23d, with our packs on our backs and a lunch tied to our belts, we bade our kind friends good-bye. The sky was somewhat cloudy with indications of a storm in the southwest. We followed the trail made on our return yesterday to a little beyond Kepler's Falls; from there we turned off east and south. Soon after leaving the Fire Hole River it began to snow, hiding the sun, so that we had to travel by guess work, as all signs of a trail and most of the land marks were hid. Our route was through timber all the way to Heron Creek.[20] Keeping our course as near as possible, taking advantage of all the more open timber, I made out to see the gap in the rocky ridge through which the trail passes. Just before reaching the gap we came to Heron Creek waters, and crossed on to the Pacific slope. Climbing through the gap we soon came out on to a ridge, from which we got a glimpse of Shoshone Lake through the falling snow. From here we had a run down of over five hundred feet to Heron Creek and its open bottom which extends to the lake. Our run down hill was through timber, preventing one's going very fast, as there was danger of running into a tree. We soon came out on the open country and again we got a view of part of the lake. It was one field of white, hard to distinguish from the rest of the open country; we had been traveling very slowly.

It was now almost 4 o'clock, and going down toward the lake we soon turned aside, and selected a place for our camp, in a sheltered gulch with heavy timber all around us. Cutting some green logs about 4 ft. long we bedded them in the snow for a fireplace, and building a fire on this we melted snow in our cups, putting in the tea and the sugar as soon as the water was hot and adding snow until the cup was full. We returned the cup to the fire as often as we drank the tea, adding snow, tea or sugar as the tea got low, weak or wanted sweetening. We made a hearty meal.

After eating dinner we cut lodge poles, and tying four together about 10 ft. 8 in. from the butts we set these up over our fireplace; four other poles were placed around in the crotches formed by the first four, and throwing the lodge around the poles so as to bring the back of it to the wind, we tied it at the bottom of the wings; then taking two small poles 15 ft. long, the small end was placed in the pockets on the wings, the butts of the poles to the back of the lodge. Pushing up on these poles we soon had the lodge in place, and going inside we spaced the poles in a circle the size of the lodge, pushing the ends down a few inches in the snow so that they would stand firmly. Now with small wooden pins we pegged the cloth down by the loops around the bottom, pushing the pins well into the snow. Kicking a little snow over the edge we banked it up to keep out the wind. Now we spread enough spruce boughs in the back of the lodge for a good bed and cut enough dry wood to keep the fire up all night if we wished it. This was piled on each side of the entrance. Going inside we tied up the lodge and were as comfortable in our "tepee" as it was possible to be, camping out on 7 ft. of snow. We next spread the sleeping bag on the boughs, and taking off our damp or wet garments, leggings and overshoes, dried them on a line stretched over the fire. Replacing them when

THE LODGE.

thoroughly dry, we got into the sleeping bag and were soon asleep.

By 4 AM the green logs used for our fireplace had burned in two, letting our fire down into a hole in the snow. I was first up, and, repairing the fireplace, I soon had a fire going. This filled the lodge with smoke, but going outside I corrected the draft by swinging the wings around, as the wind had changed in the night. A fine snow was falling, with a gale blowing outside from the southwest.

After breakfast we packed up what we could inside the lodge, then dried that over the fire, making up our packs on the bough bed. By 6 AM we were off, traveling down Heron Creek [actually, DeLacy Creek here] with the wind in our faces until we came out on Shoshone Lake. Over this we went, for it was frozen over everywhere; not a drop of open water did we see on it. The snow on the ice was from one to two feet deep. After reaching the lake we traveled southeast. This brought the storm to our right, making it less uncomfortable to travel against. We had started in the dark. It was daylight before we got to the lake, but nothing of the surrounding country could be seen, only the shore and hills on our left. Every little while I would try the snow with my pole, striking dry, solid ice every time. Once I cleaned off a place with the intention of cutting a hole to measure the thickness of the ice, but from the appearance of the ice I saw this would be a long job, and besides the wind filled the hole fast with drifting snow, so I gave it up. I think the ice was about three feet thick. Had it been less, with the strong wind blowing, I think there would have been some movement of the ice, but not the least was noticed. Keeping well out on the lake we followed the shore about four miles to the point where we were to leave the lake. Not a sign of game was to be seen, nothing but white rabbits and now and then a squirrel track. The snow was drifted into the timber along shore in immense piles, fifteen and twenty feet deep.

Leaving the lake we went into a grove of timber, made a fire and lunched. The snow here was very deep. I could not reach bottom with my 7-foot pole. The absence of all game, the impossibility of seeing anything—for the falling snow shut out the mountains—made this a very desolate country. Shouldering our packs we struck out in an easterly direction, until we found a water course which I wished to follow up to the summit of the divide. At length we reached the top—a high country, somewhat level with groves and openings. Here for the first time I had to use the compass, the wind and snow came from so many ways at once.

I could have gone through without the compass, but believed it was best to be sure of our course, for I wished to strike the head of Sand Creek, which empties its waters into the west arm of the lake a mile above and south of the "Lake Shore Geyser," and a place known as "Warm Spring Camp."[21]

We traveled on for a while, and now and then I saw a grove that looked familiar, though I had been through here but once, in 1884. The storm increased every hour, and by 2 o'clock Jack wished to camp. I wanted to get to the Yellowstone Lake before dark, but I saw it was impossible, as we were not making over a mile and a quarter in an hour. Selecting a well-sheltered place in a grove, a short distance over on the Atlantic slope, we soon had the lodge up. This time we made a better fireplace, and cutting boughs we were soon comfortable in our "tepee," although it was snowing and blowing furiously outside all the time. This night we concluded to keep up the fire, and take turns sleeping two hours each. This we did, though I think I slept most when it was my turn to keep up the fire, which was not neglected at all.

We were up by 5:30. The lodge was covered with snow and ice, and would weigh 20 lbs. unless I could get it dry. How to do this with the snow falling fast I could not tell, but after breakfast the storm ended, and we soon had everything in shape and were on the road again. Getting out of the timber we found the sky clearing and saw Mt. Sheridan close at hand. It looked but a mile or two off, the air was so clear. We could not see any other mountain peaks from here. Keeping our course I soon saw familiar ground, and descending a sharp pitch we were on the head of Sand Creek. This we followed to the Yellowstone Lake. On our way we saw a very few rabbit trails, and one or two lynx sign. As we came out to the lake we found it frozen over and covered with snow. Again we saw Mt. Sheridan, and the mountains on the south and east side of the lake, all under snow, their white peaks far above the dark green forest, and all white except where the wind had swept the snow off their rocky ridges.

Following the shore of the lake for a mile we came to Warm Spring Camp and the Lake Shore Geysers [at West Thumb Geyser Basin]. Along here there was a little open water, but in no place did it extend over 50 ft. from the shore, and that only in one place, where a hot spring comes up out of the bed of the lake. At this place we lunched, mixing some of our condensed soup or extract of meat with the hot geyser water, we had hot soup or beef tea to order, and that without a fire. Here the water in the lake was at least a foot lower than I had ever seen it before.

After resting we traveled along the lake shore past the Paint Pots and many interesting springs and geysers. At one place where the steam from a great white pool drifted to a grove of trees, we saw two women standing on a white mound, one looking into the pool, the other out on the lake, their backs to each other. From their position and attitude they had been quarreling, for they had gathered their dresses away from each other. They were very life-like even when we passed close by. Bidding them good day we traveled on land until we had passed the Hot Springs. I did not like to trust myself out on the lake along here. I tried twice as we went along shore; would find a little ice under the snow, then again the pole would go through into the water.

As soon as I found enough ice to support us we struck out for **Bluff Point**. The wind had been increasing all the morning, and was now blowing a gale from the west-southwest. As this was offshore, we did not feel it until well out on the lake. Clouds of snow were flying in the air and along the surface of the ice. We could see only a short distance ahead in a horizontal line, but looking up we could see the bluffs and timber for some distance. We had as yet seen no game on the lake shore, except a few ducks in the warm water. After passing Bluff Point we saw what we at first took to be animals. They were 250 yds. from the shore, and the flying clouds of snow would make them come and go, appear and disappear as though they were running around. We soon found they were stumps of upturned trees on a little rocky island [Carrington Island]. Owing to the storm and the flying poudre [powdery snow], everything we saw changed thus. We would see a point ahead, then it would be entirely hid for a long time, then would suddenly show up again, now near, and then would move off until out of sight again.

From Bluff Point we struck across the bay for some heavy timber on a point about due east. This brought the wind more behind us, and proved an assistance. Some blasts were strong enough to move us ahead a little, so that at every step we could gain a little extra distance by the aid of the wind. Every few rods I sounded the depth of snow, which was from 8 in. to 2 ft. When far out from shore I once ran the pole into 6 in. of water under 8 in. of dry snow. Going on further I struck more

water. I had not felt the ice under the water and did not like to stop until I was off this kind of ground, so next time I tried the snow I used considerable force and pushed the small end of the pole through a foot of dry snow and a foot of water and snow down to solid ice. This was all I cared for. I did not mind the water on the ice as long as there was dry snow enough to keep my shoes out of it. Jack was some distance behind me and had been watching my movements, and was naturally somewhat interested. He would try every hole I did with like results, and he said his hair stood up when I did not strike ice through the water. Soon the ice was again dry under the snow, then it became again wet. When we wanted a drink of water all we had to do was to feel down until we found it on the ice, then clear a place away and dip it up. I think the ice was broken into great cakes, the weight of snow sinking the cakes in places enough to have the water come on top. Before reaching shore I thought I noticed a motion to the ice under me rising and falling, but concluded it was the waves of snow where it was deep or shallow on the ice.

We made across the bay and to the timber by 4 o'clock and selecting a camp, we were soon busy getting things in shape for the night. At this camp we broke a great piece out of our axe, taking over an inch out of the blade, besides several smaller pieces. This was owing to the frost in the axe and frozen timber. The accident made it difficult to get our camp in shape for the night, but a little after

Bluff Point: The historic name for a point of land that intrudes a little into West Thumb Bay about two miles due north across from West Thumb Geyser Basin.

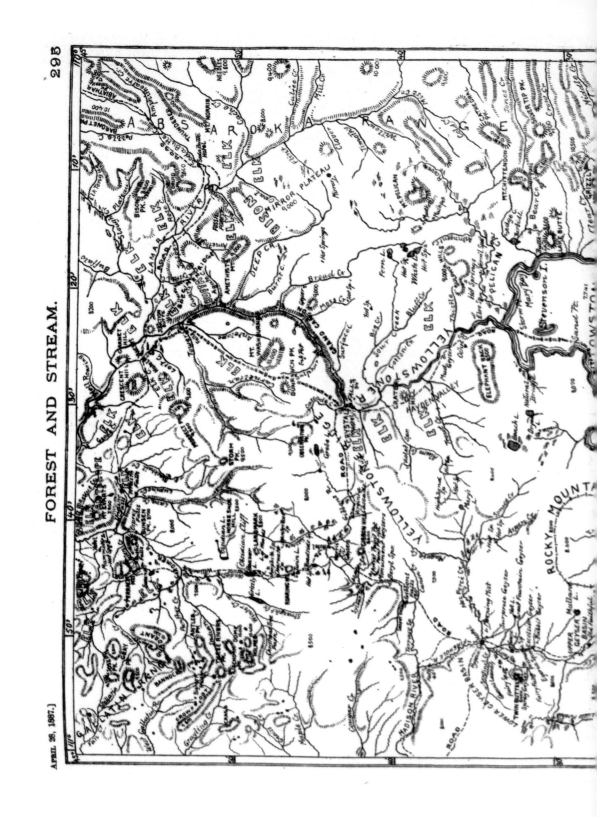

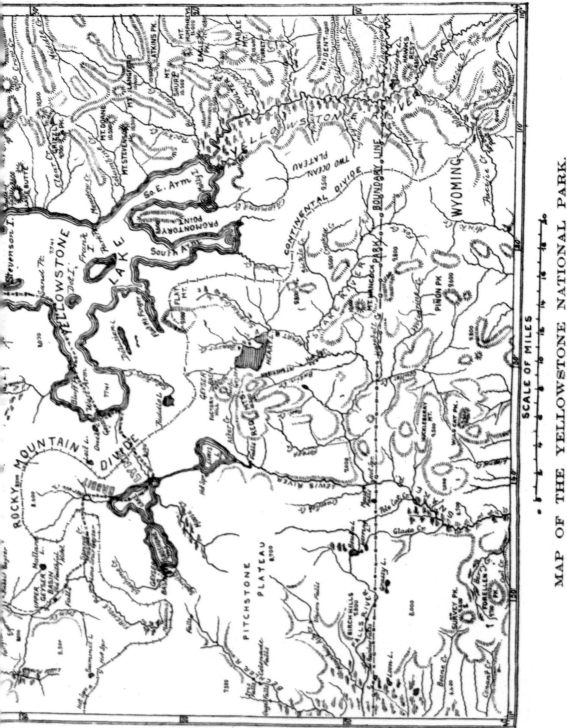

MAP OF THE YELLOWSTONE NATIONAL PARK.

SCALE OF MILES

dark we had everything snug, and passed a comfortable night. We both went to sleep in the bag, letting the fire take care of itself.

Next morning, Feb. 26, we started soon after daylight. A gale was still blowing, but more from the southwest. We made directly for the lake, as that was the best traveling. Along the shore for over a mile, there were long, narrow, open places made by hot springs, and all along this open water we saw wild ducks. We soon rounded this point, which I called Hot Spring Point, and then turned north-northeast until we came to Rock Point [just south of Sand Point], where were a great many mounds of ice above the surface of the lake. There I took to the rocks, over which the water dashed and froze before the lake itself froze up.

In all the open water I had been watching for fish, intending to catch some, if possible, to see if they were wormy in the winter as in summer, but I did not see one fish.[22] In summer I have seen thousands of fish around the hot springs on the shore of the lake, yet this trip saw none. I do not know where they are, unless out in the deep water.

We soon came to Sand Point, and here the wind quieted down a little, so that we could see Stevenson Island and the Elephant's Back. Our course was to leave the first to our right and the latter a little to our left. Had the weather been clear we could have seen Mt. Washburne, almost due north. On the east we could now just see the tops of the high peaks across the lake, and the Hot Springs on Sulphur Hill to the northeast. Soon after leaving this point we were out on the lake again, and exposed once more to the gale. As we had changed our course, we had the wind more to our left, receiving

help from it, as we had after leaving Hot Spring Point on to Sand Point. We soon found that Stevenson Island was all we could see, and often that would be hidden by the flying snow.

Pushing on, we passed it, going over a long, narrow point on the north end, then turning for the outlet of the lake. Soon we were out in the main part of the lake once more. Again I felt the raising and falling I noticed on the west arm; the further out we went the more I noticed it. I stopped and waited until Jack came up, and asked him if he noticed the motion. He said he did, but at first thought it was something wrong with himself. Before getting to the outlet I found the undulations increased still more. I expected to hear some noise as the ice rose and fell, but the wind drowned it if there was any. By 2 o'clock we were at the old cabin at the outlet. This was filled with snow and almost out of sight under high drifts. Crossing the little creek back of the cabin, where there was a little open water, we followed the wagon road. On a hill to our left was the grave of a man struck by lightning while out on the lake in a boat. He was connected with the Geological Survey.[23] The wind had drifted the snow away from the grave, leaving it in plain sight. We followed the road for a while longer, then turned aside and camped in some sheltered timber, about two miles below the outlet.

We broke camp next morning at 6:45 AM. Traveling slowly, I soon noticed more life. Besides ducks we began to see more birds, and I heard one little fellow singing as though it were spring. At the Mud Geysers we lunched; there was little here more interesting than summer. As I expected to find game ahead I hurried on to a high point overlooking the Alum Creek country, or Hayden Valley. Far off I saw a few objects that I thought were buffalo, but they were so distant that I was not sure. Before reaching Trout Creek I saw a small band of elk on the east side of the Yellowstone River—14 cows and calves.

At Trout Creek I saw a fresh trail of a large animal and, following this up, I first noticed coyote tracks both sides, and a lynx track. Soon I saw the latter going over a hill ahead, and 200 yds. further on the trail, I saw a large six-point bull elk. He was less than 100 yds. off; he was lying down and did not notice us for a moment or two. Not wishing to disturb him I turned off and crossed the creek. When he first saw us he did not get up at once, for he was evidently very much surprised to see such looking things out there, our packs and snowshoes making it very difficult for him to make us out. At last he got up, satisfied we were his old enemies, men. He was quite poor, and when going through the snow-drifts would sink in very deep, struggling through and stopping to rest every little way. The ridges and sidehills to the west were blown free from snow, giving game a chance to get plenty of feed. The elk soon disappeared over a hill. I saw 8 ravens in one flock. As they are never far from game I was sure there was more in the country.

As I came in sight of the Crater Hills I surprised two coyotes in a little draw. I got within 50 yds. of them before they saw me; they were a dog and bitch. They ran off behind a hill, but came up on top to have another look at me. I had left Jack some distance behind me, and seeing him they sneaked off. Crater Hill was as interesting as usual,

almost free from snow, its yellow sulphur vents very bright, filled with perfect crystals of pure sulphur all fresh and undisturbed by the "specimen fiend." As I was now getting into a game country I did not care to linger where there was no frost work noticeable.

Alum Creek we crossed on the ice. Some distance ahead I noticed the snow looked rough, as though horses had been pawing it over, and going to the place saw that a large band of elk had been feeding here. From the trail made there must have been over 60 in the band. The sign was from ten days to two weeks old. These elk had gone up Alum Creek to the high ridges there, where there is more feed. I regretted that I could not follow them and learn how many there was in this section of the country. Following the river down we entered the timber below Alum Creek; here was more **lynx** sign; they had run all over the country. I could see where they evidently had their quarters, as, from under overturned trees and other places, on the steep sidehills their trails lead, the snow all patted down around them. These lynxes are large enough to kill a young elk, which I am quite sure they do, as there is a great number of them. Trails could be seen where they hunt in pairs.

Soon we came to the hotel [at Canyon]. Only the top of it could be seen through the snow, it being piled higher than the eaves. Sliding down a steep incline tunneled through the snow to reach the door, we went on through the long dark hall to

Lynx still live in Yellowstone, but even their tracks and dens are very rarely seen. Listed as a threatened species.

the north end, where we had seen smoke coming from a stovepipe in a wing. Here we found Major Lyman, who was in charge of the place. Soon Mr. Al Thorne came in. He has been here since the "Schwatka explorers" came over, coming through with them from Norris; had come from the Mammoth Hot Springs to that place with a team.

An hour and a half after we arrived, Pete Nelson, the mail carrier, came in from Norris. As the telephone was in working order, word was sent to Kelley that we had arrived. Some fears had been entertained that we were lost, as there had been several very stormy days since we had left.

5.

In the evening I made inquiries about the whereabouts of the game around there. I was told of some being on the ridges near by, and then of the rescue of eight elk out of the cañon.

On the morning of Feb. 18, the Major and Mr. Thorne, while on a sight-seeing expedition, found eight cows and two heifers in the cañon between the two falls [the Grand Canyon of the Yellowstone, between Upper and Lower Falls]. There were no calves with the band. The Major thinks the lions killed them. If the lions did not there are lynxes around enough to do it. The river here is all frozen over and the snow at least 9 ft. deep in the cañon. From all indications they had been in here a long time, probably over two weeks. They had traveled around all over the river and up on the sides of the cañon in their efforts to escape, but the deep snow on the steep hillside was more than they could get through.

There being no food for them in the cañon

they had eaten the small limbs and boughs of the spruce and balsam fir trees as high up as they could reach, even eating the wood of limbs over half an inch through. The bark off dry trees and large limbs of a "quaking asp" (aspen) tree was almost devoured. Limbs over an inch in diameter were chewed off close to the body of the tree and the bark off that. The Major and Mr. Thorne hunted for the trail by which they entered the cañon; not finding this or any sign of it they decided to tramp a trail for them. The men returned to the hotel leaving their snowshoes: they tramped a trail from the little foot bridge crossing the gulch just above the hotel, down past that, through the gorge, between walls of rock, following the gulch on to Cascade Creek and out to the river. The Major was accompanied by his two dogs, Sue and Shep, who kept close to heel.

Keeping to one side they went below the elk and started them up. Two—a cow and heifer—broke past them. The cow, a very large one, went to the south side of the falls, ran up a very steep ridge forming the brink of a precipice overhanging the falls, got up to where the ice was almost perpendicular, paused a moment, looking back, when her feet slipped on the hard ice, she fell over backward, slid down on the comb of the ridge, then over the falls, and down, over 300 ft., disappearing through a cloud of mist into a round hole between an ice bridge and the falls. Thorne ran to the edge and looked over. Nothing of her was to be seen. When the two elk went below, the men stopped, expecting them to return and join the band. After the death of the cow, they started to drive the heifer back. She ran to the platform on the south side, from which tourists view the falls and cañon. When the men attempted to go near her, she would stamp and back up, until she was outside the railing and standing on ice that overhung the chasm below. Thorne went to the brink of the falls and threw boughs up at her, in hopes of driving her to the others. The Major was afraid to let the dogs go, fearing that both dogs and elk might fall over into the abyss. Finding they could not make the animal move, they left it. After much hard work running around on the elk trails, they got the eight elk started up Cascade Creek, but they missed the trail made for their escape up the gulch and went on up to Crystal Falls. While the Major with the two dogs stopped below, Thorne went up to and among them as he would domestic cows. At one time some of them broke past, almost stepping on him. All started down but one; she was wedged in between the snow and rocks. Thorne tramped a trail and by pushing and twisting her got her out of this place into another where, by helping her, he thought he could get her out. Having about 6 ft. of ⅜ in. rope with him, which he used to carry his web snowshoes, he tied this around her neck and started to lead her out, but she would not come. When he pulled on the rope she would brace herself and pull back. He said: "When I would go to leave her she would bawl for me. I went back several times, but every time I tried to lead her she'd pull back, not knowing what I wanted of her, yet would make that same noise, calling for me, when I left her." Finding he could not get her out of her trouble he left her with the intention of taking some hay to her in the morning, as there was part of a bale at the hotel.

The seven elk Thorne had turned back had gone on down the creek to the gulch, and had then there turned up the trail tramped for them, passing within 8 ft. of Major Lyman and the two dogs. The Major says they were very poor and weak. As they passed they paid no attention to him or the dogs, as by this time they had learned that they were not going to be hurt. The elk followed the trail, crossed the bridge and passed within 10 ft. of the hotel, going on out in the open country. The men were worn out with their day's work tramping around in the snow.

In the morning they started down to get the others out. They found the one with the rope on had gone out in the night following the others, or one could say, following Mr. Thorne out, as he was last over the trail. The heifer was still in the cañon. Every time they attempted to get between her and the Lower Fall or go near her, she would run to the platform and stay there. Knowing that she would soon starve if left in the cañon, they determined to make an effort to drive her away from the platform and out to the other elk. Thorne would go out on the ice where it projects over the falls and throw things at her, but she would not start away from there. He then climbed above, trying to get at her from that side, but could not. Out on the platform the elk showed fight, stamping and grinding her teeth. She had backed so far toward the edge that she had to stamp her hind feet to get a foothold on the ice. At last, as she stood there, her feet slipped and over the precipice she went. Whirling over and over for 300 ft. distance, she struck on one end of the bridge of ice, near the hole where the other fell. The poor thing must have been killed instantly. It is possible that this elk would have found her way out, but this is not probable, as snow was falling most every day. There was not enough hay at the hotel to keep her alive more than a little while. Better sudden death than starvation.

On the 28th [of February], a bright clear day, in company with Major Lyman and Mr. Thorne, we visited the two falls. Leaving the hotel we descended directly into the gulch up which the rescued elk came ten days before. We could see their trail although partially hidden by new snow. We followed this gulch down between walls of rock and overhanging snowdrifts to Cascade Creek, then on out to the river. This was frozen and covered with snow. Deciding to see the Lower Falls first we turned down stream. We soon saw signs of the elk where they had been eating off the limbs of trees. I broke off several of these, which I send to show the point of starvation which the elk had reached. We saw the trails on the side of the cañon where they had tried to force their way up through the snow, the hoof-marks on the rough ice where the cow went over, and the tracks of the heifer where she was when she plunged to instant death, and I even saw some of the boughs and sticks Thorne had thrown at her lodged on the ice.

The ice on the river projected 15 ft. out over the falls, curving down on the outer edge until out of sight. Going near the brink the most beautiful frost work in the whole park was to be seen. Words could never describe this grand sight. On the south side the whole precipice from the river up and away around for hundreds of feet was one mass of ice and frost work. Up for about 200 ft. from the river, the ice was in the form of gigantic

icicles from 1 ft. to 200 ft. long. Above this the ice was more like a great bed of flowers, on edge masses of flowers, clusters, bunches and bouquets, projecting out from the rest; globular-shaped pendant clusters of ice, the surface covered with pearly frost work like frozen dew drops, or the iridescent formation of the geysers, for 100 and 200 ft. more. All this was not without color. The flowers were delicately shaded from a dark straw color to white, the icicles a faint blue, green and yellow. The whole of the cliff was overhung with a fringe of icicles from the top almost pure white. The top of the cliff and timber back of it was coated with fine ice that glittered as the sun shone on it from over the edge of the cañon above. Two dead trees, whose ice-coated tops were in the sunshine, looked like electric lights, they were so bright. The sun striking the other side of the highly colored cañon cast a golden glow over the whole scene impossible to describe.

Going to the platform and venturing out as far as one dared, I looked down to see the ice bridge formed across the river. This reached up at least one-third of the height of the falls, and was crescent-shaped, leaving an immense hole, into which the water poured; below this bridge the river was open. The water was a deep green color, although less in volume than in October, when I was last here.

Recrossing the river we ventured out as far as it was safe, to see the precipice on the north side, but could not unless we risked our lives on the comb of the ridge, over which the first elk fell.

Going to the Upper Falls we found great ice mounds and domes at its base reaching more than half way up its face. We climbed all over the bridges and mounds. From the top of one we saw that the main volume of water ran over the left edge as we looked at it in a solid stream. The rest of the falls were now but a cascade as far down as the level of the mound; the river below these falls is very wide, forming a circular basin; half of this was filled with the mounds, their bases reaching halfway across. From both Maj. Lyman and Mr. Thorne I learned that one mound of ice, at least 45 ft. high, had formed in the last ten days.

At these falls were more ice flowers, some a dark yellow, some clinging to the rock over which the cascade ran. Some of the ice was a light straw color, shaded down to white. Part of the falls were covered with a lattice work of ice, through which the water and ice under it could be seen. Above dark rocks, covered with caps of snow, the edges of the cañon, fringed with timber, made a grand and imposing sight. We spent the day here in this cañon, going home when the sun was getting low. We climbed back up the gulch and turned aside to see some of the snow-covered buildings. In returning to the entrance I made a cut off by going over one end of the hotel to the front porch on my snowshoes.

The next day, March 1, we started for the sawmill, some two miles distant, in company with the Major, and his dogs harnessed to a sled. Two hundred yards from the hotel we came to the fresh trail of two elk going toward Cascade Creek. This I followed a short distance in order to learn how old it was. The elk had passed not over two hours before we started out. Expecting to get a shot at a mountain lion at the mill, or have a crack at a lynx, we took a .40-90 Sharps[24] along and a small revolver. We had learned of five mountain lions said to have taken possession of the sawmill, barn, tent and other buildings out there. If the sign was favorable we intended to stay all night at the mill to get a shot at the lions. We soon got there and were disgusted, for we found nothing but a few lynx tracks. Not a lion or a sign of one could be seen. The barn was crushed in. A tent just showed from under the snow. The mill was standing, but the timbers with which it was strengthened were bent and twisted and some broken. A few more inches of snow, and this too would go down. The mill is situated on a spring creek, in the northwest corner of a large meadow.

We saw several old elk trails and places where they had been feeding. Coyote, fox, martin, rabbit and lynx tracks, ran in every direction. There were many small birds. An osprey was noticed, and a few woodpeckers were seen hammering away for their dinner. A gull and a few ravens flying over the cañon made up the most bird life I noticed. We were going toward Lookout Point and the Grand Cañon. Before we got there I saw several piles of lumber, and asking the Major about it, he said "it was the **new hotel site.**" This is not the one selected back of Lookout Point, but one much nearer the cañon and considerably less than a quarter of a mile from it.

At Lookout Point we had a view of the Lower Falls, with its icy surroundings. Noticing a dark

new hotel site: The hotel where Hofer stayed at Canyon, built in 1886, was intended to be temporary, but the more permanent one, for which Hofer saw piled up lumber, was not completed until 1890.

object on the end of the ice bridge, directly beneath the platform from which the elk fell, I called the others' attention to it. We concluded it was the body of the heifer. The long distance we were from the falls spoiled the effect of the frost work. Every point, tower, pinnacle, buttress, tree and projection in the cañon was crowned with snow. As the different additions were made to the cap it would settle out over the edges until now the cap of snow was more of a hood, covering the points and hanging down on the sides half their depth. This hid the darker portions of the rock in the cañon, giving it a much lighter appearance. The steam jets in the bottom and on the sides were sending up little columns of steam, like smoke from chimneys, looking as if people were living below. The cañon was not as attractive as in summer. Now there is too much white. In returning we crossed Cascade Creek where the **Howard** wagon train did in 1877 on its way over Mt. Washburne. Here the fresh trail of the morning came down and passed up the creek. We had gone entirely around the elk.

On the 2d and 3d [of March] it snowed some; these two days we devoted to resting and looking at the cañon.

On the 4th it was snowing, but cleared a little by 8 o'clock. At 8:30, with two days' provisions, we started for our trip over Mt. Washburne. Soon after crossing Cascade Creek we crossed the trail of the two elk whose trail we had seen on

Gen. O. O. Howard pursued the Nez Perce tribe across the park in a long and often chronicled endeavor, ending when Chief Joseph and his people surrendered near the Canadian border.

the 1st. In due time we were climbing a spur of Dunraven Peak; from here, on a clear day one can see the Grand Tetons. Now the clouds hid them. Mts. Hancock and Sheridan were in sight. All the mountains on the east of Yellowstone Lake were in view. Leaving this ridge and keeping up, we soon came to the pass which takes us on to the waters of Carnelian Creek. Looking back we could see some of the country and timber in which Mr. Haynes and his party had wandered while lost. From the top of the pass we had a grand run down hill for some 500 ft. following the water course; then turning aside to the right we commenced to climb the ridge which the trail follows up to the top of Washburne. Soon we crossed an elk trail made going down hill through snow 8 ft. deep. Further on were the trails and beds of a large band of elk. Above on the ridge I saw the elk, twenty-three of them. Getting out of the timber, we found the western slopes of the hillsides almost bare, with good and sufficient grass on them to have wintered a large band of horses. Above was a band of eleven elk, six cows, two yearlings and three spikes (two year old bulls). I could not tell if this was a new band or part of the first twenty-three seen. I could see elk further up on the ridge. All had "winded us" and were moving. The eleven tried to come down and pass us on the ridge, but when within 200 yds. of us they turned back.

When I reached the summit of this ridge, I was a long distance ahead of Jack, and taking off my pack I walked out on to an immense snow drift on the east side that followed the ridge for miles. Here I sat down to rest and look for game. I could see Specimen Ridge, but not plainly, for a strong wind blowing filled the air with fine snowclouds. On all the bare ridges on this side of Washburne I could see elk scattered in bands, three, four and ten in a place. I could not see game across the river. While waiting for Jack I heard a "whining sound" to my left, and looking up, a spike bull was passing within 50 ft. I could see shreds of old velvet still sticking to his horns; he was poor and drawn up. He passed out of sight over the edge of the drift. Snowclouds hid all the mountain tops, one resting on the summit above. My intention had been to go there for a view of the country and to look for game, but the clouds rendered such a trip useless.

Running down the mountain from here, we entered a grove to camp, flushing as we did so several dark grouse. Some call them blue, others dusky grouse. We selected a camp in this grove and passed a very comfortable night. By daylight we were on the march. As we left the grove I heard the song of a small bird, a wren. As the sun rose over the mountains to the east I came in sight of game. I saw thirty dark objects across the Yellowstone about one-third the distance from Tower Creek to opposite Washburne. These I took to be bison. As we were traveling toward them for some distance I constantly watched them for some movement. I could see elk on the other side opposite the mouth of Tower Creek. Soon we crossed a sag and on to the high ground looking into Antelope Creek. All around us the snow was pawed by elk. My dark objects had turned to "sure enough" bison, yet were too far off to tell anything about them. A mile north of where the bison were was a band of fifty-four elk. Going on I saw other bands, fifteen in one, twelve in another, seven and twenty in others.

Running on down hill, the longest runs we had on the whole trip, brought us to the hill overlooking Tower Creek. On the other side of that was a band of twelve elk and one old bull off to one side. The bulls had just commenced to drop their horns. I saw one fresh one on the ridge as we came down. Here too the snow was pawed over by the elk with trails leading through the deep drifts from one feeding place to another. The snow down here was about 5 ft. deep. Following a ridge I went on alone to a butte directly over Tower Falls. Across the cañon and close to the edge, was a band of thirteen elk. There were four spikes in this bunch. Across Antelope Creek, between it and the Yellowstone, in the edge of the timber, were more elk, over twenty in the band.

I followed down the ridge to where I had a view of the falls [Tower Fall]. These are the prettiest in the Park. Now they are almost hidden by ice up to within 25 ft. of the top; masses of icicles are on each side and the brink covered by a hood of ice under a bed of snow. In the space behind the falling water could be seen icicles like stalagmites reaching up to within 10 ft. of the top. The snow had fallen off most of the towers around the falls, filling the cañon below for 25 ft. Returning to my shoes I crossed the creek above. Here there were open places. The volume of water is the same in this creek now as in August.

Shouldering our shoes we climbed the steep hill, following an elk trail to the open bench on top. From this we could see elk in every direction. I soon gave up trying to count them. I could make out distant bands on the East Fork of the Yellowstone (Lamar River) bottoms and mountain sides.

We crossed elk trails all the way to Elk Creek. Here we saw the first willows on our trip. The others were under snow. We soon came out to the Cooke City road, and half a mile further on we came to Yancy's Station.

We were kindly received. Mr. Yancy was looking for us, having learned we were coming out that way.

Here we learned people were discussing our trip, some going so far as to say they never expected to see us again. We spent the evening talking of the game in the Park, and inspected Mr. Yancy's new Winchester, a single shot, .40-caliber. This he thinks one of the best rifles he ever owned; is delighted with its fine shooting. Mr. Y. is an old hunter, and one of the best fishermen in the country. As the first mentioned sport is prohibited in the Park, he devotes some of his time to target shooting. Not far from his station is some of the best fishing in the Park.

By 8 o'clock in the morning we left Mr. Yancy's for the long 1,800-foot climb up Elk Creek to the high, open country above [Blacktail Deer Plateau]. In a quarter of an hour after leaving "Pleasant Valley" we saw elk. Nine were feeding on an open spot not half a mile from Mr. Yancy's hotel. From this time on until I started down the cañon of Lava Creek (east fork of Gardiner River), I was not out of sight of elk at any time. We climbed the hill, easily following the sleigh road until we came to a deep cut into which the snow drifts and slides, making it impassable for teams in winter, but used for a wagon road in summer. The sleigh track turned to the left, over a higher hill to avoid this cut. Going through and out of the cut we came on to Geode Creek. Elk were to be seen in every direction; cows, calves and spikes. The calves could now more properly be called yearlings. Now and then there would be a bull or two off to one side. The proportion of cows, etc., was six cows and heifers, three calves and one spike to every ten head. The bulls older than two years are never with the band, except in the running [rutting] season. Some of the older bulls have dropped their horns, commencing about the last day of February.

Before we came to Blacktail Deer Creek, Jack turned to the right, taking a trail to Gardiner, back of Mt. Evarts. I crossed Blacktail, seeing sign of game and elk on all the bare hills. The gulches were filled deep with snow. Soon I came to the head of the cañon of Lava Creek. Here are two very pretty falls, but buried under snow and ice. In the distance I could see the Mammoth Hot Spring terraces with high mountains for a background, with Electric Peak white and high above all the rest. To the left the Madison Range with its dozen fine peaks. To the right part of the Yellowstone Range [the Beartooth Mountains], most of it hid by Mt. Evarts. On this was a band of some thirty elk and a bunch of ten mountain sheep.

Running down the long grade to Gardiner River, I went up it for two miles to the springs, and from there, next day, to Gardiner. Going down I did not see the six tame sheep observed when we started out. Jack was in town, having come in the day I reached the springs. We had made the round trip through the Park, as we intended to do when we started out, 160 miles on snowshoes. Counting in addition to this the side trips made, I traveled 225 miles [in 23 days]. We camped out six nights, suffered no hardships or privation, and withal had a most enjoyable time. To be sure, we made no wonderful discoveries, for there are none to be made; the Park is too well known for that. My purpose in going through the Park was to see its winter features and to learn something about the game there. This I have done.

I can only give estimates in regard to the game. When it was possible I counted them, but still, one never sees all there are. To count all would require "a round up."

On the ridges around the Washburne there are at least 150 elk; about the falls, 50; on Specimen Ridge and the section of the Park to the north, at least 2,000; on Black Tail, Lava, Elk and Lost creeks, and country north of Tower Creek, some 1,600; in the country between Mammoth Hot Springs and the Madison Mountains [Gallatin Range], some 500. I know nothing of the number on the west side of these mountains. On Alum Creek and the country across the river there are elk, but how many I do not know. Perhaps 200 would be a large estimate, though some people put it as high as 800. In the south end of the Park I do not think the elk winter, but come in very early in the spring. Not counting these, this would give us 4,500 elk in the Park this winter. A few of the best hunters, men who do not get excited when they see a hundred elk and say there are a thousand, think there are from 7,000 to 8,000 elk in all; but I cannot think so, judging from the number I have counted in the country spoken of. One thing noticeable is the very small number of bulls older than two years old seen. On our trip not over fifteen were found. In one place where there were over a hundred cows and calves, there were but five bulls, and this, too, in a country where I could see almost all the game. We may be sure that the bulls we saw are not all there are by a long way. Some of the reasons for this disproportion of bulls to cows are these: The bulls are killed in summer because they are the best meat up to the running season. After that they are killed for their heads and horns for specimens. Then, too, a bull is easier to be found and approached than a cow, especially in the fall, for one sometimes goes up to a band of horses or a man on horseback just to see what they are, unless he has the wind of them.

Of bison I saw but thirty. I believe, however, that there are between 200 and 300 in the Park. Some people think there are not even fifty, as the high price paid for them, $50 to $75 for fine heads and hides, has induced hunters to kill them off and to take great risks of detection for the money offered.

Mountain sheep, antelope, blacktail deer and whitetail, as a rule, do not winter in the Park. There are a few sheep, some 200 antelope, but no blacktail or whitetail worth mentioning. Still, a great many have their young there and pass the summer, only going out as the snow comes. I have seen hundreds of sheep and blacktail on their way out in the fall, and returning in the spring. Last fall I knew hunters on the Gallatin River who saw, as they express it, "more blacktails coming out of the mountains in the Park this fall than I ever did before for years." Some say they think not less than 1,500 came out on the north side and west of the Yellowstone River.

Tourists through the Park, as a rule, keep to

the beaten roads, only going to the hotels, and never seeing any of the wild animals they hear so much about. Traveling as they do, nothing else can be expected. For their benefit some propose to pen up the elk in pastures for them to see as they ride along.

To see the game in this country, one must either leave the roads or visit the Park in the winter. At Yancy's (a day from either the Hot Springs or Gardiner) they would have elk on all sides of them. Thousands can be seen in a day from there. Elk may be seen within three miles of the Mammoth Hot Springs. At both these places hotels have been open all winter. A great many people with a few days practice on snowshoes, can see part or all the Park in winter and be well repaid for their trouble.

In a short time the proprietors of the hotels will find it to their interest to encourage winter travel, for, in addition to the game to be seen, certain features of the Park are much more interesting in winter than in summer.

NOTES

1. A winter trip was made the year before Hofer's by an unnamed correspondent for the *Philadelphia Times* and appears in another anthology. Whittlesey and Watry, *Ho! For Wonderland*, 114–23.
2. Hofer, "Winter in Wonderland," parts 1 through 5, *Forest and Stream* 28, nos. 11–15 (April 7 to May 5, 1887).
3. Schullery, *Yellowstone's Ski Pioneers*, chapter 4, "Uncle Billy," 50, 51.
4. Special Agent for the Department of the Interior William Hallett Phillips, quoted in Culpin, *History of the Concession Development*, 31.
5. Hough, "Yellowstone Park Game Exploration," part 1, *Forest and Stream* 42, 377.
6. "Ski Running," *Forest and Stream* 62, 64. Accessed on Google Books, October 7, 2015.
7. The route Hofer and Tansey took after climbing above Golden Gate later became part of the Howard Eaton Trail and is used as a ski trail to this day.
8. Hofer had arrived at Swan Lake Basin when he saw the first bands of elk he writes about. Electric Peak is northwest of there, so perhaps he meant to say he turned to look toward the south side of Electric Peak.
9. Hofer's Roadside Springs are located between Nymph Lake and the main road and probably include today's Frying Pan Spring. Whittlesey, *Wonderland Nomenclature*, 1046.
10. The Norris Hotel was built late in 1886. Apparently the Schwatka, Haynes, and Hofer parties stayed there, although it only opened to the public in the summer of 1887—and burned down that July.
11. Judging from its location at Norris Geyser Basin, this "safety valve" was probably Steamvalve Spring, described by nineteenth-century geologist Walter Weed as roaring with copious steam, but now dormant.
12 In the area that the Schwatka party traversed, Obsidian Creek flows through marshy Willow Park, which was sometimes called Willow Creek Park. Whittlesey, *Wonderland Nomenclature*, 1329.
13. Although it is probably true that Crow Indians did not go through the park in winter, unfortunately Hofer here perpetuates the popular myth that all Indians were afraid of the park.
14. Hofer mentions Cañon Creek Hill and Teton Hill, two high points on a southwest-heading trail that did not pass through Madison Junction as the road does now but connected Gibbon Falls and the Firehole River more directly (Whittlesey, *Yellowstone Place Names*, 247–48). By the 1920s this became another section of the Howard Eaton Trail system. See "Yellowstone Trails Blazed by New York Woman," page 233, for information about this trail.
15. Hofer and Tansey must have stayed with Mr. and Mrs. Dean in the cottage at the Lower Basin hotel, then known as the Firehole Hotel. About this hotel, see also Thomas, "Yellowstone Park Illustrated," page 159, note 36. At this point Hofer digresses to discuss Mr. Dean, the November earthquakes he felt, January temperatures encountered by the Schwatka party, and the unusually large snowfall. He then picks up his own story again.

16. Earthquakes are extremely common in the park, and the Norris area has a great many. However, most are too small to be felt. In the years after he served at Norris Hotel, James H. Dean became manager of the Yellowstone Park Association hotels (Bartlett, *Yellowstone Besieged*, 172; and Haines, *Yellowstone Story* 2: 48, 201–2).

17. The dull winter coloring Hofer observed is due to the fact that, although the refraction from deep water remains the same in winter and summer, the microorganisms in the runoff channels are less colorful in winter.

18. The heyday of Excelsior's geyser activity occurred in 1882 and 1888, when Excelsior sometimes erupted to 350 feet. "Reports to the contrary notwithstanding, there were no eruptions of Excelsior 1883 through 1887" (Whittlesey, *Wonderland Nomenclature*, 370). The Charleston, South Carolina, earthquake of August 31, 1886, mentioned earlier in the paragraph, damaged two thousand buildings and killed 60 to 110 people.

19. The Yellowstone National Park Improvement Company was the first concessaire to build hotels throughout the park, beginning with Mammoth Hotel in 1883. They first put up a tent camp at Upper Geyser Basin in 1883, and in 1885 they built a hotel, soon dubbed the "Shack Hotel." Whittlesey, "History of the Old Faithful Area," 15–16.

20. Herron (not Heron) Creek is a tributary of DeLacy Creek, which flows into Shoshone Lake; it was named for William H. Herron, a topographer on the USGS surveys under Arnold Hague in the mid 1880s.

21. They were now heading for a point on Yellowstone Lake just south of West Thumb Geyser Basin. Sandy (not Sand) Creek was the name of present Big Thumb Creek at the time of Hofer's trip. It flows through the present-day Grant Campground, but another small creek named Sandy Creek flows through Grant Village (Lee H. Whittlesey, personal communication, September 2, 2010).

22. Hofer refers to the tapeworm (*Diphyllobothrium* sp.) found in many of Yellowstone Lake's fishes and mentioned throughout the park's written history. John D. Varley and Paul Schullery explain that the worm's eggs are laid in a host, most frequently a pelican, then passed through the bird's feces into the lake, where they develop into larvae. These are then eaten by a crustacean, which in turn is eaten by the fish. The larvae pass through the wall of the fish's stomach and grow in its flesh, and when the fish is eaten by another host, the cycle repeats. Varley and Schullery, *Yellowstone Fishes*, 17.

23. In 1885 U.S. Geological Survey employee M. D. Scott was struck and killed by lightning while on the lake in a small sailboat with other USGS men. The lightning had come from a clear blue sky on an unusually warm day, and the mystery of this has never been solved. Since Mr. Scott's body had been exhumed by his family shortly after burial, Hofer would have seen only the grave site. Whittlesey, *Death in Yellowstone*, 102–3 and 332n6.

24. Sharps rifles were used by troops on both sides during the Civil War and were the favored weapon of bison hunters and mountain men throughout the second half of the 1800s due to their power and accuracy. A capable marksman could take down prey six hundred or more yards away.

A visit from a Welsh artist

The Northern Pacific Railroad tracks reached the terminus of Cinnabar in 1883. Now visitors detrained only three miles from Yellowstone's North Entrance. The convenience of this immediately ballooned park visits from an average of one thousand to about five thousand people per year. Also, the first comfortable hostelry, the Mammoth Hot Springs Hotel, was now taking in guests.

In 1884 Welshman Thomas H. Thomas took part in an excursion of the British Association for the Advancement of Science, traveling from England to Montreal and then to the Rocky Mountains. He contributed his watercolor sketches and geological specimens to a lecture about Yellowstone given in 1885 in Cardiff, Wales, by Charles T. Whitmell, another member of the tour.[1]

Interested in finding American Indian artifacts in the park, Thomas searched for them near the feature of the Gardner River near Mammoth Hot Springs now known as Boiling River. He wrote in a note to Whitmell that he had found three jasper arrowheads and numerous "small chips of obsidian, crystal, and variously coloured agates, and jasper, [that] were scattered in a rough circle, as if around the Indian engaged in his

Portrait of Thomas by Christopher Williams, 1902, National Museum of Wales, NMWA 5146

occupation." Contributing to the earliest archeological information about Yellowstone, while at the same time perpetuating the myth that Native American Indians were afraid to enter the park, he continued, "None of the arrowheads found was of obsidian, but the great majority of the chips were of that substance. This may be accounted for by supposing that the arrowheads found were lost in hunting, or dropped; while the obsidian heads, made upon the spot, would be carefully pouched and carried away. Time did not allow of following up the subject further, but the matter is of interest, as traces of Indians in the district are few, the preternatural phenomena of the Park having daunted the Red Men, who seldom penetrated a region which they declared harboured 'Bad Spirits.'"[2] Much more evidence of early peoples in Yellowstone has been uncovered in recent decades, and research into their history in the area and their attitudes toward the park is ongoing.

Thomas's two articles with engravings illustrating his Yellowstone trip appeared in a London magazine, the *Graphic*, a large format, richly illustrated weekly magazine sent to subscribers all over the world and published from 1869 until 1932.[3] A major emphasis of the magazine in its first three decades or more was the publication of serialized fiction with titles like "That Unfortunate Marriage" by Frances Eleanor Trollop. It also presented political opinion, poetry, ladies' columns, travel, and natural history.

In his articles Thomas mentions names of literary figures and otherwise reveals his erudition. Some of the details he presents, such as the heights of geyser eruptions and distances in Yellowstone, are grossly exaggerated, yet his account is lively and highly readable today, and the observations of his fellow tourists are keen. Unlike many other early writers about Yellowstone, Thomas seems to have used a guidebook only rarely. His observations are mostly very personal and often humorous. However, he made quite a few errors, some of which perpetuated errors in guidebooks.

Many of the original forty-four engravings were much larger than the format of the present volume; the hand-colored engraving of the Grand Canyon of the Yellowstone measures about nine by twelve inches. Printing illustrations in color was rare in nineteenth-century magazines. This volume includes many of the *Graphic's* engravings, which were originally arranged to fit the sixteen-by-twelve-inch pages, usually with little correspondence to the narrative.

We reproduce here twenty-six of Thomas's original Yellowstone watercolor paintings, based upon his on-site sketches. The paintings have never before been exhibited or published.[4] Referring to the "water-colour sketches" Thomas sent to his friend Charles Whitmell, he wrote, "They are almost untouched travel sketches, quite half, if not more, of the Park ones being taken on the logger-head of the Mexican saddle of my Cayuse. . . ." Whitmell adds, "Mr. Thomas need have sent us no excuse; the very want of finish in some of the pictures is one of their chiefest charms—they come, as it were, red-hot from the artist's anvil."[5]

Thomas was the son of the president of the Baptist College of Pontypool, Wales. He received his education in art in Bristol, London, Paris, and Rome, then settled for a time in London, working as an artist. By 1878 he had relocated to Cardiff, where he became a key member of the Cardiff Naturalists' Society and its president in 1888. His interests were broad, ranging from zoology to geology to the archeology, cultural life, and heritage of Wales. The National Museum of Wales, of which Thomas was a founding father, holds a collection of his artwork and miscellanea. The museum's website states about Thomas, "The strength of the Thomas material lies not in its artistic merit but in its quirkiness, its breadth, and that it represents an almost complete catalogue of the major concerns of the nineteenth century . . . in the tradition of J. W. Goethe and John Ruskin, men whose works spanned many diverse disciplines and sought to bridge the gap between science and the arts."[6]

Yellowstone Park Illustrated
1888

THOMAS H. THOMAS
born Pontypool, Wales, 1839 • died Cardiff, Wales, 1915

1.

Possibly no real New Yorker could believe it, yet there are persons who enter the United States, that Land of the Free and Home of the Brave, by other portals than that between Rockaway and Sandy Hook. We, for example, found ourselves upon the sacred soil for the first time at a place named—O Muse of Tragic Comedy! Gretna Green.[7]

From Gretna, through plains of wheat, along the Red River of the North, to Fargo, D.T. [Dakota Territory], on the North Pacific Railway, is but a couple of hours' run, and, deposited in that city, we had some hours to "lay over" before the train "moving westward," as the "folder" phrases it, arrived. We saw the stern realities of life in Fargo, during those hours, from 9 PM to 2 AM chiefly consisting of a "Theatre of Varieties" and **faro-banks**. Among the "varieties" were many young ladies in character-costume, who after their performances mingled affably with the audience, and the remembrance of one, arrayed in celestial white, with a pair of wings to her shoulders, apparently newly descended from a Teutonic **Elysium**, sucking the sherry-cobbler of bruderschaft [fellowship]

with a cowboy of exceptional length and sunburn, still lingers in our mind as a sunny memory of the Wild West.

With the usual bell-ringing our "cars" drew up at the "depôt" strictly "on time," and we were "all aboard" for the Park in the fine Pullman cars of the Northern Pacific Railway.[8] One has nothing to do but eat, drink, smoke, and sleep, and watch the wondrous panorama of wheat, prairie, cattle, river, and mountain, which seems to be everlastingly flowing past the car windows. Our first duty was to sleep, and on awaking and turning out of our berth the train came to a standstill just over a bridge crossing a wide river in which mud flats lifted their ridges like the backs of huge amphibians.

"What river is this, sir?" we asked an on-looker, as we sketched.

"The 'Big Muddy.'"

Faro bank (or simply "faro") was a popular gambling card game in England that spread to the western United States in the 1800s.

Elysium: In Roman mythology, the final resting place of heroic and virtuous souls.

"What?"

"The 'Big Muddy.'"

Pause for mutual consideration ensued, then,

"From the old country, mebbe?"

"Yes."

"Then she's what you'd call th' 'Massourah.'"

When again moving, we fell into war to the knife with our "folder," which insisted that we should leave the station of Mandan an hour before we arrived. After much anxiety of mind, we became instructed in the mysteries of "Central" and "Mountain" time.[9] On, past growing towns and cities, to Dickinson, where the depôt was crowded with cattle and real cowboys. Hence we run soon into the strange tract of the "Bad Lands," where we sketched some of its fantastic pyramids towering up against the glowing sky, and made acquaintance with that unique journal the *Bad Lands Cowboy*.

Out of Dakota into Montana, where "Sentinel Butte" stands lone. We gaze ahead near Glendive to catch our first glimpse of the Yellowstone River, which will be always near us during the rest of the journey. Then, in early morning we sight a tributary river, shining bright blue among golden cotton-wood trees, and beyond range after range of mountains, culminating in delicately shaped snow-clad peaks. That is "Clarke's Fork," and at last we view the chaos of ranges which bastion the citadel of the Rocky Mountains—the Wonderland of the world [Plate 1].[10]

Livingston, 1,034 miles west of St. Paul, was duly reached, and ere long we were speeding up the branch to Cinnabar, the conductors and a

A SKETCH IN THE "BAD LANDS"

A "BOOMING" CITY, LIVINGSTON

passenger or two whiling away the time by popping with their revolvers at various objects we passed, with an invariable non-success which was surprising, and, justified Colonel Starbottle's admiration at the "many shots as are fired and no gentleman hit."[11]

Arriving at Cinnabar, we were to drive the seven miles to the Mammoth Hot Springs Hotel. Beside the platform a number of vehicles were ready to carry travellers on. Here we became aware of facts new to us. The carriages, with their horses, were called "rigs." The drivers, "carters." It was for us to select. A fellow-passenger who took an interest in our proceedings, waving his hand, so as to indicate the whole assembly, said, "There is not one of these gentlemen as can't be fully recommended in every way." Heavens! what an assemblage of sun-baked, frost-dried, grisly faces! brown, hollow-cheeked, dark-bearded, with the skin tightly drawn over the foreheads and ropy veins meandering about their thin temples and necks. Every mouth clinging tightly round a long black cigar, and with a brown smear at the corners. Yet young men, almost all of them, in full health and energy, as the bright eyes rolling in their sunken orbits fully testified: one, at least, of this group was a Justice of the Peace "and **coram**." So far as we afterwards had to do with the drivers in the Park, the recommendation given at Cinnabar was just. All seemed to be trustworthy in essentials, and under a very rough and swaggering exterior there was plenty of shrewdness and good temper. Still we sympathised a little with the indignation of some companions when one of the drivers affably inquired of them, "Say, what gentleman's a-going to drive you fellows?"

Driving steadily along the dusty track, the small town of Gardiner is soon reached. It is one of those villages of wooden houses, common in the West, the framework and slabs of which are almost as portable as tents, while they have at first sight an architectural appearance.

One of these, painted gaily, the gable surmounted by an elk skull and horns, a sign, upon which is painted "Restaurant, C.o.d." (cash on delivery), stuck up in front, and surrounded by a group of dwellings part shanty, part tent, with other shelters, which baffle description, seems frequently to form a "city," which makes a great figure in the railway folder: the pilgrim from Europe smiles a superior smile as he enters them.

But to appreciate their real importance, he has only to get benighted twenty miles away from one, and then to use his leisure time in considering that in all directions but one gloomy forest and prairie extends, habitationless, for a hundred miles or so.

At Gardiner we are upon the border of the promised land, the "Yellowstone National Park," and, as we jog along the road, we may consider a little what the region is that we are about to enter.

One of the Dublin guide-books remarks, with truth possibly, "The **Phoenix Park** is the largest in the world, with the exception of the Yellowstone National Park in the United States," but the author does not mention that the exception has the modest dimensions of fifty-five miles by sixty-five miles.

coram: *Coram judice* is Latin for "before a judge."

Phoenix Park: In northwest Dublin, this is still the largest enclosed park within a European capital city.

This enormous tract, larger than the County of Devon, has, by a noble and timely Act of the United States Government, been preserved intact, so far as its wonders are concerned, while every facility for viewing them will be granted by means of good roads; which are gradually replacing the old trails.

To Dr. F. V. Hayden, the United States Geologist, the credit is due for the idea of setting apart this region of wonders for the pleasure and instruction of the citizens of his country.[12]

Bills for the purpose were introduced in 1871, into the Senate by the Hon. S. C. Pomeroy, and into the House of Representatives by the Hon. William H. Claygett,[13] of Montana, and with little opposition passed into law.

When we call this area a Park we must allow our imagination to work freely about the term, or, at least, we must admit of great arithmetical progression. If an English park may contain within it woods, hills, meads, lakes, and ravines, and may be divided into, say, the "home" and the "deer" park, we are to find in the Yellowstone Park all these, enlarged in ratio with the area. The woods are miles of dense forest, living or dead, wherein we may ride for hours under the tottering fire- or frost-smitten trunks, or view where the cyclones have carved their roads of ruin. The hills are mountains of 4,000 feet above the Park level, the meads are prairies, the ravines are tremendous gorges, sometimes exceeding 1000 feet of depth, the fish-ponds are lovely little lakes, lily-covered, and with beaver dams, the Great Lake is a vast sheet of water, twenty-five miles by thirty miles [about 14 by 20 miles (23 by 32 kilometers)]; the "deer" to be looked for are the great "elk" (wapiti), moose, and black tail, and the "vermin" the keepers of the Park have to watch for are bear and "mountain lion." The "rock-work" is vast cliffs of volcanic glass, and mountains of delicate stalactitic fret-work. And as for the fountains of Uncle Sam's Home Park, they are bigger than any in the world, and boiling to boot.

As our "carter," who has sketched all the scenes mentioned in lively language, begins to expatiate

MAMMOTH HOT SPRINGS HOTEL

on the fountains, his speech gathers force as he proceeds with his wondrous tale, until, over-burdened with expletive and illustrative allusions to the realm of Pluto, a slight incoherence takes place, and, turning a bend, we see before us in the evening light the huge wooden hotel of "Mammoth Hot Springs," with green walls and red roof, and beyond it the strange, pale terraces of the "White Mountain," the protruding face of the active portion of the Hot Springs of Gardiner's River, backed by dark pine-clad slopes [Plate 5].

A few minutes, and we are safely landed in the great hall of the hotel, bask in the rays of the electric light, and hear the notes of a pianoforte, whose full, strong tones can hardly be those of another maker than Steinway. Rather bewildered by these evidences of the march of progress, we proceed to that registration and colloquy with the clerk which is so great an institution in American travel, and here a disappointment occurs; when we add our home addresses—Hosh-Kosh, Mich., and Bullock-Smithy, Eng.—the clerk does not extend a hand to each, and question us earnestly as to the health and well-being of a friend of his, and ours, at each of these places; for once, only once, the American hotel clerk was not omniscient, and we felt discouraged.

⌁

An entertaining account of Mammoth Hotel employees and the arrival of the day's burden of tourists is supplied by writer Owen Wister in his 1891 diary of a trip through Yellowstone:

The stages from the train arrive soon after noon. Five minutes before they come in sight there is total silence in the wide hall of the hotel. The clerk dozes or reads the paper. The porters tip back their chairs and now and then catch a fly. Suddenly some watcher shouts "Stage!" The clerk stands upright by the register book, the porters line up near the door, a chambermaid who was leaning over the railing looking down from upstairs vanishes, and the musicians who were lolling somewhere, hasten to the piano. The pianist plunges his hands among the keys, the fiddle strikes its open fifths rapidly, and as the blistered dusty passengers, veiled women and spectacled men, are helped down from the coach, they hear the jubilant melodies of Strauss going at the rate of 100 miles an hour. (Wister, unpublished diary, transcript, 24)

⌁

As we ponder this strange thing, our hand is touched by what feels like a calf, and an odour as of a farm floats around; we turn and find a gentleman enveloped in buffalo skin who wishes also to register. We resign the pen and look around us. The hall runs apparently from end to end of the building; but, at one end, is closed by curtains. They open for an instant, and disclose the dining-room. Around huge upright stoves in the long corridor groups of tourists, carters, and hunters, most characteristic of Western ways, are seen, and in long, long perspective a line of classically shaped, vermillion spittoons extends in an array at once economically convenient and severely architectonic [Plate 3].

CHARACTERS IN HALL OF MAMMOTH HOT SPRINGS HOTEL

Georgina Synge stayed at Mammoth in 1889 and observed:

> The people were very amusing to watch, they were such a funny mixture. Officers in uniform, from the depôt, looking very immaculate; business men taking their holiday in black coats and top hats; cowboys and stage-drivers dropping in for a dinner and a wash after 'rounding up'; and every description of tourist and traveller, in every sort of 'get up' imaginable. The women were most of them very smart, some with low dresses, and flowers in their hair. These, however, we heard, were not 'transients' (the American term for the sojourner of a day or two), but were boarding there for the summer."
> (Synge, *A Ride through Wonderland*, 123)

Following the line, we soon lifted the great curtain, and, seated at a little table, were deep in the consideration whether we should select elk steak or bear from the Western dainties registered upon one of Prang's most elegant *menu* cards.[14] Our friend voted for the former; we took the latter. As it was our first experience, we tasted of each other's dish, and also tried a little moose meat. The result reminded us of the opening to Hans Andersen's story: "There were two little toy soldiers who were brothers, for they were both made out of the same leaden spoon." Similarly, we found that in the Yellowstone elk, moose, and bear-meat are brothers, for they are all made out of the same old bull.

As we made this discovery voices were heard without, speaking with that varied inflexion which, in America, proclaims the "Britisher"; the curtains swung aside and disclosed a genial English Professor and other members of the British Association. But, ah! how changed from the point-device aspect they possessed at our last meeting— brown, with sun-scars upon their noses, fly-bites round their eyes, frost chaps across their knuckles, beards of a fortnight, and garments more or less frayed off all projecting points, they presented a fearful sight to incoming tourists.

We fraternised, joy was unconfined, and, together with a German gentleman who knew the Park, we settled to the consideration of route and "transportation." There can be little doubt about the former; in regard to the second there is the question of driving or riding. For both there is every facility, and a party of say, five, can hire one of the before-mentioned "rigs," or stage waggons, upon reasonable inclusive terms. For smaller parties of gentlemen, riding may be recommended; the traveller is freer, and the ponies, called "cayuses," which are let for hire, are generally untiring and hardy, even if one here and there may appear at the morning saddling or "sinching" to have graduated at the "Buffalo Billeries."[15] The experienced at our council all advised riding, and that we should get ponies, our German friend assenting, adding, without full appreciation of the English idiom, "I would advise you to bekom* ponies. [Thomas's footnote in the original: *"Bekommen"—to get, procure.] I would myself bekom a pony when I had not a bad lek, for which I visit dese sbrings."

THE "LIBERTY CAP" (CONE OF AN EXTINCT GEYSER) AND HOTEL

We afterwards had the opportunity of seeing that good arrangements for testing the therapeutic value of the springs was made, and although this cannot as yet be fully known, sufficient success in the treatment of articular maladies, rheumatism, and cutaneous diseases has been achieved to show that, as a sanatorium, Mammoth Hot Springs has a great future before it, and will be the salvation of many a bad leg, arm, or body as a whole.[16]

A lovely morning gave us every opportunity for seeing the Mammoth Hot Springs at their best. Before the hotel spread a grey plain, dotted with clumps of wormwood, young pines, or Thuja bush.[17] In the midst stood a strange pyramidal object, some fifty feet in height, called the **"Liberty Cap"**; beyond were the Terraces of glistening white or yellow, passing into browns, still in formation. Clouds of steam were reeking up and dispersing among the pine-trees that clothed the hill-sides above. In order to understand the whole system of the Terraces it is well to descend from the hotel, which stands upon one of them, to the level of the Gardiner River, which flows about 1,000 feet below the uppermost springs, which are about two miles back from the river. Three great divisions are observable. The old Spring Terraces at, and a little above the level of the river, upon which are a few insignificant vents, and a small stream of high temperature which, falling into the Gardiner, enables the fisherman—now for the incident without which no account of the Yellowstone Park is

Liberty Cap was named for its resemblance to the conical hats worn during the French Revolution.

complete, and which we are anxious to get over as early as possible—standing at the junction of the streams, to catch a fish in the cold, and stew it in the hot water without removing it from the hook, or feeling any remorse for the cruelty of the operation [Plate 2].

From these extinct terraces a sharp rise of some 400 feet brings us to the plain upon which the hotel stands, and which, though now broken in surface and crumbled by atmospheric influences, shows that at no very ancient date it was the theatre of very imposing phenomena. At one point a deep chasm shows the position of a boiling spring of great dimensions, and the curious "Liberty Cap" remains as witness of a geyser of special interest. This isolated shaft of forty-five feet in height, with another upon which the Terraces are encroaching, named the "Giant's Thumb" [Devil's Thumb] are the only geyser orifices having a great length of tube above the surface.[18] The cone of the "Giant," of which we shall have to speak later, has a height of some twelve feet only.

But *the* "Terraces," that lovely mass of delicate and vari-coloured incrustation pierced with pools, the colour of which no pen can describe, which travellers willingly cross the Continent to see, are there above us, forming the third great platform of the "White Mountain." All portions of this are still active, but the lower part, a tract of about one hundred and seventy acres in extent, is that which comprises the special beauties which give to Mammoth Hot Spring Terraces their renown, beauties which, now that the greater terraces of Rotomahana have been destroyed, are unique.[19]

The most interesting points are three. Minerva Terrace from below the level, the Pulpit Terrace, and the former Terrace with its source, the lovely Cleopatra Spring, looked at from the slightly higher ground or what are called the main springs.

Given a fine clear day of August or September, nothing can be more strangely beautiful than the aspect of the Minerva Terrace as one struggles along in the broken-down, powdery, geyser formation, towards it.

On the left are the fine Terraces surrounding the Main Spring, on the right a mass of deposit forty feet in height, and covering perhaps, an acre. At differing levels project from the general mass huge cups, bearing a rough resemblance in form to halves of the great sponges we see in museums called "Neptune's Cups." The projections are various in size, some being as much as eight feet high, the more usual height is four to six feet. The edge of each terrace forms a perfectly straight line, telling with the utmost sharpness in contrast with the curves of the sides, with their delicate wave-like ornamentation and pedestals of slender stalactites. The general tint of the whole terrace is snowy white, varying at different points into delicate yellow and ochre tones, here and there contrasted by a rich brown. As we approach nearer, every basin is seen to be ornamented with tiny hollows and projections, all conforming to some law of harmonious overflow and deposition, and giving one the same sense of craft and workmanship as one experiences in looking at a half-effaced stone, carved with cunning knots and enlacements of ancient Celtic Art. As we look closely too, into the lovely pure surfaces shining as the water slides over them, we see that threads of more vivid, but still delicate tints are adding a beauty of tone by their presence.

As we climb the path between the two Terraces the heat becomes intense, and the glare upon the eyes intolerable; we are glad to put on blue or smoke glasses, which no traveller should be without. Arrived at the upper level, we view the Cleopatra Spring itself and the basins which surround it,

THE PULPIT TERRACE, MAMMOTH HOT SPRINGS

FORMATION AT PERIODICAL LAKE

and an effect of colour is spread out before us such as could, we imagine, be seen nowhere out of this region of enchantment. We now see how all the vast cups, the sculpture on the sides of which we have admired, are massed, one outside the other, at various levels around a central group of shallow pools extending over the whole surface of the Terrace, in the midst of which opens a spring, consummate in its beauty, of clear water of the deepest emerald, shifting into blue, changing through an infinitude of tints until it is bounded by a thin line of coral-like incrustation; outside of this is curve after curve, sweep after sweep of the same delicate formation, each curve enclosing a very shallow pool, in which silky threads stir or wave; each pool, according to its depth or coloured bottom, or reflection of sky or cloud, has its own true or passing tint, while over all, here confusing, there receiving reflection of the hues below, hangs a delicate haze of steam. Thus, looking from the higher level, the spectator has before him a species of natural *cloisonné* enamel on a vast scale, in which the delicate threads of deposit are the *cloisons* and the pure, shallow, many-hued pools the enamel. But not in Osaka, nor in the ateliers of Barbédienne[21] is there any *cloisonné* of such opaline hues and laughing tint as that around "Cleopatra's Spring [Plate 5]."

We gaze long at this wonderful surface, forgetting that it is only a part of

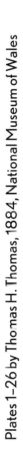

Plates 1–26 by Thomas H. Thomas, 1884, National Museum of Wales

1. "Approach to Rocky Mountains, from Yellowstone Valley W."

2. Boiling River, "Sept 20th"

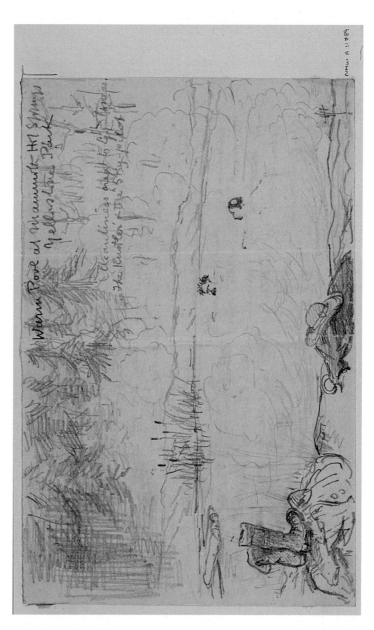

Characters in Hall of Mammoth Springs Hotel.

Hthomas.

NMW A 11492

3. "Characters in Hall of Mammoth Hot Springs Hotel"

Warm Pool at Mammoth Hot Springs
Yellowstone Park

Cleanliness next to Godliness
the Dwelling: the sky so fast

NMW A 11789

4. "Warm Pool at Mammoth Hot Springs Yellowstone Park" [Bath Lake]

5. Cleopatra Spring and Stalactite Terraces, Mammoth Hot Springs, "Sept 20th"

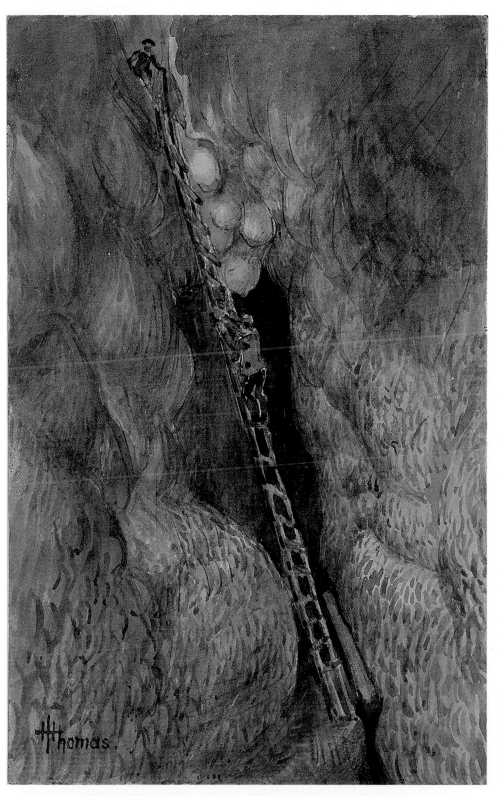

6. "Interior of an Extinct Fissure Geyser, Mammoth Hot Springs" [Devil's Kitchen]

7. "The 'Orange' Geyser and the 'Chipmunk'" [Orange Spring Mound]

8. Beaver Lake

9. Lake of the Woods

10. In a tent hotel, Norris Basin—Strange Bedfellows

11. Ford in Gibbon Cañon

12. Steam from "Hell's Half-Acre" and Lower Geyser Basin — Early Morning

Cone of "Grotto" Geyser.

13. Cone of "Grotto" Geyser

14. "Fire Hole Basin," "Sept 23, 1884" [Marshall House]

15. "Round the Stove Marshall's, Sept 22"

16. Paint Pots, Lower Geyser Basin

17. "Diana's Well" and "Castle" Geyser Plunging

18. "Old Faithful Sept 22"

19. "Giant Geyser, Yellowstone Park"

20. "Hell's Half-Acre, 22 Sept / 84"

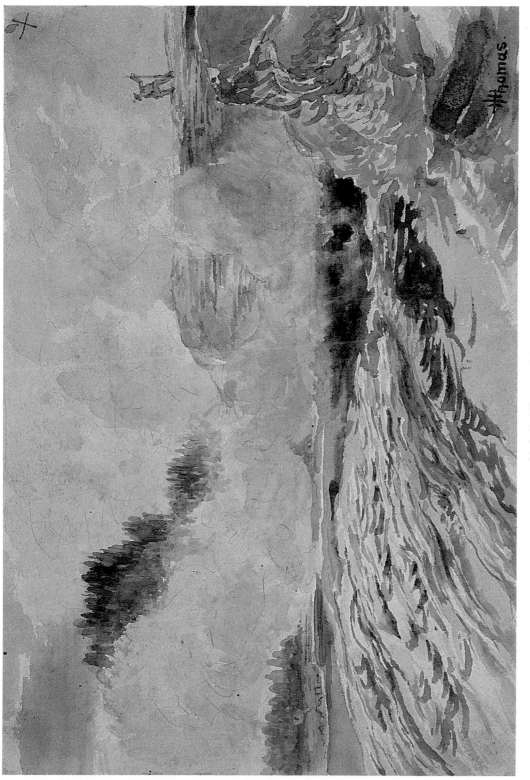

21. Gulf of "Excelsior" Geyser

22. Grand Prismatic Spring, Midway Geyser Basin

23. Queen's Laundry, "25th Sept"

24. "Hunter Yellowstone Sept. 26th"

25. "Great Falls of the Yellowstone"

26. "Yellowstone"

27. The Grand Cañon of the Yellowstone, from the Great Falls, hand-colored engraving after "Yellowstone" (Plate 26)

the beautiful panorama which is spread out before the eye, as we stand on the acclivity. Presently we find time to admire the valley to the northwards, and the worn slopes of Mount Evarts, crowned with its long rampart of cliffs over against us, before we turn again to the ascent, and to examine further the wonders of this strange mountain-side, which seems to be quivering with some mysterious life; for above us, from among the pines which have grown to a forest upon the half-extinct Terraces, we hear slight noises, and see thin wreaths of steam which betoken activity.

Not so beautiful as the Terraces when the springs are in full action, the higher region, where vast extinct terraces moulder under air, frost, and heat, and upon which the forest gradually encroaches, is full of interest, for in it may be studied the anatomy of the formations in the huge breaches which time has made in the cliffs of geyserite, leaving the internal structure open to view, and in caverns from which the boiling streams once gushed or spouted, the interior of which may now be examined.

Of the latter, our illustration of the so-called "Mammoth Cave," named from its locality and not from its size, will give an idea [Plate 6].[22] We find the opening to it upon the crest of a long ridge, small cracks along which show that the aperture is only the largest of a series which are not so roomy, but which probably mark the line of a rock fissure, along the whole extent of which waters holding minerals in solution have gushed, gradually piling a long mound of deposit, through which the waters oozed or spurted until the pressure became withdrawn, and the fissure became sealed.

A portion of one of the finest specimens of this kind of formation will be seen in the termination of the "Narrow Gauge," which we engrave from a photograph by Mr. Brooks, of St. Helen's.[23]

A rude ladder of poles allow[s] us to descend to a depth of thirty-five feet, and at the extremity of the cave we become aware of a heat considerably greater than that of the blazing sunshine above, which tells of our approximation to that mysterious fiery source of energy which exists at no very great depth, causing all the strange phenomena of this Wonderland, and which geologists tell us is probably a mass of still hot lava. The sides of the cavern as they arch over to the elliptical opening above us are coated with carbonate of lime of great hardness deposited in ribs and bosses, and at one

END OF "NARROW GAUGE" FORMATION AND MOUNT EVARTS

of the commissures of the fissure hangs a group of huge oval masses, in shape and colour like vast bladders of lard, such as the **Gastrolaters** might sacrifice to their god Manduce.

Making a circuit westward on our return, we find many curious exemplifications of the action of the Springs; at one point a pretty grotto of

THE BATHING POOL AT "MAMMOTH"—"CLEANLINESS IS NEXT TO GODLINESS"

PULPIT TERRACE—"TAKING DUTY" IN A YELLOWSTONE PULPIT

formation of pure white, streaked with red, brown, and green, is seen against a background of pines, which closely surround it. Again, hearing a strange chattering sound proceeding from a dense grove, we push through and arrive at a space covered with small mounds of geyserite, out of which tiny spurts of water are continually leaping, causing the twittering sound we heard. This is called the "Squirrel" geyser.[24]

Further on we find the "Orange" geyser [Orange Spring Mound]; a small thread of water continually leaps from the summit of a mound of a brilliant orange colour [Plate 7]. While forming, this mound, like almost all others, has enveloped the trunks of growing pines which are killed, and stand white and ghostly in the inundation of deposit.

Sketching here, we found ourselves closely watched by several pretty little ground-squirrels called "chip-munks," brown, with bodies longitudinally striped, fawn bellies, and short straight tails.[25] They would watch from behind a grass tuft, and then, for a better view, suddenly run to the end of a low branch or the summit of a hillock, and eye us with the utmost friendliness. As artists, wandering in byways of America, we must express our sense of indebtedness to the "chip-munks" for their constant and cheerful companionship.

Among these woods "back of" Mammoth Springs, there is a **warm pool** much resorted to for bathing. Repairing hither, two heads were discernible upon the reeking surface. That those cloud-borne countenances were not those of a species of cherub was presumptively proved by the presence on the bank of a monumental pair of boots, having that plenitude of verge and curve which so loudly proclaims the benefit of protective duties to the American consumer, and by a wide-brimmed hat with a neat little rosette upon the band. There could be no doubt in the mind of the observer that there floated before him, in one warm baptism blent, a "rustler" of the Occident,[26] and an Anglican priest from beyond the Eastern Ocean. It was a gracious incident, and how suggestive to the mind! [Plate 4]

Our course back to the hotel brings us again out upon the Great Terraces, and we have, upon the western side, wonders as great as upon the eastern face we ascended—the singularly perfect stalactite basins, called the Pulpit Terrace,[27] which, for purity of colour and grace of form in the separate cups, cedes to none. In the midst is the "Pulpit" itself, with its lovely decoration of what seems fair white drapery hanging in fluted folds to the base. Mr. Ingersoll's arrangement is apt, in which we see photographed a veteran of the "Grand Army of the Republic" apparently officiating, with, on the pulpit edge, according to a graceful American custom, a bouquet, composed of mallow, willow-herb and local woodland blossoms. This group appears to be quite extinct, and must moulder away in the course of a few years, to be replaced, it may be, by fresh decorations.

Our evening at the hotel was fertile in incident. A party of English tourists had come down from the Park, among their baggage a mysterious box, the contemplation of which, "with one consideration and another," induced a policeman to arrest one of the travellers for the heinous offence of deporting "specimens." This, as our German friend explained with a happy occultation of language, is "streckly verbod." An Act had been passed rendering the collection of specimens punishable, but copies of the document had not arrived, so that the action of the minion of the law was considered somewhat premature.[28]

In an outbuilding a Court was hurriedly improvised, a Justice of the Peace of somewhat battered appearance presided, the general aspect of the Court and spectators, seen by the light of two small lamps and through a cloud of cigar-smoke, might be described as rugose, and seemed to promise Justice neat, unsweetened by Mercy. The accused was a blond gentleman, whose fairness was in touching contrast to the bronze of the members of the **Vehmgericht**. The presiding

> **Gastrolaters:** Rabelais's sixteenth-century work, *Gargantua and Pantagruel*, described this fictional sect with their huge sacrifices of rich and exotic foods.
>
> **warm pool:** Bath Lake (now dry), near today's Upper Terrace Drive.
>
> **Vehmgericht:** In medieval Germany, a tribunal under the jurisdiction of the emperor; it later became secret and sometimes used terroristic methods.

magistrate made a few remarks on the heinousness of the offence so impressively that we emptied our pockets of the geyserite fragments we had therein, and, favoured by the gloom, dropped them into the invitingly open pocket of our next neighbour. After the observations of the Justice, the proceedings took a somewhat Pickwickian character; it was discovered that the Act was not yet quite sufficiently matured for operation, and that the offender had in his collections been solely influenced by scientific considerations. The Court broke up, and by detachments adjourned to the "saloon," to the discussion of the *cause célèbre* and "Old Bourbon." There we heard the decision of the Court colloquialised—

"Nary a fine, fer the Act's only come down on the wires; and he wern't a goin' to sell the sp'c'm'ns, ner give 'em to gels fer toys."

The stringent application of a law against the injury of the beautiful and fragile decorations of the geyserite formations should have every possible support. The energy of the collector is quite equal to the deportation of the "Liberty Cap" or the mound of the "Castle Geyser," and infinite injury can easily be done to the terraces and the coral-borders of the hot pools. At the same time, there are places where no injury could be caused by collection of geyserites and geological specimens, and it would be well if some responsible person under, say, the Geological Survey, were nominated to form and dispose of to museums, &c., collections representative of the very interesting minerals of the region. Otherwise the system of petty purloining, to which even the most virtuous tourist now renders adhesion, must continue.[29]

The central platform of Mammoth Hot Springs, upon which the hotel stands, has an elevation of 6,387 feet above the sea, that is, twice the altitude of **Snowdon**; but we are here only at the lowest level of the Park, and, leaving for the next "hotel," that at Norris's Basin, we at once ascend a grade of 2,000 feet in about two miles of road, and then find ourselves upon what may be called the "floor" of the great Alpine plateau, upon which the "Wonderland" is seated. As we crawl up the steep, hot, and dusty slope, we think again about the strange characteristics of the region and begin to appreciate that we are climbing into the central and mysterious citadel of the North American continent—the very heart of the Rocky Mountains—whence flows the chief stream of the greatest river of the Continent, and among the peaks and gorges of which the great cyclones gather, and are flung eastward over the thousands of miles of plain and ocean, until they break against the shores of Britain and Norway—a constant war of the gods. Kabibonokka, the ice-god of the West, is ever hurling storm and vapour against the fastnesses of Thor.[30]

As we ride up the slope we are striking nearly southward for the first of the great geyser tracts, "Norris," or "Gibbon" Basin, twenty-one miles from Mammoth Hot Springs. From the summit of the grade a magnificent panoramic view is seen looking north, along the Gardiner and Yellowstone Valleys, the crater-like summits of Sepulchre Mountains [Mountain], the palisade-cliffs of Mount Evarts, and in the distant north-east, the grand snowy "Electric Peak" towering to over eleven thousand feet [10,969 feet (3,343 meters)].

Passing the pretty little "Freda Lake," [Swan Lake] after a few miles over a somewhat open country, where the sun beats hotly upon the sage scrub, we cross the Gardiner River, keeping along Obsidian Creek towards Obsidian Canyon and Cliffs, one of the great wonders of the Park.

Ascending the creek, the valley narrows, and the road enters dense forest, until, crossing the stream, it passes a point of remarkable interest. On the right, is spread out Beaver Lake,[31] a considerable sheet of water bordered by grassy marshes, and backed up by high hills densely clad with pine [Plate 8]. The lower part of the lake is a series of old beaver-dams, showing a strange labyrinth of raised banks, enclosing pools mantled with green, with an old beaver-hut, forming a little islet on the western side. On the eastern bank the road passes under cliffs of more than two hundred feet high, exclusive of the scree below them, from which the Cañon takes its name. The lower half of these cliffs is composed of irregularly shaped columns of volcanic glass, overlaid by another mass not so clearly columnar. Huge rocks of the black cinder have fallen, and form the scree out of which the roadway has been hewn by means of huge fires lighted among the largest blocks, which were splintered when hot by dashing water upon them. The dark

OBSIDIAN CLIFF (VOLCANIC GLASS) 200 FEET HIGH

lake, the immense black vitrified cliffs set among dense forest, and the burned trunks about the screes, make the whole scene, such as **Doré** might have imaged.

From this vast quarry the Indians appear to have supplied themselves with arrow-heads; some fine implements were discovered upon an old trail by the Geological Survey near this spot, and we had ourselves the good fortune to find, near Mammoth, spots where the arrow-makers had sat and worked, surrounded by their chippings of obsidian, jasper, and chalcedony.

A little further, and the beautiful little "Lake of the Woods" [Plate 9] is reached, where, at nearly

Mt. Snowdon, at 3,560 feet, is the highest point in Wales, whereas Mammoth Junction is at 6,239 feet (1,902 m).

Gustave Doré (1832-1883) illustrated dramatic scenes for the English Bible and for classics such as Rabelais's *Gargantua and Pantagruel* and Poe's "The Raven."

A RIDE THROUGH BURNT FOREST

eight thousand feet, we approach the divide of the waters flowing to the Gardiner, and those of the Gibbon flowing to the Madison.[32] Through forest green or forest burned we press on, and, emerging upon a dislocating piece of corduroy road, cross the stream, and draw up at the row of tents which does duty for a hotel. A tent-hotel, sometimes called a "krawl," is something fearful and wonderful; there appears to be a fixed price for every item—one dollar—and, as a man must have breakfast, dinner, "supper," and bed, it means a minimum of four dollars a day. The "nourriture," in Park parlance, "grub-pile," does not differ much at the different meals, and if the traveller wants to know what meal is before him, consultation with the host or the watch is requisite. When we say a bed is necessary, perhaps we overstate the case, it would be more proper to say a moiety of a bed, for travelling in the National Park, like the poverty to which it leads, makes a man acquainted with strange bedfellows.

Our sketch gives our first glimpse of tent-hotel life at night, in which an English tourist pauses in preparations for rest to eye carefully and suspiciously a new-comer, dark-visaged, arrayed in sombrero and leathers, and whose fatigue from long riding gives him the air of revolving in his mind some crime of special violence when the candle, elegantly sconced in a bottle, shall have waned [Plate 10]. As for the furniture of the tent, it is not so bad; an ingenious adaptation in iron of

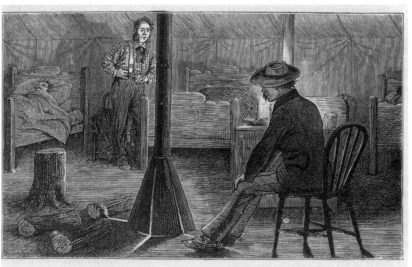

IN A TENT HOTEL, NORRIS BASIN—STRANGE BEDFELLOWS

the earthen stove, used from time immemorial by Indians, keeps the frost out, a pine stump or two stick up conveniently out of the ground, beds of considerable capacity, well-furnished with blankets, and, of course, a grass "whisk" which, in America, "always is with us." During the height of the season the principle upon which the beds are populated is said to be the addition of visitors so long as they may arrive, or until the occupants "go for their guns." The plan is simple, and relieves the authorities of responsibility.

At Norris Basin the arrangements for ablution did, perhaps, lack finish. They consisted of one basin and a pitcher. It was interesting in the morning, when the temperature still hovered about 32 deg. Fahr., to see an eager group of shiverers demanding their turn, and to hear how, when it came, they all unconsciously quoted Foote, "What! no soap?"[33]

Besides the illustrations after the sketches of our artist, Mr. T. H. Thomas, our view of Livingston is from a photograph by Mr. Edgar W. Sollas, of 32, King Henry's Road, London, N.W., that of the "Narrow Gauge" and Mount Evarts from a photograph by Mr. R. G. Brooks, of St. Helen's Lane. The "Hot Springs Hotel," Pulpit Terrace, Liberty Cap, and Yellowstone Lake from the "Mammoth" Series of Mr. W. E. Jay Haynes [F. Jay Haynes], official photographer of the Northern Pacific Railway, Fargo, D.T., and the "Preacher" and Golden Gate Road are from the Imperial Series of Mr. Ingersoll, of St. Paul, Minn. We are indebted for the use of the drawing, reproduced in color, of the Great Falls, to Professor Sollas, Trin. Coll., Dublin.

2.

At "Norris," or "Gibbon," Basin we are in the land of real geysers, not indeed the greatest, but of a size which will prepare us for what is further to be seen. The springs called by courtesy geysers at Mammoth can only base their pretensions to the name upon the minutest agreement with the meaning of the Icelandic word *geysa*, to gush—from which "geyser" is derived." Thus saith the guide-book.

The tract upon which the phenomena are exhibited covers about 170 acres, a great plain of white deposit, composed chiefly of lime and silica, with sulphur. A belt of pine-forest surrounds it, many of the trees at the edge of which stand white and dead, killed by the encroachment of the hot deposits, and partly silicified by infiltration. In the midst of this heated desert of white, an oasis or two of pines give the eye rest with their dark green. The deposit is very friable, and is crossed by many fissures, out of which steam and sulphurous vapours reek. The crust seems everywhere hollow, and reverberations are heard below, pools of scalding water are at every turn, and on some portions of the formation one is in danger at every step of a jet of steam from some vent-hole. What with the heat radiating from the soil and beating down from the heavens, Norris Basin on an autumn noon can probably challenge any locality outside **Tophet** and the Tropics in the matter of heat. Faint with heat, sick with sulphur-fumes,

Tophet is a synonym for "hell" but also a place mentioned in the Bible.

FORD IN GIBBON CAÑON

FALLS OF THE GIBBON

constantly startled by steam-jets and the crumbling of the floor beneath the feet, the time the tourist spends here is not a very happy one, but the sight of the almost constant activity within a great hollow area of the "Fountain," "Twin," and "Triplet" geysers makes amends. Here, too, are pools of boiling mud of various colours, and a geyser of the first-class as to size, called the "Monarch," may at times be seen in eruption. A small geyser in rapid action, called the "Minute Man," is close beside the road, and always lively.[34]

On, southwards, there is the pretty open country of Elk Park to be crossed, when we arrive at the commencement of Gibbon Cañon, a ravine full of strangeness and beauty. High above us, as we enter we see the steam of a group of vents, then the valley narrows, and has the character of an Alpine gorge, broken here and there by little plateaux of white, in which hot springs are seated. The River Gibbon now tears its way among rocks and then meanders peacefully in a wider bed, immense cliffs hang above shrouded by pine, the road is niched into the flank of the cliffs and has some bits where, of two evils, the traveller prefers to stumble over the boulders of the river-bed. To see a stage well-stowed with travellers coming down the grade to the ford in this Cañon is a pleasant sight for those fond of feats with the "ribbons" [the reins]—the careful descent, the anxious faces peering out from the tilt, the sudden submergence, the struggles of the team among the boulders, the pitching and swaying of the whole "rig" on the slender hickory wheels, is delightful to the spectator [Plate 11]. Here, however, as upon the thousand other nasty bits in the West, accidents rarely happen, and every one must admire the way in which Western drivers handle their unwieldy-looking teams of six or eight horses or mules, the pairs of which are termed, according to their position, "wheelers," "leaders," "point," and "swing."

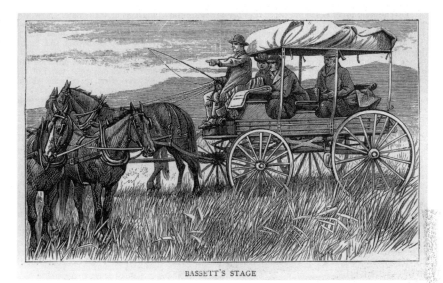

BASSETT'S STAGE

A little to the west of the ford are the Gibbon Falls, which have been so successfully photographed in his "Mammoth" Series by Mr. J. Haynes [Frank Jay Haynes]. Although one of the minor sights of this region, this Fall would be a great feature elsewhere, with its considerable volume and height of over eighty feet. What the beautiful Swallow Fall of North Wales is on a small, this is on a large scale. After baking on Norris Basin and weltering in Elk Park, the traveller pants for water-brooks, and an hotel planted among the exquisite scenery of this part of the Gibbon should be a success.

A few miles of forest ascent from the Gibbon River, and we descend to its tributary, the Firehole River,[35] the name of which prepares us for something extraordinary. From the declivity we see southward dense masses of forest, out of which pillars of cloud arise in groups, extending for many miles. They give at first sight the idea that the country is peopled, and that they are the signs of energy in manufacture; then at once there flows into the mind the somewhat appalling idea that they are really from vents of volcanic energy, perhaps capable still of suddenly changing the whole aspect of the panorama, and leaving it a chaos of fire-smitten rock, as has been the case in New Zealand.

At early morning these clouds of steam have a very remarkable appearance, standing with almost unchanging outline against the sky, as seen in our illustration [Plate 12]. If there be a gust of wind, they seem to "curtsey" to one another in a gracious manner, and then regain the perpendicular.

Soon we are on the banks of the Firehole River, and see—un embarras de richesses—on one bank a tent-hotel, prettily grouped in a meadow beside the stream, with a pine-clad butte in the background, and across a branch of the stream a real hotel, built of logs, and with apparently all sorts of conveniences surrounding it. We cross the ford, draw up at the verandah, and become a guest of Marshall and Henderson's, glad to forget that such a thing as a tent exists.[36] And here we may note the contrariety of human nature; a few nights' packing in log-houses on more or less ancient buffalo-robes makes one long for tents; and a few nights in tents, with temperature about 28 deg., restore one's belief in log-houses. But Henderson's is not a house to tire of. Our illustration will give an idea of the prettiness of the position—on a narrow island, with a shallow river of slightly tepid water, being chiefly derived from the hot springs, flowing round it, and backed by rocky hills crowned by pines [Plate 14]. Beside the house is a hot pool [Hygeia Spring], the water from which is led to the bath-house and into a washing-trough in the hotel, over which sacrilege no doubt the ardent naiad of the spring weeps copiously.

This point is central for the various routes in the Park. Northward lies the road we have traversed from Mammoth Hot Springs; from the west enters Bassett's stage [route] from Beaver Canyon, about one hundred miles away, connecting with the Union Pacific Railway and Utah; to the south are the Great Geyser Basins, Upper, Middle, and Lower, and to the east runs the road to Yellowstone

HENDERSON AND KLAMER'S HOTEL, FIRE-HOLE BASIN

Lake, the Great Falls, and the Grand Canyon of the Yellowstone.[37]

Our route is southward into the heart of the geyser tracts, and a short ride brings us to the Lower Basin by a road from which we gaze upon the great plateaus of that and the Middle Basin stretched before us, marked with clouds of steam.

Reaching the formation, we see a graceful display from a geyser, arising from a large pool, to a height of forty feet. Little noise or vibration accompanies the eruption, and it stands, an iridescent column, surmounted by millions of brilliants flashing in the sun, sharply silhouetted against the deep blue of the sky. This is the "Fountain" Geyser, which pours forth its waters at intervals of about four hours. The display soon terminates, and we pass to the great mudpools and craters, called the "Paint Pots," which are the most remarkable sight upon this plateau. These combine the sublime and the ridiculous. There is an element of terror in the heat and force which sustain in constant ebullition the great cauldron of milk-white mud, and which twist and work the rose-coloured craters. The great reservoir is filled with silicious mud, out of which white bubbles—as large as, and irresistibly reminding one of, so many bald pates—emerge, swell, and burst. Around this central mass of white, which steams and fills the air with a dead, semi-sulphurous odour, is a space of ruddy mud, fissured and cracked hideously, upon which craters of three or four feet high open their great pustular mouths, showing throats which seem to writhe in agonies of suffocation, and, after repeated efforts, succeed in disgorging red pellets [Plate 16].

Again on the bank of the Firehole River, we resist the temptation to cross a wooden bridge and visit the wonders of the Midway Basin, leaving them for our return, and pass the long margin of it as it meets the river, noting the steaming streams that sweep down its sides.

Two miles further,[38] ascending a slope, we emerge on the Upper Geyser Basin, the road passing the strangely formed mound of the Grotto Geyser—a mass of pure white geyserite, pierced by two openings, the discharges from which have caused the deposit to form masses of the strange form seen in our illustration [Plate 13]. In eruption the direction of the tubes and the form of the mound give strange variety to the fountain, which, with great lashing and roaring sounds, splashes in all directions, the greater steam, however, ascending to a height of fifty feet. The eruptions last as much as an hour.

From this point a grand panorama spreads before us—the great geyser region, grey and white in colour, with streaks of brown-dried herbage, divided by the Firehole River, which derives so much of its waters from it, and bounded by that very dense forest of pines characteristic of the Rocky Mountains. The whole basin is somewhat triangular in shape, and comprises about four square miles. Upon it open almost all the greatest geysers of the world, and the number of hot springs

ROUND THE STOVE AT HENDERSON'S

upon it is not less than fifteen hundred.

Near us is the great "Castle" Geyser, which possesses the most imposing crater in the Park. Its whole base is not less than three and a half acres in extent. Upon this is a sort of platform, which has a somewhat laminated appearance. The "Castle" towers above this platform some eighteen feet. Its energy in eruption is very great; but it seems to be rarely in full action, though continually groaning and throwing out jets to a height of from twelve to twenty feet. In the "Great Divide," by Lord Dunraven, will be found a remarkable description of an eruption of the "Castle," which gives very perfectly the mingled impression of sublimity and comicality which many of the phenomena of the Park impress upon the mind.[39]

A beautiful scene is formed by "Pool Beautiful," "Diana's Well," or "Devil's Well" [today's Crested Pool, Plate 17]—for it has all these names—in the foreground, and the great mound in the distance. The pool is most exquisitely shapen—almost perfectly circular, and confined by a charming raised rim of geyserite of almost exactly twenty feet diameter. The rim has a beautiful pearly tint and coral-like incrustation, while the heated waters it limits show every shade of emerald and azure as the bottom deepens to the central tube by which it is supplied. Such pools are frequent in the Park—sometimes opening on the great geyser plateaus, sometimes hidden away among the pines, but, whenever seen, arresting the traveller by their beauty of faery.

While looking upon this gem, a curious blowing noise heard above the growling of the "Castle" made us look southward; and there, at the other end of the plateau, half a mile away, surrounded at a respectful distance by groups of people, who looked like flies upon a surface of sugar, soared into the air an immense geyser not less than one hundred feet in height, and surmounted by a lofty cloud of steam that waved like a huge banneret, the noise of the impulsion being wafted to us—now loud, now soft—by the breeze.

We stood still, astonished at the beauty of the spectacle, when, after a strong gush, the column of water seemed to break; then another stream shot up not so high, another, and another, each less powerful, when the water ceased to leap, and only the cloud of steam rising from the drenched ground and the rivulets flowing to the river remained to show what had occurred. We had seen our

"Mrs. Finch's, Fire Hole Basin"

MRS. FINCH'S CAMP HOTEL, FIRE-HOLE BASIN

first eruption of "Old Faithful," and determined to make a nearer acquaintance at his next appearance. Meanwhile, near to us was the queer "Sawmill" Geyser in full work, a toy geyser of five or six yards high, which makes the grating noise of a saw driven at high speed through a log, and flinging up the water by what may be described as separate mouthfuls. Ascending and descending blobs often meet, and flash like a broken glass-ball.

Space would fail us to describe the many great geysers which deigned to play for our benefit, and those which would not. Geysers are most annoyingly feminine in their ways—unpunctual to a proverb, irregular in their action, promising all things by subtle indications, performing, indeed, but always either before or after their promised time. The naiad of "Old Faithful" alone is true, and she, with feminine exaggeration of good qualities, is really too exact to her sixty-five minutes [Plate 18]. The racing and chasing on the banks of the "Firehole" is absurd; we are devoutly admiring "Old Faithful," then the "Fan" at the other end of the plateau raises its lovely expansion of waters, the carters rattle their "rigs" towards her, the ponymen gallop, people on foot scurry, all perspire. On their arrival the "Fan" gives a final flirt and sinks into her pool, or gives a few little derisive skips before she becomes totally quiescent. Meanwhile the "Splendid," or "Comet," sets off roaring, as if about to begin. Everybody gathers round, and nothing comes of it; but the "Beehive," at a distance, is seen to fling its wonderful column into the air. As to the "Grand," or "Giantess," their favourite trick is to despoil the weary wayfarer of his beauty sleep, or drag him out in the earliest morn into the freezing air. But they are also feminine in that their beauty makes amends.

To give an exact idea of the appearance and action of one of the great geysers, it may be well to simply quote the description of the mound of deposit and crater of "Old Faithful," with its mode of action, as given by Lieutenant Doane and Dr. Hayden in the "Report of the United States Government Survey":[40]

"Close around the opening, which is 2 feet by 6 feet inside, are built up walls 8 feet in height, of spherical nodules from 6 inches to 3 feet in diameter; these, in turn, are covered on the surface with minute globules of stalagmite, incrusted with a thin glazing of silica. The rock at a distance appears the colour of ashes of roses, but near at hand shows a metallic grey, with pink and yellow margins of the utmost delicacy. Being constantly wet, the colours are brilliant beyond description. Sloping gently from this rim of the crater, in every direction, the rocks are full of cavities, in successive terraces, forming little pools, with margins of silica the colour of silver, the cavities being of irregular shape, constantly full of hot water, and precipitating delicate coral-like beads of bright saffron. These cavities are also fringed with rock around the edges, in meshes as delicate as the **finest lace**. Diminutive yellow columns rise from their depth, capped with small tablets of rock, and resembling flowers growing in the water; some of them are filled with oval pebbles of brilliant white, and others with a yellowish frostwork. . . . Receding still further from the crater, the cavities become larger and the water cooler, causing changes in the brilliant colouring, and also in the formation of the deposits. They are often apparently as delicate as the down on the butterfly's wing, both in texture and colouring, yet are firm and solid beneath the tread. "The eruption of 'Old Faithful' begins with some preliminary splashes or spurts— from three to a dozen or more—which appear like abortive attempts of eruption. These continue for about four minutes, becoming more and more powerful, when they are followed by a rapid succession of jets, which escape with a roar, and soon attain the maximum height of 125 to 150 feet; clouds of steam rise at times to a height of 500 feet. In a few seconds after the maximum is attained the column dies down, with occasional vigorous spurts. The water eruption lasts from four to five minutes, and the steam period is indefinite."

This description, written with scientific precision, will help to give an idea of the sublime scenes to be witnessed on this basin. The geysers named "Giant," "Giantess," "Castle," and "Grand," are of far greater force than "Old Faithful," and not inferior in beauty, while the "Beehive," "Splendid," "Comet," and others are of almost equal importance. Add to these countless smaller manifestations, and hundreds of lovely pools studding the plain with spots of colour like the eyes of huge peacock-feathers, and labyrinths of delicately woven lace-like geyserite, glistening in the fierce sunlight like the webs of Brobdingnagian spiders, and we may figure the wondrous scene.

For ourselves, the time spent on this Upper Geyser Basin was thronged with intense excitement—the stupendous energies at work, the appalling beauties of the great fountains—*"belles à faire peur"* [beauties that frighten one]—the explosions, the vibrating floor, the fantastic unreality of the whole, under the furnace heat of the sun, caused a fever of the nerves, which in part returns in writing a memorial of it.

A basin upon the borders of Shoshone Lake, some twelve miles further south, is well worthy of a visit, and the more that in reaching it the Continental Divide must be crossed. In this direction, set in the midst of the forest, is the massive cone of pure white deposit of the Lone Star Geyser, of which we give an illustration. Of its frequent eruptions, rising to a height of 50 feet, the chipmunks and blue jays are usually the only spectators.

The Midway Geyser Basin, which we passed on our route southwards, is but two miles off, and, keeping on the west side of the Firehole River, vents and springs are to be seen throughout our ride thither. [The party was now returning northward toward Marshall's hotel.] It occupies the tongue of land between the Firehole and its tributary, Iron Spring Creek.[41] Here we do not seek, at present, for geysers, but are upon a land of great boiling springs—the Egeria, the Prismatic Pool, and the

"Caldron," alias the Excelsior Gulf [Excelsior Geyser], and "Hell's Half-Acre." [See Plates 20 and 21.]

The Western mind is elastic as to the application of names, especially in cases of Plutonian nomenclature, and thus it is difficult to localise the last name; some allege that the Prismatic Pool is the "Half-Acre"; others, indeed the majority, so denominate the whole weird plateau, oblivious of the fact that it occupies a space of a mile in length by a quarter-mile in width. Upon this space open two huge and consummately lovely boiling pools,[42] the "Turquoise," a deep, blue-tinted, almost square sheet of water, measuring 100 feet in diameter; and the greatest and most beautiful spring in the park, oval in form, and measuring 250 by 350 feet [75 by 100 meters], an area upon which every beauty of colour seems to gather, and which is well-named the "Prismatic Spring." Bounded by a delicate lip of purest white coral, supported by little terraces of coloured deposit, this fairy pool shows a shallow border of pale lemon and fawn colour. As the water deepens gradually it shows every tint of sea-green and blue, until in the profound central portion the deep Atlantic indigo hue is reached, a continuous gentle pulsation renders every tint shifting, while above hangs a bright canopy of steam, receiving, reflecting, refracting all the tints of the iris in never-ceasing movement [Plate 22]. This exquisite jewel is set in the midst of a mournful plain of ash-coloured deposit, about which shallow steaming streams meander, and from which mouldering logs of half-silicified pine protrude.

At a short distance, and in stern contrast to the beauty of this Spring, the awful Gulf of the Excelsior Geyser, now dormant, opens. It is

THE "LONE STAR" GEYSER

a chasm of rugged outline, measuring some **330 feet by 200 feet**. Here there has been no gradual formation of mound or cone, but the impetuous monster beneath has hurled up the strata bodily. The sides of the pit overhang, and many masses of rock are on the point of sinking into the abyss. At about twenty feet below, the boiling contents of the cauldron are in eternal tumult, and seem to threaten another of the stupendous eruptions which, down to 1881, used to shake the whole region, and change the Firehole River into a boiling flood of twice its normal volume. The

330 feet by 200 feet: Excelsior Geyser Crater actually measures about 300 by 250 feet (90 by 75 m).

seething waters now shake the neighbourhood of the pit with constant vibrations, and huge columns of steam arise to hundreds of feet, sweeping all around the awful hollow in suffocating masses, through which, now and again, a glimpse of the dark blue scalding waves may be caught, or, at the opening, where the overflow descends to the river, which we engrave, a clearer view may be obtained by the observer, screened from the hot vapours by the rocks of the slope. After the earthquake which devastated Charleston, this geyser is said to have been again in activity.[43]

We return to the fork of the Firehole to Marshall's hotel, glad to regain the shelter of a house. We do all the damage we can with that hateful implement the nickel-plated knife, the bane of American travel, to the "grub-pile" of elk and moose meat with various "fixings" which is laid before us, and drink our tea thankfully. A hint of that unbelief in the reality of "wild meat" which we have previously expressed, brings our host over to us with a face of great solemnity, he beckons us out, and taking us to a young forked pine before the house, he indicates, with a dramatic gesture, a moose skull fixed in the cleft. "That," he said, "is the head of the moose off of which you have had your supper." It was evening, the wind sighed among the pines, and as we gazed reverentially upon the relic, one of the empty eye-sockets became slowly obscured by what appeared to be, nay, certainly was, an eyelid, and a wink of great impressiveness was materialised by some sarcastic spirit.

We turned and visited the log-hut beside the hotel, upon a beam of which appeared the word "Saloon." Leaning against the bar stood a hunter, tall, with a head and frame not unlike the great Abraham Lincoln, King of Men [Plate 24]. He was picturesque, in rough shirt, leathers, sombrero, and belt of cartridges. At his elbow were the two little glasses necessary in the exhibition of "Old Bourbon"; they were empty—one usually sees them so. One glass is placed before the patient filled with whiskey, the other with water. The former liquid instantly disappears, and is closely followed by the latter. Thus, the patient is considered to sustain the most exhilarating form of shock with the least constitutional disturbance.

Returning to the heat of the stove in the hall, we found a representative group of all sorts and conditions of men, prospectors, "pilgrims," "tender-feet" and "rustlers" from the district, an American and an English professor, a lady novelist, etc., such as meet in these places [Plate 15]. The travellers discuss routes, hear of the glories of the places they have missed seeing from the lips of those who have seen them, and listen with due amazement to the stories of "buffler" and "bar" which the denizens of the Yellowstone region can "sling" on small provocation—some true, even if amazing, others evidently "manufactured out of whole cloth," as some person of little faith may delicately express his sense of doubt. Or, again, the company may smoke all the evening in that American perfection of silence that the comparatively garrulous Britisher may emulate, but never equal.

When leaving the Fork of the Firehole River for the eastern portion of the Park, the traveller leaves the greater areas of volcanic activity, and has before him as principal objects wonders of other character: the greatest Alpine lake in the world, the extraordinary course of the issuant stream, pouring over precipices, carving out gorges of enormous magnitude, and placing before the eye, in the course of only thirty miles, a succession of scenes so varied, so grand, and in such dramatic sequence of silver lake, rich vale, thundering fall, stupendous cliff, and appalling ravine as must live in every traveller's mind as one of the grandest spectacles of the

HAYDEN VALLEY AND RIVER YELLOWSTONE

world; one which to many seems to belittle even the wonders of the western portion of the region.

Riding twenty miles eastward from Henderson's [traveling on today's Mary Mountain Trail], by hot pools, through glade and forest, and passing the beautiful little St. Mary's Lake,[44] on the divide between the Yellowstone and the Madison, at an elevation of 8,000 feet above the sea, the road branches north and south. Following the latter through the peaceful scenery of wood and mead in Hayden's Valley, beside the broad Yellowstone River, a glimpse of which will be found among our illustrations, a reminder of our wanderings on the other side of the Park is reached at the Mud Geysers. Of these the "Giant's Caldron," a veritable Malebolge, is the most remarkable.[45]

Mr. C. T. Whitmell [who visited Yellowstone in 1883], in an elaborate paper read before

ON THE SHORES OF THE YELLOWSTONE LAKE

the Cardiff Naturalists' Society, thus describes it: "Thirty feet across, as many deep, and narrowing as it descends, it presents a yawning crater, in which the boiling slate-coloured mud rises and falls with a deep rumbling sound. After the paste

"SULPHUR MOUNTAIN" AND PLUNGING POOL

is sucked back into the orifice, there comes a jarring noise as of some explosion, and out surges again the horrid mixture, flinging its heavy spray against the walls of the crater, which is sometimes filled nearly to the top, steam meanwhile escaping in large volumes. There is something very alluring, and yet very horrible, in the sight."[46]

A few miles more, and the foot of the Yellowstone Lake is reached—an inland sea of 150 square miles area, of bluish-green water, clear, sweet, and pure, surrounded by forest, above which stand the snow peaks of the great Yellowstone range. Our illustration shows Mount Sheridan. Hot springs and pools of great beauty stud the shore at several points, and there are minor sights of interest, as the Natural Arch, etc.; but little is really known to travellers of the **300 miles** of coastline,

300 miles: The very irregular shoreline actually measures about 140 miles (225 km).

and to young Englishmen fond of adventure, nothing could be much pleasanter than to float their canoes upon this beautiful sea and explore its inlets.

Returning along the Yellowstone river, the fork of the road is soon reached near Crater, or Sulphur Hills, and we are en route for the Great Falls and Grand Painted Cañon of the Yellowstone.

Sulphur Hill, which we illustrate, is one of a group of detached mounds of about 150 feet in height, composed of silica and sulphur, probably deposited by a spring, of which the crater remains.[47] The chief centre of activity now is the Yellow Sulphur Pool at the base—a very beautiful emerald boiling pool, which ever and anon gushes to the height of five or six feet. Its basin is a fantastic mass of delicate yellow sulphur crystals, which overarch the pool, rendering the ground around unsafe, as the ponies well know, and will on no account approach too near the edge.

On through beautiful park and woodland, and the road soon again follows the course of the river, overshadowed by fine pine and various deciduous trees. We are near the Upper Falls. The river, after its fourteen miles of dalliance among the woods and meadows, narrows its stream to the opening of a pine-clad ravine, then breaks into a rapid, and falling over a ledge of 150 feet [109 feet (33 meters)], seems to take a moment's respite in the dark-green pool at the foot of the Fall, under the shadow of the dark rocks and pines. Rushing hence, it again breaks into white foam down a rapid, then gathering into a clear mass of glassy olive-green water, flowing with extreme swiftness, the river, 100 feet wide, flings itself over its "Great Fall" of 350 feet [308 feet, Plate 25]. At the edge there is a flash of diamond and emerald, then the whole descending surface breaks into a tissue of frosted silver, and with a tremendous roar, re-echoed from the huge cliffs of the Cañon, becomes mixed with the iridescent cloud of spray which fills the hollow.

From the "Great Fall" the river hurries down the descending floor of the "Great Painted Cañon" for a mile and a half, amid a scene of the strangest beauty. The cliffs that rise beside the Fall, and which have been cut by the river, have a height of 800 feet, and, by rising of the edges and descent of the floor, this is increased, until at the distance mentioned, the Cañon is 1100 feet. Upon this spot it would seem that the "Prince of the Power of the Air" determined to excavate and carve his grandest palace.

Through white and pink and yellow strata of geyserites and sandstones the strenuous river bit its way, then the heat of the summer blistered and crumbled the cliffs, rivers of rain and melting snow fluted and moulded them, and the winter frost put its expansive fingers into every crevice, and dragged down huge morsels.[48] But under and through the softer rocks were foundations and dykes of adamantine lavas, which were slow to carve, and which stand as obelisks of the temple. Now, standing beside the fall, we see the work accomplished, yet still in progress. As seen in our coloured illustration [Plate 27; see also Plate 26], the view from

this point is scenic in the extreme, the cliffs, steep declivities, and buttressed slopes stand arid, only a few pines finding foothold here and there. The rocks, black, brown, ochre, yellow, white, pink, are carved into strange forms, and in the midst rises one great tower of blood-red, so placed as to accent the pictorial effect, to enhance which still more, the summit has been made a resting-place by **eagles** which hover round. At "Point Lookout," a mile below the western side of the Fall, the Cañon is crowned by masses of white rock, and the view looking up and shut in by the cliffs between which the Falls plunge is of equally extraordinary character. We engrave a view from one of Jay Haynes's grand photographs. Masses of rock, almost white, form the foreground, below which oblique descents show very varied tints from pink to brown, and the pyramidal rock, stained red by iron, stands out prominently. We can hardly, at first, appreciate the enormous depth of 1100 feet into which we gaze, but the whole Cañon seems to widen and deepen momently and gives us a startled sensation as if the huge chasm were yawning slowly open before our eyes. The contrast between the purity and variety of the colours in the Cañon, and the dark green stretch of forest which covers the upland landscape seen beyond the Fall, gives to the whole an aspect of strangeness, to which the magnificent falling sheet of water, with its cloud of spray, and the winding emerald and blue line of the river flowing so far below, add elements of beauty.

eagles: The birds that most commonly nest in Yellowstone's Grand Canyon are ospreys.

Around "Point Lookout" the river bends, and the Cañon, painted no more, becomes narrow, its walls, in parts, almost vertical, and among its cliffs of darkest grey and brown there are scenes of awful grandeur.

From the Great Falls, where there is a tent hotel, now, perhaps, replaced by a **building**, a trail runs north along the Great Cañon by Mount Washburn, the summit of which, 10,300 feet high, easily reached, affords a magnificent panoramic view [10,243 feet (3,122 meters); see the Earl of Dunraven's description on page 53]. The trail descends into Pleasant Valley, to a log house, where the hospitality of a hunter named Yancey

may be proved, and one may, on occasion, have ocular demonstration of the cervine origin of the elk steak.

Tower Falls, upon Tower Creek, a tributary of the Yellowstone, may be seen en route from Yancey's to Mammoth Hot Springs, a ride of twenty-seven miles. A narrow, but powerful stream, confined between two lofty columns of worn volcanic breccia, plunges 130 feet unbroken into a narrow, darksome gorge among fantastic towers and pinnacles of rock.

Within a few miles of the Mammoth Hot Springs the Gardiner River is again struck near the Gardiner Falls [on Lava Creek, now called Undine Falls], one of the minor but very picturesque sights of the region.

Five miles more and we draw rein once again on the plateau before the Springs Hotel, and luxuriate in all the resources of civilisation, having completed the usual "tour" of the Yellowstone National Park—the American Wonderland.

——And? Yes, one's face is blistered with the fierce noons; one is a little stiff from the freezing nights, slightly bruised by the dislocating gait of the faithful "cayuse." One has had enough of rice and prunes under canvas and of cold meat in the "corrals"; but where are there brighter skies and blither air? That it has been given to one to see the beauty, the grandeur, and terror of this region of "Wonder-beauty" before the tourists troop through it in unbroken procession, laus Deo.

building: The first permanent Canyon Hotel did not open until 1890, six years after Thomas's visit.

Our engravings are from sketches by our artist Mr. T. H. Thomas, and photographs, that of Mrs. Finch's Camp by Mr. Edgar Sollas, 32, King Henry's Road, N.W., "Bassett's Stage," by Mr. R. G. Brooks, of St. Helen's. The Great Falls, Falls of the Gibbon, and Grand Cañon of the Yellowstone are from the Mammoth Series of Mr. F. Jay Haynes, official photographer to the Northern Pacific Railway, D.T., and the Formation at Periodical Lake and "Lone Star" Geyser are by Mr. Ingersoll, St. Paul, Minn.

We are indebted for the loan of the drawing from which our coloured illustration [of the Great Falls, not reproduced in this volume] is reproduced to Mr. C. T. Whitmell, M.A., of Cardiff.

NOTES

1. Whitmell, "American Wonderland," 77.
2. Whitmell, "American Wonderland," 96.
3. Thomas, "Yellowstone Park Illustrated," *Graphic*, 15/– 65 and 189–96, August 11, 1888, and August 18, 1888, respectively.
4. Paintings by Thomas H. Thomas reproduced in this volume are from the archives and by permission of the National Museum of Wales, Cardiff.
5. Whitmell, "American Wonderland," 78.
6. National Museum of Wales article about Thomas: http://www.museumwales.ac.uk/articles/2007-09-20/The-unique-prints-and-drawings-of-T-H-Thomas/, accessed December 7, 2015.
7. Thomas was then in Manitoba, Canada, on the U.S. border. In Gretna Green, Scotland, beginning in 1753, boys could marry at age fourteen and girls at twelve without parental consent. Thomas is pointing out the bliss but potential tragedy of such early marriage.
8. The Northern Pacific Railroad (as it was called in 1884) was reorganized in 1896 after a bankruptcy under the name Northern Pacific Railway. Waite, *Yellowstone by Train*, 147n1.
9. U.S. time zones became necessary only after completion of the transcontinental railroad in 1869. Thomas's puzzlement about Central and Mountain time is not surprising, since time zones had only been adopted by U.S. and Canadian railroads in November 1883, the year before Thomas's visit.
10. This area east of Livingston is truly a gateway where the vast plains along the Yellowstone River all the way through Montana give way to views of mountains to the north and south. See also the painting by Albert Hencke in the article by Lenz (page 168). Clarks Fork actually enters the Yellowstone River nearly one hundred miles east of here.
11. Colonel Starbottle was the hero of at least two Bret Harte stories about a Southern gentleman lawyer in the Northern California of the 1860s and his murderer client.
12. Hayden, to whom Thomas gives credit for the idea of setting aside Yellowstone, was only one of the several men who explored the area in 1870 and 1871 and subsequently urged Congress to establish the national park.
13. William Clagett, as correctly spelled, was newly elected as delegate from Montana Territory to the House of Representatives in 1871 and thus was probably not the primary author of the park bill but had considerable help from others in its drafting and passage. Bartlett, *Nature's Yellowstone*, 198, 201.
14. The Taber Prang Art Company of Boston pioneered the process of chromolithography in the United States, the only process available for bulk printing of multicolored pictures until about the 1930s. Saunders, *Glimpses of Wonderland*, 21.
15. Buffalo Bill (William Cody) toured nationally and then internationally with his Wild West show for over thirty years beginning in 1883. Real cowboys riding bucking broncos were a part of the show.
16. Numerous references to the potential value of Mammoth Springs for therapeutic uses occur in late nineteenth-century writings about Yellowstone, but no concessionaire took up the challenge of establishing a sanatorium.
17. Thomas observed plants at Mammoth similar to Old World ones he knew: wormwood is a species of *Artemisia*, as is the American sagebrush, and thuja bush is in the cypress family, as is Mammoth's juniper.
18. Like many early observers, Thomas was incorrect in calling Liberty Cap and Devil's Thumb extinct geysers and saying that the material was geyserite (silicon

dioxide). He confesses later (in part 2) that he has his information from a guidebook. The Mammoth Terraces actually have no geysers, active or extinct, because the spring water is not hot enough. The terraces are made of travertine (calcium carbonate), which not only builds formations much faster but is more friable than geyserite.

19. The large Pink and White Terraces on the North Island of New Zealand at Lake Rotomahana were destroyed in a volcanic eruption that killed at least 108 people in June 1886; this occurred between Thomas's visit to Yellowstone and the appearance of his article. The terraces "were completely blown away by the explosive Mt. Tarawera–Rotomahana–Waimangu volcanic eruptions." And, in the aftermath, "new and equally fascinating thermal features were formed" (Bryan, *Geysers of Yellowstone*, 437). The Mammoth Terraces are not the largest extant ones in the world; since Roman times, if not before, a vast area at Turkey's Pamukkale (meaning "cotton castle") has been building up similar terraces.

20. The engraving labeled "Formation at Periodical Lake" on page 112 shows the center of the east edge of Main Terrace. Although that name is no longer used, it describes perfectly the cyclical nature of Mammoth's hot springs (Whittlesey, *Wonderland Nomenclature*, 1028).

21. Barbédienne was a foundry in Paris that cast excellent bronze sculptures.

22. Tourists were taken into this cavity, usually called Devil's Kitchen, for many years. Park guide George L. Henderson had inserted a ladder into the cavity earlier in the summer of 1884. Devil's Kitchen was closed in 1939, when the Park Service realized that the gases that killed many small birds and rodents were unhealthy for humans as well. See Anne Bosworth Greene's experience at Devil's Kitchen, pages 263–65. This type of natural cavity is called a solution cave, according to geologist Keith Bargar (Bargar, *Geology and Thermal History . . . Mammoth*, 27).

23. Narrow Gauge Terrace (pictured on page 137) is today described as a fissure ridge. Thomas's next paragraph refers to the descent into Devil's Kitchen (his "Mammoth Cave"). The opening at the top of Narrow Gauge is only a crack.

24. Squirrel Springs is a feature under the ridge of the same name at the far southwestern edge of the terrace area near today's Snow Pass Trail.

25. Both the least chipmunks and the golden-mantled ground squirrels of Yellowstone have stripes on their bodies, but the chipmunks are smaller and also have stripes on their cheeks.

26. The *Shorter Oxford English Dictionary*, 1955 edition, gives us this information about a rustler: "U.S. a. An energetic or bustling man, 1872. b. A cattle-thief, 1882." Which definition did Thomas use in 1884?

27. Pulpit Terrace, mentioned and pictured in many early accounts, disintegrated and is no longer recognizable, although its former location is known.

28. Thomas is referring to the law that had just passed in March 1884 by the Wyoming legislature to place the portion of the park's land that lay within Wyoming Territory under that territory's jurisdiction. Law enforcement until then had been very lax and disorganized, as the incident related here illustrates.

29. It should be noted that, in spite of the sermon in this paragraph, Thomas admitted to picking up arrowheads near Boiling River—three miles inside the park's boundary—(see page 102 and Plate 2) and that his friend Charles T. Whitmell, in his lecture to the Cardiff Naturalists' Society, mentions Thomas's "specimens" being displayed along with the lecture. The park's Superintendent Philetus W. Norris (from 1877 to 1882) himself sent specimens to Washington, one of which is still displayed in the Smithsonian National Museum of Natural History.

30. Thomas refers here to Kabibonokka, one of the four wind-gods in American Indian mythology (possibly Ojibway or Algonquin) mentioned in Longfellow's "Song of Hiawatha," published in 1855. However, Kabibonokka was the god of the north wind, not of the west. Thor was the Norse god of thunder.

31. Beaver Lake filled with sediment over the decades when beaver became scarce in Yellowstone; it is now just a swampy area.

32. The road built in 1878—now a poorly maintained backcountry trail—went southeast after passing Beaver Lake, skirted Lake of the Woods, and followed Solfatara Creek nearly to Norris Geyser Basin. Today's road takes a more westerly route to Norris, crossing the drainage divide at Twin Lakes.

33. This line comes from English actor and playwright Samuel Foote's nonsense prose, "The Great Panjandrum" (1755), written to test a rival actor's claim that he could memorize any text at a single reading: "So she went into the garden / to cut a cabbage-leaf / to make an apple-pie: / and at the same time / a great she-bear, coming down the street, / pops its head into the shop. / What! No soap? / So he died, and she very imprudently married the Barber; / and there were present / the Picninnies, and the Joblillies, / and the Garyulies, / and the great Panjandrum himself, / with the little round button at top; / and they all fell to playing the game of catch-as-catch-can, / till the gunpowder ran out at the heels of their boots."

34. Minute Man (now simply Minute) Geyser was a popular feature, and today's walkway near it was the main road in Thomas's time. However, the geyser was severely vandalized and, as a result, is not very interesting today.

35. The road Thomas took cut southwest from the Gibbon River to the Firehole River and did not go through Madison Junction and turn south as it does now.

36. It is hard to understand Thomas's description of hotels in the area without some knowledge of the human history of the junction of the Firehole River and Nez Perce Creek. The tent-hotel mentioned at the beginning of Thomas's paragraph was erected earlier in the summer of 1884 on the north bank of Nez Perce Creek by Carroll T. Hobart, General Manager of the Yellowstone National Park Improvement Company, purposely competing with Marshall's Hotel.
Neither of Marshall's Hotels was on "a narrow island." In 1880 G. W. Marshall built the first hotel in Lower Geyser Basin on the west side of the Firehole River. In 1884, the year of Thomas's visit, Marshall and George G. Henderson built another hotel on the river's east or right bank, usually called the Marshall House; this second hotel was on the strip of land that falls between the Firehole River and Nez Perce Creek, which Thomas took for an island. By the time his article was published, the second hotel had been transferred to Henderson and his new partner, Henry E. Klamer (Whittlesey, "Marshall's Hotel," 49; Whittlesey, "Hotels on the Firehole," 14–17).

37. The roads to the east and west are no longer there: Bassett's stage route, built under Superintendent Philetus W. Norris and so steep it was sometimes called the Norris Slide, used to pass over the Madison Plateau from the Madison River to the Firehole River and is not now maintained, even as a trail. The nineteenth-century road running east to Yellowstone Lake over Mary Mountain is now a maintained trail. The six Bassett brothers drove stagecoaches for park visitors from the Utah and Northern Railroad line that ran west of Yellowstone from the late 1870s to about the mid 1880s.

38. It was more than four miles from Midway Geyser Basin to the northern edge of the Upper Geyser Basin by the 1880s road, part of which is now the trail from Biscuit Basin to Morning Glory Pool.

39. The Earl of Dunraven's description of an eruption of Castle Geyser is in Wyndham-Quin, *Great Divide*, 265–68. The approximate height of Castle's cone is twelve feet (3.7 meters). But vandals among the early visitors removed large amounts of beautiful and ornate geyserite incrustations from the geyser formations, so it may have been higher at one time.

40. The Old Faithful Geyser cone and eruption descriptions are from Lt. Gustavus C. Doane's journal, cited in Hayden, *Twelfth Annual Report*, 221.

41. Iron Spring Creek joins the Firehole River (as does the Little Firehole River) at Biscuit Basin (two miles from Old Faithful), not at Midway Geyser Basin. However, the thermal features that Thomas names are at Midway.

42. Midway Geyser Basin has a third boiling pool. West of Turquoise Spring is Opal Pool, which can be beautiful and can even erupt as a geyser but occasionally drains completely. Opal may have had no water or only tepid water at the time Thomas observed two features besides Excelsior Geyser.

43. A strong earthquake destroyed much of the city of Charleston, South Carolina, in August 1886. Earthquakes at a considerable distance from Yellowstone have strongly affected geyser eruptions, but there is no documentation of Excelsior erupting in 1886, although many eruptions occurred in 1881, 1882, and 1888. Thomas seems to be repeating a rumor he had heard. ("Reports to the contrary notwithstanding, there were no eruptions of Excelsior 1883 through 1887." Whittlesey, *Wonderland Nomenclature*, "Excelsior," 360.)

44. Mary Lake, a small lake along the former road (now the Mary Mountain Trail) was actually named in 1873 for a Miss Clark, "a young lady from Chicago, with vocal gifts that all admired," according to the author

of *Rambles in Wonderland*, written by a member of her touring party, the Rev. Edwin J. Stanley.

45. Giant's or Devil's Caldron, so named by Hayden's 1872 expedition party, is now called Mud Volcano. Thomas probably recalled the word *malebolge*, literally "an evil cavern or ditch," from Dante's *Inferno*, where it is the name for the eighth circle of Hell.

46. Whitmell, "American Wonderland," 86.

47. Some confusion exists over the names Sulphur Hill and Sulphur Mountain in many early writings. The approved name of the area west of the Yellowstone River in Hayden Valley is Sulphur Mountain, although the name Crater Hills is often used for it. Thomas's Yellow Sulphur Pool is now called Crater Hills Geyser. Whittlesey, *Wonderland Nomenclature*, "Sulphur Mountain," 1210.

48. Thomas describes erosional processes that no doubt play a part in creating this and other canyons, but the major process that cut the Grand Canyon of the Yellowstone is now known to be the sudden release of floodwaters from melting glacial lakes.

Adventure at Norris Geyser Basin

George L. Henderson, *National Park Manual*, pp. 7–8, 1888

George L. Henderson "was the acknowledged expert in his day on Yellowstone, and was probably the first person to care a great deal about factual accuracy and effective communication in his speeches to park visitors"—thus, the first "park interpreter."[1] Born in Scotland about 1828, Henderson emigrated to the United States at the age of eleven. He and his Scottish wife lived in Iowa but divorced, and three years later he brought his four daughters and one son to Yellowstone, where he served as assistant superintendent from 1882 to 1885. For nearly twenty years he guided tourists through the park, gave classical names to many features that are retained to this day, built and ran the Cottage Hotel at Mammoth, wrote articles for the *Livingston Enterprise*, and garnered praise from numerous visitors for his knowledge and communications skills. After 1891 he wintered in Chula Vista, California, but still summered in Yellowstone. Henderson died in 1905.

*B*eyond the Spiteful [Vixen Geyser in Back Basin] and separated from her by a belt of pines are the Norris Sinks, where my unfortunate animal getting into the unfathomable slime slowly sinks, every effort to extricate itself but adding to the certainty of more quickly reaching the end. Here the writer on one occasion was driving from the Monarch[2] in a heavy shower, the whole basin being veiled in dense fog.

My companions were Dr. and Mrs. J. W. Joyce of Cincinnati and Miss Lambie of St. Paul. I took the wrong side of the pine ridge and to my consternation found myself entering the sinks. Old Dan, one of the best animals that wore a collar in human service, sank to his knees and, with a groan of despair, lay over on his right side. The other [horse] had as yet good footing, but was so terrified that his restless motion was gradually working the horrid mud underneath into soft mush. I sprang from the carriage and held the fallen horse firmly to prevent all ineffectual struggles. The two ladies were soon on safe ground among the trees and the doctor, with a coolness that did him credit, managed to loosen the tugs and clear the harness.

The nigh horse was instantly out of danger. In the meantime I had sunk to the knees and knew that when the next thin crust gave way a bottomless abyss was all that I could expect. The doctor held the tongue aloft and my chief danger now was in being caught by Old Dan when he should make his leap for life. The dumb brute seemed to have reasoned it all out. With a cautious movement he raised his head and seeing where Dave [the other horse] stood he wisely aimed for that locality, and in doing so resorted to the only possible way to save me, for had he made a single forward movement of two feet we would have inevitably disappeared and perished together. The crust that held me up had also sustained the fore part of his body and with a movement impossible to describe, he crawled a few feet on his knees where, finding the substance firm, he was able to drag his hind legs out of the slime, making a snoring sound as the ooze flowed into the space made by his body.

There was joy indeed and a clapping of hands as the noble beast stood once more on solid footing. All this transpired so quickly that it was impossible to realize how little time it had taken. With a picket rope attached to the hind axle the carriage was extricated and we were soon standing beside the Vixen. One of the braces of the tongue was bent so that the wood had opened, revealing a fibre so tough that a knot might have been tied on each as if they had been linen threads. Such was the material used in the Quincy carriages that are so famous wherever used. These bent threads held together until we reached the forks of the Firehole, where an iron patch was put on and the bend forced back to its normal position. Old Dan could never be induced to pass the ridge again that separated the VIXEN from the SINKS.

1. Whittlesey, *Storytelling in Yellowstone*, 121. For a biography of Henderson, see chapter 9 of Whittlesey's book.
2. A large and popular geyser in early Yellowstone days, located in Back Basin at Norris, Monarch Geyser has been dormant since 1913, but Vixen Geyser still erupts frequently.

Feats of an avid cyclist

Rapid transit of some kind . . . will reverse the present order of having to ride in a continuous cloud of dust over a road so rutted and cut up by ten thousand wheels that if you have a weak spot in any part of the vertebral column the jerks will find it out.
Park guide George L. Henderson,
Yellowstone Park: Past, Present, and Future, 1891, p. 12

Frank D. Lenz's account of cycling through Yellowstone in 1892 is only a small part of his extensive report of a planned solo world bicycle tour. Installments of his report appeared in *Outing* magazine every month from August 1892 through July 1896.[1]

Lenz set out on his trip on June 4, 1892, leaving from New York City, where, as he wrote, people "crowded around me in such numbers that I found it impossible to mount my wheel, much less make the start."[2] Before reaching Yellowstone in late August, he had cycled some 1,700 miles. When possible, he followed wagon roads or railroad tracks—even bumping over the ties at times. In North Dakota's Badlands, cactus needles punctured both his tires. Nearing Montana, he was invited to spend a day at the Eaton Brothers' ranch,[3] where he rode a horse but did not enjoy the jolting, apparently finding bicycle riding to be smoother.

Frank D. Lenz and his safety bicycle (courtesy of Archives and Special Collections, Mansfield Library, University of Montana: 11926)

A few days later Lenz rode along the Yellowstone River toward Yellowstone Park. He passed through the town of Billings, still a departure point for tours of Yellowstone—and dear to the heart of this anthologist, who lived her first eighteen years there.

It is not surprising that Lenz makes quite a few errors of geography while whizzing through the park in five days, since he could not have had time to take many notes. He did not allow himself to tarry in the geyser basins, and his tour included only the road segments from Gardiner to Norris and what is now called the Southern Loop of the Grand Loop Road. The present segments between Canyon and Tower junctions and between Tower and Mammoth Hot Springs were not yet completed.

Lenz was not the first man to tour Yellowstone by bicycle. W. O. Owen and two other members of the Laramie Bicycle Club claimed that honor in an account appearing in the June 1891 issue of *Outing* and reproduced in Paul Schullery's collection, *Old Yellowstone Days*.

Lenz must have been in superb physical shape. He mentions the abysmal condition of the roads and acknowledges late in his account that the ride through Yellowstone was not a pleasant one. Of two places with elevation changes of around one thousand feet, he mentions only that one is "a continuous up-grade and the road very dusty" and the other has "heavy sand and continual up-grade." Another cyclist, Lyman B. Glover, detailed his complaints about Yellowstone's roads in 1896:

> The mountain road laid with obsidian sand, filled in with powdered geyserite, plowed into impassable furrows by the wheels of the stagecoach and the hunter's outfit, is a proposition calculated to make the stoutest heart quail. Upon such a footing the cyclist can neither ride up nor down hill. The shifting obsidian sand skews his wheel about and the gaping precipice at the side contents him to walk laboriously up or down the steep incline, happy if a firmer interval of bench land permits the luxury of riding for a little while.[4]

If Lenz made rather a large number of factual errors in his telegraphed reports, it is not surprising. He could not have carried many maps or guidebooks, nor could he connect to the Internet!

Frank Lenz entered history—or at least the part now preserved in the *New York Times* archives—when, as captain of the Allegheny Cyclers of Pittsburgh, he cycled to New Orleans in 1891. The next year, he headed west alone, launched on what was to become more than fourteen thousand miles of a world tour "a-wheel," with *Outing* magazine and the Victor Bicycle Company sponsoring his tour.[5] Lenz managed to send reports from telegraph stations, even from remotest China and Persia, and *Outing* continued publishing his story just as he had sent it.

By autumn 1896 Lenz was missing in Asiatic Turkey, but *Outing's* publisher kept up hopeful reports through January 1897. The *New York Times* became interested in what had happened to him and printed reports over a period of eighteen months that varied in their details as to place, nationality, and number of assailants. One story had it that "he had been seen by two Turkish soldiers riding along an Armenian road on his machine, and a dispute arose between them as to whether the strange object was man or devil. To settle the controversy they fired at the cyclist and he fell from his wheel." Another: "The natives thought his wheel was of silver, and murdered him and broke up his bicycle and divided the different parts." It was finally determined that Lenz was indeed murdered in rural Turkey. Compared to his tragic end, his difficulties riding through Montana and Yellowstone were minor!

Lenz's World Tour Awheel

1893

born Philadelphia, Pennsylvania, 1868 • died Turkey, 1896

From Miles City to Yellowstone Park

I struck the Valley of the Yellowstone at Glendon.[6] Had not this valley become famous as the gateway to the wonders of our great National Park, it would to all time be memorable for its associations. The arena in which was worked out what was probably the last act in the great drama that brought the land of the red man under the developing influences of civilization, the battlefields and resting-places of Custer and many of his gallant band, the region which Sitting Bull fired, like Moscow,[7] but failed to hold, must ever touch the chords of sentiment and patriotism. Nor, indeed, does the fame of the Valley of the Yellowstone rest either upon the great marvel-land to which it leads or its historic associations; for it bears, in the great railroad which threads its sinuous course, the towns which dot its river, and the myriad cattle which it sustains, evidences of the enterprise and industry of our nation.

Who would think, standing beneath the shadow of the handsome court-house of Miles City, surrounded by its schools, bank and hotels, that a few years ago all its great surrounding pastures and rich valleys were the home of the once countless buffalo, and that from the ashes of the destruction of that traffic Miles City should rise, phoenix-like, to become probably the greatest cattle center in the world. It is named after General Miles, whose brilliant campaign in 1877 against the Nez Percés opened up so much of the valley to settlement. He built Fort Keogh, about two miles and a half west of here. I visited the Fort in company with Claude U. Potter as escort. It is the most important post in the Northwest, is delightfully situated, and affords ample accommodation to about one thousand officers and men. An excellent brass band furnishes music, and on certain evenings in the week gives concerts.

Miles City, like all Western cities however remote, has its bicycle club. Fifteen wheelmen, most entertaining, make a thoroughly sociable club.

On the morning of August 17th I had my wheel nicely cleaned to continue the journey West along the banks of Yellowstone River. The wind was blowing with terrific force, and when I reached the ferry, where I intended to cross, the wife of the ferryman informed me that the wind was too strong to risk the boat across. I sat down and patiently waited for an hour for the wind to subside. At last a lull came on, and I was soon shoving my machine up a steep and deep gravel road to the top of the hill on the north bank; once the top reached, the wind fairly whistled from the west. The headwind I rode against for thirty-eight miles at Leamington, Canada, along the north shore of Lake Erie, was steady, but to-day's wind came in tremendous puffs, carrying me clear off the road, and my eyes kept filling with dust. Many miles of this would surely exhaust any wheelman.

The first ranch that hove in sight I stopped at, tired out, only *ten miles west of Miles City* [italics original]. The occupant was a bachelor, cooking, sleeping and living in one room. But E. C. Stoneing was a hospitable man, and had lived here for years. He was formerly a government scout and courier, and at one time was companion to Buffalo Bill. Many interesting stories he told as the wind blew outside, until sundown. The old fellow kindly gave me his bed, while he slept on the floor. The coarse straw in the mattress and pillow kept working through the muslin during the night, annoying me not a little, but I was also kept awake by the coyotes howling dismally without.

Arising early, I partook that morning of a plain breakfast, prepared by the old man, and then started west at 7:30. The air was cool and calm. The road continues following in sight of the Yellowstone River. The hard wind the day before had blown the dust and sand off the road. The bearing of the wheel now being cleaned, it seemed to run easily. I quickly passed ranches, with herds of horses and cattle, which usually stampeded off at sight of me. By noon I reached Cold Spring Sheep Ranch, and by sundown Rancher P. O.,

eighty miles for the day. The road was mostly level and good riding—only three hills in the entire stretch. Up these the roads followed the gravel beds of dried-up streams, which made it impossible to ride.

The road next day improved to Junction City, a small village on the Yellowstone. Here I ferried across the river to the Crow Indian reservation, as usual waiting an hour for the ferryman. The Crows are good-natured Indians, and have always been the best of friends with the whites. They ford the Yellowstone on their horses, and daily come to settlements on the north side of the river. Some of them make good farmers, raising cattle and horses in large numbers. I met an old buck and his squaw, who motioned to me to stop, to enable them to examine the wheel more closely; and I don't know what feature of it astonished them most. The spring fork saddle, the adjustable gearing and the brake specially interested the buck, and I shall never forget the blank astonishment of these red people when I took out the pump and proceeded to pump up. "The Victor" fairly raised the phlegm of the buck, and that is an achievement indeed; it takes something akin to the marvelous to do that.

The road now follows along the N. P. R. R. [Northern Pacific Railroad] through the reservation, sometimes running inside the fence, along the track; at other times through some fenced ranges, making it quite frequently necessary to let down poles and open gates. At Bull Mountain the road winds along some cliffs, one of the most picturesque spots on the Yellowstone River. The hills or buttes are now sparsely covered with small pines, showing that the long prairie would soon end.

From Bull Mountain to Pompey's Pillar is another flat stretch. Pompey's Pillar, a mass of yellow sandstone rising abruptly to a height of 400 feet, and with its base covering nearly an acre of ground, has quite an interesting history. Capt. Meriwether Lewis and Capt. Wm. Clark, U.S.A., on their three years' exploration of this territory for the government in 1804–1807, then known as the "Louisiana purchase," because it was acquired of Napoleon Bonaparte by payment of $15,000,000, stopped here. Their colored cook, named Pompey, died while at this point and was buried on the top of this rock, which, curiously enough, is covered with quite a deep soil. This rock has a very striking appearance, looking at a distance like a huge pillar. The inscription and date (July 25, 1806) still remain.[8]

The sun was just setting as I wheeled up to the Huntley section-house for the night. The road next morning started up a hill four miles long. From the top I had a splendid view of the valley. A spur of the Rockies could be faintly seen in the distance, fifty miles away. A short distance farther the road joins the Fort Custer trail to Billings, a town just ten years old and containing already a population of 3,000 souls. It is a supply town for a radius of about 100 miles, including valuable mines, and is quite a wool market.

From Billings west the road is on the north side of the Yellowstone again. The scenery now is all grandeur and beauty, such as we hope to get in wheeling through Switzerland. Through **Laurel Park City**, to within four miles of Stillwater, is level bottom, making excellent wheeling, although somewhat dusty—or rather it would be

excellent wheeling were it not for bridgeless irrigating ditches, which frequently cross the road and necessitate dismounting. Near Stillwater the road turns up a ravine, and a mile's walk up a steep hill and a terribly steep ride down the other side over layers of rock prepared my appetite for a good supper.

Next day I reached Big Timber, at the confluence of **Big Boulder and Big Lumber Creeks** with the Yellowstone. Continuing along the Yellowstone River, the valley road is excellent to Merrill. To keep the valley it is necessary to cross over the river on the railroad bridge to Reed's Point section-house. From here Crazy Mountains can be distinctly seen in the distance, thirty miles away, the tops partly covered with snow. They became more and more distinct from Greycliff to Big Timber on the Boulder River. This stream is well named. Round boulders of every size simply cover everything, including the town itself. But there is a wheelman even there. After riding 1,200 miles of dreary prairie this is like entering a new country. Mountains are visible within twenty miles of here—west and north and south. The riding next day to Livingston, through the valley of the gate of the mountains, was very good. In some places there were many loose stones, however, and within four miles of Livingston it was very stony until

Laurel and **Park City** are two separate towns west of Billings.

Big Boulder and Big Lumber Creeks: The Boulder River enters the Yellowstone from the south, and Big Timber Creek enters it from the north at the town of Big Timber, Montana.

the Yellowstone was crossed into town. Livingston, although only ten years old, is a very thriving town. It is situated at the base of the mountains, 4,600 feet above the sea-level.

Two wheelmen accompanied me from Livingston to the first cañon. The wind was blowing through here at a tremendous rate against us. I had so far been riding my wheel geared to fifty-four inches, but I had my wheel arranged to gear down to forty-five inches for mountainous country. The strong wind compelled me to change it. Bidding the Livingston wheelmen good-by, I continued on a good road down the valley through the mountains along the Yellowstone River. Several ranchmen have settled in this happy valley [Paradise Valley], where the soil is good for raising crops and cattle, and the mountain scenery changes at every bend in the river. Emigrant is a small hamlet twenty-four miles from Livingston, where the hungry wheelman can satisfy the inner man. The long dry seasons thoroughly dry up the road, and in some places the dust lies two to four inches thick.

"The Gate of the Mountains"

"Yankee Jim Cañon"

Continuing on comes another cañon, much narrower than the first ones, called "Yankee Jim Cañon," after an old Indian fighter, scout, guide and hunter who settled in the valley in 1871.[9] Yankee Jim is an interesting character—very enterprising. He constructed a wagon-road through this rocky path and for years collected toll from everybody passing into the park. He still has the gates across the road, and collects toll; for many people go through the park in camping outfits, spending two and three weeks there. Wheelmen are exempt from this toll. The old fellow informed me he thought it hard labor "working them damn'd old velocipedes all day." He turned out to be a congenial companion for the night. His stories of frontier life would fill a good-sized volume. He is a bachelor and a splendid cook.

Nature has endowed many countries with fair scenes; but we have in the Yellowstone—as it were, snatched pure and undefiled from the hand of the Creator—one of His very gems, and mean to preserve it in all its pristine loveliness.

All around the teeming multitude is transfiguring the earth, turning it to man's use, and in too many cases marring its features; but "Yellowstone," by the fiat of the nation, is to remain to us a thing of beauty and a joy forever.

It has nothing more than a figurative relation to a gem, however, for its area would make a respectable kingdom in some parts of the world, and its attractiveness, not to say productiveness would provide a princely revenue. It taxes the memory to recall—even in the works of those somewhat fervid and overwrought inventors of marvels, the early travelers—any other portion of the world presenting a greater diversity of character than do the rivers and mountains, torrents and waterfalls, hills and valleys of the Yellowstone.

The verdure of abundant nature and the blanched and alkali-withered desert blend their effects into a phantasmagoria of unequaled grandeur and unexcelled attraction to the cyclist, if he have the good sense to provide himself with a pneumatic, and the good fortune to have in it as honest and trusty a friend as my "Victor" has proved to me. It has often been remarked that between the cyclist and his wheel a more than sentimental friendship springs up. Of a verity I can indorse this, so far as the wheel that has borne my burden and cheered my pilgrimage is concerned. It has been a steadfast friend indeed, and that in direst need too. What other wheel could have withstood the wear and tear to which I have subjected my safety pneumatic "Victor"? These journeys over railroad ties and prairie grass have put it to a crucial test, and, as was my purpose, the question whether the pneumatic safety will stand the strain of a wheelman's world tour over rough and rugged wayside is forever and most favorably settled now.[10]

Yellowstone Park

Eureka! I have girdled the great wonderland of our continent, and put behind me the greatest temptation to deviate from my onward track. I would by no means have missed it, though it has cost me five precious days. There are many wonderlands in store for me in Asia and in Europe, but will there be any quite like this one in the Rockies? Think of an area of fifty-five miles in width from east to west, and sixty-five miles in length from north to south, covering about 3,575 square miles, laid out as a national park! How "little Rhody" [Rhode Island] and "peach Delaware" must swell into pride when told that the Yellowstone Park reminds [one] of them. When compared in size to any of the States, these two are usually cited as being together just large enough to be comfortably accommodated within the "park." It should be added, however, that such a disposition of the two States would leave still a margin of over 200 square miles for a national playground. But, aside from its selection as a national playground, the

Yellowstone would be noteworthy, for from the slopes of these highlands spring the rills which grow into the mightiest rivers of the United States. The springs of the Missouri-Mississippi system, as well as those of the Columbia and the Colorado, take life here, and "from the summit of Mount Washburn, the highest point of observation embraced by the park, may be seen the grim and towering walls which partition a complex of waters, forcing the flow either eastward, by way of the Gulf of Mexico, into the Atlantic, or westward into the Pacific Ocean."[11]

The tourists coming into the park from Livingston take the branch road to Cinnabar. There they are compelled to enter the stage-coach for an eight-mile ride to the Mammoth Hot Springs Hotel [a climb of nearly a thousand feet]. Of course I did nothing of the sort. My "Victor" was a good enough vehicle for me, though, I confess, it proved a pretty hard pull. It is almost a continuous up-grade and the road very dusty. Writing of dusty roads brings back the strange impressions the various travelers made upon me. I could easily distinguish by their dusty clothing and begrimed and sunburned faces those who had "made" the park from the tidily dressed and fair-complexioned new arrivals. It does not take a very long stay within these natural pleasure precincts to change one to a backwoodsman. As for myself, I must have been a sight when I dismounted at the hotel. My face and nose and ears were not only brown but peeling off, and my trusty wheel bore signs of many a gallant league's work over the alkali roads.

I topped my first day by a ride over the hill through the forest and up a terrible steep and dusty grade through the Golden Gate [another thousand-foot climb], where the west branch of the Gardiner River [Glen Creek] falls over a series of moss-grown cascades with sinuous courses, creating the exquisitely formed and splendidly colored Minerva Terrace by its magic alchemy.[12] The roadway through the "Golden Gate" is very appropriately named. Though less than a mile in length, I was told that it cost Uncle Sam $15,000 to build it.

After leaving the Golden Gate gorge the road continues along the top of the mountain, and its even surface is a great relief after the tremendous pull up from the Mammoth Hotel to the famous Obsidian Cliff or Glass Mountain, which rises, basalt-like, in almost vertical columns, from the eastern shores of Beaver Lake to a height of from 150 to 250 feet, and is probably unequaled in the world. The volcanic glass glistens like jet, but is quite opaque. Sometimes it is variegated with streaks of red and yellow. The material lends itself to the formation of a perfect road-bed. It successfully resists drills and giant powder, and only disintegrates under a process of heating by fire and then rapidly cools. No wonder that its fame and use spread wide among the aborigines, for the continent does not produce another natural substance capable of such an edge as flaked obsidian. The sacrificial knives of the Aztec priests, and other tools, were made from it.

My rendezvous for the night was to be Norris Geyser Basin,[13] a short ride for a day for me; but then there had been so much to see en route, and after arrival there would still be the geysers to see. This was to be my initiation into the mysteries of the great geyser system which Yellowstone marks as its own, at once its pride and its terror. Who can stand upon the trembling earth, with evidences all around of the mighty buried forces of nature scarce slumbering skin-deep beneath one's feet, without a sense of the mighty powers of imprisoned chaos?

Next morning I started down the road which winds through the Elk and Johnson parks,[14] and thence through the four miles of Gibbon Cañon, a narrow, rocky defile, with scarce width sufficient for road and river. The wild grandeur of this rocky chasm is, like so much else in this wonder-working district, difficult of portrayal. On one side the cliffs rise with precipice abruptness a thousand feet, on the other they are clothed with the somber pine to their tops. Here the air is filled with the fumes from subterranean caldrons, not too pleasant in aroma; there the crystal water, fresh from the snow-clad heights, pours through the hundred obstructions in its way, with swish and swirl, and glint of many colors.

Fortunately the road is all down-grade and very good for nine miles to the Fire Hole River, which one must perforce ford.[15] After that there is, by way of compensation, a succession of steep and dusty hills, almost impassable for a wheel in some places, until the Lower Geyser Basin, the midway basin, and the Upper Geyser Basin successively arrest your attention and claim your too short hours.

In the Lower Geyser Basin alone there are nearly 700 hot springs, and nigh a score of the greater giants that lay claim to the higher distinction of geysers, whilst collectively those of the three basins seem to defy computation. Suffice to note the more important in their order— the "Excelsior," of the midway basin, the sleeping monster who, when he wakes, sends forth a voice that can be heard for miles, and a volume of water that turns the adjacent river into a seething torrent, with boiling water from his raging maw.

I did not stop to see this myself, but passed onward to the Oblong Geyser, not so much because of its power, but because its formation permits a closer and better inspection than usual of the masses of crystal which, in liquid form, are ever being **ejected** from this or the other hundred mouths direct from nature's laboratory. Wondrous in delicacy, color and formation are these gems, laces and fairy frost-work, if such a term can be applied to creations in which fire plays the principal part.

"Old Faithful" holds the post of honor in point of popularity, somewhat probably from its position in contiguity to one of the hotels, but mainly from the reliability of the exhibition of his powers; for day and night through all the year round, at intervals of about an hour, he raises his graceful column, to be wind-wafted with feather-like grace, a height of 150 feet.

From the lower to the upper basin, some nine miles, the road is level enough, but I found it sandy and dusty. Here a fellow wheelman, who had rashly partaken of a drink of the pellucid but treacherous water, with results more enduring than

ejected: Geyserite eggs, knobs, and biscuits are actually aggregated from silicon dioxide precipitated from the hot spring waters.

pleasant, left me to return to Billings, his home. It is a venture, and a dangerous one, to drink from any stream in this neighborhood.

The next morning I started for fair Shoshone Lake and over the divide to Yellowstone Lake, following the course of Fire Hole River a short distance; but even in that short way had to ford the stream three times, not a very pleasant experience, for, though its name is fire, its waters are icy cold. Once more clear of the water, the road turns up a newly made ravine,[16] fairly good riding in at the start, but after the first eight miles it grew from bad to worse, and the best-natured wheel in the world would have refused to move over the heavy sand and continual up-grade which lasted to within four and a half miles of the lake, where the road improves again and is good as far as the lunch station on the lake side.

This lunch station [at West Thumb] is presided over by a **jolly Irishman**, who keeps the guests thoroughly amused by his humor and his yarns.

It is curious to see, right on the borders of the lake, bubbling hot springs; indeed in one case the cone of the geyser is within the lake and the hot water within is only separated from the cold water without by the thinnest of partitions. I had of necessity to forego much that I should very much liked to have seen. I would gladly have gone over into the Red Mountain Range and followed the Lewis [River] from the lake downward over Sherman's trail;[17] but time has its limitations, and I could not

jolly Irishman: Larry Mathews managed various lunch stations in the park over many years and is mentioned frequently as a convivial host.

even afford the lesser excursion southward round the West Bay Thumb of Yellowstone Lake.

I had lingered already longer than I could well afford, and had yet before me the Grand Cañon, which was sure to overpower the scruples of conscience and chain me a votary. True, I could have taken from here a steamer to the Lower Lake Hotel, as do most explorers, even those who have hitherto enjoyed the less toilsome stage, but that was foreign to my mission. Though most of the wheelmen who have hitherto done the park have availed themselves of the steamer at this stage, it was denied to me, for I would not ride by water wherever possible for a wheel to carry me—or, if needs be, be pushed—and I knew that where the stage went, and often where it did not go, there the Victor would carry me. I do not blame the wheelmen—indeed, after my experience, I think in the ordinary course of a pleasure trip they are to be commended for their wisdom, for the ride will tire even the most hardened.

After lunch I continued on round the lake for a good twenty miles to the hotel, and it took me nearly four hours to do it. Here I again set my face north, and next morning started down the valley with the intention of reaching the falls, eighteen miles off, and thence facing westward, back to Norris Geyser Basin and out again, by Yankee Jim's, to resume my greater journey.

The road from the outlet down the valley is, as roads in the late summer go, not a very bad one, though in some places very sandy and, need I say, dusty. However, it was infinitely better than those over which I had toiled for the past two days, and I was congratulating myself upon having passed through the most uncomfortable portion of my trip when I espied it raining on the opposite side of the river, and soon the icy-cold spray reached me. When within half a mile of a government engineer's camp, what was my surprise to see the rain change into snow. As it blew up quite strong, I made for the cook's tent for shelter, and here for three hours I thawed out my fingers and feet, which were nearly frozen. The thermometer dropped from 60° to 39° in three hours. The snow continued to fall until the grass and trees were thickly covered. Anxious to reach the hotel but four miles away, I started out, but stopped at two camps to warm up before reaching there. This was a nice state of affairs—snow-bound in the Yellowstone Park, and yet in the valley, 3,000 feet below, all was warm and dry. Some one has said of Yellowstone Park that "nature puts forth all her powers, and her moods are ever changing from 'grave to gay, from lively to severe.'"[18] I had the full opportunity of approving this writer. Surely, if my trip through the park was not a pleasant one, it was at least a memorable one, and I had seen nature changing from "lively to severe."

Next morning the sky slowly cleared, but as it was impossible to start with the wheel in this mud, I had ample time to overhaul my machine, which again was the center of attraction to the guests. I also improved the time to make a visit to the Great Falls and Grand Cañon of the Yellowstone. The best point of view for the falls is Lookout Point, a rugged precipice extending out in the cañon; but Inspiration Point, about two miles below, affords another splendid view of the cañon, both up and down. The wonders of the Grand Cañon have been

told by abler pens than mine. The truth is, language fails to do it justice.

The falls are two in number, the upper and lower; the former some hundred feet or more, and the latter 350 feet [308 feet (94 meters)]. It is not, however, either in the depth of the falls or the volume of the water which passes over them that their charm exists, but in the wonderful setting in which nature has placed them, every form of rock, every color in nature's palette, every hue of foliage, every

Painted for OUTING by Albert Hencke.

"ALONE IN THIS GREAT SANCTUARY OF NATURE."

play of light and shade, every variety of grouping, every effect which it seems possible for sun, air, water and earth to produce, is spread with lavish hand, and placed and posed with an artistic effect that almost bespeaks design. Yet the hand of man is conspicuous only by its absence here; nature, reveling in her own strength and drawing on her own resources, has planned the vista and spread the canvas; the emblazoned walls, the tessellated floor, the canopy of matchless blue, all are hers, and never can we be too grateful to those who, in a decade often scoffed at as prosaic, utilitarian, and uneducated in matters merely esthetic, could provide the funds and the protection which alike were needed to save this masterpiece of nature from the destroying vandal, the vulgar advertiser, and the pot-hunting man of the world.

While photographing the falls from Lookout Point, my cap went over the precipice sixty feet below on a ledge of rock. It was a dangerous task, but I climbed down and succeeded in getting it and returning alive. An old tourist standing above actually sat down overcome by the sight of seeing me climbing up. A misstep and I would have been precipitated 1,500 feet below into the Yellowstone River rushing through the cañon.

The next morning everything was covered by a heavy frost, the thermometer was below freezing-point, and there was a dense fog everywhere. I was determined, however, to get off that day, if possible, and although the frozen dirt road was rather rough riding it had no terrors to the rider of a pneumatic.

As far as Norris Geyser Basin it was mostly down grade, and I progressed fairly well (thirteen miles in two hours). Then the sun shone warmly; the road, improved by the snow and rain of the two days before, dried up, and I briskly wheeled off the twenty miles to the Hot Springs, the end of the circuit. My cyclometer showed just 139 miles around the park.

I should not advise wheelmen visiting the park to make the entire circuit, as from Norris Basin to the Upper Basin, and across to the lake and thence up the cañon, it is mostly poor wheeling. Work is being pushed with all possible speed, but it will be some time before this stretch can be called a good road. But those desiring to see, at least, the most important portions of the park, can wheel from Mammoth Hot Springs to the Norris Geyser Basin, over twenty miles of fairly good road, thence cross to the Grand Cañon and Great Falls thirteen miles farther, and by returning over the same route can make a pleasant and not too fatiguing tour. Adding in the sixteen miles from Cinnabar to the Mammoth Hot Springs and return, this would make a total of eighty-two miles, and to all wheelmen in search of a holiday amid the fairest and most wonderful of nature's handiwork I say, Take your pneumatic and see the Yellowstone Park awheel as I did.

Manifold as are the beauties and attractions of the Yellowstone, as seen by the every-day tourist and written of in the most accessible books of travel, it is startling, but true, that two-thirds of its area is practically unknown. Here and there an occasional enthusiast with time on his hands and the needy hardihood [robustness], some mountain climber, lone fisherman, hunter or geologist have penetrated its remoter waterways and mountains, but their stories do not reach far beyond the campfire and the hotel corridor, unless indeed, as is sometimes happily the case, they make their way into the pages of OUTING, like the story of Mr. Owen and his companions awheel there, and Mr. Guptill's graphic narrative.* [Footnote in the original: *In Outing, July 1890 and June 1891.][19] The latter, I remember, says that in the northeastern portions of the park, where I did not go, there are vast areas strewn with the fossilized remains of animal and vegetable life, and huge trunks and fragments of petrified trees, many still standing erect, preserving much of their old form and outline, deep down among the roots of which may be found clustering deposits of the most brilliant and beautiful crystallizations, varying in color from delicate shades of pink to deep cherry, while colorless amethyst and yellow quartz lie scattered in profusion. Then, again, between the Passamaria fork of the Big Horn [now called the North Fork of the Shoshone River] and the east fork of the Yellowstone [the Lamar River] is the celebrated Hoodoo Region, or Goblin Land, designations which in nowise belie the character and appearance of the locality—a region in which volcanic action and erosion have seemingly striven to outvie each other in the production of fantastic forms and shapes. To the superstitious Indian it was the abode of evil spirits; to the white man, roused from his slumbers by the weird mutterings of the voiceless air, the region presented an enigma solved by the term "Hoodoo."

In an annual report, Supt. Norris (1877–82) mentioned his exploration of the Hoodoos. He wrote that prospector Adam Miller and two companions discovered and named Hoodoo or Goblin Land in 1870, and continued:

> *In shape they are unlike any elsewhere known, being a cross between the usual spire and steeple form, and the slender-based, and flat, tottering, table-topped sandstone monuments near the Garden of the Gods, in Colorado; and while lacking the symmetry and beauty of these, surpass both in wild, weird fascination.* (Norris, *Report for 1880*, 6–8).

The story of a slightly later trip to the Hoodoos by E. V. Wilcox appears on page 203.

From Yellowstone Park to Bearmouth

Even such marvelous attractions of superb scenery and weird phenomena as fairly riot in mine Uncle Sam's unrivaled national playground, cannot hold, magnetic though they be, a lone wheelman who has yet full three-fourths of the world to girdle. Regretfully, therefore, I was compelled to bind myself by most solemn covenant to start once more upon my long pursuit of the sun westward.

There were many charming and curious features which I had not seen; but no traveler, unless his travels are to end in that wonderland, can hope to see all of the marvels of Yellowstone Park, and I know from my brief experience that I might dally an entire year and then go on unsatisfied. So I prepared my faithful steel courser for another stage forthwith. There was a choice of routes northward out of the park. A new one would surely have revealed much to repay the venture, but my run south over the Valley Road had proved its excellence for wheeling, and, as it is unquestionably the best route, I decided to travel north by it, though really re-covering the line already traveled.

The fifty-one-mile run back to old "Yankee Jim's" was accomplished comfortably and without special incident. The old boy appeared really pleased to see me again, and when we got settled down for a chat he fired off story after story, all savoring strongly of the strange, free, breezy West.

Next morning I bade him final farewell, and went on through the Yellowstone Valley. Imposing panoramas of peak and crag were disclosed as I wheeled steadily forward—scenes that pen cannot describe nor brush portray; for eyes, and eyes alone, can rightly convey to the spirit of these mountain pictures. Passing the grand bulk of Emigrant Peak, I noticed with pleasure that the grim old sentinel had received a shining silver helmet of new-fallen snow, and so I bore away another delightful memory of him. . . .[20]

NOTES

1. Lenz, "Lenz's World Tour Awheel," *Outing* 21, nos. 4 and 5, 286–90; 378–83.
2. Lenz, "Lenz's World Tour Awheel," *Outing* 20, no. 6, 482.
3. From 1879 through 1903, the Eaton family ran a horse and cattle ranch near Medora, North Dakota, and soon began to take in paying guests. They moved the ranch to its location near Sheridan, Wyoming, in 1904 and became well known for taking horseback parties from there to Yellowstone.
4. Quoted from "Cycling through Yellowstone Park," in Whittlesey and Watry, *Ho! for Wonderland*, 174.

5. See David V. Herlihy, *The Lost Cyclist* (2010), for the complete story of Lenz's adventure and the stories of other nineteenth-century world-circling cyclists.
6. Lenz entered eastern Montana Territory near Glendive. Barely settled in 1880, it grew to a fair-sized town in 1881, when the Northern Pacific tracks reached it.
7. Lenz refers to Chief Sitting Bull of the Hunkpapa Lakota Sioux tribe, who was a spiritual and political leader (not a warrior) at the time of Custer's 1876 defeat in southeastern Montana. This battle, formerly called Custer's Last Stand, is now called the Battle of the Little Bighorn. The "firing" of Moscow refers to the famous fire of 1571, when a Turkish khan set the city ablaze, and tens of thousands of people died.
8. Lenz (or his editor) had the wrong story about Pompey's Pillar. William Clark named the huge, unique rock along the Yellowstone River near Huntley for the son of the expedition's only woman, Sacajawea. Clark called the boy Pomp or Pompy (DeVoto, *Journals of Lewis and Clark*, 451). The only black man on the Lewis and Clark Expedition was York, Clark's slave.
9. James George ("Yankee Jim") took over and improved an existing road through what was then called the Second Canyon of the Yellowstone, making it passable for wagons. He lived and collected tolls there from 1874 until about 1910. He is described as a loquacious old character in many early travel accounts.
10. The safety bicycle, with two equal-sized wheels, had by 1890 become more popular than the ordinary or penny-farthing bicycle, which had a large wheel in front and a smaller one in back—a dangerous vehicle. Pneumatic tires had been used on bicycles for only a few years when Lenz made his tour.
11. This quote is not credited but came from Henry Jacob Winser's guidebook *Yellowstone National Park*, 5.
12. Here Lenz seems to be confusing the cold water falling over Rustic Falls of Glen Creek with the hot spring water of a terrace that is nearly three miles north of the falls and originates from deep below the surface.
13. When Lenz arrived at Norris Geyser Basin in summer of 1892, a temporary tent hotel had been erected to replace the Norris Hotel that had stood near the basin since 1887 but had burned down that May (Whittlesey, "History of the Norris Area," 15–19). Lenz seems to have spent very little time visiting Norris Geyser Basin.

14. The name Elk Park is still used, but Johnson Park is not. According to Whittlesey, it may be the same as Gibbon Meadows. The name was probably applied by Superintendent Norris for N. D. Johnson, whom he tried (unsuccessfully) to have appointed as U.S. Commissioner to help control crime—especially poaching—in the park.

15. The road in 1892 left the Gibbon River and headed southwest, bypassing Madison Junction and the Firehole Canyon (both passed along today's main road) before continuing south.

16. The new 1892 road left the Firehole River and turned east up the steep Spring Creek grade to cross the continental divide and descend to Yellowstone Lake. Culpin, *History of the Road System*, 231.

17. Gen. William T. Sherman did visit Yellowstone (in 1877), but it was Gen. Philip H. Sheridan's party who, on an 1882 visit, cut the trail from Jackson Hole to Yellowstone Lake. It became a road only in 1895.

18. Winser, *Yellowstone National Park*, 7.

19. Owen was the first cyclist who recorded a trip through Yellowstone. The June 1891 issue of *Outing* contains Owen's cycling report. The 1890 *Outing* article is a strong tribute to and plug for travel to the park, written by A. B. Guptill, an employee of Yellowstone photographer and concessionaire Frank J. Haynes.

20. Lenz, "Lenz's World Tour Awheel," *Outing* 21, no. 6, 444–45.

How the trout got into Yellowstone Lake

Two-Ocean Pass has long been known to mountain men. The earliest traditions speak of it as a pass in which is a spring whose waters, flowing by two channels from either side, take their way down the opposite slopes of the divide to flow at last into the Atlantic and Pacific oceans. General Raynolds, in his report of the exploration of the Yellowstone in 1868, refers to it; Jones passed through it from the east in 1873, and Hayden visited it in 1878, also from the east. Both of these writers describe the Pass, and give sketch maps of the valley and the drainage.

Billy Hofer, "Through Two-Ocean Pass," 1885

Scientists who studied Yellowstone Park in its earliest years were puzzled by a seeming paradox: there were no fish at all in Lewis and Shoshone Lakes and in many other bodies of water in the western half of Yellowstone, yet the biggest lake in the park, Yellowstone Lake, was full of trout and other fish. That the fish had not been able to ascend the streams where numerous tall waterfalls flowed down the volcanic rims was already well known. To solve the puzzle definitively, the U.S. Fish Commission sent Barton W. Evermann to the Two-Ocean Pass in 1891. His article was published in the *Popular Science Monthly* in 1895.[1]

Explorer Jim Bridger probably visited this pass in 1825,[2] and others who saw it suspected that it was important to the movement of fish into Yellowstone Lake. Scientists who came before Evermann had visited the pass; this included Dr. Arnold Hague of the USGS—whose 1884 party was guided to the region by Billy Hofer.[3] But none of these men had fully explained the question that Evermann was sent to answer.

Another visitor to Two-Ocean Pass in 1891 was Theodore Roosevelt—at that time serving as U.S. Civil Service commissioner in Washington. Roosevelt spent a week there the month after Evermann conducted his research in the area. In those days Roosevelt was an avid big-game hunter, and his goal was to shoot as many elk as he could. He ended up killing nine, along with some grouse and ducks. He was not there for the scenery, yet he wrote an engaging description of what his party of seven men (including Billy Hofer) witnessed "from the brink of a bold cliff" on their fourth day of travel. "The wild and lonely valley of Two-Ocean Pass [was] walled in on either hand by rugged mountain chains, their flanks scarred and gashed by precipice and chasm. Beyond, in a wilderness of jagged and barren peaks, stretched the Shoshones [an old name for the Absaroka Mountains]. At the middle point of the pass two streams welled down from either side. At first each flowed in but one bed, but soon divided in two; each of the twin branches then joined the like branch of the brook opposite, and swept one to the east and one to the west, on their long journey to the two great oceans. They ran as rapid brooks, through wet meadows and willow-flats, the eastern to the

Yellowstone, the western to the Snake."[4]

Evermann received his degrees from Indiana University, culminating in the PhD in 1891, and worked as teacher and professor of biology through 1906 at schools and universities including Stanford, Cornell, and Yale. His earliest publications were in ornithology, but under the influence of then Indiana University President David Starr Jordan, he took up ichthyology. He began to work with the U.S. Fish Commission in 1888, and in 1891 he became ichthyologist of that commission. His visit to Yellowstone the same year had been preceded by that of Jordan, who was sent to study the fish of the park in 1889. Jordan recommended that fish be stocked above the waterfalls in hitherto barren streams and lakes, and this began in 1890.

Evermann served as director of the California Academy of Sciences in San Francisco's Golden Gate Park beginning in 1914, planning that museum's groups of mammals and birds. At least two names commemorate his scientific discoveries: Evermann Cove on Bird Island, South Georgia (a British overseas territory in the south Atlantic, also claimed by Argentina), and a family of saber-toothed fish, the *Evermannellidae*.[5]

Two-Ocean Pass

1895

BARTON WARREN EVERMANN

born Monroe County, Iowa, 1853 • died Berkeley, California, 1932

It was while the Great Ice King still ruled over all America from the pole to the middle United States that Lake Lahontan and Lake Bonneville spread their waters over hundreds of square miles of our western territory; Lahontan where we now have the sage plains and alkali sinks of Nevada, and Bonneville covering the greater part of Utah west of the Wasatch Mountains, but now reduced to Sevier, Utah, and Great Salt Lakes, the last shallow remnants of a once mighty inland sea. It was probably long before these great lakes had dried up, while their waters were yet fresh and sweet, that occurred an event which wrought a vast change in the physical geography of that region. Somewhere, but no one is yet certain exactly where, one or more great fissures opened in the earth, and there poured out an incredible amount of lava which covered not less than one hundred and fifty thousand square miles with one vast sheet of rhyolite hundreds, in some places thousands, of feet in thickness. Northern California, northwestern Nevada, nearly all of Oregon, Washington, and Idaho, and parts of Wyoming, the Yellowstone Park, Montana, and British Columbia were all covered by this stupendous flow.[6]

The effect of this lava flow upon the present distribution of the fishes of that region is known to have been very great, and we are now beginning to understand some of the most important factors of that distribution—a distribution which, until recently, presented many anomalies.

It has been my good fortune to make explorations in Montana, Wyoming, Idaho, and the Yellowstone Park, which have cleared up some of these difficulties. The presence of trout in Yellowstone Lake and the total absence of all fish from the other large lakes of the park was one of the most interesting of these anomalies, and it is to its explanation that this article is devoted.

It is certain that all the streams and lakes of the territory covered by the lava flow were wiped out of existence by the fiery flood, and all terrestrial and aquatic life destroyed. Many long years must have passed before this lava sheet became sufficiently cooled to permit the formation of new streams; but a time finally came when the rains, falling upon the gradually cooling rock, were no longer converted into steam and thrown back into the air, only to condense and fall again, but, being able to remain in liquid form upon the rock, sought lower levels, and thus new streams began to flow. And then the fishes in the connecting

TWO-OCEAN PASS, LOOKING EAST.

streams below, which had not been destroyed by the lava flow, began to invade the desolated region and repeople its waters.

The rhyolite, obsidian, and trachyte were very hard and eroded slowly, but when the streams reached the edge of the lava field they encountered rock which was comparatively soft and which wore away rapidly. The result is that every stream leaving the Yellowstone Park has one or more great waterfalls in its course where it leaves the lava sheet. Notable among these streams are Lewis River, the outlet of Lewis and Shoshone Lakes; Yellowstone River, the outlet of Yellowstone Lake; Gardiner, Gibbon, and Firehole Rivers; and Lava, Lupine, Glen, Crawfish, Tower, and Cascade Creeks, all leaving the lava sheet in beautiful falls, varying from thirty feet to over three hundred feet in vertical descent. The following is a list of the principal waterfalls in the streams in and about the park, each one of which is supposed to form an insurmountable barrier to the ascent of fish:

Great Falls of the Yellowstone. . . . .308 feet.
Upper Falls of the Yellowstone . . . . . 109 ft.
Crystal Falls in Cascade Creek. . . . . 129 ft.
Tower Falls in Tower Creek . . . . 132 ft.
Undine Falls in Lava Creek . . . . 60 ft.
Lower Falls in Lava Creek[7] . . . . 50 ft.
Wraith Falls in Lupine Creek . . . . . . 100 ft.
Osprey Falls in Gardiner River. . . . . 150 ft.
Rustic Falls in Glen Creek . . . . 70 ft.
Virginia Cascades in Gibbon River. . . 60 ft.
Gibbon Falls in Gibbon River . . . . . . 80 ft.
Keppler Cascade in Firehole River . . . 80 ft.
Upper Falls in Lewis River . . . . 50 ft.
Lower Falls in Lewis River[8] . . . . 30 ft.
Moose Falls in Crawfish Creek. . . . . . 30 ft.

Besides these, there are almost innumerable falls in the smaller streams and brooks, but of them we take no account. When it is remembered that nearly all these falls are within the limits of an area fifty-five by sixty-five miles, one can get some idea of the grandeur and beauty of the Yellowstone National Park. It is doubtful if any other similar area in the world affords so many magnificent waterfalls, beautiful cascades, seething torrents, and abysmal gorges as are found here. But these are among the least of the strange and wonderful things in this wonderland, where geysers great and small, mud springs and boiling paint-pots, and petrified forests so abound. With scarcely an exception all these streams and lakes are of the best of pure clear, cold water, well supplied with insect larvae, the smaller crustacea, and various other

kinds of the smaller animal and plant forms sufficient in amount to support an immense fish life. But it is a strange and interesting fact that, with the exception of Yellowstone Lake and River, these waters were wholly barren of fish life until recently stocked by the United States Fish Commission. The river and lake just named are well filled with the Red-throated trout (*Salmo mykiss lewisi*),[9] and this fact is the more remarkable when it is remembered that the falls in the lower Yellowstone River are one hundred and nine and three hundred and eight feet, respectively—by far the greatest found in the park.

The total absence of fish from Lewis and Shoshone Lakes and the numerous other small lakes and streams of the park is certainly due to the various falls in their lower courses, which have proved

UPPER FALLS OF THE YELLOWSTONE RIVER. One hundred and nine feet.

impassable barriers to the ascent of fishes from below; for in every one of these streams, just below the falls, trout and in some cases other species of fishes are found in abundance. But to account for the presence of trout in Yellowstone Lake was a matter of no little difficulty. If a fall of thirty to fifty feet in Lewis River has prevented trout from ascending to Lewis and Shoshone Lakes, why have not the much greater falls in the Yellowstone proved a barrier to the ascent of trout to Yellowstone Lake? Certainly no fish can ascend these falls, and we must look elsewhere for the explanation.

Many years ago the famous old guide, Jim Bridger, told his incredulous friends that he had found, on the divide west of the upper Yellowstone, a creek which flowed in both directions— one end flowing east into the Yellowstone, the other west into Snake River. But, as he also told about many other strange and to them impossible things which he had seen—among which were a glass mountain, and a river which ran down hill so fast that the water was made boiling hot—they were not disposed to acknowledge the existence of his "Two-Ocean Creek." Subsequent events, however, showed that the strange stories of Jim Bridger were not without some elements of truth.

Two-Ocean Pass was visited by Captain Jones in 1873, by Dr. F. V. Hayden in 1878, and by Mr. Arnold Hague in 1884. The observations made by these various explorers seemed to indicate that Two-Ocean Pass is a nearly level meadow, near the center of which is a marsh, which, in times of wet weather, becomes a small lake, and that "a portion of the waters from the surrounding mountains accumulates in the marshy meadows and gradually gravitates from either side into two small streams, one of which follows to the northeast, the other to the southwest" (Hayden).

From these reports it began to be suspected that trout, ascending Pacific Creek from Snake River, might, in time of high water, pass through the lake in Two-Ocean Pass and descend Atlantic Creek and the upper Yellowstone to Yellowstone Lake, and thus would the origin of the trout of that lake be explained. Dr. Jordan,[10] who spent some time in the park in 1889, was impressed with the probable correctness of this explanation, but did not visit Two-Ocean Pass.

In 1891, while carrying on certain investigations in Montana and the Yellowstone Park, under the direction of the United States Commissioner of Fish and Fisheries, Colonel Marshal McDonald, I was instructed to visit Two-Ocean Pass and determine definitely the conditions which obtain there.

On August 7th, with Billy Hofer [see Hofer's 1887 ski trip account on page 63], that prince of mountaineers, as our guide, we started out from the Mammoth Hot Springs with a pack train of ten pack horses and eight saddle horses. Our route led us through all the geyser basins of the park, and we reached Two-Ocean Pass August 17th, where we remained long enough to make a careful examination.

This pass is a high mountain meadow, about eight thousand two hundred feet above the sea, and situated just south of the park, in longitude 110° 10', latitude 44° 3'. It is surrounded on all sides by rather high mountains, except where the narrow valleys of Atlantic and Pacific Creeks open out from it. Running back among the mountains to the northward are two small cañons, down which come two small streams. On the opposite side is another cañon, down which comes another small stream. The extreme length of the meadow from east to west is about a mile, while the width from north to south is not much less. The larger of the streams coming in from the north is Pacific Creek, which, after winding along the western side of the meadow, turns abruptly westward, leaving the pass through a narrow gorge. Receiving numerous small affluents, Pacific Creek soon becomes a good-sized stream, which finally unites with Buffalo Creek a few miles above where the latter stream flows into Snake River.

Atlantic Creek was found to have two forks entering the pass. At the north end of the meadow is a small wooded cañon, down which flows the North Fork. This stream hugs the border of the flat very closely. The South Fork comes down the cañon on the south side, skirting the brow of the hill a little less closely than does the North Fork. The two, coming together near the middle of the eastern border of the meadow, form Atlantic Creek, which, after a course of a few miles, flows into the Upper Yellowstone. But the remarkable phenomena exhibited here remain to be described.

Each fork of Atlantic Creek, just after entering the meadow, divides as if to flow around an island; but the stream toward the meadow, instead of returning to the portion from which it had parted, continues its westerly course across the meadow. Just before reaching the western border the two streams unite, and then pour their combined waters into Pacific Creek; thus are Atlantic and Pacific Creeks united, and a continuous water way

from the mouth of the Columbia, via Two-Ocean Pass, to the Gulf of Mexico is established. Two-Ocean Creek is not a myth but a verity, and Jim Bridger is vindicated. We stood upon the bank of either fork of Atlantic Creek, just above the place of the "parting of the waters," and watched the stream pursue its rapid but dangerous and uncertain course along the very crest of the "Great Continental Divide." A creek flowing along the ridgepole of a continent is unusual and strange, and well worth watching and experimenting with. So we waded to the middle of the North Fork, and, lying down upon the rocks in its bed, we drank the pure icy water that was hurrying to the Pacific, and, without rising, but by simply bending a little to the left, we took a draught from that portion of the stream which was just deciding to go east, via the Missouri-Mississippi route, to the Gulf of Mexico. And then we tossed chips, two at a time, into the stream. Though they would strike the water within an inch or so of each other, not infrequently one would be carried by the current to the left, keeping in Atlantic Creek, while the other might be carried a little to the right and enter the branch running across the meadow to Pacific Creek; the one beginning a journey which will finally bring it to the great gulf, the other entering upon a long voyage in the opposite direction to Balboa's ocean.

Pacific Creek is a stream of good size long before it enters the pass, and its course through the meadow is in a definite channel; but not so with Atlantic Creek. The west bank of each fork is low, and the water is liable to break through anywhere, and thus send a part of its water across to Pacific Creek. It is probably true that one or two branches always connect the two creeks under ordinary conditions, and that, following heavy rains, or when the snows are melting, a much greater portion of the water of Atlantic Creek finds its way across the meadow to the other.

Besides the channels already mentioned, there are several more or less distinct ones that were dry at the time of our visit. As already stated, the pass is a nearly level meadow, covered with a heavy growth of grass and many small willows one to three feet high. While it is somewhat marshy in places, it has nothing of the nature of a lake about it. Of course, during wet weather the small springs at the borders of the meadow would be stronger; but the important facts are that there is no lake or even marsh there, and that neither Atlantic nor Pacific Creek has its rise in the meadow. Atlantic Creek, in fact, comes into the pass as two good-sized streams from opposite directions, and leaves it by at least four channels, thus making an island of a considerable portion of the meadow. And it is certain that there is, under ordinary circumstances, a continuous waterway through Two-Ocean Pass of such a character as to permit fishes to pass easily and readily from Snake River over to the Yellowstone, or in the opposite direction. Indeed, it is possible, barring certain falls in Snake River, for a fish so inclined to start at the mouth of the Columbia, travel up that great river to its principal tributary, the Snake, thence on through the

long, tortuous course of that stream, and, under the shadows of the Grand Tetons, enter the cold waters of Pacific Creek, by which it could journey on up to the very crest of the Great Continental Divide to Two-Ocean Pass; through this pass it may have a choice of two routes to Atlantic Creek, in which the down-stream journey is begun. Soon

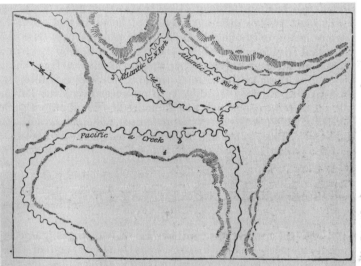

DIAGRAM SHOWING RELATION OF STREAMS IN TWO-OCEAN PASS.

SALMO MYKISS Walbaum. Red-throated trout; adult; one half natural size.

SALMO MYKISS. Red-throated trout; young; natural size.

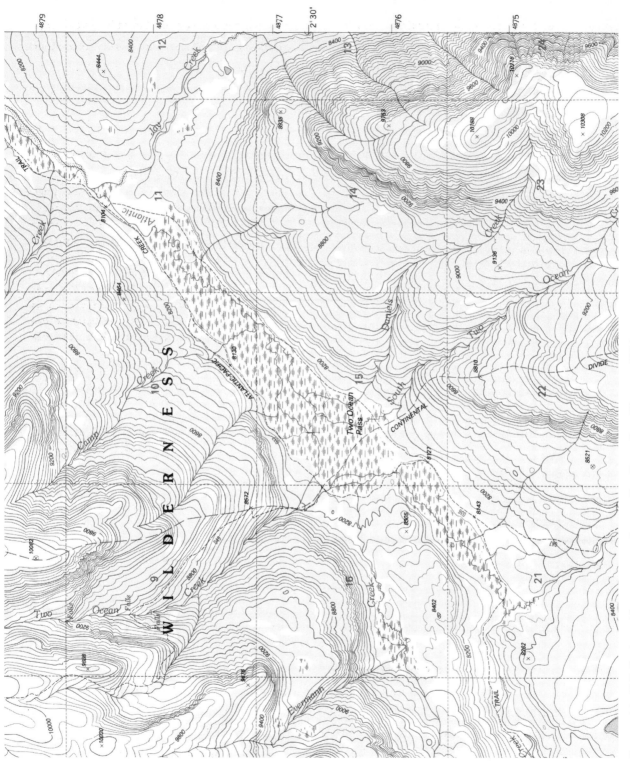

Portion of the U. S. Geological Survey topographic map, Two Ocean Pass, Wyoming, 1996

it reaches the Yellowstone, down which it continues to Yellowstone Lake, then through the lower Yellowstone out into the turbid waters of the Missouri. For many hundred miles it may continue down this mighty river before reaching the Father of Waters [the Mississippi], which will finally carry it to the Gulf of Mexico—a wonderful journey of nearly six thousand miles, by far the longest possible fresh-water journey in the world.

We found trout in Pacific Creek at every point where we examined it. In Two-Ocean Pass we obtained specimens from each of the streams, and in such positions as would have permitted them to pass easily from one side of the divide to the other. We also caught trout in Atlantic Creek below the pass, and in the upper Yellowstone, where they were abundant.

Thus it is certain that there is no obstruction even in dry weather to prevent the passage of trout from the Snake River to Yellowstone Lake; it is quite evident that trout do pass over in this way; and it is almost absolutely certain that Yellowstone Lake was stocked with trout from the west, via Two-Ocean Pass.

From the basin of Snake River above Shoshone Falls we know at least twelve different species of fishes, but of all these the trout is the only one which has been able to pass over the Continental Divide and establish itself in Yellowstone Lake and its tributary streams, for no other species is known from those waters. But these twelve species are, as a rule, fishes of intermediate altitudes, rarely ascending into streams so cold as Pacific Creek. The only one which accompanies the trout into Pacific Creek is the blob (*Cottus bairdi punctulatus*), which we found even in Two-Ocean Pass, but it has never been seen on the Yellowstone side of the pass.

NOTES

1. Everman, "Two-Ocean Pass," 175–86.
2. Alter, *Jim Bridger*, 76.
3. Hofer, "Through Two-Ocean Pass," part 4, 62.
4. Roosevelt, *Wilderness Hunter*, 207–8.
5. Memorial resolution to Barton Warren Evermann, http://historicalsociety.stanford.edu/pdfmem/EvermannB.pdf, and California Academy of Sciences Evermann Collection, Biographical Note, http://researcharchive.calacademy.org/research/library/special/findaids/evermann.html, both accessed September 16, 2014.
6. Twentieth-century geologists determined that huge freshwater lakes Lahontan and Bonneville date back tens of thousands of years, while the multiple lava flows in the northwestern United States mostly date back millions of years.
7. Evermann's "Lower Falls in Lava Creek," now called Lower Undine Falls, is described as about forty feet high and very difficult to access. Rubinstein et al., *Yellowstone Waterfalls*, 57.
8. Lower Falls in Lewis River is now called Lewis Canyon Falls (Lower). Rubinstein et al., *Yellowstone Waterfalls*, 53.
9. Evermann's "Red-throated trout" is the cutthroat trout; the two Yellowstone species are the Yellowstone Cutthroat (*Oncorhynchus clarki bouvieri*) and the Westslope Cutthroat (*Oncorhynchus clarki lewisi*). Varley and Schullery, *Yellowstone Fishes*, 54–58.
10. Sent to Yellowstone in 1889 by the U.S. Fish Commission, Dr. David Starr Jordan studied the fish population, wrote a report cataloguing the native fishes, listing barren waters, and advising the government as to which waters were suitable for stocking. In his autobiography, *Days of a Man*, Jordan wrote, "According to popular idea each animal species has been somehow placed in the surroundings best suited to its development. On this theory failure to fill with trout the crystal streams of Yellowstone Park must be regarded as a strange oversight on the part of Mother Nature" (Jordan, *Days of a Man* 1, 341). Jordan became the first president of Leland Stanford Junior University in 1891.

Rules and Regulations of the Yellowstone National Park

Hiram M. Chittenden, *The Yellowstone Park: Historical and Descriptive*, pp. 354–56, 1895

The following and eminently proper rules have been prescribed for the government of the Park and the protection of its multifarious objects of public interest and noble game:

1. It is forbidden to remove or injure the sediments or incrustations around the geysers, hot springs or steam vents; or to deface the same by written inscription or otherwise; or to throw any substance into the springs or geyser vents; or to injure or disturb, in any manner, or to carry off any of the mineral deposits, specimens, natural curiosities or wonders within the Park.

2. It is forbidden to ride or drive upon any of the geyser or hot spring formations, or to turn loose stock to graze in their vicinity.

3. It is forbidden to cut or injure any growing timber. Camping parties will be allowed to use dead or fallen timber for fuel.

4. Fires shall be lighted only when necessary, and completely extinguished when not longer required. The utmost care should be exercised at all times to avoid setting fire to the timber and grass, and anyone failing to comply therewith shall be peremptorily removed from the Park.

5. Hunting or killing, wounding or capturing of any bird or wild animals, except dangerous animals, when necessary to prevent them from destroying life or inflicting an injury, is prohibited. The outfits, including guns, traps, teams, horses or means of transportation used by persons engaged in hunting, killing, trapping, ensnaring or capturing such birds or wild animals, or in possession of game killed in the Park under other circumstances than prescribed above, will be forfeited to the United States except in cases where it is shown by satisfactory evidence that the outfit is not the property of the person or persons violating this regulation, and the actual owner thereof was not a party to such violation. Firearms will only be permitted in the Park on the written permission of the superintendent thereof. On arrival at the first station of the Park guard, parties having firearms will turn them over to the sergeant in charge of the station, taking his receipt for them. They will be returned to the owners on leaving the Park.

6. Fishing with nets, seines, traps, or by use of drugs or explosives, or in any other way than with hook and line, is prohibited. Fishing for purpose of merchandise or profit is forbidden by law. Fishing may be prohibited by order of the Superintendent of the Park in any of the waters

of the Park, or limited therein to any specified season of the year until otherwise ordered by the Secretary of the Interior.

7. No person will be permitted to reside permanently or to engage in any business in the Park without permission, in writing, from the Department of the Interior. The Superintendent may grant authority to competent persons to act as guides, and revoke the same at his discretion, and no pack trains shall be allowed in the Park unless in charge of a duly registered guide.

8. The herding or grazing of loose stock or cattle of any kind within the Park, as well as the driving of such stock or cattle over the roads of the Park, is strictly forbidden, except in such cases where authority therefor is granted by the Secretary of the Interior.

9. No drinking saloon or bar-room will be permitted within the limits of the Park.

10. Private notices or advertisements shall not be posted or displayed within the Park, except such as may be necessary for the convenience or guidance of the public, upon buildings on leased ground.

11. Persons who render themselves obnoxious by disorderly conduct or bad behavior, or who violate any of the foregoing rules, will be summarily removed from the Park, and will not be allowed to return without permission in writing from the Secretary of the Interior or the Superintendent of the Park. Any person who violates any of the foregoing regulations will be deemed guilty of a misdemeanor, and be subjected to a fine, as provided by the Act of Congress, approved May 7, 1894, "to protect the birds and animals in Yellowstone National Park, and to punish crimes in said park, and for other purposes," of not more than one thousand dollars or imprisonment not exceeding two years, or both, and be adjudged to pay all costs of the proceedings.

An educator tramps the distance

Few Americans would now plan to walk around the entire Grand Loop Road of Yellowstone Park[1]—certainly not in six days nor on today's busy roads and without even a day pack to carry one's food and belongings. Even an extremely fit person would find walking more than thirty sometimes-steep miles per day a challenge.

But think back to conditions in the park a century and more ago. Roads were quite primitive and vehicles were horse-drawn and moved relatively slowly. Hotels, grocery stores, and restaurants were few but were located near the most interesting places to see, and camping was allowed wherever you wished. Wild animals almost always stayed out of the way of humans, since they had not become habituated to them. So walking on the roads was at least practicable.

An extremely strong and hardy hiker, Charles Hanford Henderson covered amazing distances, considering the high altitude, strenuous hills, and poor conditions of the roads. He rarely complains of steep roads nor of being exhausted—only about the people he met who could not believe he could walk so far. Writing about his unique experience in an 1899 issue of *Outing*,[2] Henderson shows us how at a walking pace (albeit a rapid one), he had

time to notice natural phenomena along the way, and not just those at major points of interest. The reader *does* wonder from the way he writes whether Henderson may have been a rather stuffy person— or was he pulling the reader's leg with declarations such as, "The art of naming is still somewhat crude in the West"?

Henderson received a bachelor's degree from the University of Pennsylvania in 1882 and continued his education at the University of Zurich, receiving a doctorate in 1892. Henderson then embarked on a career teaching science and education. At the time of his Yellowstone adventure, he had held various teaching and journalism positions and had founded the Marienfeld Summer School in New Hampshire.

His lifelong interests led Henderson to write a number of popular books published by Houghton Mifflin between 1902 and 1914 with such titles as *Education and the Larger Life* and *The Children of Good Fortune: An Essay in Morals*. In the early twentieth century he was a rival of educational philosopher John Dewey; later in life he wrote about the ills of American industry and the causes of social unrest.

Through the Yellowstone on Foot
1899

C. Hanford Henderson
born Philadelphia, Pennsylvania, 1861 • died Daytona Beach, Florida, 1941

It is not the purpose of this article to describe the Yellowstone Park. That would take a book—a big one. Moreover, it has already been done. The purpose is simpler; it is to describe a tramp through it.

One gets there, as all the world knows, by leaving the train at the forlorn little town of Cinnabar.[3] On a certain Monday morning, in the latter part of August, we all tumbled out of the train there and into the stages, or, rather, all but one very tall young gentleman with a turn for walking, who had made up his mind to do it on foot.

Now, to walk successfully one must attend to certain details. The most important detail is one's dress. The common mistake is to wear too heavy clothing and too much. This is disastrous. Better venture upon the trip, as I did, wearing the lightest underclothing, a summer traveling suit, a straw hat, and light shoes. A special caution is needed against heavy shoes. They have wrecked many a promising expedition. It is much better to go tripping daintily along, picking one's way, if need be, than to wear tiresome clod hopper shoes, and step on every sharp stone you see. In my hand I carried a light umbrella (to kill rattlesnakes and frighten off bears) and a modest little paper bundle, in my pocket a package of soda crackers, in my heart many things. Nevertheless, it was very light. This is also important.

On the whole, I found this equipment very satisfactory. Occasionally I was a trifle too cold and occasionally a trifle too hot, but on the average I was very comfortable.

Cinnabar is on the northern edge of the Park. It is about **eight miles** from there to the Mammoth Hot Springs. It took me two hours and forty minutes to walk it.

The road enters the Park at Gardiner through a rocky and picturesque gorge. It was about two o'clock in the afternoon when I found myself on the top of a plateau above the river and in the midst of the Mammoth Hot Springs. It is quite a settlement. The tourists have the biggest building, the hotel, a yellowish green and rather characterless affair, on one side of the parade ground, and on the opposite side Uncle Sam is the chief tenant, the military post consisting of a dozen or more buildings. They have bright red roofs and

eight miles: Henderson climbed from the elevation of Cinnabar at about 5,200 feet (1,585 m) to Mammoth Hot Springs at 6,239 feet (1,902 m).

stand side by side, after the fashion of soldiers. The **parade ground** itself is an attractive bit of open sand, several acres in extent, and rests on this shelf of a plateau above the river. Back of it—that is, to the west—rise the white and glistening terraces of the hot springs. In front is the gorge. Surrounding it there is a grand circle of mountains. One has the sensation of being literally in the lap of nature. The dust subsides, and one turns to the investigation of the hot springs. It is a weird place. One picks one's way among the unique, the grotesque, perhaps the terrible. Directly in front of the hotel there are a number of sinister-looking openings, in evident communication with the nether world. They would swallow one without the least compunction. Some are explorable, but the results would be small, a probable total of darkness, dirt, bad odors, and bruised extremities. Avoiding these pitfalls, one turns to the west, makes one's way among streams of almost boiling water up a gentle slope and stands in the near presence of the famous Mammoth Hot Springs.

What shall one say of them? The first effect is disappointing. In truth, so is the last. Dickens would have said that they look as if they had been up all night. In the disappointment one does not at first realize the beauty of Minerva Terrace and Jupiter Terrace and other stalking grounds of the gods. But gradually better counsels prevail. One's appreciation adjusts itself, and one spends a happy afternoon in exploring the springs.

parade ground: The former military parade ground at Mammoth is now covered with a thick growth of sagebrush.

The first celebrity encountered is the Liberty Cap, a curious, conical mass of sinter, some fifty feet high and twenty feet broad at the base. It is built up of overlapping layers, and has evidently been the crater of a very respectable hot spring. Now it is dry, and crumbles before the elements. The general color tone is a good old ivory. Above, it is au naturel. Below, it rises from a smooth white floor, pounded hard by the broad soles and martial tread of hundreds of excursionists.

Back of the Liberty Cap there is another and a smaller cone, the Devil's Thumb. The art of naming is still somewhat crude in the West. Passing this, one comes to the Hot Springs proper. These rise, terrace after terrace, some thirteen in all, and spread themselves over nearly two hundred acres of ground. The terraces are retreating in form; that is to say, they are broader above than below. This permits many beautiful shapes. Sometimes they extend in long lines, like a heavily carved marble cornice. Sometimes it is a succession of fluted stems, and one can find the lily of both France and of Florence. Frequently the terrace rounds into a pedestal-supported bowl, and one stands before a baptismal font or perhaps a pulpit. Pools of bubbling, boiling water rest on the top of the terraces. Their outlines are a succession of graceful curves; their sides the resting place of dainty forms of stone bubbles and of mineral turf. Their depths are the home of pure, intense color. For the most part this is blue; sometimes it is green, more rarely amber. It is a very live color, and one, in an artistic sense, feasts upon it.

Meanwhile one is getting further up the hill. The water is wanting. One stands in the presence of a suspended activity. The crumbling sinter, built into well-defined ridges and running in all directions, bears witness of the past. These volcanic activities are as shifting as one's own mood. They advance and retreat, increase and decrease, appear and disappear, and all in a very short space of time. Do we speak of the eternal mountains? It is a misnomer. The forces of nature are forever removing them and casting them into the sea.

It was Monday night, and it was necessary to be back in Livingston to start eastward by Saturday night. This left but five days in which to make the tour of the Park. The stage takes six.

I was told that it was impossible to walk. I suggested that I had walked many miles in the South and in Switzerland. That might be, they said, but in the Yellowstone the climate does not permit it. The American climate needs broad shoulders. I had eight thousand miles of it during the summer, and the number of consequences for which it is held responsible is truly appalling. The hotel people added a pathetic tale of a young Englishman who had left a bundle there a few weeks before and had never returned for it.

Thus edified I went to bed, and I said in my haste something about all men.

Tuesday I woke early, and at the same moment the Jonathan Edwards[4] in me was also very wide awake. Puritan blood is stubborn. It is a red flag to be told you cannot do a thing that you know you can do. A few minutes after seven I spread my wings and flew into the sweet morning air. The sun was shining gloriously. Each breath was an inspiration. On general principles, I believe my feet touched the ground from time to time, but my memory is rather that of swimming through the air, of floating over a series of low ridges, of rising through a picturesque gorge, and of stopping, quite in surprise, at a rocky pass known as the Golden Gate, to find that I had gone four miles in a little over fifty minutes. The road through the gorge is almost Alpine in its beauty. One must pause a moment and look over the stone parapet at the side, down into the rushing stream below and back through the rocky walls, upon a group of noble mountains.

Beyond the Gate, a new experience. One comes upon a spacious mountain prairie—Swan Lake Basin[5]—hemmed in on all sides by mountains as lofty as Etna. A cold wind is blowing. The blood goes rushing through the veins. The exhilaration increases. It is a mood requiring action; one can scarcely help running. One spreads one's hands and salutes the morning and the universe. It is Ave Maria—Hail to the Great Mother! One finds one's self. One becomes a king. The kingdom is all Nature. An occasional tent speaks of human occupancy, but they are too far apart to crowd. A wagon passes, but it is too small to interfere. The great, dominant, unchangeable thing is Nature.

Imagine the vulgarity of having a guide with you at such a moment, pouring statistics into your ears!

The road passes into the forest, skirting Obsidian Cliff, a steep mountain of volcanic glass, and making its way along the borders of the beaver lakes. At high noon—the contracting parties being Nature and myself—I rubbed my eyes. And the occasion was this: I stood before the tents of the Norris lunch station. I had walked twenty-two miles in less than five hours. At least they said it was twenty-two miles, and my watch said it was less than five hours. I think the real distance may be eighteen miles. The discrepancy is chargeable to that generalization which I reached the night before.

As an introduction to geyserdom, the Norris Basin is full of interest, but after the Upper Basin it seems quite ordinary. The Norris geysers are all small, mere sprouting hot springs, yet they come upon one like old friends, recalling past lessons in geology and Bunsen's theories. It seemed wonderful then that the old Heidelberg doctor should have crossed over to Iceland, and with his accurate French thermometers and his admirable German patience should have found out why the geysers spout and play with such regularity.[6]

It is another five hours' walk from the lunch station to the Fountain Hotel. The road crosses a broad prairie, and then follows the Gibbon River through a fine canyon, past the beautiful Gibbon Falls, and over a series of wooden bridges to the valley of the Firehole River. Here one passes a **permanent cantonment of soldiers**, and then crosses a dismal flat, half prairie and half marsh,

> **permanent cantonment of soldiers:** In Henderson's time a soldier station and a guardhouse were located at the north end of Fountain Flats and just south of Nez Perce Creek.
>
> The elegant **Fountain Hotel** (1891-1917) was about one-half mile northeast of Fountain Paint Pot.
>
> **Hell's Half-Acre:** applied at times to both Excelsior Geyser's crater and the entire area of Midway Geyser Basin.

to the **Fountain Hotel**. This last stretch of road seemed quite interminable, for by that time the tramp was very tired.

At the hotel I had occasion to repeat my generalization. I also met with some discourtesy. Although disinterested, they prefer that you should come in the regular way—by the stage. But by this time one is philosophic. After dinner, when one is no longer wet—it had rained in the afternoon— and tired and hungry, and one sits before the great log fire in the hall chatting with one's fellow tourists, there comes a sense of comfort and contentment so profound that one is no longer disturbed by the thought of that poor Mammoth Springs saddle horse that cannot travel in a day as far as a city man can walk, or, indeed, by any other Yellowstone improbability.

Wednesday morning a heavy mantle of fog and steam hung over the entire dismal marsh, and produced a very wash-day sensation. The location of the hotel is bad. It is too intimate with the geysers. The road leading away from it and to the Upper Basin is also very hydropathic. It meanders among waters, hot and cold. It is better when the Firehole River is reached, and best of all at **Hell's Half-Acre** [pictured in Plates 20–22]. There the great clouds of steam rising from the Excelsior Geyser and the other pools piled up their whiteness against an intensely clear blue sky.

The beauty of these giant pools of boiling water is terrible. You cross the Firehole River on a foot-bridge. The river itself is steaming. You wander among the pools. You lose yourself in clouds of steam. A constant booming is in your ears. In the obscurity you almost run into a pool. You back off, only to stumble upon three sinister figures. You shudder. They may catch you and throw you into the boiling caldron. There is no one to prevent. Your blood runs hot and cold. The wind carries the steam in another direction. Your evil spirits are only three campers. You laugh, but there is a shiver in the laugh. It counts nothing that you have known better all along. The place has seized upon your imagination. You are living in a grotesque and abnormal world. You come to expect grotesque and abnormal things to happen. You stand and look into the deep pool of the Excelsior. Its troubled waters are blue and boiling. They are some fifteen feet below you. The walls of the caldron are roughly perpendicular. They have the appearance of a cliff seen at some distance. You catch but occasional glimpses of these details. Great volumes of steam are constantly rising above the bubbling incantations. You are in the presence of a noisy mystery. It has a curious fascination. It is horrible, but you go nearer and nearer—to the very brink, indeed—and you are tempted to throw yourself in, much as you would be tempted to jump from a high tower. One can only resist this evil gravitation by a strong effort. I drew back, fighting my way against the opposing horror. I ran down the slope, across the foot-bridge, and back to the stage road. In my heart I felt a child's glee to find myself in God's world again, and to see the sun shining.

But the road has quieter beauties also. It follows the river, sometimes along the bank, sometimes making little detours through the forest. A silver fox ambled across the road and through the timber with that amiable gait peculiar to his family. He was a beautiful creature, but distrustful. He was in a hurry to be off.

At the Upper Basin, one is in the heart of geyserdom par excellence. Here are to be found the wonderful spouters whose names are known the world over. They are eloquent spouters, speaking a universal language and telling of eternal law under their apparent caprice. A footpath wanders here and there, and takes the traveler where he most wants to go. The sun is shining. The formations covering the low slopes near the river are white and glistening. The steam is too tenuous to hide the view; the world becomes objective again. There are things to be investigated. Even the guidebook is no longer offensive. It is interesting to know how often the different geysers go off, and how long their eruptions last, and how high the water is thrown. There are the Castle and the Beehive, the Lion and the Lioness, the Giant and the Giantess, the Grand and the Splendid—in a word, the appropriate and the inappropriate. Best of all, there is Old Faithful. He is a model geyser. Once every hour, or, to be more accurate, once every sixty-five minutes, he goes off, morning, noon, and night, and he does it well. He sends the boiling, steaming water up into the transparent ether as high as a tall church steeple. The fountain plays for several minutes. In Le Conte's *Geology*[7] there is a picture of the geyser in action, and a man running away from it, in evident alarm. Underneath is the legend: "Old Faithful (after Hayden)." In college days we used to omit the parentheses, and take the frightened individual to be the good old Doctor.

The regulation tourists spend the day at the Upper Basin and go back to the Fountain Hotel for the night, a poor arrangement, except from the point of view of the receiving teller. It makes them travel over the same stretch of road three times. By avoiding this, I gained a day on the **stage people**.

It is about eighteen miles over to the Yellowstone Lake, to the Thumb lunch station. The tourists who leave the Fountain Hotel on the second morning stop there for luncheon, and then go eighteen miles further on to the Lake Hotel for the night. I meant to reach the Lake Hotel Wednesday evening by taking a rowboat from the Thumb, or, failing in this, to stop at the lunch station over night. At the Upper Basin they told me there was no rowboat at the Thumb, and that no one stopped there over night; that even the servants went to the Lake Hotel. This sounded improbable. Even a gentleman is not apt to send his servants off eighteen miles every night to sleep, much less a corporation avowedly on the make. When I got to the Lake Station [at West Thumb], about five o'clock, I found a rowboat and a printed tariff of charges. I also found that the three servants stopped there permanently; but this, I believe, was the last official untruth I met in the Yellowstone. I stopped asking questions.

In a quiet way the walk was very pleasant. The road lay through the forest, and passed over the

---

stage people: Until 1904 there was only a small hotel at Upper Geyser Basin, too crude for those taking the stage.

shingle: Rounded pebbles larger than gravel that occur by a sea or lake.

famous paint pots: The Thumb Paint Pots, praised in many early writings, have gradually cooled. Now they are overgrown with plant life and no longer colorful.

Continental Divide by inclines so gentle as seldom to be tiresome. At one point there is a fine outlook—the Shoshone view—which takes in a vast extent of forest and mountain, with the beautiful Shoshone Lake in the distance. It was pleasant, too, descending toward the Yellowstone [Lake], with the long afternoon shadows lying across the path and an occasional glimpse of the water from between the trees. The Thumb lunch station is beautifully located on a gentle slope of ground rising directly from the lake. All along the shore are numerous hot springs, the possible cones of extinct geysers. They form little mounds above the line of **shingle**; sometimes they are nearly or quite surrounded by the waters of the lake, forming tiny peninsulas and islands. Occasionally they are entirely submerged and show themselves only by bubbles. One can easily catch fish in the lake, and, turning, cook them in the boiling water of the springs. Near by are the **famous paint pots**, perhaps the best in the Park, seething masses of pink and red and brown and green and yellow, each distinct in form and color, pure monochromatic mud pies, stirring themselves.

It is fortunate to reach the lake at sundown, and later to have the moon, for then one sees the lake at its best. It is almost Italian in its beauty, a broad stretch of clear water, a few low wooded islands, a range of hills on the opposite shore, and back of them a line of lofty mountains, still white with snow. At sunset, in the gloaming, by moonlight, it is very beautiful.

I had to give up the project of rowing around to the Lake Hotel. The people at the Thumb seemed afraid of the water. The only thing that could happen, a sudden breeze, would do no harm to a steady-going rowboat.[8] But there still lingers about the Yellowstone some of the mysterious terror that sprang out of the fever and hardships of the first explorers. A corporal and private are stationed near the lunch station, and the private did offer to row me, but when the corporal remarked that he had much better stay at home and get sobered up for once in his life, I concluded that I did not want him to. So I stopped there for the night.

The corporal proved a good-hearted fellow. He told me quite naively that he had heard a professional walker was doing the Park on foot for a wager, and they all allowed there must be something in it!

It is always cold at the Thumb during the night. Water froze to an appreciable thickness inside one of the tents. We were glad to spend the evening in-doors, or rather in canvases, with only occasional glimpses at the moon. The company was democratic. It included the entire population of Thumb Bay, six in all—the corporal, the private, the manager, the cook, the kitchen boy and a contented tramp. We were not without amusement. We played a noisy game called "hearts." We had sixteen candle-power illumination; that is to say, we had a chandelier made of four crossed laths tacked together, and bearing two lighted candles at each end. The affair was raised and lowered by a cord and pulley attached to the ridge-pole of the tent. In effect it was something like a flattened Christmas tree.

I slept in a tent that night, and had the kitchen boy for roommate. The moon-light made the walls faintly luminous. A soft glow pervaded everything.

One did not have to sleep to dream. A bear came out of the forest and snuffed around the tent near my bed.

The next morning I left camp. The road skirted the lake for some distance and then struck off through the forest.[9] An inquisitive fawn remarked the expedition. The walk was charming. I wandered off among ideal footpaths, stopping occasionally to gather wild flowers or tiny mountain strawberries. It was a capital place to go sylvestering. The road lay buried so deeply in the forest that it should have been the haunt of some of Uncle Sam's big game. But none appeared. It is one of the disappointments of the Yellowstone that one sees so few animals. One hears so much about them that one comes to have a vague expectation of going out after breakfast and seeing the national game pass in procession, two by two, and labeled with the common and scientific names, after the manner of the trees in Independence Square. But nothing so interesting happens. The woods and fields are silent.

⌒

A visitor using the alias L. Louise Elliott in about 1912 echoed Henderson's remark about the scarcity of animals:

> I understand now as I never did before why so many people are disappointed when they come here. It is because of the fact that it is called a park and they come with the expectation of seeing a man-made park, similar to those of the cities, only on a much larger and vastly grander scale; with the curiosities all conveniently grouped, and the animals collected in large numbers in enclosed corrals.

They forget that it is merely a district controlled by the Government and preserved as far as possible in its wild and natural state, and that the wild animals, native to this territory, are permitted to roam at will over miles and miles of country, and that the greater part of them come down to the mainly traveled districts only when forced to do so by hunger, when the snow gets deep and the grazing poor. (Six Weeks on Horseback, 117)

⌒

It is about eighteen miles from the Thumb to the Lake Hotel, and it took nearly six hours to walk it. After leaving the forest, the road skirts the lake for several miles in approaching the hotel and gives many beautiful outlooks. One gets a good appetite for luncheon.

The road leaves the lake at the hotel and follows the west bank of the Yellowstone River for another eighteen miles [through Hayden Valley], until the Great Falls and the Canyon Hotel are reached. It was a happy afternoon's walk. The sun was shining. The air was cool and bracing. It was a delight simply to be alive. At one point, all the trees had lost their leaves and stood out against the afternoon sky bare and naked, like the trees in **Slocomb's** etchings. It brought a curious October feeling. One meets numbers of camps and campers.

Frederick Alfred Slocombe (1847-1920) was a British artist who specialized in naturalistic landscapes.

Hunting is strictly forbidden, so that fishing is the only outlet. The fish are certainly fine, the best of salmon trout, great spotted beauties. Looking upon their shining freshness, the animal in me said they must be very nice to eat. The poet in me said they were much too pretty to kill.

Later, when the sun was about an hour above the horizon, the forests ceased altogether. For several miles the road crossed a wide plateau, overlooking the narrower valley along the river. This was the best part of the walk. The all-out-doors feeling was very strong. Picture to yourself a broad, undulating plain, without a single tree, extending for miles in front of you, back of you, to the left of you. To the right, the ground falls away, forming steep cliffs. Below, there is a green and level meadow, then the Yellowstone, and on the opposite bank, low, rounded hills. The plain is bounded by a line of forest. Beyond rise the august mountains. Add to this the great vault of the sky, the intense color of the sunset, the absence of all life. Standing in the midst of this vast loneliness, there came into my heart a great flood of feeling. I bared my head. The air and sunshine bathed my person. It was a baptism. I extended my hands. I stood alone in the presence of the Eternal. My heart leaped with exultation. I wished for nothing.

At times the meadow widens, and one comes upon a truly pastoral scene. The green is dotted with hayricks and men are busy with harvesting.[10]

Everything softens with the approaching night. Camps are being made here and there. One could readily fancy that their fires were altars and the delicately curling smoke an offering of incense to the great World-Soul.

At sunset the road left the plateau and entered a narrow, sulphurous valley, only wide enough to hold the road and the river. It was a hideous place. The foul odors called up all sorts of disagreeable images. A little snake glided across the path. I fished him out of the grass with my umbrella. It was a rattlesnake.[11] I killed him. I was glad that this happened in that hellish little valley rather than up on God's plateau. Night came on. The warm, golden colors of the sunset gave place to the pale silver tints of the moonlight. The moonbeams danced upon the waters of the Yellowstone. They flitted through the fir trees at the side of the road. The camp fires were red and glowing. The brighter stars were shining. It was serene and beautiful and illusory. I was very tired.

The last two miles of the walk involved some climbing and some pain. I got to the Canyon Hotel a little after eight. Dinner was over and I could get nothing but a cup of coffee and a piece of bread and butter. This was poor comfort after walking thirty-six miles, and they charged me a dollar for it. I mentioned the very limited menu. They made it fifty cents. Even then, I felt that I had not robbed them.

It would be almost impossible to exaggerate the coloring of the Yellowstone Canyon. No falls in the world have so unique a setting. The walls of the canyon are very steep. They are sculptured into all sorts of fantastic shapes. They are alive with color; here a dazzling white, there a warm brown; between the two, nearly the whole chromatic scale—creams and yellows, pinks, reds and orange, greens and grays—a wealth of pigment not found in any artist's paint-box.

There are few who have not seen pictures of the Yellowstone [waterfalls]. The falls are getting to be almost as well known, pictorially, as Niagara. Yet they come upon one as an entire surprise. Everything is so vast that it takes some time to realize the immensity. Gradually the scales fall from one's eyes. The grandeur becomes appalling. The river, that was flowing along tranquilly enough the afternoon before, plunges at the Upper Falls down an almost perpendicular distance of 140 feet. Then a swift, short run, and the Great Falls are reached. Here the waters leap into the abyss, 360 feet below, a mass of silver foam [Upper Falls is 109 feet (33 meters) and Lower or Great Falls is 308 feet (94 meters)]. But meanwhile, you are hundreds of feet above, on the edge of the canyon. The tiny thread of water you see below you is in reality a good-sized river. You are face to face with a marvel whose size keeps you always at a distance.

From the Canyon Hotel the poor stage people go jolting over to the Norris Basin, and then back over their former road to the Mammoth Hot Springs. But your happy tramp is wiser. He leaves the stage road and follows a glorious mountain trail that stretches northward for twenty-three miles along the edge of the canyon, and around the eastern and northern slopes of Mt. Washburn, to Yancey's Camp.[12] The trail is perfect. The day is perfect. One's mood is perfect. It would be difficult to be happier.

Best of all, one is alone with Nature. The life of thought and feeling flows on uninterruptedly. The outer world ministers to it, but never breaks in upon it. Perhaps this constitutes the charm of the day.

After getting fairly clear of the hotel, I met no one until sunset and Yancey's. Scarcely an animal crossed my path, except the fretful porcupine; I almost stumbled over him. Later, a timid doe looked at me from a distance. But this was all. It was a day of intense aloneness.

It was easy to follow the trail, for the travel is sufficient to keep it fairly distinct. When it was at all doubtful, I trusted to my sense of direction, a woodman's gift, and had no trouble.

The sun was setting when I reached Yancey's, and came again into the folk-world. It is half ranch, half hotel. The house is of squared logs. It is plain and clean, and the fare is good.

From Yancey's to the Hot Springs, it is a final walk of eighteen miles. The road is high and open, and gives a series of magnificent mountain views. For the most part it follows the foot-hills overlooking the Yellowstone valley. After several hours I met a camping party, and asked them how far it was to the Springs. The women did not know. The men were very ill-natured. They said it was twenty-five miles. In reality I found it to be seven.

By noon I was sitting on the porch of the hotel waiting for the stage to carry me over to Cinnabar. I was sitting there very contentedly. The Jonathan Edwards in me, the artist, the poet, the geologist, the Indian—all were satisfied. I had done what they said I could not do. I had been in the presence of great beauty, I had experienced keen pleasure, I had been profoundly interested, I had lived for six days in the open. What more could I wish?

NOTES

1. Yellowstone's Grand Loop Road covers approximately 152 miles (245 kilometers), including the Canyon to Norris road (the center of its "figure 8"). It passes close to the majority of interesting features in the park and was first completed in 1905.

2. Henderson, "Yellowstone on Foot," *Outing* 34, no. 2 (May 1899): 161–67.

3. The Northern Pacific Railroad branch line had reached Cinnabar in 1883, but it did not go the last three miles to Gardiner until 1903 and even then was not completed in time for President Theodore Roosevelt's visit to the park that April.

4. Jonathan Edwards (1703–1758) was a brilliant, devout, and ascetic Protestant pastor, philosopher, and theologian in early eighteenth-century New England, known for taking joy from the beauties of nature.

5. From Mammoth Junction through Kingman Pass (Golden Gate) to Swan Lake is an elevation gain of 1,028 feet (313 meters). Kingman Pass is the official name of the road up Glen Creek built in 1883–84 by Dan C. Kingman and his team of engineers. Kingman later became chief of the U.S. Army Corps of Engineers. The name Golden Gate comes from the color of its ancient volcanic tuff, stained yellow by iron oxide.

6. Stating that Norris Geyser Basin's geysers "are all small, mere spouting springs," Henderson was apparently unaware of the two-hundred-fifty-foot eruptions (although rare and erratic) of Steamboat Geyser, first recorded in 1878. "The old Heidelberg doctor" would have been the nineteenth-century German physicist, chemist, and inventor Robert W. E. von Bunsen. He formulated a widely accepted theory to account for the activity of Iceland's geysers.

7. Joseph LeConte's *Elements of Geology* was published during Henderson's undergraduate years. LeConte, 1823–1901, was the first professor of geology and botany at the University of California at Berkeley and a major collector of fossils for their museum of paleontology.

8. Had Henderson known at the time of his tour how many people would drown in the lake during the following century, he would not have regretted being unable to row to the Lake Hotel. About forty people have lost their lives in the lake—although only three before 1898, the year of Henderson's walk around the park. Particularly in the afternoon, sudden storms can

create waves as high as six feet, and the water is so cold that hypothermia can kill even a strong swimmer in twenty minutes or less. Whittlesey, *Death in Yellowstone*, 179.

9.   The nineteenth-century road, rather than following the lakeshore all the way from the junction at West Thumb to the one at Fishing Bridge as the present road does, cut straight through the woods from the northernmost point of West Thumb Bay to the Natural Bridge near today's Bridge Bay area.

10. The Hayden Valley was one of several sites in the park where hay was cut to feed resident livestock in the park's early years.

11. Encountering a rattlesnake would be very unlikely in Hayden Valley. Only in the high desert area of the park between Mammoth and Gardiner have rattlesnakes been found; however, garter snakes are fairly common.

12. The section of the Grand Loop Road that crosses Dunraven Pass on the western slope of Mt. Washburn was not yet built in Henderson's time. He followed an old trail on the east side of the mountain.

A ride through Yellowstone backcountry

In 1897, E. V. Wilcox and his party rode from Bozeman through the beautiful Boulder River valley of southern Montana to enter northern Yellowstone through the Beartooth Range. From there they took a difficult route to the Absaroka Hoodoos, which span the eastern border of the park. Wilcox had probably read Superintendent Philetus W. Norris's account of his 1880 visit to the Hoodoos and had certainly read the U.S. Geological Survey's report of the area, but very few white men had seen this remote place by the time of his trip. Even today, few people visit the Hoodoos due to their difficult access.

Wilcox chose a group of hardy companions but tells us little about them and nothing about himself in his *Land of Sunshine* article,[1] choosing instead to describe in fine detail his traverse and his surroundings. The route Wilcox chose—from south of Big Timber, Montana to the Hoodoos—followed very rugged Indian trails. Part of this area is now designated as the Absaroka-Beartooth Wilderness. The anthologist has not encountered any other historical account in which adventurers approached Hoodoo Basin from the east.

F. W. Traphagen, a colleague of Wilcox at Montana Agricultural College (now Montana State University–Bozeman), was the photographer and presumably the "professor" Wilcox mentions.

Having prepared for college at Sugar Grove Seminary in Pennsylvania, Wilcox earned his bachelor's degree in one year and his doctorate three years later (1895), both from Harvard University. Wilcox was a professor of zoology and veterinary science from 1896 to 1899 at Montana Agricultural College, then became an editor for the U.S. Department of Agriculture. He later directed the Hawaii Agricultural Experiment Station and wrote for *Country Gentleman* magazine. He collected numerous specimens in Montana, Wyoming, and Idaho; a species of penstemon and a gilia, both Rocky Mountain flowers, were named for him.

Wilcox wrote books on subjects like raising farm animals and avoiding plants poisonous to stock. But he was a man of diverse interests, serving as president of a Washington, D.C., Shakespearean Society in 1941 and taking on the subject of Far Eastern poverty after extensive travels in Asia. In 1947 he published his eleventh and final book, *Acres and People: The Eternal Problem of China and India.*

A Visit to the Hoodoos of Wyoming

1901

EARLEY VERNON WILCOX
born Busti, New York, 1869 • died Washington, D.C., 1955

In parts of the country, especially in the Northwestern States, peculiar erosions are found which are known as "Hoodoos." One of the largest and most interesting groups of these grotesque geological formations is located just east of the Yellowstone Park in **Big Horn County**, Wyoming. As these Hoodoos are very seldom visited, and as the meager published descriptions seemed marvelous almost beyond belief, a small party, of which the writer was a member, decided to visit this region.

The party was outfitted in Bozeman, Montana, and consisted of a guide, his two sons, a professor, a doctor, a preacher, and the writer. We engaged a packer and a cook, and our pack train consisted of nine saddle horses and nine pack horses. We rode about eighteen miles the first day and made camp just east of the Bozeman tunnel [a railroad tunnel opened by the Northern Pacific Railroad in 1883], at the top of the divide between the Yellowstone and the Missouri, at an altitude of about 5,000 feet. The following day we passed through Livingston and traversed the dry plains in the direction of the Absaroka Mountains.

Our third day's journey took us to the Natural Bridge on the Boulder River, about twenty-five miles from Big Timber [see map, page 205]. This is well worthy of a greater **pilgrimage** than it receives. The Boulder is here a dashing mountain stream about fifty feet wide. It disappears in an immense whirlpool into the limestone rock, and flows in a subterranean channel for about 300 feet. The lower end of the tunnel opens out on the face of a perpendicular wall of solid rock which is 150 feet high. The river bursts forth from the tunnel at a height of about forty feet from the bottom of a precipice, and falls into a large rock basin, from which it disappears again in the rock and runs in its hidden course for a distance of [a] quarter of a mile. During high water the tunnel is not large enough to receive the whole river, and the overflow passes

Big Horn County had just been formed in 1896 from three other counties. In 1909, all the territory including Yellowstone Park, the Hoodoos, and east to the town of Cody became Park County.

pilgrimage: The Natural Bridge on the Boulder River collapsed in about 1989, but this beautiful part of Gallatin National Forest is still well worth a visit.

in a channel worn in the surface of the rock, dashing over the brink of the precipice at the same time that the lower portion is bursting out of the tunnel part way down the cliff. In the bottom of the upper bed, which was dry at the time of our visit, we discovered an opening into a cavern in the limestone. By the aid of two picket ropes we descended into the cavern and found it to be of considerable size. At flood times the water evidently passes through this cavern also.

From the Natural Bridge we proceeded up the

Lower End of Natural Bridge. (Height of Cliff, 150 feet). Photo by F. W. Traphagen.

Boulder along what had been described to us as "a good wagon road." We had to walk, however, a considerable part of the distance, as the horses were unable to make their way over the rocks with a rider. Supper had to be cooked and eaten that evening in a dashing rainstorm. Our baking powder biscuits were thoroughly soaked and we had to dip them in a sort of emulsified bacon grease. But a mountain appetite is not easily disturbed.

We were now skirting the mountains which surround the Lake Park region,[2] and we purposed entering this country by the most practicable pass. We broke camp early in the morning and proceeded up the beautiful, heavily wooded cañon of the Boulder. An old prospector, with a flintlock rifle, informed us that he had seen three bears in a huckleberry patch a few miles up the river, but had not cared to attack them with a flintlock. After riding for about an hour we suddenly caught sight of the ears of a bear above the huckleberry bushes. We finally succeeded in killing all three bears. The rest of the party, however, had demonstrated the great penetrating power of steel-jacketed bullets

The map opposite shows the mountainous and sometimes trackless course the Wilcox party followed—covering more than 150 miles between the Natural Bridge and Hoodoo Basin, including their aborted excursion into Sunlight Basin. The map shows only a few of the hundreds of lakes in the vicinity of the Beartooth Plateau. In 1891 the Department of the Interior created the Yellowstone Park Forest Reservation (now part of Shoshone National Forest). The Hoodoo Basin was thus inside the forest reservation in 1897 but became part of Yellowstone Park when the boundary was adjusted in 1929 to include the entire Lamar River watershed.
Source: Traced by Linton A. Brown from USGS and U.S. Forest Service maps, 2015.

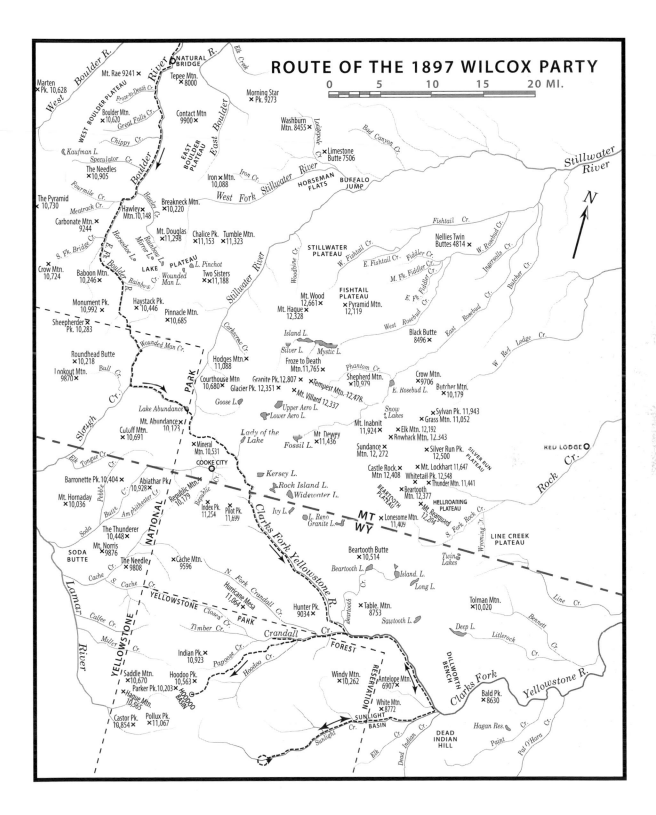

ROUTE OF THE 1897 WILCOX PARTY

0   5   10   15   20 MI.

N

Marten Pk. ×10,628
Mt. Rae 9241 ×
West Boulder R.
Boulder R.
Natural Bridge
Tepee Mtn. × 8000
Elk Creek
Morning Star × Pk. 9273
Natural R.

WEST BOULDER PLATEAU
Froze-to-Death Cr.
Boulder Mtn. ×10,620
Great Falls Cr.
Contact Mtn 9900 ×
East Boulder
Washburn Mtn. 8455 ×
Lodgepole Cr.
Bad Canyon Cr.

Chippy Cr.
EAST BOULDER PLATEAU
Limestone Butte 7506 ×
Stillwater River

Kaufman L.
Speculator Cr.
The Needles ×10,905
Iron × Mtn. 10,088
Iron Cr.
West Fork Stillwater River
HORSEMAN FLATS
BUFFALO JUMP

The Pyramid × 10,730
Fourmile Cr.
Breakneck Mtn. ×10,220
Fishtail Cr.
Nellies Twin Buttes 4814 ×
W. Rosebud Cr.
Ingersolls Cr.

Carbonate Mtn. × 9244
Meatrack Cr.
Hawley Mtn.10,148 ×
Haulla Cr.
Mt. Douglas ×11,298
Chalice Pk. ×11,153
Tumble Mtn. ×11,323
STILLWATER PLATEAU
W. Fishtail Cr.
E. Fishtail Cr.
Fiddler Cr.
M. Fk. Fiddler Cr.
E. Fk. Fiddler Cr.
Butcher Cr.

S. Fk. Bridge Cr.
Rainbow L.
Mirror L.
Woodbine Cr.

Crow Mtn. 10,724
Baboon Mtn. ×10,246
E. Fk. Boulder R.
Rainbow R.
LAKE PLATEAU
L. Pinchot
Wounded Man L.
Two Sisters ×11,188
Mt. Wood 12,661 ×
FISHTAIL PLATEAU
Pyramid Mtn. × 12,119
West Rosebud
Black Butte 8496 ×
East Rosebud
W. Red Lodge Cr.

Monument Pk. × 10,992
Haystack Pk. ×10,446
Pinnacle Mtn. ×10,685
Mt. Hague 12,328
Island L.
Silver L.
Mystic L.

Sheepherder × Pk. 10,283
Wounded Man Cr.
Roundhead Butte ×10,218
Hodges Mtn. 11,088
Froze to Death Mtn.11,765 ×
Phantom Cr.
Shepherd Mtn. ×10,979
Crow Mtn. ×9706
Butcher Mtn. ×10,179

Lookout Mtn. 9870 ×
Bull Cr.
Carbsense Cr.
Courthouse Mtn 10,680 ×
Granite Pk.12,807 ×
Glacier Pk. 12,351 ×
Tempest Mtn. 12,478 ×
Mt. Villard 12,337 ×
E. Rosebud L.

Slough Cr.
PARK
Goose L.
Upper Aero L.
Lower Aero L.
Snow Lakes
Sylvan Pk. 11,943 ×
Grass Mtn. 11,052 ×

Lake Abundance
Mt. Abundance × 10,173
Cutoff Mtn. ×10,691
Mineral × Mtn. 10,531
Lady of the Lake
Fossil L.
Mt Dewey ×11,436
Mt. Inabnit 11,924 ×
Elk Mtn. 12,192
Rowback Mtn. 12,343 ×
SILVER RUN PLATEAU
RED LODGE O

Elk Cr.
Tongue Cr.
COOKE CITY O
Sundance × Mtn. 12,272
Silver Run Pk. × 12,500
Rock Cr.

Barronette Pk.10,404 ×
Abiathar Pk. ×10,928
Republic Mtn. 10,179
Kersey L.
Castle Rock. × Mtn 12,408
Mt. Lockhart 11,647 ×
Whitetail Pk. 12,548 ×
Thunder Mtn. 11,441 ×

Mt. Hornaday ×10,036
Pebble Cr.
Amphitheater Cr.
Index Pk. × 11,254
Pilot Pk. × 11,699
Rock Island L.
Widewater L.
BEARTOOTH PLATEAU
Beartooth Mtn. × 12,377
HELLROARING PLATEAU

NATIONAL
Butte Cr.
Soda
Republic Cr.
Ivy L.
L. Reno Granite L.
MT WY
Mt. Rearguard 12,204 ×
Lonesome Mtn. × 11,409
S. Fork Rock Cr.
Wyoming Cr.
LINE CREEK PLATEAU

The Thunderer 10,448 ×
Clarks Fork Yellowstone R.
Beartooth Butte × 10,514
Beartooth L.
Island. L.
Twin Lakes

SODA BUTTE
Mt. Norris ×9876
Cache Mtn. × 9596
Long L.
Tolman Mtn. ×10,020
Line Cr.
Bennett Cr.

The Needle × 9808
Cache Cr.
S. Cache Cr.
N. Fork Crandall Cr.
Hurricane Mesa 11,064 ×
Hunter Pk. 9034 ×
Table. Mtn. 8753 ×
Beartooth Cr.
Sawtooth L.
Deep L.
Litlerock Cr.

Lamar River
YELLOWSTONE PARK
Closers' Cr.
Timber Cr.
Crandall Cr.
FOREST

Calfee Cr.
Miller Cr.
Indian Pk. × 10,923
Papoose Cr.
Hoodoo Cr.
RESERVATION
Windy Mtn. × 10,262
Antelope Mtn. 6907 ×
DILWORTH BENCH
Clarks Fork

Yellowstone River
Saddle Mtn. ×10,670
Hoodoo Pk. ×10,563
Parker Pk.10,203 ×
Hague Mtn. 10,565 ×
HOODOO BASIN
White Mtn. × 8772
Bald Pk. × 8630
Yellowstone R.

Castor Pk. 10,854 ×
Pollux Pk. ×11,067
SUNLIGHT BASIN
Sunlight Cr.
Elk Cr.
Dead Indian Cr.
DEAD INDIAN HILL
Hagan Res.
Paint Cr.
Pat O'Hara Cr.

in various trees. This episode not only gave us bear skulls and skins as trophies, but some fine bear steak which proved a very acceptable variation from bacon. The old female was of a deep black color, while one of the cubs was black and the other brown. Both cubs were males.

Thus far we had been following the middle fork of the Boulder. We now took a trail which led up one of the branches, and camped in a beautiful basin at an altitude of about 8,500 feet. The next day being Sunday, we gave the horses a needed rest and climbed a peak 11,000 feet in height [probably Monument Peak]. Here, for the first time in our trip, we found everlasting snowbanks. The Alpine plants and insects of this peak were very interesting and of great variety. We made a full collection of the plants, among which there proved to be twenty species new to science. Later in the day we descended the peak and traveled over a pass into the Lake Park country. This is essentially a plateau, 9,000 to 10,000 feet high and for the most part well covered with grass. One of the most attractive features of this region is the abundance of small lakes with clear cold water and plenty of fine trout. There were also fresh signs of mountain sheep, deer and elk. Our next march took us along Slough Creek, and we camped at Lake Abundance, near Cook City. Plenty of good trout were to be had in the lake and some rather tough ducks, but almost any fresh meat was agreeable for the sake of variety.

From Lake Abundance we crossed the divide and went down Clark's Fork. This, like all mountain streams in the region, furnished ideal conditions for trout; but there are no fish in the river or any of its branches above the falls, which are located at the point where Dead Indian and Sunlight Creeks unite with the main fork.

We traveled two days down this stream and at last reached the falls. The three rivers which unite at this point all run in cañons cut in the solid rock to a depth of about 400 feet. Near Cook City, and upon the south side of Clark's Fork, are located two high peaks of magnificent appearance, separated by a deep abrupt chasm, but constituting a sort of twin mountain. They are called Pilot and Index Peaks; their tops seemed inaccessible.[3]

Finding the Sunlight Creek to the Hoodoos too difficult, we went back to Crandall Creek and camped near the spot where Crandall and his companions were treacherously shot by Indians.[4] After photographing two or three supposed graves of Crandall, we finally found the real one and piled several stones upon the grave to mark the place.

We had supposed that from this camp we could reach the Hoodoo plateau in one long march; since it was only about twenty miles, as we estimated by the geological survey maps, though the trail was a difficult one. But it took us four days of hard work to reach our main objective point.

Saturday morning we started early, to reach the Hoodoos the same afternoon. Upon breaking camp, the bear skins were packed on the mule for the first time. As soon as she sniffed the peculiar odor of bear at such close quarters, she attempted to get away from her imagined enemy, but we overtook her about four miles from camp. We proceeded up the main fork of Crandall Creek. The valley grew narrower, until we entered a cañon and were forced to ride in the creek; and after another mile we came to impassable cascades with perpendicular walls on either side; so we were forced to go back to our previous camp. After a reconnaissance we climbed the ridge on the south side of the south fork of Crandall Creek and followed it all day. This is the historic trail down which the Nez Perces came when they succeeded in eluding the United States troops at the cañon of Clark's Fork [in 1877]. At five in the afternoon of the third day we arrived on the brink of the cañon of Hoodoo Creek; across which, about five miles distant, the Hoodoo plateau was plainly in view. We found that we must descend 1,500 feet and climb an equal height on the opposite side to reach the plateau. The sides of the cañon were so steep that several hours' hard work with pick and shovel was necessary before we could get the animals down. The following morning we descended a zigzag course, and, leading the horses and also holding on to their tails, took them safely down one by one. Then came the climb on the opposite side, which was the most difficult one of the whole trip. We had to make steps in a snow bank in order to cross it, and even where there was no snow, we had to rest every few steps. The guide and the writer were the first to reach the plateau. Our camp on the plateau was at an elevation of 10,300 feet. We shot an old blue grouse cock here but at such an altitude it was impossible to boil, fry, or otherwise reduce the flesh to an eatable degree of tenderness. Soon after our arrival on the plateau a thunderstorm burst upon us with terrific fury just as we sat down to supper. The course of the flashes of lightning was horizontal.

It is perhaps impossible adequately to describe the Hoodoos. It was remarked by several of the party that the Hoodoo Basin contains more of interest than the Yellowstone Park. **Hoodoo Peak**, which rises to an elevation of nearly 12,000 feet, is located at the northwest corner of the plateau. From its top one can see, away to the north, the Granite or Beartooth Mountains, with **Granite Peak** rising to a height of 12,800 feet, the highest point in Montana, and with immense snowfields and small glaciers even on the southern exposure. To the southeast the horizon is formed by one of the most magnificent ranges of the Absaroka system, while far to the south the Tetons present an imposing spectacle with their chief peak, **the Grand Teton**, reaching a height of 14,800 feet. The main Hoodoo basin is located in an immense cañon on the south side of Hoodoo Peak. The most interesting group of Hoodoos, however, the group which apparently was not visited by the Geological Survey parties, is to be found on the southeast and east slopes of the peak, and is about three miles distant from the main Hoodoo Basin.

The whole region is of volcanic origin, being largely composed of basic **breccia**. The softer parts are readily eroded and carried away by the water, while the hard parts remain standing in the form of "Hoodoos" of all sizes and of every conceivable shape. It requires no imagination to

Hoodoo Peak in the Absaroka Range is 10,563 feet (3,220 m) high.

Granite Peak, located in the Beartooth Range, is 12,807 feet (3,904 m) high.

The Grand Teton's elevation is 13,770 feet (4,197 m).

breccia: Rock made up of sharp fragments cemented in a matrix of fine sand and sediment.

see chickens, cathedrals, towers, palaces, camels, goats, men and women, done in breccia. The figures vary in size from the merest hummocks to columns of 200 feet in height. One group was particularly striking and lifelike—of a number of large columns, of which one stood apart from the rest. Upon the main group were mounted several female figures in most fantastic drapery. On the isolated column was an immense bust of a man about fifty feet in height. His giant arm was extended and the clenched fist rested upon the column. He had upon his head a twisted turban and wore a most grotesque solemn expression. There were no commandments on stone tablets, but the gentleman was evidently laying down the law to his assembled harem, and he was named, accordingly, the "Hoodoo Chief." We had great expectations of the Hoodoos and were agreeably surprised. They were far more interesting than we had imagined.

As from the Hoodoo plateau we searched the distant snowfields of the Granite Mountains with our field-glasses, regret was felt that we had not made a side trip to the Grasshopper Glacier of that region.[5] This glacier is not of great size, but is especially interesting from the fact that it contains tons of grasshoppers frozen into the ice far below the surface. They are probably the Rocky Mountain locust, but they crumble so rapidly on being exposed to the

"Hoodoo Column, 200 Feet High" and The Hoodoo Castle." Photos by F. W. Traphagen.

air that the species could not be determined from specimens brought by the party which visited the glacier. Photographs of the glacier show that the grasshoppers are imbedded in two strata of the ice.

On leaving the Hoodoos, the expedition passed down Miller Creek and Lamar River into the Yellowstone Park. We stopped on Cache Creek near Death Gulch, visited Soda Butte, and spent some time on Amethyst Creek and in the Fossil Forest. One camp was made at Tower Falls, and on the way we received at Yancey's our first mail from home.

One day's journey along the cañon of the Yellowstone brought us to the lower falls, and here we were surprised to find ourselves under arrest by order of the military authorities of the Park. On the day of our march from Tower Falls to the Great Falls of the Yellowstone, two armed highwaymen had held up six stage-coaches on the road from the Cañon Hotel to Norris Basin and robbed the passengers. Naturally we knew nothing of the affair, having come from the opposite direction. During this day's journey our party had become separated. In crossing a boggy meadow, alone, my horse broke through the sod and broke a strap by which my gun was slung to the saddle. At this moment I saw two men slowly riding out of the woods. I supposed them to be the professor and the doctor, who had not been seen since morning, and [I] immediately shouted; whereupon the men wheeled their horses and disappeared in the forest. I dismounted, took my gun from the case, readjusted the case, and after leading my horse across the meadow, rode on more rapidly in order to overtake the guide.

This little episode had unexpected developments.

It seems that the two riders were the highwaymen. A messenger had been sent to summon troops and was riding on the trail along the side of the meadow when I shouted. He did not see the horsemen, and supposed I was shouting at him. His mind was full of the recent robbery; and when I took my gun from its case he concluded that I was about to try a shot at him. So he put spurs to his horse and rode at his best speed for three miles, when he met the soldiers and informed them that he had barely escaped being shot by one of the robbers.[6]

When the soldiers arrived at the Cañon hotel, they found us boldly encamped near the river, nine men strong and eighteen horses. We were at once directed not to break camp pending further orders from the superintendent of the park. We were kept under military arrest for nearly thirty-six hours after the superintendent knew who we were, and for reasons which we were quite unable to discover. The soldiers seemed to know nothing of the park except the regular wagon road over which tourists are taken. We were told that every possible exit from the park was guarded, but when we said we intended to leave the park by the Bannock Pass, the sergeant confessed that he did not know its location.[7]

As we rode over this pass we found a fresh, well beaten elk track, and on the Gallatin side of the pass, at the foot of **Three Rivers Peak**, saw a band of about 150 elk. From Three Rivers Peak to Bozeman we traveled more rapidly, covering the

Three Rivers Peak is at the heads of Grayling, Indian, and Panther Creeks in the northwestern quadrant of the park.

whole distance in three days and riding fifty miles on the third day. Thus we may briefly describe our route as eastward along the whole northern boundary of the park, southward to the Hoodoos, and westward through the park, returning by the Gallatin Cañon. The trip occupied us for twenty-five days, and we traveled over 500 miles of mountainous country.

From a botanical standpoint I never saw a richer country. On the Hoodoo plateau there are to be found in August not only a great variety of alpine plants in full bloom, but also such plants as *Dodecatheon* [shooting star] and *Claytonia* [spring beauty], which at lower altitudes are among the earliest spring flowers. Upon this plateau it freezes every night. While we were there a half inch of ice formed during the night. All the plants here are frozen so that they may be broken off in the early morning, and the ice rattles off from them upon one's boots. The fringed gentian [*Gentian detonsa*] may be frozen so rigidly that the petals can be broken in the fingers. As soon as the sun appears, however, the plants thaw out and are uninjured.

In the mud near the edges of the snow banks, buttercups [*Ranunculus* sp.] and *calthas* [mountain marsh marigold] grow in great abundance. These plants also force their way through the snow, and it is not an uncommon thing to see them flaunting their gay flowers above the surface of the snow.

The Hoodoos may be approached either from the Yellowstone Park or from Crandall Creek, and for the geologist, zoölogist, botanist, photographer or tourist, the region presents attractions which are seldom equalled.

U.S. Dept. of Agriculture, Washington, D.C.

NOTES

1. Wilcox, "Visit to the Hoodoos of Wyoming," 209–23.
2. Lake Park is probably the high mountain area full of small lakes just northeast of Wilcox's route, marked Lake Plateau on the Gallatin National Forest Central map, U.S. Department of Agriculture, 2012.
3. The first ascent of Pilot Peak was achieved on August 12, 1932, by Hollis Mees and Robert McKenzie. They used no climbing gear.
4. Crow Indians murdered prospector Jack Crandall and his companion Dougherty near this creek in 1869. They left the heads on the points of picks. Haines, *Yellowstone Story* 1: 81.
5. Grasshopper Glacier, in which millions of grasshoppers had become embedded in the ice, is about eight miles north of Cooke City, in the Custer National Forest just on the border of the Gallatin National Forest. It became a tourist destination in the early twentieth century. Of the several other disappearing glaciers where grasshoppers are embedded in the Rocky Mountains, two are in the Beartooth Range.
6. The stagecoach robbery that prompted Wilcox's troubles took place on August 14, 1897; coach passengers were robbed of cash, jewelry, and watches, but the robbers were apprehended two weeks later and served time for their crime. Haynes, *Yellowstone Stage Holdups*, 10–14.
7. The Bannocks and other tribes crossed the park annually to hunt buffalo in what became southeastern Montana. Bannock Pass is where their trail crossed the Gallatin Range from the Gallatin River drainage to the Panther Creek–Gardner River drainage.

A journalist tours on horseback

Thirty years after the park was established, the majority of visitors traveled by horse-drawn coach and followed a set route through the park. Still, a few people continued to ride horseback in small parties. Ray Stannard Baker, who probably visited in 1902, entered from Yellowstone's South Entrance. (The South Entrance Road was roughed out in 1892 but substantially improved in 1902.)[1] Visitors like Baker stayed in the hotels or camped wherever they wished.

Baker gives us a lively account of his turn-of-the-century horseback tour.[2] He describes the "human procession" he finds in the park and also reveals his considerable sensitivity to wilderness. Accompanying Baker's text were unusual drawings of characters and scenery by artist Ernest Blumenschein, who traveled with Baker.

In closing the account of his trip, Baker tells us uncritically about the coach travelers and the "dusty campers," who, in his day, traveled with horse and wagon and were often called "sagebrushers." A man named H. Z. Osborne told this story about Adam Deem of the Yellowstone Park Association's transportation department:

> [Deem assigns] the passengers to their respective coaches, and as they are thrown into each other's society constantly for the five days of the trip, it is of no little consequence to the individual that he be parceled off into an agreeable crowd. I asked Deem how he managed that part of the business.

"Well," he said, "I try to get all the pleasant people together. Then I pick out all the cranks and kickers, and put them all into a carriage by themselves if it is feasible. I have been at this business so long that I can tell a crank as far as I can see him. The minute they go across the floor to register I pick out the cranks, and mentally begin to assign them to carriages for the next day. I give the pleasant people the most accommodating drivers, and to the kickers I give some crusty old frost-bitten driver that will fire it right back at them. In that way everything moves as smooth as glass."[3]

After spending his youth in Wisconsin, Baker received a bachelor's degree from Michigan Agricultural College, spent a year in law school, then became a reporter for the *Chicago News Record*. A few years later he joined the staff of *McClure's Magazine*, where he still worked at the time of this Yellowstone report, although it was the *Century Magazine* that published it. He became an editor of *American Magazine* in 1906 and wrote numerous books, primarily on social issues.

Baker's best-known work stemmed from his position as President Woodrow Wilson's press secretary during World War I. The last two volumes of his biography of Wilson (*Woodrow Wilson, War Leader* and *Woodrow Wilson, Armistice*) won the 1940 Pulitzer Prize for biography.

A Place of Marvels:

Yellowstone Park as It Now Is ("The Great Northwest Series")

1903

Ray Stannard Baker
born Lansing, Michigan, 1870 • died Amherst, Massachusetts, 1946

[The account here offered of the aspects of Yellowstone Park, as it is now under government supervision, will be read with particular interest by those who remember the first magazine papers to bring the subject prominently before the public. They appeared in the early numbers of this periodical, within one and two years of the discovery of this remarkable region. Ex-Governor N. P. Langford's two papers on "The Wonders of the Yellowstone" were printed in this magazine for May and June, 1871;[4] in the November issue of the same year Truman C. Everts described the incidents of his "Thirty-seven Days of Peril" while lost in the Yellowstone, having become separated from the Langford company;[5] and to the February number of the following year (1872), Dr. F. V. Hayden contributed a fully illustrated paper on his adventurous visit of the previous year.[6]—THE EDITOR.]

At first, approaching the Park, we felt the pressure of our desire to reach the ultra-natural attractions which have made this a place of marvels for all the world—the remnant volcanoes dying out in geysers, the strangely ebullient pots of mud, the thundering earth-rents discharging clouds of sulphurous steam, and the many other evidences of a world in the process of making. But as we proceeded—we had come in by the little-traveled south entrance of the Park, through Idaho and Wyoming, along the splendid Tetons, the wildest of wild country, desert basin, and mountain pass—we seemed to forget the objective point of our journey in the natural glory of this Rocky Mountain wilderness, the every-day joy of the road, sleeping underneath the trees, bathing in the noisy streams, tramping off alone through beguiling bypaths of desert and cañon. Here the wilderness is so commanding and omnipotent that the dim, winding human trail among the rocks and sand seemed almost of yesterday's making, giving us the feeling of the intrepid discoverer. Think of coming suddenly to an opening among the trees and, all unexpectedly, beholding a fine, brawling stream tumbling down a mountain-side, or a snow-clad mountain peak with the sun upon it, or an elk or a deer starting from the very road, pausing a moment with startled alertness, then bounding off, a flash of brown and white, through the woods!

So long we loitered among these beauties, common to all the Rocky Mountains, that we were slow in reaching the wonders of the Park itself. Perhaps these days of adjustment to the wild and natural prepared us the better for what we were now to see.

In the morning of our second day within the Park we beheld afar off a valley rolling full of steam. It was as if a city lay hidden there, with smoke rising through the bright, cool air from a hundred busy chimneys. For a moment, so vivid was the impression, we almost expected to hear the city noises and smell the city smells; then we felt again, not without a pleasant sense of recovery, the solemn quiet of the forest spreading illimitably before our eyes, the splendid mountain-tops, the glimpses of blue lake, the charm of the winding road.

But the populous and smoky city of the imagination was now the eager desire of the heart. Certain sulphurous odors, suggestive of volcanic activity, had come to our nostrils; we had already seen a number of smoking rivulets oozing out of the earth near the roadside and creeping down through varicolored mud to the brook, and we had dismounted to dabble our fingers in the tepid water of our first hot spring. Now we rode out of the forest, and there before us, on the shore of Yellowstone Lake, stretched the bare volcanic formation, a glaring white in the sunshine, steam rising from a score of grotesque mud-cones and boiling pools—nature's imitation of a smoky city [West Thumb Geyser Basin].

Here is a veritable miniature volcano, crater and all; a wooden sign names it a paint-pot. We stoop over and look into the steamy crater: a lake of pink mud is slowly rising within, rumbling and emitting sulphurous smells. Opening suddenly, it hurls the hot mud in air, splashing it almost into our faces, and slowly subsides with much grumbling, to repeat the operation again in a few minutes, as it has been doing these fifty thousand years and more.[7] Not beautiful, but mysterious, curious, uncanny.

Here is a placid hot pool a dozen feet wide, set like a white-rimmed basin in the hard formation, with water so clear that one can see the marvelously colored sides extending deep into the earth—evanescent blue, cream-color, pink, red   attrac-

THE MAN WHO BUILT THE ROAD

tive because so strange. A Chinaman has planted his laundry where he can dip up water heated by the earth's eternal fires for his washtubs. His clothes-line, with a brave array of new washing, cuts off a large portion of the volcanic landscape. Down at the lake-brink a number of girls are trying, with unaccustomed fishing-rods, to perform the feat, without which no visit to the Park would be quite successful, of catching a trout and cooking it, wriggling, in the hot pool behind them. A few rods away are the lunch-stations of the transportation companies, where the regular visitors in the big coaches stop for a meal, or possibly to stay for a night on their way around the Park. At each wonder-center such a station may be found, buzzing with visitors, every one in ecstasies over the geysers, setting up cameras, snapping buttons, filling little bottles with hot water or little boxes with pink mud, all very jolly, all expecting to be astonished, and all realizing their expectations. Indeed, a nameless exhilaration seems to affect every Park visitor, so that everything seems especially beautiful, especially marvelous—perhaps the effect of the clear, pure air, or the altitude: for we are here more than seven thousand feet above the level of the sea.

They tell one that the Thumb—this point of Yellowstone Lake is thus described—is nothing.

"Wait until you reach the Upper Geyser Basin! Wait until you hear the Black Growler at Norris! And wait, oh, wait, until you see Old Faithful in eruption!"

And so one mounts his horse with a cheerful sense of pleasures to come, and half a day later rides into the fuming valley of the Upper Geyser Basin, the greatest of all the centers of volcanic activity. As one emerges from the forest, Old Faithful is just in the act of throwing its splendid column of hot water a hundred and fifty feet in air, the wind blowing out the top in white spray, until the geyser resembles a huge, sparkling, graceful plume set in the earth. The geyser holds its height much longer than one expects; but presently it falls away, rallies often, throws up lesser jets, and finally sinks, hissing and rumbling, into its brown

"On Hymen Terrace"

cone; leaving all the rocky earth about it glistening, smoking with hot water. The little crowd of spectators on the convenient benches press the buttons of their kodaks once more, and hurry to the next geyser on the list. All this valley smokes with pools and hot rivulets flowing into the Firehole River; there are many curious, grotesque cone formations very appropriately named, each bearing its label on a white stake. And on the hill stands the big, ugly eating-house, swarming with tourists, and a store where one may buy photographs of the wonders, and souvenir spoons, which will help to convince the friends at home that no wonder has been missed.

Beyond the Upper Basin one cannot escape a veritable succession of marvels. At the Fountain there are many strange forms of geysers and hot springs, often gorgeous in coloring, surrounded by water-formed rocks in many curious and beautiful designs, and veritable caldrons of bubbling mud, and bears in the garbage-piles, and I know not how many other wonders. At Norris there are growling, jagged holes in the earth, belching forth huge volumes of hot steam, which, having killed and bleached all the verdure of the near mountain-side, has given the whole valley an indescribable air of desolation, as if the forces of nature had gone wrong—the very work of the devil, after whom so many of the marvels are named. Farther along one shudders under the brow of Roaring Mountain, makes a wry face while sipping water from the Apollinaris spring, wonders at the Hoodoo rocks [at Silver Gate], or admires the gorgeous colored pulpits and terraces of the Mammoth Hot Springs.[8]

And yet after all these things, amazing as they are, one turns again to the road and the mountains and the trees. Undue emphasis may have been laid upon the odd, spectacular, bizarre—those things, dear to the heart of the American, which are the "biggest," the "grandest," the "most wonderful," the "most beautiful" of their kind in the world. But the Park is far more than a natural hippodrome. The geysers appeal to one's sense of the mysterious: one treads on the hollow earth not without an agreeable sense of danger, thrills with the volcanic rumblings underneath, waits with tense interest

Drawn by Ernest L. Blumenschein.   Half-tone plate engraved by F. H. Wellington

for the geyser, now boiling and bubbling, to hurl its fountain of hot water into the air; one is awed by these strange evidences of a living earth, guesses and conjectures, as the scientists have been doing for centuries, and then, somehow, unaccountably weary of these exhibitions, turns to the solemn, majestic hills, to waterfall and marshy meadow, to the wonderful trail through the forest. For, after all, the charm of the Park is the charm of the deep, untouched wilderness, the joy of the open road.

Indeed, the very name Park, associated as it is with smooth lawns and formal, man-guarded tree-groups and stream-courses, seems out of place when applied to these splendid mountain-tops. Here is a space nearly sixty miles square—a third larger than the State of Delaware, and, with its adjoining forest reserves, which are really a part of the public wilderness, nearly as large as Massachusetts or New Jersey. Visitors see only a narrow road-strip of its wonders, though the best; upon vast reaches of mountain and forest, lakes, rivers, geysers, cañons, no man looks once a year; probably many areas have never been seen by human eyes. The United States regular soldiers who guard it keep mostly to the roads, the boundaries of the Park being for the most part so wild and rugged that even poaching hunters could not cross them if they would.

It was a carping German traveler who complained that this Park was no park. "Look at your dead trees and burned stumps in

A PIONEER

the woods," he said, thinking perhaps of the well-groomed, man-made forests of his native land, "and your streams, full of driftwood. It is not cared for."

And Heaven help that it may never be cared for in that way! Not a park, but a wilderness, full of wild beauty and natural disorder, may we keep the place as nature left it, disturbing no land-slide where it lies, no natural dam of logs and stones heaped here by mountain freshet, no havoc of wind-storm or avalanche. The windfall, with its shaggy spreading roots full of matted earth and stone, rapidly being covered with grass and moss, and the river-bed full of bleached driftwood, each has its own rare quality of picturesqueness, its own fitting place in this wild harmony. There is beauty even in the work of the forest fire, which has left whole mountain-sides of freshly scorched pine foliage, a deep golden red smoldering in the sunshine; and many a blackened bit of forest, longer burned, leaves an impression of somber shadows, of silence and death, which cannot be forgotten. One even comes to begrudge this wilderness its telephone poles, its roads, and the excellent stone embankments which keep them from slipping down the mountainsides into the swift streams below; for they detract from its wild perfection. We may behold nature in its softer and more comely aspects almost anywhere; but every year, with the spread of population in our country, it becomes more difficult to preserve genuine wilderness places where hill and forest and stream have been left exactly as nature made them. Already our indomitable pioneers have driven the wilderness into the very fastnesses of the mountains, so that only remnants now remain. And this great Yellowstone Park remnant has been fortunately set aside by the government for the enjoyment and inspiration of the people forever.

And not only for the enjoyment of the people, but for practical use as well. Nothing gives the American keener joy than to plan a pleasure and then find that he has also developed a business opportunity. So Yellowstone Park, set aside for the wonders of its geysers and its great cañon, turns out to be the very continental fountain of waters. Here in the tops of the Rockies, within the Park or near it, rise the greatest of American rivers. At one spot the traveler may stand squarely upon the backbone of North America, the continental divide: at his right hand a stream flows outward and downward, finding its way through the Snake and Columbia rivers to the Pacific Ocean; at his left a rivulet reaches the Yellowstone, the Missouri, the Mississippi, and thence the Gulf of Mexico. And to the southward of the Park rise the head-waters of the Platte and the Colorado rivers, and to the northward the head-waters of the Missouri. Protecting these mountains, preserving the forest, excluding cattle and sheep, help to conserve and maintain the water-supply and keep the flow of all these rivers steady and sure, a need which grows greater with every year's development in the irrigated desert land.

We come, at last, to the final glory of the Park, the splendid cañon of the Yellowstone. Yellowstone Lake, a deep basin of snow-water, 7721 feet above sea-level, debouches at its northern end into the narrow Yellowstone River. Flowing for a dozen miles or more through a wild and rugged country, this turbulent stream comes suddenly to a rocky ledge, over which it leaps 112 feet downward into a resounding gorge. Gathering itself in a huge, swirling pool, foam-flecked, it flows onward a few hundred feet and takes another tremendous leap, this time 311 feet, straight into the awful depths of the Grand Cañon. So great is the fall that most of the water, bending over the brink of the precipice, smooth, oily, and green, is dashed into spray, widening out at the base and drifting against the steep cañon walls, which the constant moisture has clothed with soft green mosses and other minute water-growths. Thence it collects in a thousand gleaming rivulets, gathers in brooks and cascades, and gushes back into the river-channel. From the summit of the awful precipice above the falls one may trace the stream along the depths of the cañon—seen at this distance a mere hand's-breadth of foamy water broken by varied forms of cascades, pools, and rapids, and all of a limpid greenness unmatched elsewhere.

Niagara is greater, more majestic in the plenitude of its power, having twenty times the flow of water; but it cannot compare with these falls in the settings of cañon and forest, in the coloring of rock, water, sky—all so indescribably grand, gorgeous, and overpowering.

Somehow I had thought of the cañon as rock-colored, gray, somber, perhaps like the gorge of Niagara; and it was with a thrill that I first saw it in all its savage glory of reds and yellows, greens and blues. Surely never was there such a spectacle. Imagine, if you can,—but you never can,—a mighty cleft in the level earth a third of a mile wide, its brinks sharp, precipitous, reaching over twelve hundred feet downward; sometimes almost perpendicular, sometimes banked with huge heaps of talus or buttressed with spindling pinnacles and towers often surmounted with eagle-nests, and all painted, glowing with the richest color—vast patches of yellow and orange, streakings of red and blue, with here a towering abutment all of red, and there another all of yellow. At the bottom flows the gleaming green river, and at the top the dark green forest reaches to the cañon-edge, and sometimes, even, rugged and gnarled pines, the vanguard of the wood, venture over the precipice, to find footing on some ledge, or to hang, half dislodged, with angular dead arms reaching out into the mighty depths; a resting-place for soaring eagle or hawk. The sides of the cañon, being not of solid rock, but of crumbling, soft formation, have furnished plastic material for the sculpturing of water and wind, which have tooled them into a thousand fantastic forms. One's eye traces out gigantic castles, huge dog forms, bird forms, titanic faces—all adding to the awful impressiveness of the place.

For miles the cañon stretches northward from the lower falls. From numerous well-guarded

AN ENGLISH TOURIST

outlooks the spectator, grasping hard upon the railing lest the dizziness of these heights unnerve him, may behold a hundred varied views of the grandeur, looking either toward the falls, which seem to fill the cañon-end like a splendid white column of marble, or off to the northward, where the stupendous gorge widens out, loses some of its coloring, admits more of the forest, and finally disappears among rugged mountains.

Everywhere the view is one that places the seal of awed silence upon the lips; it never palls, never grows old. One soon sees all too much of geyser and paint-pot; of this, never. At first the sensation of savage immensity is so overpowering that the spectator gathers only a confused sense of bigness and barbaric color; but when he has made the perilous descent to the cañon bottom below the falls, when he has seen the wonder from every point of view, he begins to grasp a larger part of the whole scene, to form a picture which will remain with him.

One turns away from the cañon not with the feeling with which he left the geysers and the mud-pots, yet contented to go back to the simple, familiar beauties of the trail. Occasionally it is well to feast on a grand cañon, but these hills and streams are much the better steady living. These soothe and comfort.

Next to the natural wonders

of the Park, one will be most interested in the human procession which passes constantly up and down within it. Gradually, after days spent steeping one's self in the wild and lonely glory of the wilderness, he will come again to watch the people riding, tramping, all in ceaseless course, around the Park, each taking his wonders in accord with the eccentricities of his temperament.

It is hardly safe in these days to define a wilderness, it contains so much that is unexpected. We must refuse to be convinced by the unsatisfied one who finds incongruity in the ugly red hotels, the yellow coaches, the galloping tourists, the kodaks.[9] After all, every age is entitled to its own sort of wilderness, and ours seems to include the tourist and the hotel; the traveler is today as much a part of the Rocky Mountains as the elk or the lodgepole pine. No picture of the modern wilderness would today be complete without the sturdy golf-skirted American girl with her kodak, the white-top wagon, the Eastern youth turned suddenly Western, with oddly worn sombrero and spurs. It was a shock to one traveler's sensibilities (but it converted him) the day he went poetizing up a faint trail through the deep wood. "This," he was thinking, "is the forest primeval; this is the far limit of the wilderness. Surely no human foot has ever before trod upon this soft timber grass!" I think he expected momentarily to see a deer or a bear spring from its secure resting

place, when, lo and behold, a party of girls! Here they were miles from their hotel, tramping alone in the woods, getting the real spirit of things, and as safe, bless them! as they would have been at home. He found he had yet to learn a few things about a modern wilderness.

But most of the tourists remain pretty snugly in their coach-seats or near the hotels. One meets them in great loads, some wrapped in long linen coats, some wearing black glasses, some broad, green-brimmed hats. Wherever they may come from, they soon acquire the breezy way of the West, and nod good-humoredly as they pass. Occasionally one sees them devouring their guide-books and checking off the sights as they whirl by, so that they will be sure not to miss anything or see anything twice. Usually they come in trains, a dozen or twenty or even forty great coaches one after another, and when they have passed one sees no more of them until another day.

And such fun as they have, such acquaintances as they make, and such adventures as there are! One old gentleman, accompanied by his stenographer, after each excursion sat on the piazza, guide-book in hand, and dictated an account of what he had seen. And then there is the tourist who has brought a fine new pair of field-glasses through which he is constantly seeing more wonderful things than anyone else; the old lady with the lunch-basket; the young person who is

absorbed in altitudes, and who wishes to be constantly informed how high up she is now.

And then there are the dusty campers with white-top wagons or packhorses trailing slowly along the roads or making camp at the streamsides. Many of them have been through before; many are from near-by Montana or Utah, and have come for their regular summer outing, turning their horses to graze in the natural meadows. We met one young married couple thus spending their honeymoon, looking from the front of their wagon, a picture of dusty joy.

NOTES

1. Construction of the South Entrance Road is described in Culpin, *History of the Road System*, 355.
2. Baker, "Place of Marvels," 481–91.
3. Osborne, *A Midsummer Ramble*, as quoted in Whittlesey and Watry, *Ho! For Yellowstone*, 132.
4. This editor's note was in the original *Century* article. *Scribner's Monthly* became the *Century Illustrated Monthly Magazine* in 1881. Langford's *Scribner's* article appears on page 9 of this volume.

5. Truman Everts's story has been reissued in a fully annotated version as *Lost in the Yellowstone*, edited by Lee H. Whittlesey (2015).
6. Hayden, "Wonders of the West—II," 388–96.
7. "Fifty thousand years" must have seemed to Baker a suitably long time. West Thumb Bay itself was formed in a hydrothermal explosion some 200,000 years ago, but the paint pots could have been spouting mud even before that. No one can say just how long the Yellowstone region has had mud pots, hot springs, and geysers, only that those within the caldera must have appeared since the last caldera eruption 639,000 years ago. How do geoscientists determine such a precise date? Here is a much-simplified explanation of the argon-argon radiometric dating technique used for this determination. They measured the amounts of two isotopes of the element argon present in a very small crystal of the predominant rock produced by the last caldera eruption. Then they determined the age of the erupted rock and the eruption itself from these measurements (Lanphere et al., "Revised Ages for Tuffs," 559–68).
8. Pulpit and Hymen Terraces, both favorites with photographers and writers in the nineteenth century, have dried and then crumbled to the point of being unrecognizable. However, so-called Lower Hymen Terrace was very active and beautiful from 1992 to 2008 and may become so yet again.
9. By 1888 film was replacing plates as the medium for photography, and George Eastman's company introduced the name "Kodak" with the slogan: "You press the button—we do the rest." In 1900 "the first of the famous BROWNIE Cameras was introduced. It sold for $1 and used film that sold for 15 cents a roll. For the first time, the hobby of photography was within the financial reach of virtually everyone." From Kodak website, "History of Kodak: Milestones."

An intrepid mother

For the past century the vast majority of family visitors to Yellowstone Park have loaded up a car, minivan, or recreational vehicle at home and spent a few days or weeks camping or staying in motels and hotels while they see the geysers, the animals, and the scenery. A century ago Mrs. N. E. Corthell had neither our modern conveniences nor our speed of travel, but she took her large family to Yellowstone anyway, with children ranging in age from sixteen down to seven or eight, accompanied by no other adults until Mr. Corthell joined the family for the homeward trip. Her story first appeared in a 1905 issue of *The Independent* magazine.[1] Although most of this account takes place

outside of Yellowstone, it is valuable for its graphic portrait of the Wyoming many visitors traversed at the turn of the last century and its historic record of an independent woman's accomplishment.

One of the Corthell daughters, Mrs. John A. Hill (Evelyn), wrote her own account of traveling to Yellowstone in an automobile, "Twenty-Four Years After," which was published in a 1928 book along with an extended version of her mother's *Independent* account. The book contains a short foreword by Evelyn's father, Nellis E. Corthell, where he describes how he learned that his wife had planned the trip in his absence and had already acquired a wagon for it. He vigorously protested

The N. E. Corthell family shortly after their trek from Laramie to Yellowstone and back. The three girls surrounding their father are, *left to right*, Evelyn ("Daughter"), Gladys, and Miriam ("Mim"). The four boys around their mother Eleanor ("Nellie") are, *left to right*, Robert ("Robin"), Irving, Morris, and Huron. Photo courtesy of Alan ("Corky") Corthell, son of Robin.

the trip and expressed apprehension, but finally he gave in—and paid for the pair of big road horses, the spring wagon, and other travel expenses. A version of Mrs. Corthell's story, edited and combined with parts of the 1928 book, appears in *Adventures in Yellowstone*, by M. Mark Miller (2009).

Eleanor Quackenbush arrived in Laramie, Wyoming Territory, as a schoolteacher in 1882. She first found employment in the nearby railroad center of Rock Creek but soon moved to Laramie to teach. In 1885 she married attorney Nellis E. Corthell. Mr. Corthell, a native of New York state, became an authority on water rights and was the owner of the *Laramie Republican Boomerang* from 1890 to 1911. Their seven children, born in nine years, were Evelyn, Morris, Miriam, Gladys, Robin, Huron, and Irving.[2] Mrs. Corthell refers to them by nicknames in her story.

Raising children was only one of Corthell's interests. She was secretary of the Wyoming Press Association from 1896 to 1898 and on the editorial staff of the *Laramie Boomerang*, women's edition, in 1900. During World War I she and her husband both volunteered to go to France with the Red Cross but were rejected, because their four sons were in the army. Son Robin was wounded, but all returned home.[3] Mrs. Corthell was a strong supporter of women's rights, writing in 1915 to her daughter Miriam, then living in New York City, "I see so much in the Times about the Suffrage Campaign and I wonder if you are helping ever so little. To let it be known that you were born to the privilege and right of voting, and now you are deprived of it should make a point if you *feel* it an injustice."[4] She was referring here to the right of women in Wyoming Territory to vote, which was granted by their legislature in 1869—way ahead of the national women's suffrage (nineteenth) constitutional amendment, ratified in 1920.

Asked for biographical information about Nellie Corthell, her grandson Alan ("Corky") Corthell wrote, "She was a strong-willed person with firm beliefs in women's role in politics and the evils of alcohol. . . . Eleanor fit into the Wyoming political environment very well. Eleanor and Nellis were both confirmed Democrats and railed against the big trusts that oppressed the country. They believed that much of Wyoming could be made to bloom like the Garden of Eden, and devoted a lot of time and effort to make it happen."[5]

A Family Trek to the Yellowstone

1905

ELEANOR ("NELLIE") QUACKENBUSH CORTHELL
**born Black River Falls, Wisconsin, 1860
died Laramie, Wyoming, 1932**

[One of the most original and delightful vacation trips we have heard of recently is that of a Wyoming mother who with her seven children, the eldest son barely sixteen, traveled in a wagon from the southeastern part of the State to Yellowstone National Park in its northwest corner, a total distance of about 1200 miles. They lived out of doors two months, and crossed mountains and deserts where for many days they saw no one. We have asked the enterprising little woman who planned and carried out this unusual expedition to tell about it, for it is very encouraging to parents who are wondering how they can give their children a cheap and healthful vacation.—editor.][6]

Nearly half a life-time I have lived in Laramie, with all the while a great longing to see the wonders of the Yellowstone—in season, out of season, when the house was full of babies, even when it was full of measles. As the older children outgrew marbles and dolls, I conceived the bold idea of stowing them all in a prairie schooner and sailing away over the Rocky Mountains, deserts, forests and fords to the enchanted land five hundred miles away. My husband offered strenuous objection of course to the crazy project, but could only fizz and fume and furnish the wherewithal, for the reasons advanced he found irresistible; such an ideal vacation for the children—a summer out of doors seeing their native State! A chance for their botany, geography, zoology, to be naturalized. To be drivers and cooks would throw them on their own resources somewhat, a valuable education in itself. So economical, too! Such a fine opportunity for stretching of legs and lungs, with the Park at the end! Reasons to turn a man's head, you see, so when the boys wrote along the wagon top "Park or Bust," that settled it, and we started July 4th, 1903.

The first day out was glorious, so we camped without tent or stove, for the small boys were "heap big Injuns," who scorned the ways of civilized folk—in fair weather. They whooped along on the warpath, gravely examined every old trail, read the sky, sent the "stinging fatal arrow" after jackrabbits, clamored for pioneer talks, then rolled up in blankets around the campfire with only the stars overhead.

From Laramie down to the bridge where we made our first camp, a distance of thirty-three miles, there was one road only; beyond the bridge there were a dozen. Which one led to Little Medicine crossing, our most direct route to Shirley Basin, we didn't know and couldn't find out, for one may travel a whole day beyond the bridge and not see a house or an individual.

So we took the wrong road, went out of our way ten miles, and had to make a dry camp at Como, arriving in Medicine Bow the third day at noon. From here we drove north over the same road among the same Freezeout Hills, through which the "Virginian" piloted Owen Wister on his way to the Goose Egg Ranch,[7] reaching the old Trabing place about four o'clock. It was apparently abandoned, save that freighters were stopping here this one night. They courteously offered to camp outside and give us the house, but we were afraid of strangers, afraid of everything, in fact, and after a hasty supper moved on and spread our tarpaulins on the bare plain, arriving at the home of my friend, Kirk Dyer, the next morning.

I told him of my foolish suspicions—that the freighters, having lost their horses, might have designs on ours, etc. He rebuked me sternly, and read me such a lecture as I shall never forget.

"Country people are honest," said he, "and you must take it for granted. Away from the railroad this far, you are safer than on the streets of Laramie, and you will get a square deal everywhere. Trust people and don't harbor suspicions."

Such a delightful day as the children spent riding horseback and eating Mrs. Dyer's cream biscuits. We turned west from here and camped in Shirley Basin, just one hundred miles from home and five days out. So far the trip had been "better than my dreams," as the "Virginian" would say, tho in dreams I had traveled in automobiles. The next day was different. We were driving gayly along through a fine meadow, when suddenly the wagon sank in mire. The horses tugged to pull it out, the kingbolt snapped and off they walked, with the front wheels. My driver-boy quietly stepped over the dash-board and walked off after them.

For one despairing moment I thought the end of all things had come when my wagon parted in the middle. Noting my forlorn face one youngster concluded it was time to laugh, for he exclaimed: "Gee, mamma! This isn't a bit exciting. The horses ought to have run away and smashed a few kids." Seeing how much worse it might have been I thanked my lucky stars and calmed my fears.

Now, Shirley Basin is the land of the Good Samaritan, where every ranchman is your friend and neighbor, who pulls you out of the mud, mends your kingbolts and fifth wheels, agrees with you in politics, praises your husband, and treats you to ice cream in the evening, so the accident makes pleasant memory.

After circulating around and among Seminole and Ferris mountains, we finally wound up in Alcova, exactly a week from home. This is where the Platte River flows through a mountain cleft and where the "Pathfinder" dam is to be made which will flood Platte Valley and the Valley of the Sweetwater.

Now I must tell our troubles. We had forgotten the pocketbook when we started. Imagine my predicament. A mother totally unused to business or cares outside her own domain, 150 miles from home, with seven children and two horses to provide for and not a cent of money? Fifty miles from telephone or telegraph! We discovered our loss twenty miles out from Laramie, but just then met friends driving in, who promised to have it forwarded promptly; and we went serenely on our way into this dilemma.

We were put to our wits' end to get oats, as yet our only necessity. The driver suggested that we trade off a hammock; daughter thought we could better spare bacon; being a hot day, little Tad generously offered his overcoat as a basis of trade, and the driver and I walked over to a ranchman's house nerved up to try a bargain until—we saw the man, who was a perfect stranger. Then we realized it would be like asking the President to swap a sack of oats for a side of bacon. No, we must put dignity into our need, so quaking like two criminals, I ask Mr. Blank for oats and to "send the bill to my husband, please." A fleeting, quizzical flutter of his eyelid brought out the wretched blunder of the pocketbook.

"But, my dear madam," said he, "you must not be traveling with all those children to care for and no money." Then he brought from his desk a generous sum, saying, "Your husband can send me his check when convenient." My troubles were over, but was ever a deed more chivalrous "in days of old when knights were bold"?

Next morning we drove into the ruts of the old Oregon Trail at Independence Rock, where the trail finds the Sweetwater. This hill of granite, standing isolated on the plain, was a prominent landmark on the overland route. The annual rendezvous of fur traders, trappers and Indians occurred here. The Mormons left their names on it. The Whitman wedding party sojourned here, and here a great celebration took place July 4th, 1850, at a rendezvous, when General Fremont was carried to the top and made a speech. This rock is covered with thousands of names, one as early as 1819.

Everybody is growing handy, even expert, in camp work. The boys can skin a cottontail or dress a sage hen equal to Kit Carson himself, while daughter can prepare a savory dinner or pack a mess box good enough for an army general. The children are eagerly interested in everything they see, hear or can catch. Tad announces that we have seen nine horned toads, caught six, mailed three and have two packed in little tablet boxes with which to surprise (?) the chum at home. Query: Where is the medicine that was in the boxes? Well, if they spill the tablets, they will have to drink sage tea when sick. Marvelous cures of many kinds in bitter sage.

The immensity of Wyoming is beginning to dawn on them. They hunt, swim, explore, and so learn to enjoy the special, individual flavor of each locality. But all grow tired of the illimitable sage— one million acres after another. Why do these vast plains bear one species of wood only, and that so abundantly?

We are over two hundred miles from home now and approaching the Beaver Hill dragon.[8] We have heard so much about it, tho, we are braced for trouble. With a strong steel brake and a seventy-five-foot picket rope fastened behind for the children to pull back on, and me boosting on the underside to help the wagon over sidling places, out on that steep, windy comb, we came down safely, tho the stage coaches had blown over three times the week before.

A rare stroke of luck! The Shoshone Sun Dance was **on the tapis**—in a tepee as we drove into Fort Washakie. Fifteen hundred Indians were gathered here for the solemn ceremony. There was a large tepee on a common surrounded by quite a village of small ones. Half of this big tepee, or dance lodge, was filled with stalls made of green branches. The other half was occupied by tom-tom players and singers.

In each stall were two young braves dressed in modest loincloth and much paint, who in turn, while blowing a whistle, danced to the central pole and back in time to the music. Thus while sixty or more young men were entered for the dance, half alternated with the other half every fifteen minutes. This they continued from Tuesday night until Friday morning, almost without food, drink or rest. As an added test of endurance a great feast was going on outside all Thursday afternoon, which they must smell but not taste.

The Shoshone Indian reservation [Wind River Indian Reservation] is as large as a good sized Eastern State, and for seventy miles we had the whole country to ourselves. When the loneliness of the wide, treeless plains grew oppressive the children sang "Good Old Summer Time," or else they made "fudge." They sang from pure joyousness, for this free outdoor life is sweet to nature's own boys and girls, school-housed and book-ridden all winter. Each is a different kind of plainsman from the rest; one gets things with his gun, one with his hook, one with his bow, one with his hands. The latter is the naturalist, of course, engaged just now in switching a couple of water snakes into a beer bottle, with which he proposes to ornament his temporary totem pole. Every time the wagon stops, up springs a tiny dance lodge, a tom-tom is improvised, and Indian ki-yis revive the weary plain.

To-night, July 26th, we feel like a band of heroes. We forded Dinwoody, the ugliest tributary of Wind River. The water didn't flow quite over the horses' backs, because they are big horses. Yet it wasn't the deep water alone, but the swift mountain current, and huge, slippery upsetting boulders that made the ford dangerous. We forded the Wind and its tributaries eleven times after getting above its deepest water, and then—Dubois.

Here between the Indian reservation and the forest reserve is a narrow strip of

Where the Holdbacks Held Back, as Sketched by One of the Children

Government land, standing on end, along the upper canyons of the Wind, where young settlers are trying to make homes. The choicest locations were taken up long ago, one of them by a ranch-man named George B. West, said to be the original of the "Virginian." He wouldn't own up that he changed the babies [as related in *The Virginian*], but did go so far as to say that he attended that particular dance on the old Gallatin ranch. Like the "Virginian," he will talk on any subject except that of his own exploits.

Dubois has the distinction of being farther from the railroad than any other post office in the country, so they say. It is two hundred and fifty miles from here to Rawlins or Casper, and over four hundred to Laramie.

The responsibility, the anxiety of the long journey, are laying hold of me until I'm nearly overwhelmed. Four hundred miles from home! And only one letter! What may have happened in all these weeks? Suppose a child should sicken! There's one at home would never forgive me should any of them be injured. Will the horses hold out? The food? Already two spokes are broken and wrapped together with baling wire. My bold driver says we shall go on if we have to drive into the park with every spoke bound up in baling wire. And the dangers anticipated did add a certain zest. "Give ma something to fret about and she's happy," observed our twelve-year-old philosopher.

After the fords, our problems narrowed to a question of food, with the continental divide looming in the distance. How to cook enough for all those hungry children and still get ahead fifteen or twenty miles a day, where bread could not be bought. The capacity of my oven was two tins of twelve biscuits each. These I filled three times every night when dark overtook me. That made seventy-two biscuits, three apiece every meal, but those boys wanted ten each—and there was the problem.

The final spurt that brought us over the divide was strenuous, but repaid us grandly. It is fine to climb a thousand feet to look about you, but when you have mounted ten thousand feet to gaze abroad over the crest of the continent, the Atlantic slope behind, the Pacific slope spreading before you in range after range, with intervening valley, and gorge, and river, and lake, with the Grand Teton gleaming over all, magnificent, inspiring, your soul is filled with exaltation.[9]

Yet it is a **pokerish** kind of pleasure trying to enjoy the ravings of the demons from the bottomless pit at the "Thumb" [West Thumb Paint Pots]. As for me, I was kept busy counting the children. Every time one of them moved I was certain he would stumble into one of the boiling, walloping vats of mud; that it was delicate rose, emerald green, or heavenly blue mud did not reassure me in the least. But the children simply laughed. Even the youngest pertly informed me he had not come all the way to Yellowstone Park to fall into a mud hole. Still the horrid smells and the horrible groans and growls, and the gaping mouths clear to Hades aroused such emotions of terror in me that in sheer desperation I hurried over to the lake.

on the tapis: under discussion

pokerish: "ghostly, eerie," from the now rare word *poker* for hobgoblin or demon.

From here we telegraphed the anxious one and rested in the sweet peace that reigns over this corner of the park. And then, the Grand Canyon of the Yellowstone! Mere words cannot picture this wonderful vision, so I will only say that after we had spent a day sight seeing it seemed almost sacrilegious in me to return to camp, and go to baking beans; but we needed a change from Van Camp's, so there was nothing else to do. I wouldn't speak of it now, only that was how we came to have a visit from a bear. The beans were not done at bedtime, then I put in more wood, thinking they would be just right for breakfast.

About midnight there was a great clatter of falling stove. Sure enough, a bear had tipped it over trying to get my beans. He was trying so hard to get the oven door open that he never noticed our excitement. Not until I went out and threw things at him would he give up trying to find the combination of the oven door and go away, and not until then did we hear a peep from Shep. We never thought of being afraid. But I used all my ingenuity in hiding the bags of bacon and sugar so he wouldn't get them. The next forenoon we spent taking a long look into the canyon. On our way back we stopped at Canyon Hotel, where we received our wished for message from the father of the family: "Will meet you at Mammoth Hot Springs August 8th." August 8th was to-morrow, and Mammoth thirty miles away. The mere thought of seeing our beloved so soon lent wings to our feet, new life to our hopes and joys, so that surmounting the divide which separates Yellowstone [River] from Norris Basin was not so much work as needed exercise for holding us down to earth.

The prospect of losing half my responsibilities sent my spirits floating skyward.

We arrived in camp twelve minutes ahead of the stage from the railway station at Gardner. How we rushed to make camp homey! The driver unhitched and had the horses feeding instantly; daughter, Tom and babe set the tent; Tad brought wood, Glad water, and Mim speedily had a roaring fire; while I popped my biscuits in the oven, sliced bacon, seasoned corn, opened a jar of jam and a can of tomatoes, and set the coffee simmering. Daughter watched the fire, Glad spread the cloth, Mim tidied the mess box, and the boys put the bedding to air in the hot sun. Then we all had time to primp a little, the while wondering what father would bring, for shoes and hats had seen hard service.

But he never minded our weather-beaten appearance, tho we had been roughing it five weeks, having traveled just six hundred miles; we all looked good to him, and the wonderful "Springs" reflecting the joy of the occasion gleamed in the beautiful tints of the rainbow.

Now a new spirit has entered camp. The man of business has come to take his family home. We have to hurry. Oats are increased three-fold and thirty miles our speed. Then, ho! for the geysers! The Black Growler, a hissing, hideous monster we admire for his titanic and satanic power, but hastily pass on to cool, solid ground.

Like everybody else, we loved Old Faithful and the Morning Glory, we feared Excelsior, we admired the Giant, Bee Hive, Punch Bowl and a hundred other yawning chasms and smiling springs and spouting geysers. But the horrible rumbling as if an earthquake were imminent and the smell of brimstone made me eager to get my brood into the valley of safety beyond the Yellowstone.

We left the Park for Laramie over a new road recently completed by Captain Chittenden, through Sylvan Pass and Shoshone Canyon to Cody. This is the crowning joy of the trip. The park swarmed with people. Wherever we pitched our tent there hundreds had camped before us, to say nothing of the crowded hotels and Wylie tourists. But here in the heart of the mountain forest surely we are the first white woman and children to go over the trail, to fish in Sylvan Lake, to climb Grizzly Peak, to camp within the sacred haunts of **"Wahb,"** once lord of the Wind River Range.

Altogether we traveled twelve hundred miles, stood the journey well and never, never had such a wonderful, delightful summer. One must love the life to say that, must crave the outdoors and thrive on it. The sand was never too deep, the waters too high or the way too long. Every obstruction made the goal a dearer prize and we have lived our precious summer over and over.

Cold, thirst, hunger, fatigue, loneliness, I wanted the children to feel them all deeply, that their sympathy with the deprivation and isolation of the noble hearted army who blaze the way for civilization may be keen, true and sometimes helpful.

It is a trip anybody can take. It cost us only $25 apiece for the two months outing. We met people from Kansas and Salt Lake traveling just as we were. We had $15 worth of medicine along and never took a dose. The ammonia bottle was broken, also the camphor. The children emptied the witch hazel out in order to put specimens in. They plastered the arnica salve on the pony, and the dog ate the cold cream, and we shared our eight bottles of mosquito dope with ranchmen where we stopped. The wagon created some amusement on our arrival, for it bore the inscription, "July 4th, *Park or Bust*" on one side, and "September 1st, *Park and Busted*!" on the other. The children know their State as no book could teach them, and will have lifelong memories of the grandest scenes the world can produce.

LARAMIE, WYOMING.

NOTES

1. Corthell, *Independent*, 1460–67.
2. Obituary of Mrs. Nellis E. Corthell, *Laramie Republican Boomerang*, August 22, 1932, sent to the anthologist by Tamsen Hert, University of Wyoming associate librarian.
3. Personal communication, Corthell granddaughter Sally Hill Mackey, October 31, 2007.
4. Quoted by Ms. Mackey (Oct. 31, 2007) from Nellie's letter to her daughter Miriam, October 1915.
5. Personal communication, grandson Alan ("Corky") Corthell, October 19, 2007.
6. This editorial note appears in the original article.
7. *The Virginian: A Horseman of the Plains*, is the 1902 novel by Owen Wister, often considered to be the father of all western novels and movies. It is largely set at a ranch near Medicine Bow, in southern Wyoming.
8. Beaver Hill, also called Beaver Rim, is a steep cliff twenty-eight miles southeast of Lander, Wyoming.
9. The Corthell family crossed 9,544-foot (2,909 meters) Togwotee Pass for their view of the Tetons.

Wahb: The bear in Ernest Thompson Seton's popular 1899 storybook, *Biography of a Grizzly*.

Yellowstone and the Teacher

"Wylie-Way" in Yellowstone,[1] ca. 1907

Have you seen the gushing geysers of Iceland and Thibet, the mud pots of Java, the multi-colored hot springs of New Zealand or the lakes of Switzerland and the Canadian Rockies? Have you seen the waterfalls of the Yosemite and the Zambezi, the glass cliffs of Italy, the petrified trees of Arizona, the snow-crowned Alps or the Grand Cañon of the Colorado River? Perhaps not. Very few are the fortunate world travelers who have gazed upon all this varied and widely separated scenery. A pursuit of these treasures would take one from the Arctic circle to darkest equatorial Africa, from the highlands of Asia to the Sierras of California, and entail an expenditure of time and money that places it beyond even the hope of any but the wealthy and leisure class.

Now be it known that there exists at the very top of the North American continent, high up in the Rocky Mountains, a region whose limits encompass natural wonders like those enumerated above—an epitome, in short, of them all. This region is the Yellowstone National Park. Here Nature exhibits, as in a great museum, collections of her rarest handiwork: mud pots, geysers, hot spring terraces, mountain lakes, cataracts, cliffs, petrifactions, lofty peaks and mighty cañons. Even one of its multitudinous attractions would make a town in the Mississippi Valley world-famous. And Yellowstone is more than a vast scenic sanctuary. It is the largest big game preserve in the world. Elk, deer, antelope, big horn and the American bison live in their natural state and divide attention even with the great spouting geysers. Truly this is the "Wonderland" of all the world.

And be it further known that Yellowstone can only be visited successfully during the summer months—from the middle of June until the middle of September. It is significant that the calendar limits of its accessibility coincide almost exactly with the limits of the teacher's summer vacation period. When the teacher is engrossed in the arduous duties of the classroom, Nature covers "Wonderland" with a mantel of snow and ice; when the teacher is free to travel, Nature lifts the covering and exposes a pine-embowered, verdure clad fairyland.

The teacher's vacation trips should be at once recreative, pleasure-giving and educative. Life close to Nature in cozy tent cottages, association that fosters jollity and cheeriness, and the exhilaration of sight-seeing will bring the teacher nightly to resting beds where sleep is real; and each morning will usher in a day of cumulative wonder and delight. Surely Yellowstone is the teacher's ideal vacation trip.

1. This brochure promoted the Wylie Permanent Camping Company to teachers and college students. Superintendent of Bozeman schools William W. Wylie began leading inexpensive tours through the park in the early 1880s and sold his concession to Montana State Senator A. W. Miles in 1905.

An enterprising horsewoman

Mrs. Robert C. Morris, born Alice Parmelee in New Haven, Connecticut, about 1865, was descended from a Revolutionary War soldier in the Connecticut militia. In 1890 she married Robert Clark Morris, a New York City lawyer interested in international law, and in 1897 she published *Dragons and Cherry Blossoms* about her trip to Japan. Mrs. Morris was an avid horsewoman who became enamored with the scenery of Yellowstone Park and spent many summers at the Silver Tip Ranch just north of the park. In 1917 she conceived, financed, and carried out her remarkable plan to explore and map an interconnected loop of trails throughout the park and environs. Here we reproduce the article about her from the February 10, 1918, issue of *New York Times Magazine*.

Alice P. Morris had been in touch with park officials for several years concerning her interests in clearly marking the north boundary of Yellowstone and in improving and expanding trails in and around the park. By 1916 trail mileage totaled 402 miles—but not all were suitable for equestrian traffic. In a pamphlet intended for park visitors that she wrote in 1918, "Yellowstone Trails," she mentions spending "summer after summer at a mountain ranch on its border," and says of the work she did in 1917, "I rode for 4 months and travelled 15 hundred miles or thereabouts on horseback." She calls Yellowstone's famous bears "greedy groups about the dump-heaps near the hotels." Describing the existing trail that follows the eastern shore or Yellowstone Lake she writes, "Along the pebble beach grow immense luscious wild raspberries, as big as one's thumb, and in such undisciplined profusion that one may lean almost casually from the saddle and pluck them as one rides!"[1]

Her previous twenty-nine-page typed report, "Notes on Trail Study in Yellowstone Park 1917," sent to Park Supervisor Chester A. Lindsley, was much more matter-of-fact and mostly impersonal. But of the same route along Yellowstone Lake she allowed herself to say, "[The trail] comes out on a hill from which can be had an extensive view of the Upper Yellowstone valley. Also from this point moose and elk can be seen feeding in the small ponds in the valley." And a little farther south, "The mountains to the east are extremely rugged and picturesque. 'The Trident' and Colter Peak loom into the sky in most impressive manner."[2]

What became of this report that Mrs. Morris worked out so carefully in 1917? No evidence of action taken on her work turns up in a search of Yellowstone Park archives. One can speculate, however, that there could have been several reasons for this.

1. Lack of funds: A U.S. House of Representatives bill (H. R. 31/65/1, author unknown) dated April 2, 1917, requested a $50,000 appropriation for a system of trails and bridle paths in Yellowstone. This was the exact date of President Woodrow Wilson's request to Congress for a declaration of war with Germany.

2. The years 1917 and 1918 saw considerable administrative turmoil due to the gradual turnover

of park control from the U.S. Army to the new National Park Service (NPS), which was created on August 25, 1916, but not funded by Congress until April 17, 1917. As an example of this turmoil, a letter from acting director of the NPS, Horace M. Albright, to Chester A. Lindsley on October 23, 1917, urging that road work be transferred from the army to the Department of the Interior, stated, "The Engineer Corps of the Army has a vicious policy . . . which makes continuous development of the Yellowstone Road system according to a well-defined plan impossible."[3]

3. Soon after automobiles were first allowed in Yellowstone on August 1, 1915, park officials realized that saddle horses and horse-drawn vehicles were not compatible on park roads. They rightly guessed that the vast majority of visitors would arrive by auto; in 1918, for example, of the park's 35,039 tourists, 808 came in horse-drawn vehicles. The number on horseback is not known but must have been very small. Thus, improved bridle paths were not a high priority.

4. Two other Yellowstone enthusiasts contributed to the literature on trail construction in the same general time frame as Mrs. Morris's report. In June 1917, Milton P. Skinner, at that time an overseer for the Corps of Engineers, submitted his own report on potential trail building with a list of cost estimates. And Howard Eaton, a Wyoming rancher who led extended pack trips through the park for nearly forty years beginning in 1883 (including women since 1902), seems to have marked many trails.[4] It was Eaton to whom the NPS dedicated a completed system of trails on July 19, 1923.

Yellowstone Trails Blazed by New York Woman

Mrs. Robert C. Morris Has Laid Out Complete System of New Paths for the Government, Opening the Park's Wild Beauty to Horseback Riders

1918

ALICE PARMELEE MORRIS
born 1865, New Haven, Connecticut • death date unknown

It is almost two years since, in the words of official statement, "the Yellowstone National Park was opened to automobiles," and the fear has been general that the coming of the motor cars and the passing of the ancient stage coaches would rob that wild and magnificent mountain land of much of its charm, and, indeed, of its enjoyment. But the fear that "the Yellowstone would be spoiled," that opportunities for pack trains and horseback riding would be less, turns out to be just the opposite. They will be more.

The National Park Service of the Department of the Interior has recently accepted a complete mapping of projected trails through the vast extent of the Yellowstone National Park. Work is to begin on the actual cutting of the trails as soon as possible. Back of its neat lines and dots and tracings lies a great amount of rugged, courageous, brilliant

Mrs. Morris starting on her long trip

work. It is the sort of work which any one would think must be done by a forester or a professional mountaineer or surveyor.

But it was not. It was done by Mrs. Robert C. Morris, a New York woman who has a ranch on the borders of the park and spends her Summers in the Yellowstone because she loves it and who gave the whole of last Summer, and rode fifteen hundred miles on horseback, to plan the Yellowstone trails.

To introduce Mrs. Morris's work and the plan of the National Park Service, the following paragraph is quoted from the introduction to her official report:

> In these days of speedy pleasure vehicles, horses have been relegated to the background. There are, however, sections of our Western country, one of which is the Yellowstone National Park, which cannot be advantageously visited except by using horses. For even with its excellent system of well-kept roads, offering to the tourist an interesting automobile trip, only a comparatively small portion of this great domain of 3,300 square miles may be covered in this way, the greater part of it being reached only by the use of horses on trails and bridle paths.

There are many persons who prefer to visit the Yellowstone National Park leisurely in order to better appreciate its beauties and obtain healthful exercise and recreation, and previous to the opening of the park to automobiles these tourists used their own camping outfits with horse-drawn vehicles or pack trains. Since the advent of automobiles, however, there has been less opportunity for them to enjoy a visit of this sort; as the roads are not so available for the purpose as formerly, and it was with a view to continuing to make the park attractive to them as well as to the automobilists that the Department of the Interior determined to prepare information of the existing trail system and as to possible trails for future development.

Mrs. Morris began her work in June. Completed, it is in two parts—the "Map and Description of the Trails in and About Yellowstone Park" and the "Notes on Trail Study in Yellowstone Park." The first was the official report of existing trails. The second offered suggestions for connections and complete

Part of the pack train which covered 1,500 miles

trail marking. The map showed both.

What Mrs. Morris has done is to map out an elaborate system of trails through the park which will make it possible for visitors to ride through the most beautiful and picturesque portions of the great "reservation," journeying in an unhurried and enjoyable fashion, seeing much that cannot be seen from the motor roads alone, and never once traveling on the motor highways. What is more, the trails are arranged so that trips can be made in a day, a week, a month, or more. For—and here is one of the most valuable features of the work—the trails "system" is not simply one circle of bridle pathways; the trail is not one, but three. There is a circular trail that connects the hotels—that is "the loop," and every lover of Yellowstone Park will rejoice at the prospect of the loop's completion. Then there are series of circular trails that radiate from the hotels themselves like the spokes of a wheel—for short trips, these. Finally, for the longest journeys of all, is the outer circle that will wind its way through the wild country to the borders of the National Park; parts of this trail already exist as "fire lanes" in the wilderness; the rest of the outer circle was planned by Mrs. Morris on her Summer ride.

The new trails will not simply skirt mountains. They will go over them, sometimes cut through wonderful wild passes. To find and mark the mountain trails Mrs. Morris led her pack train over mountains whose height ranged anywhere from 5,000 to 10,000 feet. And, as one must realize at once with a little consideration of the problem, the trail routes were not always directly found. In talking of her Summer's work Mrs. Morris chanced casually to mention one snow-covered mountain peak that she had climbed four times! At last she found a way through, and the trail was blazed. Naturally, too, a great deal of the wilderness riding led through snowfields and up narrow, shaded, snow-filled valleys.

"My hope is that the completion of a system of trails will open the park to a great many people who otherwise might not think of going there at all," she said. "What could be more beautiful than a Summer journey with pack horses through that glorious country! And it is perfectly safe, you know. The guides are all men who are well known, the horses are gentle and trustworthy, and women and children can spend a magnificent holiday with horses and camping outfits on the trails. I cannot imagine greater pleasure, and I hope that thousands of Americans are going to discover it.

"We got up every morning at 5," she went on, "got the pack outfit off, mounted our horses, and rode until noon. But to say that we 'rode' doesn't give an accurate picture of my day. I was very busy, blazing the trail, finding the best way, working out the route. Sometimes we were waist-deep in snow. And," she added, casually, "there were a good many rivers to ford; sometimes the horses had to swim.

"At 12, or thereabout, we stopped for luncheon, usually by a beautiful stream, or perhaps by the side of a lake. We lunched and rested until about 1, then mounted again and rose to our day's destination. We generally reached it about 4.

"I always followed the regular system of making a point for the day's goal and arriving there. That is the only way to get anything done. System was necessary in this, as it is in anything. We

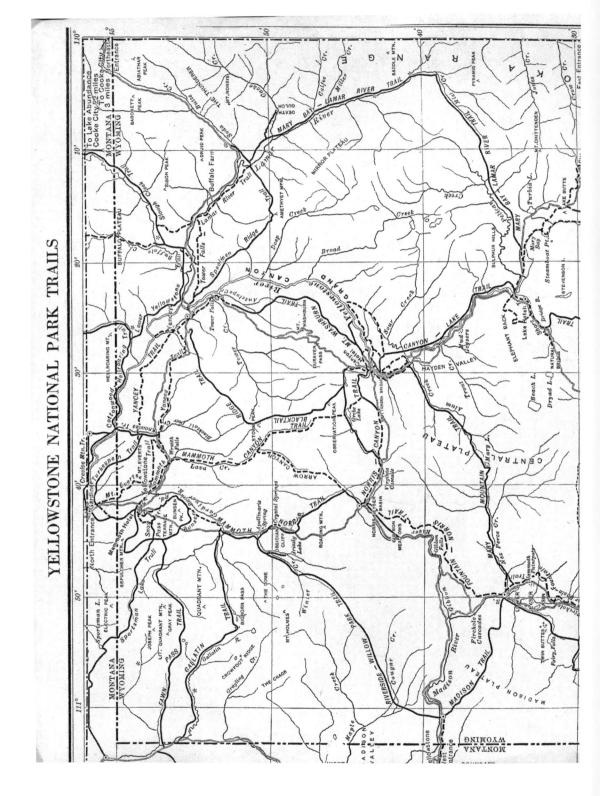

YELLOWSTONE NATIONAL PARK TRAILS

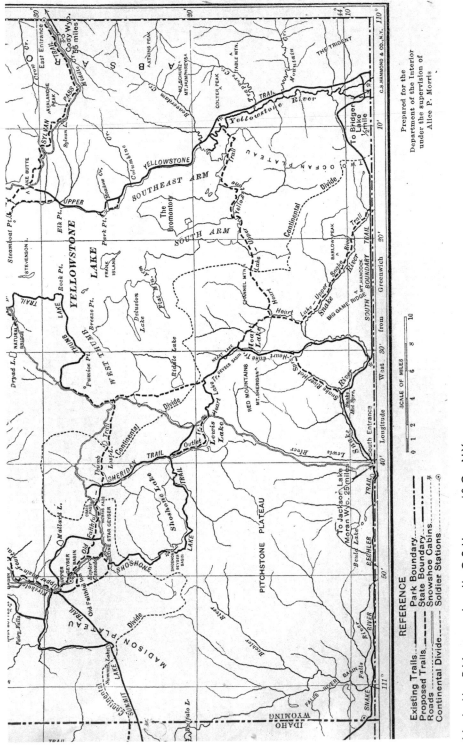

Map by Alice P. Morris, produced by C. S. Hammond & Co., N.Y.

usually arrived at our destination, as I said, about 4. That was the plan. But sometimes we got there at 3 and sometimes not until 8. My work, as a matter of fact, usually kept me busy until about 9 in the evening. But I was always ready to get up at 5 next day. Work? Of course it was work, planning the trails. But it was the most stimulating and inspiring kind of work you can imagine."

Some idea of the expert woodsman's knowledge to which Mrs. Morris makes but offhand reference may be gleaned from the notes of her "general recommendations" to the National Park Service. One is: Recommend that specifications be drawn as to what constitutes a standard trail in Yellowstone Park, and that such specifications be used as a basis for construction and inspection of new trails. Specifications to read about as follows:

Trails should be cut six feet wide through timber and graded three feet wide on all side hills and through rough ground. Also that overhanging branches be removed from trees. Small stumps and snags should be cut below the level of the ground, if possible, and the trail should be reasonably free from sharp turns, sudden declivities, and loosed stones. All trails to be constructed should be run out with a hypsometer or some such instrument and staked in order to establish an even grade. Recommended that the maximum grade on any trail constructed be 10 per cent, very few grades being over 8 per cent.

But the thing Mrs. Morris continually emphasized was the enjoyment of it all—her own enjoyment in blazing the trails and the enjoyment for others that she hopes will result.

"I know the Alps," she said. "I have lived in them and loved them. But the Alps seem very tame and 'cultivated' beside our Rockies. Ever since the Summer, years ago, when I went up from New Mexico to 'see Yellowstone Park,' it has been the most wonderful place in the world to me. And I want other women to know it and enjoy it as I do. Why, there's joy in the very rain of those mountains! And it is so easy to get horses and camping outfits and start out," she added. "At the northern and eastern entrances—Gardiner, Mon., on the north, and Cody, Wyo., on the east—one can get guides and the entire equipment, as well as horses."

NOTES

1. Morris, "Yellowstone Trails," 1.
2. Morris, "Notes on Trail Study 1917," 14, 15.
3. Albright to Lindsley, Army Box 1, File 341, Yellowstone National Park archives.
4. Kensel, *Dude Ranching*, 105n2.

How Buffalo Jones Disciplined a Bad Grizzly

William T. Hornaday, *The Minds and Manners of Wild Animals*, p. 130, 1922

William T. Hornaday (1854–1937) was first a hunter and taxidermist for the Smithsonian Institution, but in the 1880s he became concerned about the impending extinction of bison. He dedicated himself to conservation, writing several books, including *The Extermination of the American Bison*. He helped found the National Zoological Park, and in 1896 became director of what is now the Bronx Zoo.

In 1902 C. J. ("Buffalo") Jones was hired as game warden to help restore Yellowstone's bison herd, but he also tackled bear management. Yellowstone bears had begun to be a nuisance, but tourists continued to enjoy watching them for some seventy years. Other signs of the bears' popularity were the teddy bear—named for "Teddy" Roosevelt following an incident in 1902 when the president refused to kill a captured black bear—and Ernest Thompson Seton's stories of Wahb in *The Biography of a Grizzly* (1899), Johnny Bear in *Lives of the Hunted* (1901), and others with appealing bear drawings. Jones found the Yellowstone job to be impossible for one man, and he was a difficult man himself. He resigned his commission in 1905.

The most ridiculous and laughable performance ever put up with a wild grizzly bear as an actor was staged by Col. C. J. ("Buffalo") Jones when he was superintendent of the wild animals of the Yellowstone Park. He marked down for punishment a particularly troublesome grizzly that had often raided tourists' camps at a certain spot, to steal food. Very skillfully he roped that grizzly around one of his hind legs, suspended him from the limb of a tree, and while the disgraced and outraged silver-tip swung to and fro, bawling, cursing, snapping, snorting and wildly clawing at the air, Buffalo Jones whaled it with a beanpole until he was tired. With commendable forethought Mr. Jones had for that occasion provided a moving-picture camera, and this film always produces roars of laughter.

Now, here is where we guessed wrongly. We supposed that whenever and wherever a well-beaten grizzly was turned loose, the angry animal would attack the lynching party. But not so. When Mr. Jones' chastened grizzly was turned loose, it thought not of reprisals. It wildly fled to the tall timber, plunged into it, and there turned over a new leaf.

An artist on her own

This artist set out to see the park by joining a tour group, fulfilling a promise to a "Literary Person" to paint watercolor views of Yellowstone for a publication she does not name. Anne Bosworth Greene gave very few specifics about her trip, but it probably took place in 1906, with her transportation and lodging provided by the Wylie Permanent Camping Company. In the essay presented here, Greene mentions at least six works painted in Yellowstone.

Three of Greene's paintings, those that appeared in a 1913 book titled *Romantic America* by Robert Haven Schauffler, are reproduced here along with the text Schauffler wrote to accompany them. Schauffler almost certainly is Greene's Literary Person; he subtitled his chapter about Yellowstone Park "God's Old Curiosity Shop." He had a writing career spanning at least forty years and was a prolific writer of poetry, histories of American holidays, biographies of musicians, and travel essays for magazines and books.

The same summer that Greene toured Yellowstone, she visited and painted scenes of Yosemite National Park. Although Yosemite had been set aside under California state control in 1864 and became a national park in 1890, it had just come under full federal control in 1905, the year before Greene visited. In her book *Lambs in March*, Greene devotes two chapters to Yosemite and one to Yellowstone.[1]

In the chapter titled "Attempting Yellowstone," Greene chronicled three adventures that today would be considered headstrong and foolish if not absolutely forbidden: descending into the canyon (once with a rope and once without), walking out alone at night with no light, and staying in Devil's Kitchen at Mammoth for a prolonged painting session.

Born in 1876 to American parents, Anne Bosworth lived on a rural estate with servants and a governess in Chippenham near Bath, England. She had learned to read by the age of five and was conjugating irregular French verbs at six or seven, but her greatest interests centered around animals, especially horses and dogs.

When she was still a child her family moved to Springfield, Massachusetts. In 1900 she married Dr. Harrie M. Greene, who died young, leaving her with one daughter, Lorna, born in 1907. She developed an interest in painting and studied in Boston at the Eric Pape School of Art. Later she chose Provincetown, Massachusetts, for her studio but soon relocated to a farm in South Woodstock, Vermont, where she began to write stories and books about living on her farm, most centered around animals. Her books written in the 1930s include two about her travels in Europe with daughter Lorna, who died at age twenty in an automobile accident.

A *New York Times* reviewer of Greene's earlier (1923) book, *The Lone Winter*, remarked: "She has a beguiling way of seeing something that interests her, beginning to write about it, and then just wandering on as fancy leads her pen, with memories, piquant notions, quaint ideas, surmises, and all in a style that never fails to be interesting."[2] Greene painted throughout her life and participated in several exhibitions from 1911 on. Beginning in the 1930s, she spent winters in the artist colony of Tryon, North Carolina, returning to summer on her farm in Vermont.

Attempting Yellowstone
1928

ANNE BOSWORTH GREENE
born Wiltshire, England, 1876 • died Hanover, New Hampshire, 1961

1.

The sky was gray; a few flakes of snow wandered irresolutely down. I strolled along, surveying with a somewhat saturnine eye this region I had come West to render in art: the scrubby evergreens, the stretch of prairie beyond, the cold, sullen loneliness of it all; and I began to feel sincerely sorry for my fellow-worker, the Literary Person, who was to produce literature out of it. . . .

Sixty miles to the Geyser Basin! All around me passengers gabbled enthusiastically as we entered a promising gorge; reddish-purple walls arose, and a yellow stream chattered. This was as it should be. There should be no dallying on scenery's part. National parks were to have plenty of it. That was what they were parks *for*.

But the gorge soon dwindled. Toward noon we began to climb, and with no stop for lunch-hour were conveyed steadily, ruthlessly along up an endless hill through woods. It was the strangest woods, neither aisled nor arched; along its edge uprooted firs had fallen, crisscross and topsy turvy like matches tumbled anyhow into a box; and it was a satisfying moment when at last tent-tops, together with a flaming sunset, showed above the dark spruces.[3]

Bare, bright sunshine lay on Geyser Basin next morning. The valley was dotted with parties out to inspect the "formation," and knapsack on my back I prowled prospectingly about, keeping as far as possible from the sound of megaphones and information. Pools, large and small, interrupted one's progress; some were sapphires and some were emeralds; all had topaz edges; and one looked down through their unbelievable clarity as into the heart of a jewel a mile deep. But out of a jewel, exquisite though it be, one can hardly construe a landscape.

"This is a *mental* place," I murmured, coming to a stop by the steamy mouth of a geyser and leaning despondently upon it. "A geologist would be frightfully happy here. A sculptor might get designs for fountains, a movie-man could do crowds and geysers; but what, will you tell me, is a person to paint? Portraits of hydrants? I'm sure," I continued irreverently. "I've seen hydrants spout quite as imposingly as these geysers—though they don't steam, of course. Still-life, perhaps? These pools, now, and flowers growing so distressingly close to them? That little one, my dear, with a rim of orange rock, and blue gentian leaning over hot water—there's a subject for you! . . . No," I decided, rising from my moist seat and closing my half-folded easel, "this is a mental place. The Literary Person will have a lovely time; he'll describe for weeks; I'm going on." So I strode determinedly around a rocky corner; and came full upon the Emerald Pool.

EMERALD POOL

It lay in a secluded glade, a large, quiet, shapely pool, with only the slightest film of steam loitering above it. Beyond its golden margin pale trees, like frail souls arising, trembled in the light wind, gazing flutteringly down into this age-old wonder whose cavernous center was now deepest sea-green, now a jeweled blue. Scarcely moving from the spot where I stood on its water-worn rim, I set silently, fervidly to work. I was supposed to be working in black and white, but—Color? Of course one would use color. Color was the very incredible soul of the thing before me; and deep within the pool, sun-reflections quivered on the recessional gold of curving walls, or lost themselves in unfathomable shadow.

Robert Haven Schauffler[4] wrote about Emerald Pool:

> Its dreamy depths, as one gazes down through an essence almost too pure and precious to couple with the thought of hydrogen and oxygen,—seem haunts most fit for the mermen and the other elusive water-folk that Boecklin loved to paint. The cool enticement of its depths is belied by the testimony of the fleeces of steam endlessly filming and dissolving on the surface. The greens are all strange hues that never were on land or sea,—unhuman greens which fairly cry out for those creatures that swim through the labyrinthine depths of Teutonic mythology. If we had only discovered it a few centuries ago, Emerald Pool might have given rise to one of those American legends of which we are to-day so sadly destitute. But one hopes that on summer eves to come our poets shall dream more magic things beside this pool than remain to be dreamed beside any haunted stream that ever bewitched the Old World (Romantic America, 148–51).

The afternoon wore along. It grew very still. The frail trees had ceased their trembling; their delicate shadows had stolen out to touch the margin of the pool. The sun sank, grayness fell upon the glade; the film of steam rose less lazily from the shining water; and it was a subdued and chastened person who at this dimming of the light rose stiffly from her camp-stool around one of whose wooden feet a steaming pool was slowly spreading. Were we then, camp-stool and I, starting a geyserette of our own? We hastily withdrew.

As I wandered along a rocky path, sunset was tingeing the jets of steam, and the valley lay in silent unmegaphoned peace. A frosty July evening was evidently setting in, and soon I knew only the thoughtlessly placed and impracticable geysers would be truly warm. How agreeable it would be to have one of the steamy things right inside one's tent!

And I wondered very much where the Literary Person might be.

"I do hope," I murmured, smiling absently at a wet and vacant geyser-mouth I was passing, "he hasn't fallen into Lake Tahoe; I hear it's a hundred and seventy feet deep." For he had been there, writing, and now I was waiting for at least a letter of suggestion. The Yellowstone gave one a strangely helpless sensation; I should just now have found it entirely soothing to be led out into landscape by a large, firm person who would say sternly:

"Do you see *that*? Sit down then, Silly, and paint!"

It is at times a bit perplexing, I find, working for absent geniuses. They have exceedingly distinct ideas, and one day perhaps after you have been laboring alone at their behests for weeks and weeks at white heat and in the most savage and uncomfortable spots, they arrive, turn over your things coolly and remark:

"*That* will do nicely, I think—reduced down small, of course," and, "Please, what is *this* intended to be?" and, "Oh, but I wanted something quite different done from *there*, you know!"

But you didn't know; and the half-humorous dread that you may not know, drags at your brush ever afterward. . . .

Strolling about the piny lanes of camp that evening, I collided amiably with numbers of my fellow-campers—mostly feminine, and of enormous conversational powers. They apparently talked all the time, discourse of the "Oh Sal, ain't it great!" order; and they almost all had false teeth; so for the next day's drive, I found to my great contentment that I had been allotted a seat in a yellow buckboard containing only a party of four, a Chautauqua lecturer, his wife, aunt, and niece; and, compressing easel and camp-stool beneath my feet, I listened with an ever-lightening heart to fragments of repartee between my companion and his ladies.

Still in the viewless woods of the day before we drove leisurely along, but this second morning passed as if by magic. Humorous disputation raged hotly back and forth. The Chautauquan (known as "Benjy" to his family) had a lively and twinkling, though somewhat bilious gray eye, a mop of light-brown hair, and, in spots, a very broad English accent. He was from Chicago, and upon all subjects he was violently discursive. Just now he was full of mirthful invective against camp life. He was convalescent from an illness, it seemed, and so, "They lured me into this!" he confided, with a dramatic flop of hair and much gesturing at his broad-smiling ladies.

"Geyser soup!" he shouted, "and geyser coffee this morning. They make everything out of geyser. Only it's cold geyser. They haven't even the intelligence to let it stay hot. I'm shivering still. I never want to see a tent again. I—but can you tell me any intelligent reason," he demanded of the world in general, with wildly interrogative eyebrows, "why a man shouldn't be allowed to shave in geyser—nice hot geyser, if he wants to?"

And then he turned his omniscient attention to the landscape. . . . Pooh! these "Nat" parks. Not *half* as interesting as New England. New England now, *that* ought to be a Nat park.

"That's all it's good for!" he crowed, turning triumphantly to me. "Manufacturing? . . . Pooh! Little bits here and there. Should all be done somewhere else anyway—in some hideous place. . . . No, make it into a Nat park!

"It's a thousand times more beautiful than *this*," he said, gesturing earnestly at our environment. "I'm going to write a lecture about it," he cried enthusiastically, sitting up so straight and tall that a malevolent bump of the buckboard sent him crashing into its top. "Damn. I *beg* your pardon—but I am! I'm going to make a petition out of it! I'm going to present it to Congress! I—"

"If you have them make *my home* into a national park—" I began in all seriousness, also sitting up and glaring at him with frank wrath, "I . . ." and then for some unknown reason we dissolved into utter laughter. We laughed, the whole buckboardful of us, till we leaned back helpless in our seats; till we became actually warm and comfortable from mere laughter and, wiping our eyes and gasping feebly, were pulled over the crest of the long hill, where we saw that the tiresome woods had broken at last.

Across a vast and shining lake of blue and silver stood a majestic range; the snowy Tetons.[5] Two lofty peaks presided, lonely against the sky, and in thought I followed the **Virginian** into their haunted solitudes, beneath the music of their pines; breathing frosty air and forest scent; knowing their silence—where even a pine-needle is noisy when it drops; and as I dreamed, a something lifted within me, an everlastingness seemed to dawn, a glimmer to play and lighten about my spirit. . . . Slowly, we passed on.

A boat or two floated on the lake—water-bugs on immensity; it was all one could do not to spring from the wagon and unfurl one's camp-stool on the spot. Snow-mountains always affect me with a sort of delirium, partly of the eye but mostly, I do believe, of the soul; a feeling hard to bear without immediate expression of some kind. The Sierras had been bad enough; the Tetons were going to be worse. No limitedness here; only immensity, and gleams, and far-off snowy divineness.

Facing this and half-hidden by pines was a trim camp. Its tents were gay little abodes, cheery with pink-and-white chintz, and in one corner a small stove with a kettle purring upon it. Stewart Edward White[6] opines that "tent-stoves are little devils, either red-hot or stone cold"; but my tent-stove was an angel from heaven.

The Virginian: A Horseman of the Plains, Owen Wister, 1902.

YELLOWSTONE LAKE

I ran out under the pines. The water was gleaming pink, the sky above it a miracle of color. Silvery-rose against a pale-green horizon stood the Tetons; crabby, pink cloud-wisps curved into the evening blue. Directly over the loftiest peak soared a streamer of pink exactly like a rosy geyser in action; and as I stood rooted in contemplation, behind me sounded a mocking, vibrant voice:

"Geyser sunset, you see!"

Benjy, having emerged from the tranced state into which the rest of us had fallen, was his absurd self again. Disregarding him, I rushed away to my tent and snatched up an armful of materials. Gloaming or not, a five-minute, thumb-nail note of that sea of color I must and would have.

That evening a sweet air wandered overhead through the swaying pines, the tourists gathered about a bonfire, and the lines of illuminated tents, each with a cheerful chimney-pipe protruding from its rear and a small blue stream of smoke ascending, resembled little lighted steamboats drawn up at a nocturnal wharf.

As there was no other place for it, my easel, next morning, stood in full view of camp; and all day long successions of tourists strolled by. Comments were mysteriously murmured, or prolonged, whispered colloquies took place behind me—just exasperatingly not in hearing. Toward the end of the afternoon, however, with the Tetons growing more glorious every instant, I was becoming very happy and working furiously (for the stream of onlookers had ceased) when suddenly a fresh supply appeared; this time soldiers and their girls. Their comments, ingenuous and frankly unmuffled, I found far preferable to the stifled well-bred murmurs I had suffered under during the day; though one couple, halting behind me arm in arm, as I was frowning at my palette in the dimming light, stood in silent contemplation so long that I grew absurdly worried and self-conscious, and found myself doing the silliest things with an absent-minded brush.

"Makin' pictures, ain't she?" was the young soldier's discriminating remark. A long, assimilating pause followed; then:

"Settin' out here—a nawful long time, she's ben," volunteered the girl. "I seen her out here this mornin'." To which, with no pause whatever, came the swift masculine verdict:

"Golly! Too lonesome a job for me!" and turning with one accord, they swung off in pursuit of more social matters.

Schauffler on Yellowstone Lake:

Late that afternoon, afloat on Yellowstone Lake, I thought I had never seen another body of inland water combining such majesty of sweep with so much strongly individualized beauty. Drenched in the alpenglow the snow summits of the Absarokas towered above the shore. Over the waters hung a vast, purple loving-cup of cloud. Purple draperies hovered over the firs that clothed the western side to the very beach and half hid a flare of camp-fire. Little Stevenson Island became a thing enchanted. And without warning there sprang up in the four quarters of the heavens four different sunset pageants. It was as if the sky would not be outdone in generosity by a lake which had in store, wherever one turned, a different tale of beauty or of grandeur (Romantic America, 152, 155).

2.

Next day's drive [along the lake and through Hayden Valley] was much enlivened by elk. Elk feeding in meadows; a herd of them swimming a river, their leader splashing out and staring boldly at us; a stream of elk fleeting exquisitely up a hillside, or elk lying domestically down, like contented cows, in the sage-brush. And the sight of them there, free and happy, somehow became a luxurious part of one's contentment. It gave one a restful feeling, as if for an hour or two one had slipped back into the Golden Age; for these creatures on that splendid background were as beautiful, as refreshingly unworldly and unexploited as the Tetons themselves—and almost as expanding to the spirit.

That night my tent, exhilaratingly perched on the very edge of a steep slope, commanded through great pines a vista of the white stream and winding canyon [the Grand Canyon of the Yellowstone]; and it was to a wild song of rushing pines overhead and the pleasant purring of the great fall that I dropped to sleep—the flawless sleep that comes to one in such a place and air. Allured by its beauty, the Chautauquans had decided to halt a while in this spot. Benjy liked this open-air idea, he proclaimed; jolly air in the Yellowstone anyway! Must be the altitude. Everything was the altitude. And, by Jove, your tent was hot in the morning! . . . It was pleasant to have Benjy really charmed at last.

Our tents certainly were hot in the morning, by reason of a surreptitious five-o'clock boy who lighted your fire, sagaciously feeding it spoonfuls of oiled sawdust till the exulting blaze roared so that you leaped up in alarm to turn it off—an excellent scheme for getting a person up in the morning, when a hot breakfast awaited you. Otherwise, it sat about gathering a retributive chill. The Chautauquan, I observed, was ever obediently on time. He esteemed his breakfast, did Benjy. In fact he enormously enjoyed a multiplicity of things—among them his discursive self.

"I'm a fearful egotist, you know," he informed us radiantly. "My wife *tells* me I am. I'm such a mawss of egotism I can scarcely *live*!" and he beamed delightedly upon us.

Was it not agreeable then, I reflected, to have a self-confessed egotist about? A professionally happy creature, basking in his own glow? For Benjy with his subjective radiances was a boon to all of us; on gray mornings he positively lit us up, and was a match for any sunshine.

At the canyon most of my subjects were at the pleasing distance that necessitates horseback riding, so once more I joyfully visited a corral and went prying around for a not too docile mount. The "hoss-wrangler," I found, was absent, but two cowboys in furry chaps and gay red neckerchiefs put me up on a powerful bright-yellow beast, who, they gleefully murmured, would "give you somethin' to look after—ef that's what you want, ma'am!" Grinning, they stood watching us as the animal, after a preliminary whirl of joy, departed with stupendous leaps up the field. His spirit was delightful, but his leaps dislodged too much scenery for my purposes; so, with difficulty persuading him to "come about," I took him down the field again, this time in moderated leaps. He refused to halt by the corral, however, and was gathering himself to leap its impassibly high fence, when the two cowboys, with a sudden cessation of grins, dashed up and seized him, assisting me down with kind and gallant words, from which I escaped into the haven of the corral. Browsing happily about in its medley of horse-colors, I finally selected Judy— good, fat, cream-colored Judy, an easy-rocking old dear with a perpetual lope and a wary eye for precipice edges; and soon, with much flopping of paraphernalia and Judy's cream-colored mane, we were galloping across the high bridge that spans the river[7]—a stream here running smooth, deep green

and quiet to its great leap. Judy's unneeded reins swung from one hand and my largest panel from the other; for to-day we were to slay our thousands, Judy and I; the thousands, that is, of rock points and precipice angles that are included in any glimpse of Yellowstone Canyon.

It is a blossom of a canyon, colored like a bunch of sweet-peas. A garden of tea-roses might suggest it; or, architecturally, the upper detail of Milan Cathedral, if played upon by pink and lavender and primrose lights. At its head fluffs the whiteness of the falls, and deep in its blossoming, minareted folds lies the green and silver of the stream. Upon this vision our winding road, companioned on one side by pine woods and roar, on the other by bumblebees and Alpine flowers, led us suddenly out. Judy flung up her head, staring absorbedly down-canyon. Probably it was not the first time she had cantered whole-heartedly out to that rim and halted a gasping rider on the edge of nothing; I am sure she deeply enjoyed doing it; and she continued to stare recommendingly up and down until I towed her back into a bit of pine woods, and unloaded her.

⌒◦⌒

Schauffler on the Canyon:

> *Artist Point held in store for me one of the surprises of my life. The writers and painters and promoters of colored photographs had prepared me for the utmost riot of color allowed by the liberal laws of Nature,—a pictorial hue-and-cry, an anarchy of paint. They had led me to look for a gorge rather more thickly pasted with shrieking primary*

hues than Matisse's pal-
ette,—a sort of brass band
transposed into pigment with
the strident cornets, the nar-
row-dissecting piccolo, the
cymbals, trombones and
big bass drum all at the full
stretch of unbridled frenzy.
But what was my amazement
to find instead, a well-bal-
anced, mellow orchestra of
color, never obstreperous,
never allowing a blatant tone
to emerge into relief.

LOOKING DOWN THE GRAND CANYON OF THE YELLOWSTONE

A third of a mile away on
the opposite wall were broad,
tranquil slides of cream and pink, orange
and rust color. Downstream they grew more
yellow and jagged. Where the pinnacles of
Inspiration Point were relieved against far
cliffs of royal purple, the ponderous quietude
of the canyon was brought out the more by
an occasional spot of sharp color. A thousand
feet below ranted the foam-checkered green
*of the river (*Romantic America, *156–57).*

᜵

My establishment was soon set up in a niche
between some pink and yellow rocks. It was the
fairest of mornings, not a cloud in the blue; I was
glad of a plain sky, when all around was detail
enough to satisfy a scientist. How, I puzzled,
restraining my active charcoal, was one to "generalize" that sculptured intricacy, those carved and
statuetted minarets, those superimposed and pro-
cessional peaklets with which the canyon's sides
abounded? Even the **eagles' nest** a little way below
me, on the tip of one of the minarets, exposed itself
in obvious detail, a mass of coarse sticks whereon
the poor little St. Anthony of an eaglet, lying on
its gridiron in the hot sun, gave a pathetic squirm
whenever one of his comfortable, well-aired parents sailed by overhead, never even slowing up to
inquire. . . . But though it must be bad to sleep
thus on detail, it could be worse than to sit end-
lessly squinting at the conglomerate thing, trying
to draw it and yet not draw it; and if I did not
immediately (and summarily) generalize, I told
myself fiercely, I should be here, drawing, until

> **eagles' nest:** Many early writers mentioned eagles
> in the canyon, but, in most if not all cases, the birds
> nesting there are ospreys.

time itself had done a job of softening for me, and Judy, in her pine-wood, was a little heap of art-dedicated bones.

But I continued to simmer obediently on hot rock. One consolation with a water-color is that you can always put washes over parts you don't like, so, rising wearily at the end of the day I murmured:

"You'll have a fine time with this, my dear— washing, you know. Perhaps," I added ominously, "you'll want to put it in the river before you're done!"

At the sound of my actual (though gloomy) voice, a cheery little "hoo-hoo!" came from the pine woods; and soon we were cantering once more over our upland road where blue shadows lay across the wild flowers, bumblebees had long since retired, and even the roar was soothingly recessional.

For many days Judy and I pursued the trail of our minarets; sometimes heartily tired of them, of heat and brightness, of the waterfall that confronted us like a derisive tongue emerging from pink rock jaws; tired, even, of unending color. Judy, stamping intolerantly, laid bare a large quantity of newly revealed pine-roots, while I worked on in the fiery glow of my yellow rocks, with little but a subsiding conscience and eagles for consolation.

The old birds did not like me there, so near the nest. They often gave, before plunging dinnerward into the canyon's depths, a preliminary swoop or two in my direction, uttering harsh cries and staring at me so closely that I could look straight into the cruel, unwinking, topaz eyes, and it was a relief when, apparently deciding that I was altogether of earth and could not harm their lonely child,

they would abruptly sweep away to the business of dinner-getting.

This, to one perched safely aloft, appeared a dubious matter. The torrent was a mad and leaping thing, and only a very rash, tough and foolish fish, it seemed, would reside in so raging a spot; but after a dropping dive the big bird usually emerged successfully—a madly flapping thing, clutching in his claws a shining morsel for small son on the minaret. . . . And when son somehow surmised that a meal was en route—when he saw it actually wheeling above, how he tumbled about on those crude sticks, lunging and whimpering more like a clumsy puppy than like a young bird. Parent back-watered furiously with his great wings, lit, and sat attentively on the edge of the nest—the only attentive thing I saw the old birds do—cramming bits of fish into his offspring's beak until whimperings ceased, and the baby lay quiet once more on that heartless bed. . . . It did seem as if it would have been worth the expenditure of a few wing-flaps to slip a bit of moss under that little fellow! The old eagles never seemed in the bustling hurry that bird parents usually are, but sailed and sailed above the canyon and its wooded rim, with (apparently) leisure for moss-gathering or anything else. Perhaps the nest was made ribby and unpleasant so that the eaglet would be glad to leave it; for at his very first trial, what a horrific plunge awaited him! I wondered, very much, if a fledgling had ever pushed himself, of his own accord, into that frightful space—or if a nervy pair of parents did the pushing. He had no possible room to practise in, on the tip of his minaret; it must need a powerful faith to launch a child off above that deadly gorge—for they seemed fond,

I thought, of the little whimpering thing. I grew rather fond of him myself.

But in spite of these distractions, work, I saw to my joy, was progressing. Rising hastily one day, as is my habit, to survey the almost-finished panel, a twirl of my coat-tails upset the camp-stool and sent it gliding down the steep, graveled slope. It slid, and turned, and slid, with the greatest propriety; doing the thing quite beautifully, and nearing the edge from which space fell emptily away. A tooth of protruding rock, however, caught it just in time; and there it lay. The slide was of fine, glittering gravel; a most lovely color, heliotrope shading into mauve, though here and there in the wake of my camp-stool, silvery streams were running.

I looked wildly about. Must one, then, stop work this radiant morning? Could I sit on the ground with the panel in my lap? Alas, it was far too large. The nearly finished picture regarded me tauntingly; a bit needed here, a touch there—it was maddening. Experimentally, I set one heel in the slide; it seemed to give fair foothold, and without more pause I started, though cautiously, down. Of course the fluent gravel began to go with me; of course I clutched it and found nothing to hold by. I sat down, digging in frantic heels; it was of no avail. Just as my camp-stool had gone, so I was going, faster and faster toward the canyon's brink. Human scrabblings availed no more than wooden inertness. . . .

Sweeping along, I clutched at the tooth of rock; it stopped me, but not the sliding gravel, and I clung desperately to my sharp-edged refuge as the slide pulled and pulled, streaming over the edge into the canyon's depths. Luckily I had thought to hook my errant property over one arm; so on the lavender torrent we lay together, camp-stool and I, deeply wishing we had never come. At last the thing slackened; gradually stopped. Gingerly, inch by inch, fearing every instant to start it sliding again, I pulled myself above the tooth of rock, summoning courage to take my hands from it, to use it as a foothold and start to swarm slowly, flat on my face, across the ghastly openness of the slide where there was not even a pebble to hold by. After what seemed an ignominious age of panting and creeping, my cheek intensely pressed into the hot gravel—*how* I should hate to be a caterpillar!—I attained a stretch of coarser gravel, of less violent grade, over which I dashed in frantic leaps, carried down often, sinking despairingly above my knees, but coming nearer my goal of blessed rocks and the one, little, gnarly cedar which all the time had been vainly holding out its twisted arms to me.

At last I grasped it. How marvelous, just to *grip* something again; to feel the scaly bark under my hands, and smell the baked fragrance of the stiff foliage brushing my face as I swung up among the craggy rocks!

Sitting limply up again, I looked back over the tinted slide. My deep-plowed footsteps were already smoothed out. Here and there, as before, silvery seams were running and a rain of belated pebbles rattled on the crags below; but for the most part the thing was quiet—as quiet as a quicksand after it has successfully swallowed somebody. I had gravel in my hair, and gravel up my sleeves; grains of it were ground into my cheek; and somehow I have never enthusiastically liked even lovely heliotrope gravel since.[8]

Later, as Judy and I went cantering home at a little better than our usual pace, my completed panel swinging by a strap, I noticed that the groups of soldiers on the canyon road were more than ever demonstrative. Often they had laughed at us, or called out vague words which I had made a point of trying not to hear; but to-day they positively shouted. I looked away indignantly, touching Judy with my heel; soldiers are impudent creatures, I reflected—later learning that it was flatly against rules to canter around these curves, and the misunderstood cavalrymen had every day been politely requesting me to slow up a bit, whereat I had regularly responded by cantering on faster than ever!

When I woke, rather late the next morning, I found that a blankness had fallen upon me. My job was done. I was going to miss it grievously. Judy and I had no longer any excuse for cantering to the canyon's rim, my plan now being to go into its damp depths and do one sketch looking up. The nearest way was by a steep and scrabbling path close to the falls—**Uncle Somebody's Hole**—where you eventually slid down a rope over a forty-foot drop and landed at the bottom. Guides were supposed to let you down, but I didn't want a guide bothering about; I failed to see why I could not do my own letting. You simply snared your rope around a stump and went.

Uncle Somebody's Hole: From 1898 to 1906, "Uncle Tom" Richardson ferried visitors across the river above the falls, then showed them how to descend into the canyon. Uncle Tom's Overlook and Uncle Tom's Trail are named for him.

Having cajoled the coil of rope from a reluctant and worried camp-manager, I hung it on my shoulder and departed. Coming to the predestined stump and looking over, I was a trifle daunted. The crags were sharp, the cliff curved inward; even toe-hold would be dubious. But cool shadow lay in the cleft far below, the swift river raced alluringly; I *did* want to get down there and paint! Leaning over, I dropped my easel and camp-stool down—as an encouraging preliminary; gripped the rope and started. Once or twice I obtained foothold on a bit of crag, but the enterprise was far more unpleasant than I had expected, and, glancing rather worriedly at the expanse of dangling rope up which I must return, I made my way among wet and enormous boulders to the edge of the torrent.

It was an entertainingly frantic torrent. Huge and darkening clouds of spray flew up from the foot of the falls, but above the shadow-line the tops of the cliffs were bright with sunshine, and I set anticipatingly at work, only to find that colors, in this spray-filled dampness, ran prohibitively. Sky trickled over pink peaks, pink peaks descended into green river; so after finishing a brief black-and-white (and when the last tourist had departed) I approached the cliff again, wondering incidentally if the guides might have gathered up my rope with their own.

It still hung there; its hempen complexion much darkened by spray, its whole aspect ominous and unhelpful. A rope is a disgustingly supine thing: "The Lord helps him that helps himself—" this one seemed to be proclaiming, as it dangled uninvitingly before my eyes. . . . In the history of old castles and medieval romance there have been times when the sight of a rope was a glad thing; but this was not one of them. Attaching the ever-inconvenient easel and camp-stool to my knapsack, I started up; a fly upon the cliff wall—but a fly with a disproportionate load on its back, and a paucity of needful legs.

Half-way up I stopped, panting. My arms, it seemed, were being pulled out. There was a loud singing in my ears, and a queer daze coming over me as I hung there—a feeling that it would be altogether jolly to let go of that rope—and see what would happen. Just then the one boot by which I had toe-hold slipped from the wall; the shock of it was the tonic one needed. Rousing myself, I took firmer hold and worked deliriously, without pause, to the top, at last falling upon pine-needles and good brown earth. Above me the stump, adorned with its rope necklace, presided somewhat grimly over my fortunes, staring stolidly down at me; in fact as I lay there, thankfully inert, it had almost the bullying demeanor of one who acidly remarks, "Well! what did you go down for, then?"

Meekly accepting the stump's rebuke, I coiled the heavy rope and departed, with no Judy to console me. I missed that good creature if I went without her; there was a comfortable fat understandingness about Judy, as there often is about stout people, and I hastened instinctively down to the corral to find her. Her pink nose was prominent at the bars; she looked pleased to see me. Hay was rustling, horses of all colors capering about; a refreshing homeliness pervaded the scene. The hoss-wrangler, in his cowboy outfit, getting out his saddle preparatory to taking the horses to their night pasture, nodded pleasantly.

"Saw a bunch of elk last night, ma'am," he said, leading a horse out for grooming; "must've been a hundred of 'em. Playin', they was. Moon was bright, I could see 'em plain. Purty sight, ma'am. . . . Would you like to ride out an' see 'em?" he inquired a trifle bashfully, but looking up from his labors with a friendly smile. Startled, though much flattered, by this unprecedented invitation, I evaded decision by an objection about taking tired horses out at such an hour.

"Blue ain't done nothin' all day—I kin get you any horse you want, ma'am," he replied gallantly, "but he's stiddy for night work. . . . Moon rises early, this evenin'," he added; and the agreement was made.

During supper, as I meditated on the nature of the engagement I had made, I began feeling a trifle queer about it. Reason (1), it was an unconventional way of going out—even to see exonerating elk in their native wilds; (2) that I had no idea where or for how long we were going; (3) that I had told no one at camp I was going; and (4) that though I thought hoss-wranglers as a rule were trustworthy persons, yet you can never quite . . . etc.

Also I was aware of another source of worry far more distinct than these—a worry that on a ride with a real cowboy I should never be able to "keep up my end"; that somehow, somewhere, one would inevitably do the thing that would stamp one as a tenderfoot and an incompetent. . . . Striding down to the corral, I prepared at least to mount my blue-roan horse as agilely as Eastern methods permitted, when I found myself being mortifyingly helped into the saddle—a blow indeed to all one's Western preconceptions! Usually, when alone, I put a casual toe in the stirrup, Judy swung to meet me, and we were half-way to the canyon road before I troubled to catch the other, and dangling, stirrup. . . . But this was a special occasion; doubtless these were special methods to match.

We rode into a dusky back trail, the cowboy mounted on a colossal bay whose only gait appeared to consist of repressed, but enormous, sidewise bounds; while beside him the "stiddy" Blue was also agitated, doing his best in the way of competitive leaps. I sat him interestedly; the herd, with jingling bells, frolicked on before us. As we thundered across the bridge I commented on the huge size and apparently needless state of mind of my companion's horse.

"He just wants handlin'," remarked the young wrangler, holding the enormous animal down with one skilful, gauntleted hand. "Got him for work around camp, but—feelin' kinder good, I reckon—he broke the waggin to pieces this mornin'. I'm going to take him out nights for a while."

At a grassy track that led away over an upland, we turned in. Afterglow still burned in the west and a few stars twinkled uncertainly. It was a particularly baffling light to ride by.

"Makes me think of Alaska," said the cowboy, suddenly breaking silence. "Queer light there all the time. Fellow gets lost if there ain't any stars out. An' golly, the moss-quitos! We had to wear head-nets over our hats, an' sometimes the critters was so thick on 'em you'd nigh smother. . . . I got so I plumb hated the smell o' them moss-quitos."

Bearing in mind Wister's revelations of cowboy tale-telling, I merely nodded serenely to this recital. By this time the soft clamor of the bells was very far away. A few dim forms could still be seen drifting up a misty glade, but for the most part the herd seemed scattered and gone.

"Aren't you afraid you'll lose them?" I asked.

"No, ma'am. They range two-three miles up an' down here, but they don't git clear away," said the cowboy, smiling. "I've got a tent somewhar up here on the mesa, but I don't calc'late to be in it any. They keep a-feedin' along, an' by two o'clock I have to begin to round 'em up again. They's lots o' fog comes in towards mornin'. Takes me three hours sometimes to git 'em all in, and they have to be back in camp by five."

Blue was now hopping sidewise, in imitation of his companion, up a rise composed of broken ridges and graveled washes, clumps of bushes often concealing the nature of the ground beneath them—the worst I had ever taken a horse over at such a pace. For a miracle, neither of them stumbled; the cowboy, placidly sitting his foam-flecked mount, was gazing serenely about. I found Blue increasingly hard to hold. "Does he—always pull like this?" I panted, gripping the reins lower on the hot neck as Blue plunged and foamed.

"No. He's dead-wood, git him away from the hosses," said my companion pleasantly. "I reckoned if you'd like, ma'am, I'd show you the country over on this side before the moon come up. Indians call it Devil Valley. It's got a sort of crust on it—all hot underside, an' steam comin' up out."

I did not mention that I had already been sufficiently steamed and hot-crusted in the Geyser Basin, but rode obediently on over the top of the ridge, and plungingly down the other side; a sense of strangeness coming gradually over me. Where, with this unknown escort, might one be going? And why, especially in a diabolical half-light, should any one desire to ride upon hot crust? But the horses had dashed upon smoother footing now, and I soon began to relish the rush of wind in my face, the incessant hoof-thunder beneath, the lovely dimness and uncertainty of everything. Suddenly my companion shot ahead into the dusk.

"Crossin' the river hyar!" he called back, and there was a gigantic splashing as he searched for a ford. Blue was frantic at this separation; he reared, he sat down mutinously on his tail, he hopped wildly about, till a shout directed us and we spattered in.

"Nice cool water in this hyar river," remarked the dim shape before us; "hosses like it. An' yet the steam's a-comin' up all around."

Indeed, it was writhing unpleasantly from the dusky plain. Its sulphurous odor was stifling. We plowed silently along; in front I could hear the cowboy's horse floundering and splashing.

"Guess I hit the wrong crossin'," I heard him mutter, and all at once poor Blue sank into smothering bog, struggling, in miry leaps, apparently for his life.

"Oo!" I said tensely, though quite to myself, distastefully lifting my stirrups out of the mud, and trying desperately to swing Blue around.

"Yes ma'am—a little soft," came an unexpected voice in my ear as a dark shape lunged alongside, and with much heaving and bounding of his powerful beast, the wrangler hauled us out on solid ground again. Blue had time to pant and blow and recover himself while, without

comment, the cowboy searched for another ford, which washed our mud off nicely; then we walked the wet horses quietly toward the upland once more, my companion still bafflingly silent. Guiding Blue as well as I could over the rough ground, and resolving—much against a discursive disposition—not to be outdone in this or any other Western attribute, I was equally stolid, though wondering a little as to the nature of the young wrangler's entirely inward thoughts.

Topping the long rise, I saw a glow above the dark fir woods; and through a notch in the timber an immense moon, very round and golden, was solemnly regarding us. On the dimly golden turf beside us pranced two enormous shadows, their tips disappearing, far away, over the edge of the mesa. From a distance came a reassuring tinkle of bells, and as we rode toward the dark woods the cowboy, to my surprise—I thought him extinguished for the evening—turned and pointed.

"This hyar notch," he whispered, leaning toward me, "is where the elk was playin'. We'll go round a piece and come up by the timber."

The horses, as if they felt our need of quietness, moved stealthily along the edge of the woods in the shadow, scarcely a twig snapping under their artful hoofs. As we reached the corner of the notch, across the glade something moved—and there in full moonlight was a magnificent elk, his antlers brilliantly outlined against the shadow. The notch itself was a sea of moonlit backs and tossing heads, big black ears, and shadowy small creatures running along the edge of the throng.

"Them's the calves," murmured the young wrangler. "Want me to rope one for you?"

"*No!*" I breathed in a horrified whisper. Presently several "cows" (I do wish they would call these lovely creatures some more poetic name!) strolled out into the clear moonlit space and stood a moment, moving their heads delicately about; and then they began to play. Their motions at first were tentative, leisurely, and full of grace, but soon they were daffing sportively at one another with their heads; then two of them reared up and pranced delightedly about, making passes at each other with their slender forelegs. The moon, soaring above the woods, poured its light upon them, deepening the shadows that danced beside them; down the glade in dimmer moonlight the dusky babies raced back and forth. Two more bulls had joined the sentinel, and all three stood proudly gazing, their antlers turning slightly as they watched.

Sometimes Blue quivered beneath me, giving his head a tiny, noiseless shake; or a breeze passed softly through branches overhead; but I felt as if it might all be a dream—of silence and mystery and wild happiness. The moon soared and soared; the graceful creatures still played in its light.

"It must be getting late," I murmured unwillingly—and making a wide detour, we swung out again on the moonlit mesa. Barring irresistible roping proclivities, the cowboy had been an ideal comrade; he had sat his dark steed in restful silence; and now I could not but notice the splendor of this limber rider beside me in the gray moonlight, a sombrero shadow across his keen face, and behind him, as I glimpsed it over a flying mane, the tossing background of mesa and scattered fir-trees. We rode and rode; after a glorious gallop the mesa dipped suddenly, and we drew the horses to a prancing walk.[9]

"Please don't go any farther with me," I urged. "I can see the canyon road below us, now."

"I'll take you right back to camp, ma'am, I reckon," he said quietly. "There's Blue to look after, you see. Ef I didn't take him back with the hosses, he'd holler all night. . . . But you've sure ben settin' him this evenin'," he added; pensively and unexpectedly, half as if to himself, and leaning over to tighten a cinch-strap.

"Oh—have I?" I gasped naively—astonished out of any possible wits; and as we trotted upon the echoing bridge, to my further amazement he turned a beaming dark face suddenly upon me and let out, in a sort of burst, "An' you ain't no tenderfoot, neither, ma'am—let me tell you that!" and exploded in joyous laughter.

I was more than astonished; I was dumb, jogging mechanically along on a now subsiding Blue. At times I had dimly fancied that my laborious efforts to approach cowboy standards might serve to mitigate cowboy scorn; but to find oneself thus not only tolerated, but openly approved, was beyond one's most hyperbolic dream. We trotted decorously along the moon-chequered road, the soft light doing wonders with the canyon; then turned into the darkness of the pines, where the cowboy, once more his inscrutable self, took Blue's rein from my hand, lifted his sombrero gravely and clattered away into the shadows of the trail.

Finished at last with the canyon, I took reluctant leave of it. The Chautauquans had long ago departed and Judy, I am sure, regarded me as a fixture. I held her kind nose against my cheek in farewell; whatever I had been able to accomplish here was due in part to this good friend, and I told her so. Somewhat like her master, the horse-wrangler, she gazed down at me with gently tolerating brown eyes; but as I retreated up the slope from the corral I saw, as I glanced back, a pair of cream-colored ears still lifted intently toward me above the bars.

3.

Although immense mule-drawn freight-wagons rumbled by, along the valley road, my next camp [Swan Lake Flat's Wylie Camp], poised in the midst of loneliness and immensity, was environed only by sage-brush plains, a sage-clad ridge above dense fir woods, and a ring of snow-peaks. The air here combined whiffs of snow-purity, tang of sage, and the inescapable breath from **fir and balsam**.

Also the bears were uncommonly pleasing. One grows to have a fastidiousness even in bears, here in these wilds where they are offered in lavish variety. There had been a sufficiency of them at the canyon, pampered, garbagy bears prowling about edible heaps in the woods; but here they appeared to us in more unstudied ways. A minister's wife related at breakfast how she had confronted one, only the evening before, on a narrow bridge. Almost paralyzed with fright yet conscious that it is wiser not to turn one's back on a wild animal, she had crept agonizedly along, hugging her rail of the bridge and eying in horror the approaching beast—who, following her tactics exactly, pressed close to his edge and sidled by, also fearfully eying the minister's wife.

The cook too had a pet brown bear that came for tidbits, sitting up and smiting his furry stomach dramatically; and once I came upon him in a patch of sunshine, blinking and gobbling, and waving his nose in the senseless, weavy way bears have, the cook meanwhile casting goodies to him and relating proudly how she had to hide her sugar and molasses, and how one day, in spite of her pains, this unconscionable pet ate up five hams and a jar of apple-butter on her. I ought to have done a drawing of him, but he went away; and I loathed the garbage-heaps and the slinky looks of the poor moth-eaten bears that were busy at them, so much that I never did any bears at all, which was, editorially speaking, I suppose, a sin.[10]

Altogether, this camp had its piquancies. It did not, however, have saddle-horses; a grievous lack for a far-wandering person with express-loads of stuff to carry; so one gray, sweet-smelling morning I shouldered my things and tramped away through sage-brush and delicious exciting unknown wild flowers (every one of which looks as if it had strayed from a conservatory) toward the Golden Gate—a boon to the illustrator. In the distance were draped the folds of a most Japanese mountain [Electric Peak], purplish-gray, or grayish-green; no geisha-peak of gaudy hues but one showing the refined tints of the robe of a high-born Japanese lady. Near by canyon walls towered, an exposition of gorgeous yellows, sulphur, orange, and tawny gold; a skillful road clung to one of the walls, and, tramping down it, I looked out for a sightly and yet modest spot in which to set up an easel.

> **fir and balsam:** The trees would probably have been Douglas fir and Rocky Mountain juniper, since there is no balsam in the park.

Not caring to work absolutely in the path of coaches, I clambered out upon one of its outer ledges and began. Also the rain began; the first rain I had met in a long time. The distance was shutting in; little by little, the Japanese mountain withdrew its tinted robe. Perforce, at last, I put up a sketching umbrella (after much searching for a rock crack for its brass-shod toe) and sat in sheltered dinginess, the rain pattering cozily overhead. Just then, behind me, sounded the clattering of a stage. There was a shout, a clanking of harness, and an abrupt roar:

"Put down that fool umbreller—scarin' my hosses!"

And the coach resumed its way, the driver glaring back red and wrathful over his shoulder.

Deeply as I dislike to obey when roared at, I still less enjoy frightening poor silly stage-horses, so I furled my protector and trudged up the canyon again. It was so very beautiful in that rain. Yellows simply shone, from the grayness. Anyway I love to paint in the rain, and in the sunshiny West, where as a rule,

> *The sky, eachwhere, did show*
> *full bright and fair,*

one so seldom could. So the walls lavished their golden regards provokingly upon me till I emerged from the last curve and was out again among the freshened tints of the wild flowers. They were charmingly drenched. They had shut their eyes, some of them, against the shower, and

the sky, eachwhere: A line from the second stanza of late sixteenth-century English poet Edmund Spenser's poem "The Visions of Petrarch."

the attendant bumblebees had taken cover; but their wet sweetness was bewildering. As for the sage, it was simply going mad as to fragrance, and I trudged through it with wet boots and a heart overflowing with joy. The snow-peaks were prettily blurry as the gray storm flitted among them, while lines of rain slanted, like rain in a Japanese print, upon the dark border of fir woods.

Later in the day the rain stopped; though the sky was still lowery, and thunder was about. But the Silver Gate, I learned, was only a mile or two below the site of my morning's work, so I set off again down the lively gold of the canyon into a drear, sinister region of dead-white boulders and burnt stumps of trees. Two towering cliffs furnished an excellent studio-cranny, and in this strategic crevice I labored, an actual grin of pleasure distorting my greedy countenance. I had been horribly interrupted of late; peace and silence seemed heaven-sent, and I managed to achieve the portentous rocks of the gate and a fold or two of the Japanese robe before thunder muttered too ominously among the mountains. Hearing the rumble of a government-freight wagon, I hastily clapped-to my easel, much desirous of catching a ride up the long miles to camp. To my surprise the soldier driver drew up instantly at sight of me, staring at me with an alarmed face that soon relaxed into a hospitable grin. I was helped into the hooded seat, and the six mules started entertainingly along. The young soldier at first paid necessary attention to his driving, but after we had exchanged a commonplace or two, surprised me by bursting out, with a boyish chuckle:

"You cert'nly scart me, ma'am, down there by

the turn—steppin' out of them rocks!"

"Scared you?" I asked, wondering.

"That's a hold-up place, ma'am. Feller held up a string o' fourteen coaches there last year.[11] He hid in that crack in the big rocks. The turn's sharp there, an' every coach that come along, he'd stop 'em, out o' sight from the others. Big, tall feller he was, with a mask on. Spoke polite to the folks—made 'em walk along and drop their stuff in a bag he had. Then he made his get-away, an' they ain't got him yet!"

"Dear me!" I said, sitting up interestedly. "And—so you thought I was a highwayman, did you?"

"I sure did," said the boy, grinning. "Kinder dusk down there—an' all them things you wuz carryin'; they've warned us t' keep an eye out there, anyway. . . . I wuz just goin' to pull my gun, ma'am," he added simply.

Digesting this revelation, I leaned back again, soberly eying my equivocal puttees and paraphernalia in general.

"*Now* you see!" I thought severely to myself. "You nearly had a gun pulled on you. . . . Idiot, sitting down in a highwayman's crevice to *paint*!" for it was rather a blow to find that my innocent niche was an abode of violence—a place where jewels had been tearfully poured at the relentless feet of a creature in a black mask. . . . Well, I thought, if he had come banditing and hold-upping along while *I* was there, he wouldn't have gleaned much but tubes of paint; unless he had been one of those Beau Brummel bandits—an especially despicable variety—with a taste for wash-drawings. And I should have hated to give up my drawing;

particularly now I knew the nice gunpowdery sort of place it had been done in.

After a vain attempt that evening to beguile a nonexistent saddle-horse out of the camp-manager, I set out for a stroll along the high ridge back of camp, finding a trail that wandered obligingly through waist-high sage. The sky was partly cloudy; I faced a magnificent triplet of pink-tipped thunder-heads, but behind me Vega, in a clear patch, was winking above the forest-tops. On one side of my ridge lay a wide valley, guarded by snow-peaks and holding the shining river; on the other was the dark of the fir woods.

Although it was growing dusk I strolled on and on, lured by the vision of those great, mounting, rose-tipped clouds, among which flashes of lemon-colored lightning were playing; and trying to memorize them for a sketch. The ridge presently dipped, the fir woods withdrew a little, and along a trail out of the wood came a herd of horses gamboling, with jingling bells; after them jogged a sedate pair of cowboys with scarlet neckerchiefs, silver-bossed bridles, and Indian saddle-blankets. Rather dressy, I thought, for just going out for the night with a herd of horses! Perceiving me, they swerved and galloped eagerly up, inquiring if I had lost my way, but being reassured as to this, visibly relaxed in their superbly decorated saddles, and after gallantly reiterating that they "would like t' stay round" and see me safe home (the last thing I wanted them to do!), only that they "must take thet bunch to pasture, across this hyar river an' two mile out under them snow-mountains"—they swept off their sombreros, wheeled their chafing ponies, and dashed away after their charges, now gamboling up the further bank of the stream.

My trail rose and rose. Dusk had fallen in the valley where the river still gleamed and from which came a steady but dwindling tinkle of bells. Color was dimming on the thunder-heads, the snow-peaks had gone gray, but my ridge, being friendly with the sky, still held a little light and I was startled by close sight of a leaping thing in front of me, clearing the sage in easy scallops. At the height of one of these arcs a pair of dark ears rose against the horizon; a jack-rabbit! loping pleasantly homeward—if he had a home. He behaved as if he had. He was exceedingly serene, and not in the slightest hurry, keeping only comfortably ahead of me as I hastened my steps after him, so that for a long time I had the keen pleasure of intimately watching him as he loped systematically along, his fawn-colored back and round white tail rising above the pallor of the sage, then fading down again; the whole heart of the great dim world around me seeming to center in the curvings of this confiding wild thing, who gathered the wan evening light on his graceful length.

Suddenly speeding up, however, he veered away down the hillside and was lost. My ridge had ended; I found I was standing on the tip of it, with a steep and darkling descent on three sides. Lightning was still jabbing busily at the three fat thunder-heads; presently across the edge of the woods far below moved several dim shapes, stealing delicately along; disappearing in the gloom. Deer, I fancied. Mystery lurked everywhere; a delicious spookiness. There were strange small stirrings in the brush, lone notes from the woods; and once, just above my head, a sudden *whoof-whoof* of wings as some belated creature hastened through the dark, warm air.

Turning hastily to find the source of an odd scraping sound in the sage behind me (I never did like sounds behind me), I was dumfounded at the realization that there was nothing whatever visible of my homeward way. I was staring at a wall of blackness. Vega, on whom I had depended, was engulfed; and that darkest thing in all the outdoor world, a night of thick clouds, had set in.

At first there appeared no difference between the blackness of earth and sky, but as I bent low, remembering an old trail legend, I could barely catch (by not quite looking at it) a revealing gleam across the tops of the sage. Presently I could make out the fir woods—merely a darker smudge on darkness; and, toward the mountains, caught the faintest ghost of a tinkle that must be, I felt, the herd in their distant feeding-ground. My heart leaped to them. *Now* one could not be lost! Smudge of pine woods on one side, presumable tinkle on the other; all one had to do was to go on—and turn down the notch, where camp was. It was a long way. My jack-rabbit had been a worse lure than any will-o'-the-wisp. *He* went of course into a cozy hole, with things to eat, and maybe a wife and babies to welcome him; leaving his absent-minded admirer considerably adrift in the sage.

Starting swiftly on my way, I promptly fell down a bank, or gully; and sat up resentfully feeling the ground around me. It was not at all a worthwhile bank; I had merely been striding obliviously along and had stridden off into space. Reaching for a handkerchief with which to brush off sand and lichen, I discovered that I could actually see this bit of accessory whiteness; it made a spot of positiveness in the tiresome dimness about me, and thereafter I held it in my hand. When my eyes began swimming in my head from steady staring at the dark, I treated myself, as a weary traveler takes a pull at his flask, to a look at this small beacon traveling beside me, and felt revived at once. By frequently squinting over the tops of the sage I was able to foresee the slope of the ground, and fell into no more gullies.

But it was hard work. The sage tore and held me, objecting to every step, and from this enforced intimacy I grew very tired of this once-delightful shrub whose dew-wet scent, unpleasantly keen, seemed to penetrate the very crevices of one's brain. Unduly executive, its jabby branches thrust and stabbed, their stubby tips rasping one's wrists and knuckles. As far as I could discover, I was still on top of the ridge; it seemed absurd not to strike the trail; but the sage met me at every turn, evidently preferring to keep me plunging and scrabbling in its midst.

As I halted now and again, in this hot and panting progress, the tiny, far-away tinkle came to my ears: those free and happy horses, under the cool snows! How furiously, had they known, would those young wranglers have come galloping over the plain and splashed across the river to my rescue! It was too far for any call to reach them; yet in the weariness and fever of this scrambling fight I was once almost minded, in a weak and idiotic moment, to experiment with the vaunted powers of the feminine shriek and send a simply tremendous one in their direction.

But surely, by this time, I must be nearing that notch in the timber above camp. Camp! Unbelievable thought! Was there really anywhere such a haven of unscrabbling peace?

A sudden crashing halted me; a trampling in the sage near by. Brush crackled, and the ground beneath me shook, as that thudding tread came on. Wildly wishing to run, I stood stupidly rooted, my blood freezing as I listened. . . . And then a still more horrible thought occurred to me—it might be not only a bear, but a grizzly. Grizzlies often prowled about in these very woods; and as I was desperately striving to tear my tongue loose from the roof of my mouth, to shriek, to do *something*!—the crashing stopped. There was heavy breathing—a sudden snort, and with a "whoof!" a great hot thing rushed by me, once more shaking the ground, crushing down brush under his weight.

Could he be running—*away*?

Yes! I could hear him frantically smashing into the prickly dead-wood of the forest—a great creature, almost as frightened as I, fleeing hysterically, at a whiff of human scent, to the shelter of his beloved woods.

Faintly, still weak from the relaxing of a terrible strain, I staggered on, the sage now quite as tall as I, and far more equal to its job of hindering. The notch in the woods was indeed before me; wrestling grievously, I neared its lower edge. Now surely, one could find the trail.

Crashing resultlessly here and there, I at last decided to enter the woods blindly. If there were bears—well, there just would be bears. Steering for what looked like a lightening in the tangle, I plunged whole-heartedly into an uprooted tree, dead and prickly, the gleam of whose barkless limbs had lured me into its abominable clutches.

As I endeavored to back tactfully out of it, a branch hooked me under the collar; two more gripped me executively round the knees; another ran efficiently up my sleeve, while still others trifled with my hat and poked maliciously at my eyes. I absolutely laughed. Move cautiously as I might, a new arm of the creature seized me; an octopus of the woods. Without imperiling one's sight it was impossible to free oneself, so summoning all my resolution, and all my available breath, I shouted, "Camp ahoy!" and as the unseemly sounds went rudely echoing away, felt myself flushing a furious crimson. . . .

But all my qualms vanished when a moving light began bobbing below, and from the shadows a reassuring, indeed a divinely beautiful human voice called huskily, "Yes ma'am—I'm coming!"

"Just think of being 'ma'am' to anything again!" I muttered, with a faint flicker of reviving mirth; a sense of long hours at the mercy of a large, dark, and insubordinate wilderness being still vividly upon me.

Lantern rays moved nearer.

"I'm here!" I remarked plaintively. I was growing very tired of the octopus's clutch at the back of my neck. Back and forth the light resultlessly bobbed.

"If you'd tell me where you are, ma'am," argued the voice, "I'd try to find you."

"Here!" I repeated brilliantly; "over this way. In a tree. I can't move, or I'd—"

"Don't you try, ma'am!" came the voice gallantly; "I'll get there!" and at last, in a yellow glow of light, the actual, haloed, incomparable face of the camp-manager dawned through a gap in the branches. It was a matter of minutes to disentangle me from the octopus's clutches—being a thorough beast, he had done his job well; but only that of an instant to conduct me into the trail, some ten or twelve feet distant from the scene of my hopeless crashings. Abasedly, and very much at the manager's heels (he had been sitting up, worrying about me), I trotted down the delightful openness of the path to camp. Never was there vision more magnificent than the homely interior of my tent, with its steaming kettle; never couch so luxurious as the camp bed into which I tumbled. Woods, bears, sage, and silence, all merged into a fuzzy haze, then faded deliciously away.

Gay sunshine was already mellowing my canvas walls when I woke. This morning's drive was to be my last in Yellowstone; I gazed memorially about as we bowled through the early-morning gorgeousness of the Golden Gate, down into the region of towering silver rocks. Not without expectation, too, I awaited a second sight of the highwayman's crevice. A peaceful slot it looked, as we whirled past; an ideal spot for a retiring easel; when suddenly a series of shouts arose. . . . Our driver pulled up, the coaches in front of us stopped, and with but one thought in our minds, my fellow-passengers and I gazed fearfully ahead. A stream of up-going coaches had also halted, while beside them a man, his face in shadow under a wide black hat, sped swiftly, searching each stage as he passed. Intense silence reigned. For what might he be in quest? . . . And then, with an irrepressible gasp of relief and mirth I lapsed back in my seat.

It was the Literary Person! now hastening quite wildly along. I leaned down. "Well!" I began, "*where* are you—"

"Oh!" he interrupted, beaming and breathless, shaking my hand across the wheel-top. "*There* you are! I had to stop all these coaches to find you. I'm going on at once," he continued, the true, mad light of the highbrow shining in his eye. "I've an idea. I must go where I can write. I shan't be able to see you at the springs, but there's one thing I want you to be sure to do—the Devil's Kitchen. It's ripping! Sorry I can't be there—but you'll see what to do. . . . The Devil's Kitchen—do me a big one of that. Good luck!"

"Wait a minute!" I cried. "The Devil's Kitchen? Is this to be in color? What sort of a—"

"You'll find it!" he called back happily. "It's bully!"

As we started, a quite audible gust, or sigh, arose from our company of tourists, and a pleased murmuring followed. This, then, was the outcome of all our thrills—a literary hold-up.

Steaming up the steep and rocky slopes that afternoon, therefore, a full outfit clanking anticipatively on my back, I approached the entrance to the Kitchen. It was down a hole, then! Into the rocky jaws I clambered, and down a series of ladders, a beam of sunshine slanting along beside me.[12]

So far it was a fairly cheerful hole, but insufferably hot. Films of sulphurous steam wandered up from gruesome depths, the air grew more and more stifling. Water dripped from the walls, a greenish twilight darkened; more and thicker steam clouds rolled lazily up.

Holding tight to my possessions, I halted on the last murky verge of the abyss and peered fearfully down; then up. The remote sunbeam was yellowing the twilight shining on the dripping walls; and just above me three darkish creatures suddenly dashed about in the gloom. Bats! and tropically large ones. The steamy heat in which they lived was surely an expanding element; they looked tremendous as they surged soundlessly about, miraculously saving themselves from contact with the rocky walls. Bats always fascinate me: I love the bony drawing of their queer, Gothic wings and as for the objectionable mousy part of them, it is quite touchingly insignificant—chiefly a pair of alert ears like two round blots topping a bit of solider shadow. While they flitted about, I settled my easel on a rock platform, dusky, yet commanding an up-going composition (the only composition there was in the horrid place) of rock and rock-steps ascending from green, shadowy darkness to the golden radiance of the sun-beam; and thence to a bit of sky.

The bats were immensely helpful. They were just the touch of life I wanted. I put them all in. The largest of the trio, taken by uncanny fits of interest in my work, would suddenly poise before me, as I had never known a bat to poise before—head on, and mousiness rather unpleasantly prevailing. Had I not known him to be **quite blind**, I should have said he then looked at me sharply in the eye; and at these moments he seemed, to my

> **quite blind:** Bats can actually see quite well, especially at night.

fascinated gaze, fully as large as a sea-gull. (I think he was as large.) Scarcely a yard away, he hovered steadily on his sculptured wings, uttering a series of little sharp squeaks. Was he trying to frighten me away? I gleefully placed him at the forefront of my sketch, arranging his less-confident companions where they evidently preferred to be—in the rear.

Then I rose, drawing a suffocated breath. How stifling this cavern was! Streams were running from my eyebrows, my white-silk blouse was wet through; but the sketch must go on. For two hours already I had existed in this steaming hole; another hour would do it. Dashing up the ladders for a fresher breath, I then returned, gingerly pulling out the sleeves of my soaked blouse, and settling once more in the greenish twilight.

This *was* a devil's kitchen. At that very moment one was being deliberately stewed in it. Sulphurous and vile were the emanations from its infernal brew, gurgling far, far below; one might easily swelter to an indistinguishable morsel in that brew—a mere, silk-and-linen addition to the satanic menu; and how delighted my unfriendly bats would be!

Stirred by these meditations, I set still more feverishly at work; after a time becoming aware of a sound of voices. A shadow fell annoyingly over the sunbeam, and in the sky-hole were the heads and shoulders of two tourists, peering wonderingly down. I knew exactly how they felt; and these two gentlemen lingered, much and justifyingly in doubt.

"Hot, ain't it, Bill?" remarked one.

"Gee, yes!" muttered the other; but put a knicker-bockered leg over and began to descend.

Then he paused, gazing downward. In my steaming dusk far below I smiled blandly though invisibly up at him, putting out one white-clad arm to pull back a flange of my easel and make room. To my amazement the tourist scrabbled up the ladder and hurled himself into the light of day.

"Gosh, there's something down there!" he gasped. "Something white. I saw it move!" An agitated muttering followed. Aghast at the vision of my everyday, white-bloused self in the rôle of ghost or spirit, I rose impulsively, calling up to them:

"Do come down! I'm just painting down here—" and listened intently.

But the sky-hole was empty. The sunbeam lay once more uninterrupted on the rocky wall, and from the upper distance came a sound of running feet. . . .

Dazedly I sat down again, my charcoal quiet in my unbelieving fingers. . . . Was it possible two grown men had run away in broad daylight, from something at the bottom of a sulphurous hole? Was the world of spirits then so real a thing in the popular mind that at my mere, unexamined gesture these two need take to their preposterous heels? Did they not hear what I said—or, hearing, take me all the more for a siren posted on that glooming verge?

"Oh!" I decided, jumping up and irately gathering my things; "I'm *going*! I won't stay down here—being taken for a spook!"

Slam-bang went the easel. Suffocated both by wrath and sulphur I climbed the long ladders, only to be seized with a violent shivering at the first touch of the summer breeze, and a painful blinking at the flood of light. The world was so bright, so strangely shimmering with color and pleasantness! Devouring it with new eyes, I trotted down the slopes, conscious not only of having done the boss his Kitchen and thrown in an assortment of unspecified but entirely beautiful bats, but of also having qualified as a successful spook: achievement enough, one felt, for a July afternoon.

But my bats, personally precious, indubitably pictorial though they were, were decreed by cautious editors to be imprudent elements in an illustration. No one, they said, would want to go to the Yellowstone if they saw those bats. . . . Now whether that was a reflection on bats *per se*, on my explicit rendering of them, or on the courage of prospective tourists, I have never been able to determine; but after my own experience with Bill and his confrere at the sky-hole, I was ready to believe almost anything, and to cooperate cheerfully in a complete obliteration of bats.

After some days before the orange-tinted terraces, my easel was given its final fold. Such glories were not for black-and-white to imitate. Color everywhere shone and clamored, and color, at the last, definitely withdrew one's hand. Pausing one evening on a smooth, daffodil rim by a pool that reflected the sky and just one fair cloud, I sent a mute farewell to snow and distances, then stepped blindly down and down into the purple, light-twinkling cup of the valley.

From far away came the long, unfeeling whistle of a train.

NOTES

1. Greene, "Attempting Yellowstone," final chapter of *Lambs in March*, 229–74.

2. *New York Times* review of Greene, *The Lone Winter*, April 8, 1923, 7.

3. Greene mentions firs and spruces at Upper Geyser Basin, but the trees in that vicinity are all lodgepole pines. Greene probably entered from the West Entrance and went directly to Upper Geyser Basin.

4. Robert Haven Schauffler (1879–1964), born in Brünn, Austria-Hungary (now Brno, Czech Republic) to American missionary parents, studied cello, but after his education at Northwestern, Princeton, and Berlin Universities he became an editor and writer. His writing career spanned both world wars—he earned a Purple Heart in World War I.

5. One can see Shoshone Lake and the Tetons in the distance at one spot along the road from Upper Geyser Basin to West Thumb. In Greene's next paragraph, she mentions the Tetons again as being visible across Yellowstone Lake from West Thumb, where Greene's tent camp must have been located, but from there one sees the peaks of the Absaroka Range, not the Tetons. Greene may have derived her error about viewing the Tetons from Yellowstone Lake from her Literary Person, Robert Haven Schauffler, who wrote, "Then on to where were visible the distant sharp peaks of the Tetons, sacred to the memory of Owen Wister's Virginian" (Schauffler, *Romantic America*, 152).

6. Greene cites White, "Camp Equipment," 676. Stewart Edward White wrote western nature and travel books throughout the first half of the 1900s.

7. Lt. Hiram Chittenden, officer in charge of roads and bridges from 1891 to 1905, built the first bridge to cross the Yellowstone River above the falls—the high Melan Arch Bridge—in 1903. Culpin, *History of the Road System*, 52.

8. Would Greene have ventured down the canyon wall to retrieve her camp-stool—or undertaken her descent to "do one sketch looking up" described a bit later—if she had known how many people have died falling into the canyon? Whittlesey's *Death in Yellowstone* (144–50) tells us there have been more than forty such deaths in the history of the park.

9. After reading and rereading the story of Greene's romantic ride in the moonlight and wondering just where the wrangler and she would have gone, I have concluded from studying maps that they probably rode southeast from the Chittenden Bridge, crossed Sour

Creek, and encountered the elk on one of the hills near Wrangler Lake (which may have received its name from wranglers' use of the area as nighttime pasture). Orville Bach, Jr. describes Sour Creek as "a sluggish stream that drains several thermal basins upstream," and says the area has "plenty of mosquitoes" (Bach, *Exploring the Yellowstone Backcountry*, 234).

10. Greene's attitude toward bears contrasts markedly with that of her contemporary artist, Ernest Thompson Seton.

11. According to Jack Ellis Haynes in *Yellowstone Stage Holdups,* five holdups took place in the park—in 1887, 1897, 1908, 1914, and 1915. Although Silver Gate may seem a likely place for such a crime, none of them occurred there in the first seven years of the 1900s. Other details of Greene's holdup story correspond quite well to those of the 1914 event that took place between Old Faithful and West Thumb. Perhaps Greene added this fantasy after her 1906 trip but before her book was published in 1928.

12. Visitors descended into the Devil's Kitchen (located on the Upper Terrace at Mammoth Hot Springs) until 1939, when the National Park Service closed it because of the danger from carbon dioxide inhalation.

About the Names

The writers in *Through Early Yellowstone* used various alternate and outdated names. For example, the Firehole River was often called the Fire Hole or Fire-Hole, and Greybull, a town in Wyoming, was sometimes written as Graybull. Rather than explain and give the correct spelling at each occurrence, we present this reference chart. Many of the authors must have read the same guidebooks, and the guidebook writers must have copied from one another, since they often perpetuated the confusion.

Artemesia **Correct:** Artemisia	Latin species name for sagebrush, still frequently misspelled.
Barronett, Barronette **Correct:** Baronett	Baronett's Bridge near Tower Junction, serving miners just beyond Yellowstone's northeast corner beginning in 1871, used the correct spelling of Jack Baronett's name. Barronette Peak, viewed from the Northeast Entrance Road, carries an officially approved misspelled name.
Boseman **Correct:** Bozeman	City in southern Montana named for John Bozeman, who established a trail in 1864 connecting the Oregon Trail to the Gallatin Valley.
Boteler, Botteller **Correct:** Bottler	Frederick, Henry, and Phillip Bottler were brothers who settled in Paradise Valley in the 1860s and, with their mother, hosted numerous travelers passing their ranch.
Cañon **Correct:** Canyon	Early writers in English used the Spanish form, but the current spelling came into vogue about 1900.
Clarke, Clarke's Fork **Correct:** Clark, Clarks Fork	River named after Capt. William Clark of the Lewis and Clark expedition. The Yellowstone River tributary named for him is the Clarks Fork of the Yellowstone, with no apostrophe, but there is also a Clark Fork of the Columbia in western Montana.
Cook City **Correct:** Cooke City	Town outside the northeast corner of Yellowstone Park named in honor of Jay Cooke, financier of the Northern Pacific Railroad, at a time when area miners hoped that the N.P.R.R. would build a branch line.
Coulter **Correct:** Colter	John Colter was the earliest white man known to have traversed Yellowstone (about 1807), while John Coulter was the botanist accompanying the 1872 Hayden Expedition to the area.
Evarts **Correct:** Everts	We know that Truman Everts changed the spelling of his name from Evarts to Everts, while his father, son, and granddaughter all used the "a" in spelling their names (Whittlesey, personal communication, November 3, 2014). Although the reason he changed the spelling is not known, he may have known about a contemporary often in the news, William Maxwell Evarts, who was attorney general under President Andrew Johnson and later Secretary of State under President Rutherford B. Hayes.

Gardiner River **Correct:** Gardner River	The river was named for Johnson Gardner, who trapped beaver in the area in the 1830s. The town took his name but spelled it Gardiner, probably due to mispronunciation. Town officials have not wanted to change the spelling.
Hell's Half Acre **Correct:** Midway Geyser Basin and Excelsior Geyser	An outdated name used variously in early writings for both the basin and the geyser.
Kepler's Falls **Correct:** Kepler Cascades	The cascades near Old Faithful Village were named for Kepler Hoyt, son of Wyoming Territory's Governor John W. Hoyt. Father and twelve-year-old son visited the park in 1881. Johannes Kepler was a seventeenth-century German astronomer, known for his laws of planetary motion.
Nez Percés **Correct:** Nez Perces	The commonly used name for the tribe that calls themselves the Nimi'ipuu means pierced nose and was given them by French Canadian voyageurs. Some wore decorative pieces of seashell through the septum of the nose. The name is no longer spelled or pronounced in the French manner.
Reynold, Reynolds **Correct:** Raynolds	Capt. William F. Raynolds led an 1860 party that was unsuccessful in its attempt to find a route through the Absaroka Range to enter the Yellowstone region.
Sepulchre **Correct:** Sepulcher	Sepulcher is the spelling approved by the U.S. Board on Geographic Names for the Yellowstone mountain, although the preferred dictionary spelling of the word is sepulchre.
Shoshonee **Correct:** Shoshone or Shoshoni	The tribe's name has often been spelled ending in "e," but according to the late Park Historian Aubrey L. Haines, the preferred spelling ends in "i" when referring to the people and "e" for place names (Haines, *Yellowstone Place Names*, 9). However, most sources spell the name Shoshone. In Wyoming the place name is usually pronounced show-SHOWN, and in Idaho show-SHOW-nee (Whittlesey, personal communication, June 15, 2015).
Tower Falls **Correct:** Tower Fall	The name was used with an "s" until 1928, when the U.S. Geological Survey changed it to the singular on a topographic map.
Washburne **Correct:** Washburn	Gen. Henry D. Washburn served the Union in the Civil War and was a member of the House of Representatives. In 1870 he was surveyor general of Montana, when he was chosen to be the leader of that year's expedition to the Yellowstone area. The spelling of his surname probably became confused with that of Elihu B. Washburne and three of his brothers, who were prominent Illinois Republican politicians between 1853 and 1893.
Yancy **Correct:** Yancey	"Uncle John" Yancey built and ran a log hotel and saloon near Tower Junction from about 1885 until his death in 1903.

Bibliography

Abbreviations

AHC American Heritage Center, University of Wyoming

GPO Government Printing Office

YHRC Yellowstone Heritage and Research Center

Allen, Margaret Andrews. "A Family Camp in Yellowstone Park." *Outing: An Illustrated Monthly Magazine of Recreation* 7 (November 1885): 157–59.

Alter, J. Cecil. *Jim Bridger.* Norman: University of Oklahoma Press, 1962.

Bach, Orville, Jr. *Exploring the Yellowstone Backcountry.* San Francisco: Sierra Club Books, 1991.

Baker, Ray Stannard. "A Place of Marvels: Yellowstone Park as It Now Is," *The Century Magazine* 66, no. 4 (August 1903): 481–91.

Bargar, Keith E. *Geology and Thermal History of Mammoth Hot Springs, Yellowstone National Park, Wyoming.* U.S. Geological Survey Bulletin 1444. Washington, D.C., GPO, 1978.

Bartlett, Richard A. *Nature's Yellowstone.* Tucson: University of Arizona, 1974.

———. *Yellowstone: A Wilderness Besieged.* Tucson: University of Arizona, 1985.

Bonney, Orrin H. and Lorraine G. Bonney, eds. *Battle Drums and Geysers: Part II, The Discovery and Exploration of Yellowstone Park; Lt. G. C. Doane's Journal: First Official Report upon the Wonders of the Yellowstone.* Houston, TX: Bonney and Bonney, 1970.

Bryan, T. Scott. *The Geysers of Yellowstone.* 4th ed. Boulder: University Press of Colorado, 2008.

Chittenden, Hiram M. *The Yellowstone National Park: Historical and Descriptive.* Cincinnati: Robert Clarke Co., 1895.

Clawson, Calvin C. *A Ride to the Infernal Regions: Yellowstone's First Tourists.* Edited by Eugene Lee Silliman. Helena, MT: Riverbend Publishing Co., 2003.

Cook, Charles W., David E. Folsom, and William Peterson.

The Valley of the Upper Yellowstone: An Exploration of the Headwaters of the Yellowstone River in the Year 1869. Edited by Aubrey L. Haines. Norman: University of Oklahoma Press, 1965.

Corthell, Mrs. N. E. (Eleanor). *A Family Trek to the Yellowstone.* Laramie, WY: Laramie Printing Co., 1928.

———. *The Independent,* June 29, 1905, 1460–67.

Cruikshank, Margaret A. "Notes on the Yellowstone Park, August 1883." Manuscript. Vertical Files: History—Visitors, YHRC Library, Yellowstone National Park, WY.

Culpin, Mary Shivers. *"For the Benefit and Enjoyment of the People": A History of the Concession Development in Yellowstone National Park, 1872–1966.* Yellowstone Center for Resources, YCR-CR-2003-01, Yellowstone National Park, WY, 2003.

———. *The History of the Construction of the Road System in Yellowstone National Park, 1872–1966, Historic Resource Study,* Vol. 1. Division of Cultural Resources, Rocky Mountain Region, National Park Service, no. 5, 1994.

DeVoto, Bernard, ed. *The Journals of Lewis and Clark.* Boston: Houghton Miflin Co., 1953.

Elliott, L. Louise. *Six Weeks on Horseback through Yellowstone Park.* Rapid City, SD: Rapid City Journal, July 1913.

Evermann, Barton Warren. "Report on the Establishment of Fish-cultural Stations in the Rocky Mountain Region and Gulf States." Bulletin U.S. Fish Commission for 1891.

———. "Two-Ocean Pass." *The Popular Science Monthly* 47 (June 1895): 175–86.

Everts, Truman C. "Thirty-seven Days of Peril." *Scribner's Monthly* 3 (November 1871): 1–17; published as *Lost in the Yellowstone,* 2nd ed., edited by Lee H. Whittlesey. Salt Lake City: University of Utah Press, 2015.

Ferris, Warren A. *Life in the Rocky Mountains.* Edited by Paul C. Phillips. Denver: Old West Publishing Co., 1940.

Forest and Stream. Obituary of N. P. Langford. November 4, 1911, 684.

"Gilded Age" (no author). Wikipedia article, note 2; accessed July 18, 2015.

Graham, Charles T. Lithograph, "The Yellowstone in Winter—A Surprise," *Harper's Weekly* 31, no. 1581 (April 9, 1887): cover.

Greene, Anne Bosworth. "Attempting Yellowstone." In *Lambs in March*, 229–74. New York: The Century Co., 1928.

Guptill, A. B. "Yellowstone." *Outing: An Illustrated Monthly Magazine of Recreation* 16, no. 4 (July 1890): 256–63; *Outing* 18, no. 3 (June 1891): 175–82.

Haines, Aubrey L. *Yellowstone National Park: Its Exploration and Establishment*. Washington, D.C.: United States Department of Interior, National Park Service, 1974.

———. *The Yellowstone Story*. 1st ed., 2 vols. Boulder: Colorado Associated University Press, 1977; rev. ed., Boulder: The University Press of Colorado, 1996.

Hampton, H. Duane, *How the U.S. Cavalry Saved Our National Parks*. Bloomington: Indiana University Press, 1971.

Hassrick, Peter H. *Drawn to Yellowstone: Artists in America's First National Park*. Los Angeles: Autry Museum of Western Heritage, 2002.

Haupt, Herman, Jr. *The Yellowstone National Park*. New York: J. M. Stoddart, 1883.

Hayden, Dr. Ferdinand Vandiveer. *Twelfth Annual Report of the United States Geological and Geographical Survey of the Territories: A Report of Progress of the Exploration in Wyoming and Idaho for the Year 1878*. Washington D.C.: GPO, 1883.

———. "The Wonders of the West—II: More about the Yellowstone." *Scribner's Monthly* 3, no. 4 (February 1872): 388–96 (not attributed).

Haynes, Jack Ellis. *Yellowstone Stage Holdups*. Bozeman, MT: Haynes Studios, Inc., 1959.

Hedges, Cornelius. "Yellowstone Lake." *Helena Daily Herald*, November 9, 1870, 2.

Henderson, A. Bart. *Journal of the Yellowstone Expedition of 1866 under Captain Jeff Standifer; Also Diaries Kept by Henderson during His Prospecting Journeys in the Snake, Wind River, and Yellowstone Country during the Years 1867–72*. Unpublished document. Yale Collection of Western Americana, Beinecke Rare Book and Manuscript Library, New Haven, CT [probably 1872].

Henderson, C. Hanford. "Through the Yellowstone on Foot." *Outing: An Illustrated Monthly Magazine of Recreation* 34, no. 2 (May 1899): 161–67.

Henderson, George L. *National Park Manual*, 1888 edition.

Edited by M. A. Bellingham. YHRC Library, Yellowstone National Park, WY.

———. *Yellowstone Park: Past, Present, and Future, Facts for the Consideration of the Committee on Territories for 1891, and Future Committees*. Washington, D.C.: Gibson Brothers, 1891.

Hendrix, Marc S. *Geology Underfoot in Yellowstone Country*. Missoula, MT: Mountain Press Publishing Co., 2011.

Herlihy, David V. *The Lost Cyclist: The Epic Tale of an American Adventurer and His Mysterious Disappearance*. New York: Houghton Miflin Harcourt, 2010.

Hofer, T. E. ("Billy"). Letter to H. M. Albright, April 27, 1926. YHRC Archives, File 171.1 (1926), Box H-1, Yellowstone National Park, WY.

———. "Through Two-Ocean Pass." *Forest and Stream* 24, nos. 1–15 (January 29 to April 30, 1885).

———. "Winter in Wonderland." *Forest and Stream* 28, no. 11 (April 7, 1887), 222–223; no. 12 (April 14, 1887), 246–247; no. 13 (April 21, 1887), 270–271; no. 14 (April 28, 1887), 294–295; no. 15 (May 5, 1887), 318–319.

Hornaday, William T. *The Minds and Manners of Wild Animals*. New York: Charles Scribner's Sons, 1922.

Hough, Emerson. "Forest and Stream's Yellowstone Park Game Exploration." *Forest and Stream* 42 (13 nonconsecutive parts, May 5 to August 25, 1894).

Irving, Washington. *The Adventures of Captain Bonneville*. New York: G. P. Putnam, 1849. First published in 1837 under the title *The Rocky Mountains; or, Scenes, Incidents, and Adventures in the Far West*.

Johnson, Patricia Condon. "Truman Ingersoll: St. Paul Photographer Pictured the World." *Minnesota History* (Winter 1980): 123–32.

Jordan, David Starr. *Days of a Man: Being Memories of a Naturalist, Teacher, and Minor Prophet of Democracy*. Vol. 1. Yonkers, NY: World Book Co., 1922.

———. *Reconnaissance of the Streams and Lakes of the Yellowstone National Park, Wyoming, in Interests of the United States Fish Commission*. Washington, D.C.: GPO, 1890.

Kensel, W. Hudson. *Dude Ranching in Yellowstone Country: Larry Larom and Valley Ranch, 1915–1969*. Glendale, CA: Arthur H. Clark Co., 2010.

Kodak website. "History of Kodak: Milestones." http://www.kodak.com/ek/US/en/Our_Company/History_of_Kodak/Milestones_-_chronology/1878-1929.htm, accessed April 23, 2015.

Langford, Nathaniel P. *The Discovery of Yellowstone Park: Journal of the Washburn Expedition to the Yellowstone and Firehole Rivers in the Year 1870*. Edited by Aubrey L. Haines. Lincoln: University of Nebraska Press, 1972. First published 1905 by F. J. Haynes.

———. "The Wonders of the Yellowstone." *Scribner's Monthly* 2, nos. 1 and 2: (May 1871): 1–17; (June 1871): 113–28 (not attributed).

Lanphere, M. A., et al. "Revised Ages for Tuffs of the Yellowstone Plateau Volcanic Field." *Geological Society of America Bulletin* 114, no. 5 (2002): 559–68.

Leclercq, Jules. *La Terre des Merveilles*: *Promenade au Parc National de l'Amérique du Nord*. Paris: Hachette & Co., 1886. Translated as *Yellowstone, Land of Wonders: Promenade in the National Park of North America* by Janet Chapple and Suzanne Cane. Lincoln: University of Nebraska Press, 2013.

LeHardy, Paul. "Reminiscences," Autobiography of the Life and Adventures of Paul LeHardy de Beaulieu, Viscount. Typescript. AHC, Laramie, WY.

———. "La Terre des Merveilles: Souvenirs d'une exploration au bassin du lac Yellowstone," *Revue de Belgique* 19, 1875. Translated by Dorothy Medlin. Vertical file: History—YNP—Explorers, YHRC Library, Yellowstone National Park, WY.

Lenz, Frank D. "Lenz's World Tour Awheel." Parts 1, 4, 5, and 6. *Outing: An Illustrated Monthly Magazine of Recreation* 20, no. 6 (September 1892): 482; *Outing* 21, no. 4 (January 1893): 286–90; *Outing* 21, no. 5 (February 1893): 378–83; *Outing* 21, no. 6 (March 1893): 444–45.

Miles, Arthur W. "'Wylie-Way' in Yellowstone." Marketing brochure. Salt Lake City, UT: Wylie Permanent Camping Company, ca. 1907.

Morris, Alice Parmelee (Mrs. Robert C.). "Notes on Trail Study 1917." Typed manuscript. Facilities and Maintenance Collection, YHRC Archives.

———. "Yellowstone Trails." Typed manuscript, 1918. YHRC Archives.

New York Sun, quoted in *Current Literature: A Magazine of Contemporary Record* 28 (June 1900): 264.

New York Times Magazine, "Yellowstone Trails Blazed by New York Woman," February 10, 1918, 7.

Norris, Philetus W. *Calumet of the Coteau*. Philadelphia: J. B. Lippincott & Co., 1884.

———. *Report upon the Yellowstone National Park, to the Secretary of the Interior, for the Year 1880*. Washington, D.C.: GPO, 1881.

Organic Act Creating Yellowstone National Park, or "Act of Dedication." U.S. Statutes at Large, vol. 17, chap. 24, 32–33, 1872.

Osborne, H. Z. *A Midsummer Ramble: Being a Descriptive Sketch of the Yellowstone National Park*. Los Angeles Evening Express [probably 1889].

Owen, W. O. "The First Bicycle Tour of the Yellowstone National Park," *Outing: An Illustrated Monthly Magazine of Recreation* 18, no. 3 (June 1891): 191–95.

Potts, Daniel T. Letter to brother, Robert T. Potts. Reprinted in *Niles Weekly Register*, October 6, 1827.

Price, Sir Rose Lambart. *A Summer on the Rockies*. London: Sampson, Low, Marston & Co., 1898.

Raynolds, William F. *The Report of Brevet Brigadier General W. F. Raynolds on the Exploration of the Yellowstone and the Country Drained by That River*. Washington, D.C.: GPO, 1868.

Rollins, Alice Wellington. "The Three Tetons." *Harper's Monthly Magazine* 74 (May 1887): 869–90.

Roosevelt, Theodore. *The Wilderness Hunter*, originally published 1893. New York: G. B. Putnam Sons, 1910.

Rubenstein, Paul, Lee H. Whittlesey, and Mike Stevens. *The Guide to Yellowstone Waterfalls and Their Discovery*. Englewood, CO: Westcliffe Publishers, 2000.

Russell, Osborne. *Journal of a Trapper*. Edited by Aubrey L. Haines. First published by L. A. York, 1914. Lincoln: University of Nebraska Press, 1965.

Saunders, Richard L. *Glimpses of Wonderland: The Haynes and Their Postcards of Yellowstone National Park*. Bozeman, MT: printed by author, 1997.

———, ed. *A Yellowstone Reader: The National Park in Folklore, Popular Fiction, and Verse*. Salt Lake City: University of Utah Press, 2003.

Schauffler, Robert Haven. *Romantic America*. New York: The Century Co., 1913.

Schullery, Paul. *The Bears of Yellowstone*. Worland, WY: High Plains Publishing Co., 1992.

———, ed. *Old Yellowstone Days*. Originally published, Boulder: Colorado Associated University Press, 1979. Albuquerque: University of New Mexico Press, 2010.

———. *Searching for Yellowstone: Ecology and Wonder in the Last Wilderness*. Boston: Houghton Mifflin Co, 1997.

———. *Yellowstone's Ski Pioneers*. Worland, WY: High Plains Publishing Co., 1995.

Schullery, Paul, and Sarah Stevenson, eds. *People and Place: The Human Experience in Greater Yellowstone*. Yellowstone National Park, WY: Yellowstone Center for Resources, 2004.

Schullery, Paul, and Lee Whittlesey. *Myth and History in the Creation of Yellowstone National Park*. Lincoln: University of Nebraska Press, 2003.

Seton, Ernest Thompson. *The Biography of a Grizzly*. New York: The Century Co., 1899.

———. *Lives of the Hunted: Containing a True Account of the Doings of Five Quadrupeds & Three Birds and, in Elucidation of the Same*. New York: Charles Scribner's Sons, 1901.

"Ski Running," *Forest and Stream* 62 (January 23, 1904): 64. Accessed on Google Books, August 4, 2015.

Stanley, Edwin J. *Rambles in Wonderland*. New York: D. Appleton and Company, 1880.

Stegner, Wallace. *Marking the Sparrow's Fall: The Making of the American West*. Edited by Page Stegner. New York: Henry Holt and Co., 1998.

Synge, Georgina. *A Ride Through Wonderland*. London: Sampson, Low, Marston & Co., 1892. Reprinted Whitefish, MT: Kessinger Publishing Company, 2010.

Thomas, Thomas H. "Yellowstone Park Illustrated," *The Graphic: An Illustrated Weekly Newspaper* (London), no. 976 (August 11, 1888): 157–65; no. 977 (August 18, 1888): 189–96.

Trumbull, Walter. "The Washburn Yellowstone Expedition." *The Overland Monthly* 6, no. 5 (May 1871): 431–37; no. 6 (June 1871): 489–96 (not attributed).

Varley, John D., and Paul Schullery. *Yellowstone Fishes: Ecology, History, and Angling in the Park*. Mechanicsburg, PA: Stackpole Books, 1998.

Waite, Thornton. *Yellowstone by Train: A History of Rail Travel to America's First National Park*. Missoula, MT: Pictorial Histories Publishing Co., 2006.

White, Stewart Allen, "Camp Equipment." *Outing: An Illustrated Monthly Magazine of Recreation* 49 (October 1906–March 1907): 676.

Whitmell, Chas. T. "The American Wonderland, The Yellowstone National Park," *Cardiff Naturalists' Society Report and Transactions* 18 (1885): 77–106.

Whittlesey, Lee, H. *Death in Yellowstone: Accidents and Foolhardiness in the First National Park*. 2nd ed. Boulder, Colorado: Roberts Rinehart Publishers, 2014.

———. "A History of the Old Faithful Area with Chronology, Maps, and Executive Summary." Unpublished document. YHRC Library, Yellowstone National Park, WY, 2007.

———. "Hotels on the Firehole in Yellowstone, 1880–1891, and the Origins of Concessioner Policy in National Parks." Unpublished document. YHRC Library, Yellowstone National Park, WY, 2012.

———. "Marshall's Hotel in the National Park." *Montana: The Magazine of Western History* 30, no. 4 (Autumn 1980): 42–51.

———. "A Post-1872 History of the Norris Area: Cultural Sites Past and Present." Unpublished document. YHRC Library, Yellowstone National Park, 2005, with additions 2007.

———. *Storytelling in Yellowstone: Horse and Buggy Tour Guides*. Albuquerque: University of New Mexico Press, 2007.

———. *Wonderland Nomenclature: A History of the Place Names of Yellowstone National Park*. Microfiche. Helena: Montana Historical Society, 1988.

——— *Yellowstone Place Names*, 1st ed., Helena, MT: Montana Historical Society Press, 1988; 2nd ed., Gardiner, MT: Wonderland Publishing, 2006.

Whittlesey, Lee H., and Elizabeth Watry. *Ho! For Wonderland: Travelers' Accounts of Yellowstone, 1872–1914*. Albuquerque, NM: University of New Mexico Press, 2009.

Wilcox, Earley Vernon. "A Visit to the Hoodoos of Wyoming." *Land of Sunshine* 15, no. 4 (October 1901): 209–23.

Winser, Henry Jacob. *The Yellowstone National Park: A Manual for Tourists*. New York: G. D. Putnam's Sons, 1883.

Wister, Owen. Unpublished diary, June–September 1891. Transcript, box 1, accession no. 290, Owen Wister Papers. AHC, Laramie, WY.

———. *The Virginian: A Horseman of the Plains*. New York: Macmillan, 1902.

Wyndham-Quin, Windham Thomas, Fourth Earl of Dunraven. *The Great Divide: Travels in the Upper Yellowstone in the Summer of 1874*. First published by Chatto and Windus, 1876. Edited by Marshall Sprague. Lincoln: University of Nebraska Press, 1967. Accessed on Google Books, September 30, 2013.

Index

Page numbers in italics indicate illustrations. Italicized numbers followed by an *m* indicate maps. YNP refers to Yellowstone National Park.

Bluff Point, 87

Blumenschein, Ernest, xv–xvi, 211, *213, 214, 215, 216, 218, 219, 220*

boating: dangers of, 90, 101, 200n8; Hofer and, 61, 62; on Yellowstone Lake, 101n23, 196–97, 200n8. *See also* ferries

Boiling River, xii, *Plate 2*, 65, 102, 158n29

Bonneville, Benjamin, 33–34

Boseman. See Bozeman MT

Boteler, Fred. *See* Bottler, Fred

bottle in tree, 69

Bottler, Fred, 14, 53

Boulder River, 67, 167, 203–4, 206

bourbon drinking customs, 140, 152

Bozeman MT, 56, 57, 202–3, 209, 211

Brackett, Mr., 67, 73

breccia, 156, 207–8

bridges: in bear incident, 257; on Boulder River, 203, 204; Chittenden Bridge, 254, 256, 265n7, 265n9; on Firehole River, 81, 83, 194, 195; foot, 58, 92, 195; on Gardner River, 68; on Gibbon River, 194; Greene's adventures and, 248, 254, 256, 265n9; ice, 92, 94, 96; log, tree, or wooden, 58, 83, 93, 194; Melan Arch Bridge, 265n7; on Missouri River, 104; in poetry, 23; railroad, 104, 167; snow, 82, 83; snow-covered, 70, 76, 83; on Yellowstone River, 94–95, 167, 248, 265n7, 265n9. *See also* Natural Bridge

Bridger, Jim, 8, 10, 49n19, 178, 183, 184, 187n3

Brimstone Basin, 32, 48n15

British Association for the Advancement of Science, xi, 102, 109

bronchos. *See* horses

Brooks, R.G., xi, *137, 145*

Brown, Linton A., *205m*

buffalo. *See* bison

Buffalo Bill. *See* Cody, William

"Buffalo Billeries," allusions to. *See* Wild West Show

Buffalo Creek, 184

Bull Mountain, 166–67

bumblebees, 248, 250, 258

Bunsen, Robert, 194, 200n6

Burnt Hole River, 41, 49n25

buttercups, 210

Cache Creek, 209

Calcite Springs, 46, 49n27

"Caldron." *See* Excelsior Geyser

Calthas (mountain marsh marigolds), 210

cameras. *See* photography

camping: Baker party and, 212; during early 1900s, 190; food of, 227; LeHardy and, 51; during present-day, 4, 221; use of dead timber for, 188; worries of, 227

Camp Sheridan, 67

candles, xiii, 64–65, 83, 142, 197

Canyon Creek Hill, 76

Canyon Hotel, 5, 156, 198, 199, 228

carbon dioxide, 158n22, 266n12

Cardiff Naturalists' Society, 103, 153, 158n29

carnelian, 32

Carnelian Creek, 96

carriages and coaches, 108, 144–45, *145*, 170, 211, 214, *220*; accidents of, 161, 258; blown over by wind, 226; robberies of, 209, 210n6, 259, 266n11; routes of, 159n37; as transportation to YNP, 2, 3, 106, 159n37, 170; within YNP, 3, 4, 108, 110, 214, 262–63. *See also* wagons

Carrington Island, 87

carters. *See* drivers

Cascade Creek, 22, 92, 93, 94, 95, 96, 181

cascades: on Crandall Creek, 206–7; on Firehole River, 40; on Gibbon River, 181; on Glen Creek, 170; Kepler's Falls and Cascades, 83; Virginia Cascades, 181; on Yellowstone River, 23, 24, 25, 182, 217. *See also* waterfalls

Castle Geyser, xiv, *Plate 17*, 42, 58, 59, 147, 148, 150, 159n39, 195

Catlin, Nelson, 57, 58

cavalry, 3, 62

cayuses. *See* horses

chalcedony, 32, 141

chemical analysis, 28, 38, 47

Chief Joseph, 96

Chief Sitting Bull, 165, 176n7

chipmunks, 138–39, 150, 158n25

Chittenden, Hiram M., xvi, 8, *213*, 229, 265n7

Chittenden Bridge, 254, 256, 265n9

chromolithography, 157n14

Cinnabar MT, 3, 102, 105–6, 170, 174, 191, 200n3

Clagett, William H., 107, 157n13

Clark, Mary, 159–60n44

hand-tinters of pictures, xii

Haupt, Herman, 2, 56

Hauser, Samuel T., 10, 20, 24

hay and haying, 93–94, 198, 201n10

Hayden, Ferdinand V., 2, 107, 149–50, 160n45, 183, 195, 212

Hayden Valley, *153*, 198, 201n10; wildlife in, 247

Haynes, F. Jay: *Falls of the Gibbon*, *144*; getting lost, 67, 74, 96; as Guptill employer, 177n19; on Hofer excursion, 70; photography, xi, *110*, *112*; on Schwatka expedition, 60, 67, 73, 74

Hedges, Cornelius, 2, 10, 29, 58n5

Hell Broth Springs. *See* Washburn Hot Springs

Hell's Half-Acre, xiii, xiv, *Plate 12*, *Plates 20–22*, 80, 151, 194

Hencke, Albert, xv, *168, 173*

Henderson, A. Bart, 1, 48n14

Henderson, Charles Hanford, 4; as hiker, 1, 190, 193–94

Henderson, George G., 159n36

Henderson, George L., 4, 158n22, 161

Henderson and Klamer's Hotel, xiv, xv, *Plate 14*, 145–46, *146*

Herron, William H., 101n20

Herron Creek, 84, 101n20

highwaymen, 209, 210n6, 259

Hobart, Carroll T., xiii, 159n36

Hofer, Elwood ("Billy"): background of, 60–62; chess playing, 81–82; on crossing snow-covered lakes, 69, 85, 86–90; equipment and provisions of, 63–64, 69, 83; fall through snow, 72; and game census, 4, 60, 61, 99; as guide, 4, 85–86, 178, 183; and Haynes party, 74; Indian-style lodge of, 63–64, *64*, 84–85, *85*, 86; Schwatka expedition and, 66–67, 68, 69, 73, 74; ski-making abilities of, 61, 64–65; in snow slides, 67, 83; thermometer readings of, 68, 77, 79, 100n15. *See also under* boating; elk

Homestead Act of 1862, 1

Hoodoo Basin, 204, 207

Hoodoo Creek, 207

Hoodoo Peak, 207

Hoodoo Plateau, 206, 210

Hoodoos, xv, 4, *175*, 202, 206–8, *208*

Hornaday, William T., 239

horned toads, 225

Horr, Henry, 4

horseback riding: automobiles' effect on, 232–33; Baker party and, 211, 214; Greene and, 248, 252, 253–56; Morris and, 231, 233–34; pictured, *142, 219, 233, 234*; Wilcox party and, 202, 204, 206, 207, 209. *See also* pack trains

horses: carriage pulling, *145*, 161–62; fording rivers, 51, *144*, 144–45, 226; as easily scared, 154, 258; Greene and, 248, 249, 252, 253, 256–57; herding of, 254, 259; for hire, 110, 248; of Indians, 18; as pack animals, 14, 31, 57–58, 183, 203; on Wilcox party, 204

"hoss-wrangler," 253–56, 265–66n9

hotels, 4–5, *5*, 91–92, 95, 145, 152, 194, 199. *See also* Mammoth Hot Springs Hotel; tent hotels

hot springs: C. H. Henderson and, 195; of Iceland, 46–47; Lenz and, 172; pictured, cover, *41, 154, Plates 2, 5, 7, 17, 22, 23*; therapeutic value of, 110, 157n16; Thomas and, 150–51; Washburn expedition and, 18, 21–22, 26–28, 31, 39. *See also* Crater Hills; West Thumb Geyser Basin; *individual names of hot springs*

Hough, Emerson, 60, 62

Howard, Gen. O.O., 96

Howard Eaton Trail, 99n7, 100n7

huckleberries, 204

Huckleberry Hot Springs, 49n18

Humboldt, Alexander von, 47, 49n29

Hunt, Capt. Wilson P., 33

hunters, xv, *Plate 24*, 152

hunting: ecology and, 61; for food, 14, 15, 16, 52; Indians and, 210n7; reasons for, 99; rifle-pit for, 29; rules and regulations about, 188, 198

Hygeia Spring, xiv, 146

Hymen Terrace, xvi, *214*, 220n8

ice: effect of, on plants, 210; in geyser basins, 72–73, 78, 80, 81; in Grand Canyon of the Yellowstone, 92–93, 94; interesting shapes of, 61, 70–72, 78, 82, 94; mounds of, 71, 82–83, 94–95; on Shoshone Lake, 85; skiing on, 69, 71, 86–90, 91; at Tower Fall, 97

Icelandic geysers, 46–47, 194

icicles, 81, 83, 92, 94, 97

Independence Rock, 225

Index Peak, 206

Sepulcher Mountain, 68, 140
Seton, Ernest Thompson, 229, 239
Shack Hotel, 4, 101n19
Shaw & Powell, 5
Sheehan, Con, 66, 67, 68–69, 70, 79
Sheridan, Philip H., 177n17
Sheridan wy, 176n3
Sherman, William T., 177n17
shingle (pebbles around springs), 196
Shirley Basin, 224
shooting star (*Dodecatheon*), 210
Shoshone Canyon, 229
Shoshone Indian reservation (Wind River Indian Reservation), 226
Shoshone Lake: in winter, 84–85; lack of fish in, 178, 182–83; views of, 196, 265n5
Shoshone Mountains. *See* Absaroka Mountains
Shoshone River (called Big Horn by Lenz), 175
Shoshone Sun Dance, 226
Shoshoni, 1, 226
silence: among people, 108, 152, 255; of canyon, 23–24, 218; of forest, 245
silicious deposits, 47, 83, 143, 149
silicious mud, 146
Silver Gate, 215, 258, 266n11
Silver Tip Ranch, 231
Sitting Bull. *See* Chief Sitting Bull
Skinner, Milton P., 232
skis, Norwegian, 61, 64–65, 70, 78
"Sky-Pilot," xiii, *Plate 4*, *138*
slate, 31, *31*
Slocombe, Frederick Alfred, 198
Slough Creek, 206
Snake River, 32, 49n23, 183–85, 187, 217
snakes, 199, 201n11, 226
snow: beauty added by, 96; danger from, 69; depth of, at Canyon, 92; depth of, at Gibbon Canyon, 76; depth of, at Norris, 71; depth of, at Upper Basin, 81, 83; layered with water and ice, 87; at Mammoth, 66; measuring depth of, 65, 69, 85; records of, 77; shapes made by, 70–72
snow bridges, 82, 83
snowfall, 68, 77–78, 83
"snowshoes." *See* skis, Norwegian
snowslides, 67, 74, 76

snowstorms: in summer, 37–40, 173; in winter, 75, 84, 96
Soda Butte, 209
soldiers, 209, 216, 246, 252, 258–59
Sollas, Edgar W., xi, xii, 105, *105*, *148*
solution caves, 137, 158n22
sounds, 195, 227, 228–29
Sour Creek, 265–66n9
South Entrance and South Entrance Road, 211, 212
South Fork of Atlantic Creek, 184
Specimen Lake, 82
Specimen Ridge, 96–97
specimen fiends (Hofer expression), 77, 91
specimens, collection of, 21–22, *22*, 31, 48n14; rules against collection, 139–40, 158n29, 188; storage of, 51, 229. *See also* arrowheads
spellings, 267–68
spires, 18, 19, 48n9
Spiteful Geyser. *See* Vixen Geyser (Spiteful Geyser)
Splendid Geyser, 82, 149, 150, 195
spring beauty (*Claytonia*), 210
Squirrel Geyser, 138
squirrels, 158n25
Squirrel Springs, 158n24
stagecoaches. *See* carriages and coaches
stalactite basins, 139
stalactites, 111
Stalactite Terraces, *Plate 5*
stalagmites, 149
Stanley, Edwin J., 159–60n44
Starbottle, Colonel (fictional character), 106, 157n11
stars, 254, 259
Steamboat Geyser, 71, 72, 200n6
Steamvalve Spring, 72, 100n11
stereoscopic photography, xii
Stevenson Island, 90
Stickney, Ben, 10, 24
Stillwater River, 167
St. Mary's Lake (Mary Lake), 153, 159–60n44
stoves, *Plate 15*, *147*, 245, 246
Sullivan, Mr., 79
sulphate of soda, 47
sulphur, 10, 32, 49n27; in Devil's Kitchen, 263–64; fumes of, 143, 264; liquid, 46, 49n27; in springs, 18, 26; in Mud Volcano area, 27, 28–29, 31
Sulphur Caldron Group, 27–28

Trout Creek, 91

Trumbull, Walter A.: drawings by, x, *43*; background and work of, x, 2, 7–8; descriptions by, 15–16, 28–29, 39, 45; as expedition member, 10; Indians and, 48n5, 48n7; in naming of Tower Fall, 20

tufa, 28, 39

Turquoise Springs (Pool), 80, 151

Twin Buttes, xiv–xv, *Plate 22*

Twin Geyser, 144

Twin Lakes, 69–70

Two Ocean Pass, 178, *181*, 183–85, 185, *186m*, 217

Two Ocean Plateau, 49n23

Uncle Tom's Overlook and Trail, 252

Undine Falls, 156, 181

undulation of ice, 90

Union Pacific Railroad, 3

Upper Falls (Lewis River), 181

Upper Falls of the Yellowstone, 25–26, 154–55, 217; adventure above, 51–53; in winter, 94–95; height of, 25, 199; pictured, *25, 182*

Upper Geyser Basin, *40*, 147, 150, 171, 195, 214

Upper Terrace, xiii, 137–39, 266n12

U.S. Congress: act to protect wildlife (May 7, 1894), 189; role in creating YNP, 50, 107

U.S. Fish Commission, 4, 178, 179, 182, 187n10

U.S. Geological Survey, 141, *186m*

Utah and Northern Railroad, 159n37

"The Valley of Desolation". *See* Black Canyon of the Yellowstone

vandalism, 3, 140, 159n34, 159n39, 188, 225

Victor Bicycle Company, 164, 169

Virginia Cascades, 181

Virginia City MT, 49n24

"Virginian" (fictional character), 224, 227, 229n7, 245, 265n5

The Virginian: A Horseman of the Plains (Wister), 227, 229n7, 245, 265n5

Vixen Geyser (Spiteful Geyser), 71, 161–62, 162n2

volcanic glass. *See* obsidian

volcanoes: ash from, 21; force of, in YNP creation, 10, 30, 45–46, 145, 175, 212; lava flows from, 180, 181; New Zealand, 145, 158n19

voting rights of women, 222

wagons: accidents of, 161–62, 224; Allen excursion and, 58–59; covered, 221–22, 223, 224, 225–26, 229; freight, 257, 258

Wahb (bear in storybook), 229, 239

Warm Spring Camp, 86

Washburn, Henry D., 2, 10, 14, 29

Washburn Hot Springs, 21–22

Washburn expedition, 2, 10; Indian encounters of, 15, 37, 48n5; narrow escapes of, 21–22, 27, 42; organization of, 14–15

"The Washburn Yellowstone Expedition" (Trumbull), 15–16, 28–29, 39, 45

watercolor painting, xi, 246, 249–50

waterfalls, 24, 181, 182, 250. *See also* cascades; *names of individual waterfalls*

West Thumb (of Yellowstone Lake), 172, 196–97, 220n7

West Thumb Geyser Basin, 38, 86, 213, 227

wheelmen. *See* bicyclists

White, Stewart Edward, 245, 265n6

White Mountain, 108, 111

Whitmell, Charles, xiii, xv, 102, 103, 153–54, 158n29

Wilcox, Earley Vernon, 4, 202, 209

Wilcox party, 202, 203, *205m*

Wild West Show, 110, 157n15

Willow Park, 69, 73, 100n12

Wilson, Woodrow, 6, 211, 231

Wind River, 34, 226

Wind River Mountains (Absaroka Mountains mistaken for), 32, 33

winds, 73–75, 79, 87, 90, 165–66, 168

winter (1886–87), *63*, 77

Wister, Owen, 108, 224, 229n7, 265n5

woodpeckers, 95

World War I, 222, 231, 265n4

worms in fish, 90, 101n22

wormwood, 110, 157n17

Wraith Falls, 181

wranglers. *See* cowboys

wrens, 97. *See also* dippers, American

Wylie, William, 56, 230n1

Wylie Permanent Camping Company, 5, 229, 230, 240, 257

"Wylie-Way," 230

Wyndham-Quin, Windham Thomas, 3, 53, 147

Wyoming, 9, 212, 221; laws of, concerning YNP, 139–40, 158n28; prehistoric lava flow covering, 180; size of, 225; women's voting rights in, 222

Yancey, "Uncle John," 98, 156
Yancey's (hotel), 5, 74, 100, 200
Yankee Jim and Yankee Jim's, 168–69, 176, 176n9
Yankee Jim Canyon, 168, *168*
Yellowstone Falls, 70
Yellowstone Lake, 30–31, 86–87, 247; deaths in, 101n23, 200–201n8; elevation of, 217; fish in, 4, 30, 178, 187; pictured, *153, 246*; size of, 30, 107, 154
Yellowstone National Park, 107–8, 140, 169, 182; administration of, 188–89, 231–32; altitudes in, 24, 140, 214, 247; as big game preserve, 230; bizarre and beautiful coexisting within, 152–53, 215–16, 217–18; as business opportunity, 189, 217; compared to world tourist sites, 230; as educational vacation spot, 223, 230; establishment of, 2, 7, 50, 107; exploration of, 73, 174–75; federal government and, 217, 231–32; as headwaters location, 170, 217; laws and regulations affecting, 2, 50, 107, 139–40, 158n28, 188–89; maps of, *88–89m, 236–37m*; as "mental" place, 242–43; as "modern" wilderness, 219; names in, 17–18, 151; in poetry, 54–55; size of, 106–7, 169, 216; wild, as compared to tamed parks, 107, 197–98, 216; workers in, 108, 196
Yellowstone National Park Improvement Co. (Y.P.P.), 81, 101n19, 159n36
"Yellowstone National Park Trails" (Morris), *236–37m*
Yellowstone Range. *See* Beartooth Range
Yellowstone River, 9–10, 21, 51–53, 152–53, *153*, 154–55, 182, 183
Yellowstone River Valley, 165–68, 176
Yellow Sulphur Pool. *See* Crater Hills Geyser
Yosemite National Park, xvi, 240